EXPL

GREEK ISLANDS

Anthony Sattin
Sylvie Franquet

AA Publishing

Page 2: (a) *Thíra*; (b) *fishing boat, Diafáni, Kárpathos*
Page 3: *Little Venice, Mikonos*
Page 4: *Oía, Thíra*; (b) *detail, fishing boat, Pigádia, Kárpathos*
Page 5: *Worry beads*
Pages 6–7: *Greek flag*
Page 6: *Repainting fishing boat, Leipsoí Town, Leipsoí*
Page 8: *Ólympos, Kárpathos*
Page 9: *Nydrí and islands, Lefkáda*

Written by Anthony Sattin and Sylvie Franquet
Original photography by Steve Day, Terry Harris, Rob Moore, Anthony Sattin, James Tims
Cover design by Carroll Associates
Reprinted 2000, 2002
Revised second edition 2000
First published 1997
Edited, designed and produced by AA Publishing
Maps © Automobile Association Developments Ltd 1997, 2000
Distributed in the United Kingdom by AA Publishing

The contents of this publication are believed correct at the time of printing. Nevertheless, the publishers cannot be held responsible for any errors or omissions or for changes in the details given in this guide or for the consequences of any reliance on the information provided by the same. Assessments of attractions, hotels, restaurants and so forth are based upon the authors' own personal experiences and, therefore, descriptions given in this guide necessarily contain an element of subjective opinion which may not reflect the publishers' opinion or dictate a reader's own experiences on another occasion. We have tried to ensure accuracy in this guide, but things do change and we would be grateful if readers would advise us of any inaccuracies they may encounter.

A CIP catalogue record for this book is available from the British Library.

ISBN 0 7495 2364 6

Published by AA Publishing (a trading name of Automobile Association Developments Limited, whose registered office is Millstream, Maidenhead Road, Windsor, SL4 5GD. Registered number 1878835).

Origination by L C Repro Ltd
Printed and bound in Italy by Printer Trento srl

AA World Travel Guides publish nearly 300 guidebooks to a full range of cities, countries and regions across the world. Find out more about AA Publishing and the wide range of services the AA provides by visiting our Web site at www.theAA.com

How to use this book

ORGANISATION

The Greek Islands Are, The Greek Islands Were
Discusses aspects of life and culture in the contemporary Greek Islands and explores significant periods in their history.

A–Z
Breaks down the islands into regional chapters, and covers places to visit, including walks and drives. Within this section fall the Focus On articles, which consider a variety of subjects in greater detail.

Travel Facts
Contains the strictly practical information vital for a successful trip.

Hotels and Restaurants
Lists recommended establishments throughout the Greek Islands, giving a brief summary of their attractions.

ABOUT THE RATINGS
Most places described in this book have been given a separate rating. These are as follows:

▶▶▶ **Do not miss**

▶▶ **Highly recommended**

▶ **Worth seeing**

MAPS
To make each particular location easier to find, every main entry in this book has a map reference to the right of its name. This comprises a number, followed by a letter, followed by another number, such as 176B3. The first number (176) refers to the page on which the map can be found, the letter (B) and the second number (3) pinpoint the square in which the main entry is located. The maps on the inside front cover and inside back cover are referred to as IFC and IBC respectively.

Spelling of place names
Visitors to Greece will find variations in the spelling of place names on road signs and maps. In this book the transliteration of the Greek names into Roman letters follows a recognised convention, but where another version may be more familiar (e.g., Athens, Crete, Corfu, Rhodes) this is also used. The names of the islands are given in the Greek alphabet (in capital letters) on the pages that introduce the groups of islands.

Contents

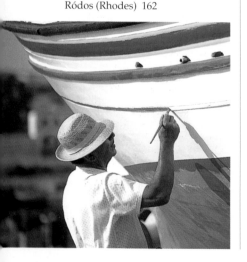

Sylvie Franquet lived in Cairo for six years. She now writes full-time and has a column in the Belgian newspaper *De Morgen*.

Anthony Sattin writes travel features and reviews books for *The Sunday Times* and is currently at work on a new book about pagan survivals in Egypt.

Our Greek Islands

Our bags had failed to arrive in Crete, the hotel we thought was going to be close to Irákleio was several miles away and beside a power station, and the dishevelled waiter had come to tell us that it never snows in April. 'Never, that is, except for now.' That was our first night researching this book.

The attractions of travelling out of season in Greece are many, including the absence of crowds, walks along windswept beaches, and an opportunity to see Greeks do whatever they do when they're not devoting themselves to tourists. There are also drawbacks, such as bad weather, a restricted choice in hotels and restaurants and a greatly reduced, unpredictable or even, in some places, shut-down ferry service.

When we returned in the height of summer it was easy to move from one island to another, but not so easy to get a seat in the good restaurants, a space on the best beaches, a clear view of the star exhibits in museums or, in many of the hotels, a quiet night. Prices had risen with the temperature, and the sense of community had changed as visitors outnumbered locals.

Greece has had a bad press in recent years for insensitive development, the destruction of its wilder corners and its rising prices. We went expecting the worst – and have not refrained from mentioning it in this guide if we found it. But most of the time it was nothing but a pleasure to travel around, to visit islands, hotels and restaurants that were new to us, to return to familiar places and not be disappointed and to revel in the freedom that the summer ferry services provide.

The history and archaeology of the Greek Islands are just as fascinating as when treasure hunters visited them more than 200 years ago. The people who inhabit them remain a curious mix of pedant and philosopher, liberal and conservative, sacred and profane. Meeting some of them and glimpsing the life they live is what draws us back to the islands again and again.

Anthony Sattin and Sylvie Franquet

The Greek Islands Are

There are more than 1,400 Greek islands, many of them merely uninhabitable rocks breaking the smooth sea surface. The islands account for only one fifth of Greece's total land mass (25,166 out of a total 131,944 sq km), yet their magical combination of brilliant light, hard land and diamond-clear air dominates many people's image of Greece.

IONIAN AND AEGEAN Greece's islands are mostly scattered to either side of the Greek mainland. To the west is the Ionian Sea, bounded by Greece and Albania to the east, Italy and the Adriatic to the north and west and the Mediterranean to the south. Within the Ionian Sea lie the Ionian Islands. To the east of the Greek mainland is the Aegean Sea, with Macedonia and Thrace to the north, the rest of mainland Greece to the west, Turkey to the east and Crete to the south. Cradled in the waters of the Aegean are the Cyclades ('the

❑ Lawrence Durrell's words still ring true: 'You should see the landscape of Greece. It would break your heart'. (*Spirit of Place*, London, 1969) ❑

Circle', from the ring they form around Dílos), the Dodecanese ('the Twelve'), in the southeast, the islands of the Northern and Eastern Aegean, the Saronic Islands, the Sporades ('the Scattered'), Évvoia, cheek by jowl with the mainland and, in the far south, Crete.

ISLAND LANDSCAPES Geology, topography and climate have combined in Greece to create some of the most stunning scenery in the Mediterranean – helped by a legendary blue sea. The Greek Islands are mostly the peaks of an otherwise submerged landmass. Their appearance is so varied that it is impossible to make generalisations: many of the larger islands have extremely fertile districts, as in the interior of Náxos, for example, while some smaller islands appear to have been worn down to the bare rock.

Other small islands, such as Paxoí and its tiny neighbour Antipaxoí, in the Ionian Sea, are very fertile; Paxoí is entirely given over to olive cultivation while Antipaxoí is dedicated to grapes. Even between neighbours, the difference can be striking: while Thásos is green and gentle, nearby Samothráki is little more than a forbidding peak jutting out of the sea.

Older Greeks swear that Poseidon sliced Évvoia off the mainland with his trident

CLIMATE Crete, Europe's most southerly land mass, enjoys mild winters and early springs on its southern coast and yet has snow on its peaks for much of the year (snow fell in the port of Irákleio as late as April in 1995). The winter islands would be unrecognisable to most summer visitors; clouds and rain strip colour from the often windswept land, the light can be dull and the sea stormy, although there are still fine days, especially on Crete and in the Dodecanese islands.

Spring comes later the further north you go and can be a joy to follow, from Crete and the Dodecanese in the south to Corfu further north. For many people, late spring and early summer are the best times to visit, when the sun is not too strong and the islands are as green and flower-filled as they will ever be, although

Agriculture still plays an important part in the islands' economy

the seas are still cold. Summers are usually hot and dry; rainfall is rare, which is one of the reasons why so many people are attracted to the islands. In September, however, although the winds pick up and the ferry service becomes less dependable, the sun is still very evident there and the blue sea is at its warmest.

❏ As Greek sailors know, Aegean winds are unpredictable and none more so than the *meltémi*. It can blow out of nowhere, get up to Force 7 or 8 on the Beaufort scale and last for an hour or a week. Perhaps more than any other single factor, the *meltémi* is responsible for the streak of resignation in the islanders' character: when control over something as basic as leaving an island is regularly taken out of your hands, what can you do but shrug your shoulders and head for the nearest *kafeneío*? ❏

❏ In ancient times, the Aegean was divided into different areas: the Thracian Sea in the north, the Mirtoan Sea in the southwest, the Ikarian Sea in the east and the Sea of Crete in the south. You may still hear these names used in some places. ❏

Times are changing for the Greek islanders. On some islands, the quiet life dependent on the olive or grape harvest has become a distant memory and new opportunities have arisen. At the same time, people from the mainland have found new value in the old island life.

THE ISLAND DREAM 'Of all peoples', wrote the German poet Goethe, 'the Greeks have dreamed the dream of life best'. Many visitors, seeing islanders going about their life – eating food grown and gathered locally, living with uplifting natural beauty, their families around them and with time to spend with each other – envy the life they have dreamed. There is another side to it, of course. Island life can be a nightmare: earthquakes have devastated islands such as Zákynthos and Kefalloniá; men plying the seas, or diving beneath them, fail to return; hardships increase as work and seafood become scarce, while every winter storms cut off the more remote

islands for weeks at a time, making food, fuel and water run short. These things do not intrude in the foreigner's rosy vision of the islands but, just as much as the summer sun, they have shaped the character of every islander you meet.

OLD HABITS Traditional island life was arranged around the seasons and orchestrated by three characters: the policeman, the priest and the teacher. In many places it still is. All three are still to be found sitting in the taverna or *kafeneío*, or strolling along the waterfront at sunset. Many of the values they stand for are still upheld – Greeks are still extremely religious and family ties are still central (how many Three Brothers' Restaurants are there?) – but life around them has changed. On many islands, students no longer need to go to Athens to be educated: television and new technology have brought the islands closer to the city, while tourism has given contact with people from all over the world. This has changed island habits. Many men no longer rely on the land or their boats for their livelihood and a woman at work is no longer a sign of a man's failure to provide for his family. But at the same time as the old ways are being questioned on the islands, another group of people are finding them of great value.

RENEWED INTEREST Earlier this century, particularly in the 1950s and 1960s when Greece was heavily influenced by the United States and the city was *the* place to live, islanders were seen as backwards. A quarter of all Greeks now live in Athens, but many of them trace their origins to

The kafeneío *is usually a men-only affair*

Young girls' expectations differ from those of their mothers and grandmothers

the islands. As the city becomes more crowded, they dream of returning: many go back for Easter and other holidays, but some find work that allows them to spend the summer near the blue Greek waters. They and some of the many Greek islanders who emigrated to South Africa, Australia and elsewhere, have become part of the summer crowd, renovating the old stone houses that year-round islanders have left for the comforts of modern homes, upholding the more traditional attitudes – and only running for the boats when the fall wind begins to bite.

MEETING THE PEOPLE In spite of the vast numbers of tourists visiting the islands, locals can still be extraordinarily

hospitable to strangers: the Greek word *xénos* means both foreigner and guest. You might not be invited into people's homes, but even on a first meeting – out strolling along the waterfront or lingering over a coffee or an *ouzo* – islanders are usually welcoming and open.

Their hospitality, like so much else on the islands, is shaped by the sea. History has taught islanders to be wary of invaders; you might be met with suspicion if you hint of any pl[an] to settle, but otherw[ise] you are welcom[ed] because you ha[ve] stopped on the [place] of which they [are] justifiably pr[oud]. On many occasi[ons you may] find yourself bein[g shown] around or told a[bout] the place with a r[ich can]dour, wit and hu[mour]

How do people survive on the Greek islands? How do they earn their money? The answer might seem simple for people who are surrounded by the sea. But as fish and sponge stocks have been depleted, islanders have had to look elsewhere for their livelihood.

SHIPPING For people who live surrounded by the sea, earning a living on it would seem to be an obvious option – and so it once was. The proximity of islands to each other made it possible for Greeks to sail early on in history and since then they have been renowned as a nation of sailors. From the late 18th century, particularly under the patronage of the Russian Czarina Catherine the Great, Greeks built up considerable merchant navies

❑ The tiny island of Oinoússes, off Chíos, is famous for its shipping families, who own as much as a third of all Greek ships. Fleeing from the Turks after the 1820s massacre on Chíos, they arrived in Sýros, were impressed by the shipyards and went home determined to set up a shipping business. 'When you're an Oinoussian', said one islander, 'from the time you're born, all you hear is ships'. ❑

– the foundation of the fortunes for which several families are still noted.

TRADITIONAL TRADE Until the 1940s and 1950s, most islands were dependent on the business (usually agricultural) from which they had always earned their living: olives, grapes or wine and wheat for trading off the island and dried and fresh fruit and vegetables, chickens, goats and dairy products for sale or barter among themselves. In some places this sort of existence is still possible, but the effect of the exodus of young men to the mainland is easily seen on many islands: fields are left to turn into scrub because the islanders are either too old or too young to do the hard work.

FAMOUS EXPORTS In 1900, currants accounted for half of Greece's total exports, while other products included lead and other ores, olive oil, wine, honey and sponges. Some of these, most noticeably sponges, have now become too scarce to be a going concern. But olives and their oil,

Not so many islanders as in the past work on small farms, like this one on Náxos

honey, wine and marble from Páros are still valuable export commodities.

TOURISM The second of Greece's three big money-spinners is the country itself – sufficiently appealing to bring more than 10 million visitors here in 1997, for example. Not surprisingly, the influence of so many foreigners has had a dramatic effect. Most visitors come to the islands in the summer months, creating seasonal jobs in hotels and other tourism-related services.

Tourism touches every part of the islands' economy: the food visitors eat boosts local farming, the wine they drink keeps Greek wineries in business (foreigners account for the majority of retsina sales), while the hotels and houses they stay in keep the construction industry running. Tourists spent approximately $3.8 billion in 1997. With so much money to be made, mainlanders are under-standably reluctant to leave the islanders to it: there is fierce competi-tion from people from the mainland, particularly Athens, who come to the islands for the season to work in restaurants or run their own hotels, tourist shops, car hire firms, or travel agencies and provide any other services foreign visitors might be willing to pay for.

Shepherds are a rare sight as more islanders head for Athens

With tourists providing a ready market, fishing is still a viable trade

BRINGING IT BACK HOME The third mainstay of the Greek economy is money sent home by Greek émigrés. Some six million Greeks live abroad, among them people as diverse as Kalymniot sponge divers working in Florida, wealthy ship owners of Oinoússes operating out of New York and other world financial centres and the 12,000-strong Ithakan community in Melbourne.

While travelling around the islands, it is as common to see churches being repaired and libraries equipped through the generosity of expatriate Greeks as it is to find their large houses shut up when the summer has ended.

15

When tourism on the Greek islands started becoming big business in the 1960s, it seemed like a beneficial exchange: foreign visitors could enjoy the islands' beauty and culture while islanders could earn some much-needed income. Now in a growing number of places both islanders and tourists are having doubts.

In summer a space on the beach is as scarce as shade

THE LOOK OF THE LAND Every visitor has an image of the Greek islands. It probably includes a small landing-place, a waterfront with a *kafeneío* and whitewashed houses on a hillside. Once commonplace, such a view is becoming increasingly hard to find in the wake of a building boom that has transformed the islands. New hotels, apartment buildings and villas appear each season, many without zoning permission. But, as one owner in the Cyclades explained, pointing to a hotel that had appeared, illegally, in front of his building, 'The planning office is far away in Sýros. It will take them forever to come to check and then they'll do nothing'.

WILDLIFE IN DANGER It is not only the views that are disappearing. The Greek islands are home to rare plants and animals which are now endangered too. Loggerhead turtles, for instance, are being forced off the beaches where they breed, in places like Zákynthos, frightened away by the noise and lights of hotels and disco-bars, most of whose customers are ignorant of the consequences of their presence. Plant life is exposed to risk too: in his introduction to *Wild Flowers of Crete* (Athens, 1987), George Sfikas writes, 'if human interference continues at the same rate without immediate steps being taken to protect nature in Crete, it will soon be ecologically destroyed'.

THE HUMAN COST Flora, fauna, the landscape – and people. Many tourists seem to believe that by paying money to visit Greece, they have bought the right to behave as they like and to find the sort of facilities with which they are familiar. In doing so they have changed life on the islands, often destroying the very things – the quiet, the undeveloped shoreline, the wildlife – that they had hoped to find here.

Greek politics are a stormy affair, providing fodder for animated discussion in many an island kafeneío. *In the 1980s and early 1990s the political scene in Greece was dominated by the elderly but charismatic and controversial leader Andréas Papandréou. Since his death in June 1996, things have been a little calmer.*

GREECE'S CONSTITUTION Under the 1975 constitution, Greece is a democracy headed by a president and ruled by an elected government with a majority in the 300-member single-chamber parliament, the *Vouli*. Members are elected for a four-year term, while the president is in office for five years.

RELATIVE STABILITY The past few years have been a time of relative political stability for Greece. Minority parties have had growing appeal, the free-spending policies of the 1980s are a thing of the past and gentle steps are being taken towards meeting requirements for membership of the European monetary union. Problems over Albania and Macedonia have been reduced to manageable proportions, though the longstanding dispute between Greece and Turkey continues to give cause for concern. (See also pages 46–9 for discussion of these issues.)

Politics are often on the kafeneío *menu*

TWO PARTIES Greek politics today is dominated by two parties, the Panhellenic Socialist Movement (PASOK) and the conservative New Democracy (ND). These two parties have been dominated in turn by Andréas Papandréou (PASOK) and Constantine Karamanlís (ND), who until recently were prime minister and president respectively. Their passings close a period that began with the fall of the colonels in 1974 and which is being called 'post-regime'. As a consequence, of these events Greek politics is likely to become less polarised.

17

❏ The Greeks, who pride themselves on having invented politics, enjoy voting and love nothing more than to settle down for a good argument about politicians and how to solve the ills of their country and the world. You have been warned! ❏

The Greek Orthodox Church touches every part of life. Priests play an important part in everyday living and are as often seen in kafeneía as conducting formal church services. Alongside the Orthodox Church, some minority religions have survived the passing of history.

EAST AND WEST The division of the Christian Church into Roman Catholic and Eastern Orthodox reflected a gap in the culture, politics and economies of the eastern and western provinces of the Roman Empire as much as a theological split. The final break occurred for two reasons: Rome's desire for supremacy in theological matters and a doctrinal difference over the divine nature of Jesus. The differences reached a head in 1054, when the pope and the patriarch excommunicated each other.

THE ORTHODOX CHURCH The Orthodox Church has some 150 million followers, but Greece is the only country where Eastern Orthodoxy is

❏ Small wayside shrines are a familiar sight on island roads. Often designed in the shape of a house or basilica surmounted by a cross, they are built in thanks to particular saints for their blessings. Inside the shrine will be an icon, an oil lamp and a bottle of oil, just as there were at the roadside shrines of pagan gods in ancient Greece. Then, as now, travellers paused to pray and to refill the lamp with oil. ❏

the state religion. During the Turkish occupation, the Orthodox Church played a crucial role, giving Greeks a sense of common identity and later providing a focus for nationalist sentiments. It was a churchman who first raised the Greek flag in defiance of Turkey in 1821 (see page 45). The Church kept Greeks in touch with their literature, art and music.

Almost all Greeks belong to the Orthodox Church. When they have something to celebrate, they go to church. When in trouble, they light candles in supplication. When afflicted, they make offerings to icons, praying that the saint will intercede for them. In a changing world it is the Church that is holding families and communities together.

ROMAN CATHOLICISM IN GREECE Although the majority of Greek Christians are Orthodox, there are small Catholic communities – a reminder of centuries of Italian influence. Catholic communities can most often be found on islands that

Saints are believed to intercede through their icons

were formerly Venetian or Genoese possessions. Tínos and Sýros, with their important Catholic shrines, are notable examples.

MUSLIM AND JEWISH COMMUNITIES

Most of Greece's Muslims are descended from Ottoman traders or from officials who settled throughout the empire as administrators. After World War I Greece and Turkey

The priest is still very much part of the village life

The church plays a social role and keeps the traditions alive

'exchanged' nationals in a swap of land and people.

Many Muslims were shipped to the nearest point out of Greece. For some that meant the Dodecanese, which were in the hands of the Italians at that time. Kós and Rhodes saw the greatest influx and today have two of the largest Muslim communities in the islands.

At one time Greece boasted one of the oldest Jewish communities in Europe, but more than 65,000 of Greece's 80,000 Jews were taken prisoner by the Nazis during World War II. Few survived the German concentration camps – less than 100 in Rhodes and none at all on Kós. The number of Jews in Greece was further reduced after the war, when many emigrated to Israel. Around 6,000 Jews live in Greece today, of whom half are in Athens.

❏ Icons have a special function in the Orthodox Church, being seen as a medium through which the divine makes itself accessible. Before making icons, both painter and material must be spiritually cleansed. During the Eucharist, the saints represented are believed to be present through their icons in the same way that the wine and wafer are Jesus's blood and body. ❏

The Greek year is punctuated by festivals. There are saints' days every day of the year and many traditional festivals are maintained locally, celebrating everything from harvest to the arts. The Lent Carnival is a time of freedom and excess. If you are lucky enough to be on an island during a festival, join in for a glimpse of real island life.

PARAMONI Below are listed the days of festivals, but remember that most religious celebrations in Greece occur on the eve of the holiday. At Easter, for instance, very little happens on the Sunday, the day of Jesus' rising. On the previous evening, however, there are candle-lit processions and prayers and, around midnight, the wonderful *Anástasi* service, ending with the greeting *Christós Anésti!* (Christ has risen).

TAKING PART Greeks are extremely welcoming to outsiders: if you happen to be on an island at a time of public celebration, feel free to join in. For religious celebrations, Orthodox church services are generally more informal than those of Roman Catholic or Protestant churches. People come and go, children run around and, provided you are suitably respectful, you will be welcome. A list of the more popular holidays

❑ For most Greeks, their name day – the day of the saint after whom they are named – is more significant than their birthday. They will celebrate and be given presents on their saint's day rather than their own birthday. This has a dual function: it ensures that everyone remembers the day and it ties the person, through their name and their saint, to the Greek Orthodox Church. ❑

and festivals is given below. The dates of some religious holidays are set according to the Eastern calendar and will change. each year. To find out more about these and civic holidays and festivals, contact the National Tourist Organisation of Greece (see page 268).

January 1: New Year's Day, Feast of St Basil (national holiday); 6: Epiphany (national holiday), Blessing of the Waters, Piréas.
February Carnivals throughout Greece, celebrations in the Ionian Islands (particularly Kefalloniá), in Athens and on Skýros, with its outrageous goat dance; 25: Ágios Riginos (patron saint of Skópelos).
March Start of Lent (national holiday), Feast of the Purification; 25: Independence Day; Evangelismós (Feast of the Annunciation: national holiday), celebrations held on Tínos and Ýdra.
April *Son et lumière* shows start in Athens, Corfu and Rhodes Town

With so many saints' days you are certain to encounter a festival

Easter is the most important festival in the Greek calendar

(until October); Palm Sunday and Easter Saturday: celebrations for Ágios Spyridon (patron saint of Corfu; also 11 August and first Monday in November); Easter (national holiday).

May 1: May Day (national holiday); 2: Ágios Georgios (patron saint of Skýros); 8: Ágios Thomás; 21: Anniversary of the union of the Ionian Islands and Greece (celebrated particularly in Corfu Town), Ágios Konstantínos and Agía Eléni; end of May: Navy Day – celebration on Ýdra of the great Independence hero Admiral Andréas Miaoúlis (1769–1835).

June Pentecost (national holiday); Athens festival of arts at Herod Atticus theatre (which runs until September); Classical drama festival (Itháki); 20: Ágios Pnévmatos (Holy Spirit Day); 29: Ágioi Apóstoloi Pétros, Pávlos.

July Rhodes wine festival, Thásos ancient drama festival (see pages 218–19), wine festival at Réthymno (Crete); 17: Agía Marína; 20: Ágios Ilías (celebrated on hilltops dedicated to the Prophet Elijah); 27: Ágios Pantelís.

August Dionysia wine festival (Náxos), Hippocrateia festival of arts (Kós), Irákleio festival (Crete), Lefkáda festival, Santoríni (Thíra) music festival; 6: Feast of the

Most celebrations occur on the eve of the festival

Metamórfosi (Transfiguration) of Jesus; 15: Panagía (Assumption of the Virgin: national holiday), Agía María, Ágios Panagiótis (notable celebrations on Tínos, Páros, Lésvos and Kárpathos); 30: Ágios/Agía Aléxandros/Aléxandra.

September 8–9: Eorti Tis Armatas (Battle of the Straits) regatta on Spétses, celebrating defeat of Ottoman navy in 1822.

October 26: Ágios/Agía Dimítrios/Dimítria; 28: Óchi day (the major patriotic festival with parades, etc; national holiday).

November 8: Feast of the Archangels Ágioi Michaíl and Gavriél; 14: Ágios Fílippos; 25: Agía Katerína; 30: Ágios Andréas.

December 5: Ágios Savvás; 6: Ágios Nikoláos; 9: Agía Ánna; 12: Ágios Spýros; 15: Ágios/Agía Ele019thérios/Elefería; 25: Christmas (national holiday), Ágios Chrístos, Agía Christína; 26: Sinaksis Theotokou (national holiday); 27: Ágios Stéfanos.

Greeks love to spend evenings talking, laughing, drinking and eating. A meal is always shared, wine flows freely and bread is abundant as both body and spirit are satisfied. Mealtimes tend to be late, leisurely and, above all, are there to be enjoyed by everyone.

LOST TRADITIONS? Greek cuisine has changed dramatically in the last 50 years as television, tourism and the modern world have put rural traditions in touch with an urban lifestyle. Food used to be simple and healthy, ingredients being dictated by the seasons. Meat and cheese were luxuries for most people. One result of the emigration of islanders and the arrival of foreigners is that in many places Greek cuisine has been reduced to the standard tourist dishes of Greek salad, *moussaká* and *souvláki*. Elsewhere, however, there are encouraging signs that the new healthy eating trend in the USA and Europe has inspired a new Greek cuisine and more restaurants are serving traditional dishes.

EATING HABITS Greeks eat little in the morning, so hotel breakfasts are often poor. It may be better to shop for a picnic breakfast of bread, fruit and rich, thick Greek yogurt with honey. In comparison with most visitors, Greeks eat the main meals of

Greek restaurants have most of what they serve on display

the day late: in Greek homes lunch is usually served after 2 pm and dinner at 10 or 11, although restaurants do serve meals earlier than that. Children are welcome and Greek cuisine offers several dishes to their taste. Many dishes are cooked in the morning, so food is often lukewarm, sometimes cold, but Greeks do not complain as they believe that hot food is bad for the stomach.

ORDERING FOOD Before ordering, Greeks ask the waiter what's cooking, as specialities are often not on the menu. You may want to look at the menu to familiarise yourself with the Greek names of food or to get an idea of the price range, but ask the waiter if there is anything else. Either go and look in the kitchen, or see what others are eating.

MEZÉDES Starters or *mezédes* are served with *ouzo* or beer as a

> ❏ 'The food... food was something he [the Greek Katsimbalis] was passionate about...Between great carnivorous gulps of food he would pound his chest like a gorilla before washing it down with a hogshead of *rezina*. He had drunk a lot of *rezina* in his time: he said it was good for one, good for the kidneys, good for the liver, good for the lungs, good for the bowels and for the mind, good for everything'.
> Henry Miller, *The Colossus of Maroussi* (London, 1942) ❏

Little snacks are one of the instant pleasures of Greek cuisine

complete light meal or at the beginning of a larger meal. As soon as Greeks arrive in a restaurant drinks are ordered, a variety of dishes is put in the middle of the table to be shared by everyone and the evening is under way. Anything served in portions smaller than a main course will do, but there are a few classics: *choriatikí* or Greek salad, *tzatzíki* (yogurt with cucumber and garlic), grilled *féta* cheese, *ochtapódi* (grilled or boiled octopus), *melitzanosaláta* (aubergine salad), *taramá* (fish-roe salad), *kalamarákia* (fried or stuffed squid), *dolmádes* (stuffed vine leaves), *gígantes* (baked butter beans), *keftédes* (meatballs), *skordaliá* (garlic sauce with mashed potatoes), *saganáki* (fried cheese), *spanakópitakia* and *tiropitákia* (spinach and cheese pastries).

MAIN COURSES Greeks are the biggest meat-eaters in Europe. The most common meat dishes are *souvláki* (lamb, veal, or pork kebabs), *brizóles* (chops), *keftédes* (meatballs), *biftékia* (Greek hamburger), and *kotópoulo* (chicken). On special occasions a spit-roast lamb (*arní psitó*), goat (*katsíki*) or suckling pig may be

available. Other traditional dishes are *pastítsio* (baked macaroni), *imám baïlnti* (stuffed aubergines with tomato sauce), *moussaká* (an oven dish with layers of chopped meat, aubergine and béchamel) and *gemistá* (stuffed tomatoes or peppers). Fish tends to be more expensive and is normally priced by the kilo. It usually comes broiled or baked.

FOR A SWEET TOOTH Traditionally tavernas do not serve desserts; at most there may be watermelon or another fresh fruit. This does not mean no desserts are available. The *zacharoplasteío* (pastry shop) usually offers ice cream, French pastries and syrupy Greco-Turkish sweets such as *baklavás* (sweet filo pastry stuffed with nuts and honey), *kataïfi* ('angel hair' soaked in honey), *galaktoboúreko* (custard tarts), and *loukoumádes* (honey puffs).

In the heat, traditional Greek coffee is often replaced by a frappé *or iced Nescafé*

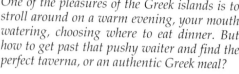

One of the pleasures of the Greek islands is to stroll around on a warm evening, your mouth watering, choosing where to eat dinner. But how to get past that pushy waiter and find the perfect taverna, or an authentic Greek meal?

LOCAL KNOWLEDGE

Greeks love going to restaurants with company or *paréa*, a group of friends or the extended family. Like Greek cuisine itself, Greek restaurants are easy-going, apart from a few more formal places in Athens and Mýkonos. The best advice is to choose a restaurant where you can see the local Greeks eating, remembering that they dine later in the evening (see pages 22–3). This may well mean giving the sea and the often tourist-orientated waterfront a miss and venturing inland. Simple tavernas, filled with Greek families, frequently produce the most delicious food and their waiters do not need to tout for business (see pages 279–83).

WHERE TO EAT An *estiatório* is the closest thing to a restaurant, sometimes with French or Italian cuisine. A *tavérna* is a straightforward place with plastic-covered tables and a menu of *mezédes*, grills and stews. A *psarotavérna* specialises in fresh fish. These can be tiny beach cabins, where fishermen cook the day's catch, or expensive waterfront tavernas with superb displays of fish, lobster and other types of seafood. A *psistariá* is a grill house specialising in char-grilled meats which often serves *kokorétsi*, a sausage made of offal, or lamb chops.

The *kafeneío* is the coffee shop where from morning till evening men sip coffee or play cards and backgammon. In small villages without tavernas the woman of the house may serve home-cooked food or offer local cheese. *Ouzéri* serve *ouzo* or wine accompanied by *mezédes*, which can be anything from char-broiled octopus to cucumber sticks. Greeks love the *zacharoplasteío* for its neon-lit counters laden with syrupy *báklavas*.

Waiters often tout for customers, but Greek families dining out are a better advertisement

The Greek Islands Were

The world of Greek mythology – of gods, demi-gods, nymphs, furies and heroes – is a complex one. Most ancient Greek art and literature drew heavily on mythology for its subjects and although many early works have been lost, enough survive to provide a precious record of these monumental stories.

IN THE BEGINNING... There were different versions of the creation myth, but one of the most widely accepted began with Chaos, the unshaped mass from which an ordered universe was formed. Chaos gave birth to Ge (or Gaia), the earth-goddess. Then Ge, without a partner, gave birth to Uranus (sky), whom she later married. Their many children included Ourea (mountains), Pontus (sea), the Cyclops, the Hundred-Handed and the Titans including Phoebe (the moon), Hyperion (a sun god), and Kronos. Ge also gave birth to Oceanus, the stream that encircled the earth, dividing the land of the humans from the underworld.

THE EARLY GODS Into this ordered world came gods who helped maintain the order. They were described as being related – a family – no doubt reflecting the growing importance of the family unit in Greek society. The founders of this heavenly family were Ge (earth) and Uranus (sky). Uranus feared his children and threw them into Tartarus, deep in the earth. Ge, wracked with pain, made a sickle and urged the Titans to strike out at their father. When Uranus next came to Ge's bed, Kronos cas-

The Cyclops Polyphemos is blinded by Odysseus and his crew

trated him, threw his genitals into the sea and became ruler of the world. But Kronos then feared that he would suffer the same fate as his father, so he ate his children Demeter, Pluto, Poseidon, Hera and Hestia. When his youngest was due, his wife Rhea tricked Kronos into swallowing a stone instead, hurried off to Crete and gave birth to Zeus. When Zeus was grown, he forced Kronos to vomit up the children in his belly and himself became ruler of the gods.

THE OLYMPIAN GODS With Kronos out of the way, the world was divided between his three sons: Poseidon was given the water, Pluto the underworld and Zeus the earth. Zeus's wife Hera, champion of heroes, is most frequently depicted as being jealous of Zeus's recurrent extramarital relations. They are seen as the mother and father of the gods, although only two of their legitimate children – Ares and Hephaistos – were admitted to the Olympian Twelve. The others were Athena, Apollo, Artemis, Poseidon, Aphrodite, Hermes, Demeter, and Hestia.

CULT FIGURES As well as the gods, a range of cult figures appeared in Greek mythology. Among those whose tales have survived into our own time are Midas, the king

was given the double-edged ability to make everything he touched turn to gold and Orpheus, whose love for the wood-nymph Eurydice led him to brave the horrors of the underworld.

THE DESCENT OF MAN Earlier Greeks accepted that man grew out of the earth, like animals, plants and all other living things, but the poet Hesiod (c8th century BC) claimed the

Poseidon and Anymone in Chaniá Archaeological Museum

gods made the first race of humans from gold, the second race of silver, the third of bronze. They were followed by the Homeric heroes and last of all by his own age, of which he wrote, 'never by day they cease from toil and woe, nor by night from being worn' (*Theogony*). It is at this point in the story of Greece that history begins to overtake mythology.

Hermes is often represented in the full flower of youth

❏ Among the best early sources for mythology are:
Homer: The *Iliad* and the *Odyssey* are the oldest surviving works of Greek literature.
Hesiod: The *Theogony* presents the creation myth and the genealogy of the gods.
Pindar: The *Victory Odes* from the Olympic Games are peopled by athletes and gods.
Aeschylus, Sophocles and Euripides: The 5th-century dramas of these Tragic Poets are based on the same sources as Pindar.
Pausanius: His *Guide to Greece* was written around AD 170.
Apollodorus: His *Library* of mythology draws heavily on Pausanius and the Tragic Poets. ❏

The religion of the Ancient Greeks was peopled with a great number of deities, connected to each other through a series of legends about the creation and early times of the universe. Many gods were personifications of aspects of the world around them (earth, night, spring) or of human life (love, discord, wisdom).

The great god was Zeus, son of Kronos, who lived on Mount Olympus with his wife Hera. His brothers Poseidon and Pluto ruled the sea and the underworld respectively. Also on Olympus were the other major gods: Athena, Apollo, Artemis, Aphrodite, Ares, Hephaistos, Demeter, Hestia and Hermes. As well as the Olympian gods, there was a host of lesser deities: the Furies, Harpies, Nymphs and Sirens. In addition, there were demi-gods: deified heroes like Heracles and Perseus, who lived on earth but became gods on their death. Ancient Greeks tried to understand the will of the gods by consulting oracles (most famously at Delphi and Dodona), interpreting dreams and looking for a variety of signs, from flights of birds to a clap of thunder.

The better-known gods of Ancient Greece include:

Aeolus God of the winds, which he kept in a cave in the Aeolian Islands.
Aphrodite The beautiful goddess of love and marriage, said to

According to Homer, Aphrodite was the daughter of Zeus and Dione

have sprung from the sea near Kýthira.
Apollo Twin of Artemis, born on Dílos. Skilled with the lyre and bow, he was regarded as the sun god (Homer called him radiant) and later also the god of all progress.
Ares Son of Zeus and Hera, the terrible god of war and lover of Aphrodite.
Artemis The huntress was a virgin goddess, often connected with the moon.
Asklepios God of medicine, worshiped at Epidáuros in the Peloponnese and on Kós.
Athena Together with Zeus and Apollo, one of the sacred trinity, often shown as the prudent warrior. As the goddess of wisdom, both practical and intellectual, she was the patron of the city of Athens.
Demeter Great mother-goddess, responsible for the fruitfulness of the Earth and mother of Persephone.
Dionysos Also known as Bacchus, he taught men how to grow grapes and was the god of wine. Dionysia or bacchanalia, riotous celebrations or orgies, were famous throughout antiquity.
Eris Goddess of arguments and sister of Ares.
Eros God of love.
Gaia Earth-goddess. Born from Chaos, she gave birth to Kronos, ruler of the earth before Zeus.
Hebe Goddess of youth.

Dionysos with panther, from the House of Masks at Dílos

Hecate Goddess of darkness and witchcraft, who roamed the earth on moonless nights with a pack of ghostly, howling dogs.
Helios A sun god, but not to be confused with Apollo. Helios rose on his chariot from the ocean in the morning and returned there at night.
Hephaistos The friendly god of fire, a blacksmith who lived on Límnos.
Hera Sister and wife of Zeus; the goddess of marriage and motherhood. The mother of Hebe, Ares and Hephaistos, she was often seen as a jealous wife – understandable, given Zeus's serial infidelities.
Heracles Later known as Hercules, he was worshiped as a demi-god for completing the famous 12 labours.
Hermes The messenger of the gods. A complicated deity, the epitome of many fine qualities but also associated with theft and cunning.
Hygieia Goddess of health, Asklepios's daughter.
Kronos Son of Heaven and Earth, he ruled the world until deposed by his son Zeus.
Luna A moon goddess.
Metis Aunt of Zeus, by whom he fathered Athena. Metis was eaten by the god when she was pregnant which is why Athena was born from his head.
Muses The nine daughters of Zeus and Mnemosyne, they were attributed to different kinds of poetry.
Nike Goddess of victory, most famously portrayed in the statue found on Samothráki, now in the Louvre, in Paris.

Nyx Goddess of the night and mother of doom, death and sleep.
Oceanus God of the ocean.
Pan God of shepherds and nature.
Persephone Daughter of Demeter. She was abducted by Pluto and became goddess of the underworld. When found by her mother, she agreed to spend part of the year underground (winter), the rest above.
Pluto God of the underworld, brother of Zeus and Poseidon.
Poseidon God of the sea, brother of Zeus and Pluto.
Priapus A fertility god, usually shown as an ugly satyr with huge genitals.
Rhea Wife of Kronos and mother of Demeter, Hera, Hestia, Poseidon, Pluto and Zeus.
Uranus God of the sky and father of the Titans, the Cyclops and, according to one legend, Aphrodite.
Zeus Son of Kronos and both brother and husband to Hera. Born on Crete, the leader of the gods presided over them on Mount Olympus.

Zeus, the supreme divinity

It is hard to travel anywhere in Greece without hearing of some of the key events in the country's long and illustrious history. The chronology below will help to put those events in context. (Note that many of the earlier dates given are approximations only.)

3200–2000 BC	Cycladic civilisation
2800–1000 BC	Bronze Age
2600 BC	Rise of Minoan civilisation
1600 BC	Height of Mycenaean civilisation
1500 BC	Thíra's volcano explodes
1450 BC	Knosós palace destroyed
1184 BC	Fall of Troy
1100–100 BC	Iron Age and Dorian invasions
900–750 BC	Creation of city-states
776 BC	Probable date of first Olympic Games
750–700 BC	Homer
650 BC	Birth of Sappho (Lésvos) Aígina mints first Greek coins
570–480 BC	Pythagoras (Sámos)
500–323 BC	Classical period
490 BC	Battle of Marathon
480 BC	Battle of Salamis
478 BC	Dílos, centre of Maritime League
460–45 BC	First Peloponnesian War
460–377 BC	Hippocrates (Kós)
458 BC	Aeschylus's *Oresteia*
456 BC	Euripides's first tragedy
442 BC	Sophocles's *Antigone*
431–04 BC	Second Peloponnesian War
425 BC	Aristophanes's *Acharnians*
399 BC	Trial and death of Socrates
380s/370s BC	Plato's *Republic*
359–36 BC	Philip II of Macedonia
336–23 BC	Alexander the Great
323–146 BC	Hellenistic period
146 BC	Romans sack Corinth, annex Macedonia and Greece
146 BC–AD 410	Roman rule
AD 58	St Paul on Rhodes
AD 95	St John's revelation on Pátmos
AD 395–1453	Byzantine rule
AD 476	End of the Roman empire (western)
AD 727–843	Iconoclasm: banning of icons in Eastern Church
AD 824–961	Saracen rule in places
AD 961	Byzantines retake Crete
1054	The Great Schism
1088	Monastery of St John founded on Pátmos
1096	First Crusade
1204	Fourth Crusade: Constantinople taken. Venetians claim right to Ionian and other islands

1210	Venetians take Crete
1309	Knights Hospitalers of St John arrive on Rhodes
1453	Constantinople falls to Ottoman Turks
1522	Rhodes falls to the Turks
1541	El Greco born in Crete
1649–69	Venetian-Turkish war, ends with Irákleio falling to Turks
1797	Napoleon takes the Ionian Islands
1799	Ionian Republic declared
1815–64	British rule in the Ionian Islands
1821–7	War of Independence
1822	Chíos massacre
1823	Solomós writes the *Hymn to Liberty*
1827–9	Aígina capital of Greece
1827	Defeat of Turkish fleet at Battle of Navaríno
1828–31	Ioánnis Kapodístrias rules
1833	Accession of King Otto
1834	Athens becomes Greek capital
1854–7	Piréas blockaded by British and French fleets
1863–1913	King George I
1864	Ionian Islands annexed
1882–93	Corinth Canal cut
1883–1957	Níkos Kazantzákis
1901	New Testament (and the *Iliad*) published in demotic Greek
1910	Venizélos becomes prime minister
1912–13	Balkans War. Greece takes Crete, Macedonia and Northern and Eastern Aegean Islands
1924	Greece declared a republic
1935	Monarchy restored
1941	Greece invaded by Nazi Germany
1948	Dodecanese Islands to Greece
1947–67	Constitutional monarchy
1953	Earthquake in Ionian Islands
1967–74	Dictatorship of the Colonels
1974	Restoration of the Republic
1974	Turks invade Cyprus
1981	Greece joins European Union (EU)

Around 3200 BC, a civilisation emerged in the Cyclades that endured for more than 1,000 years. From this period come the first recognisably Greek art and some of the country's most wonderful ancient treasures.

A SEA CHANGE Perhaps the single most important change that occurred during the Bronze Age was the development of techniques for working metals, most commonly copper. As ore was transported through the Aegean, the Cyclades found themselves at the hub of new trade routes. From these elements a distinctive culture developed.

CYCLADIC ARTS AND CRAFTS

Islanders began to live in larger communities, preferring hilly and, if possible, rocky sites for their settlements, close to the sea but easily defended. As well as metal, marble – found in excellent quality on Náxos and Páros – began to be worked into images that are among the finest creations of the human imagination. Pottery developed into an art.

Most of the objects that survive from this period were found in graves. Cycladic graves were rectangular, built of stone slabs and filled with objects that might be of use to the deceased in the afterlife: marble vessels, zoomorphic clay pots, bronze weapons and tools, amulets of clay or semi-precious stones and the marble figurines that have come to characterise Early Cycladic art.

AN UNSOLVED MYSTERY No one knows what purpose these figurines of startlingly modern appearance might have served. Were they cult figures? Divinities of life and death? Fertility figures?

The famous Faistós Disk has never been deciphered despite the endeavours of numerous experts

❏ The Cycladic era is often divided into three periods: Early Cycladic I, 3200–*c*2800 BC; Early Cycladic II, *c*2800–*c*2300 BC; Early Cycladic III, *c*2300–*c*2000 BC. ❏

The function of clay discs known as 'frying pans', usually covered with geometric designs, is also puzzling. The accepted theory is that they were used for cult purposes, but you wonder what cult could the 'frying pans' decorated with ships, in the National Archaeological Museum in Athens, have served?

Few periods of Greek history offer as many attractions and mysteries as that of the Minoans (c2600–c1450 BC). Their origins are obscured by myth, their dramatic ending has long been a matter of speculation, but what is certain is that the wonderful objects that have survived, particularly from their palaces on Crete, are proof beyond doubt of the grandeur of Europe's first civilisation.

MINOS AND THE MINOTAUR

According to legend, Crete was ruled by King Minos whose wife, Pasiphae, fell in love with a bull. From their union came a frightening creature, half-man, half-bull, called the Minotaur, for whom Daidalos, the great architect, built a labyrinth under Minos's palace at Knosós. Every nine years a group of young Athenians were sent into the labyrinth, never to be seen again.

THE AGES OF THE MINOANS It is difficult to separate fact from fiction with the Minoans. The Greek historian Thucydides (*c*460–*c*400 BC) wrote that King Minos was 'the first ruler we know of who possessed a fleet and controlled most of what are now Greek waters': this is supported by the growth of coastal settlements on pre-Minoan Crete. Other commonly accepted facts about the Minoan period include

Bull's head from Knosós

(using Professor N. Platon's period division, *Crete*, London, 1966):

Pre-Palace (2600–1900 BC): communities were established and growing, stone and metals were worked and burial rituals became increasingly elaborate.

Old Palace (1900–1700 BC): insecurity elsewhere in the region led the Cretans to unite under a few leaders, a concentration of power and wealth which led to the building of palaces at Archánes, Faistós, Knosós, Mália and Zákros. This period ended with a huge earthquake around 1700 BC.

New Palace (1700–1450 BC): the old settlements and palaces were reconstructed after the earthquake in a grander style.

Post-Palace (1450–1100 BC): Greek-speaking Achaians took over power from the Minoans.

THE OLD PALACE PERIOD After 2000 BC, several extraordinary palaces were built on Crete. Very little is known about who built them, or why, so we can only marvel at the objects found in them, such as the hieroglyphic writing (still not deciphered), the brightly coloured pottery known as Kamáres ware and the finely worked jewellery, including the famous 'Hornet Pendant' from Mália, made around 1700 BC, just before a massive earthquake destroyed all of the Minoan palaces.

THE BULL AND THE LABYRINTH The Minoans held complex rituals involving the bull, the animal sacred to the sea-god Poseidon. Decorations have shown the importance of a bull-leaping ceremony and there is a convincing theory that it was for this,

A fine gold amulet with two bees holding a drop of honey, found in the Palace of Mália on Crete

today. Knosós was once again the scene of the Minoans' most sacred rituals and seat of their power. It is from the new palaces that the great Minoan frescos have been salvaged, startling for their realism and exuberance. Similar realism appears on the surviving pottery, particularly on the jars showing octopuses, dolphins and other sea life.

Around 1450 BC, this great period of the Minoans came to an end when buildings across the island were destroyed. Was it by fire, perhaps, or a tidal wave caused by the eruption of Thíra's volcano?

once every nine years, that unwitting or unwilling Athenian youths were brought to Knosós. Another theory suggests that the labyrinth was not a place but a series of rituals or dances, a mystic approach to Poseidon, who was, appropriately, enough called the 'Earth Shaker'.

THE NEW PALACES After the earthquake, the Minoan civilisation was still vigorous enough for new palaces to be built, the ruins of which we see

Huge píthoi *like these, for storing wine and olive oil, were found in most Minoan palaces in Crete*

❏ When Theseus, son of King Aegeus of Athens, went to kill the Minotaur, Ariadne, the daughter of King Minos, gave him a ball of thread which allowed him to retrace his steps through the Labyrinth. After killing the Minotaur, Theseus fled Knosós with Ariadne, but then abandoned her, asleep, on Náxos. His punishment was immediate: sailing home to Athens, he forgot the arrangement he had made with his father: to change his black sails for white ones if he had survived. His father, upon seeing the black sails and believing that his son was dead, promptly killed himself. ❏

In the 15th century BC, power and influence shifted from the islands of Greece to the mainland, in particular to Mycenae, the Peloponnesian kingdom where, according to Homer, Agamemnon, leader of the Greeks' army to Troy, ruled. By the time Homer was telling his tales, the Mycenaeans were history and the Archaic period (c700–c500 BC) was witnessing the birth of the city-state.

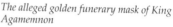

The alleged golden funerary mask of King Agamemnon

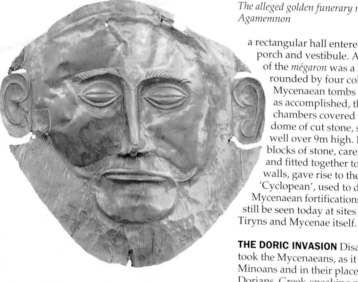

a rectangular hall entered through a porch and vestibule. At the centre of the *mégaron* was a hearth, surrounded by four columns. Mycenaean tombs were just as accomplished, their central chambers covered with a dome of cut stone, sometimes well over 9m high. Huge blocks of stone, carefully cut and fitted together to make high walls, gave rise to the term 'Cyclopean', used to describe Mycenaean fortifications which can still be seen today at sites such as Tiryns and Mycenae itself.

THE DORIC INVASION Disaster overtook the Mycenaeans, as it had the Minoans and in their place came the Dorians, Greek-speaking people from the north. The Dorians are often described as having ushered in a 'dark age', but evidence suggests otherwise. Being warriors in troubled times, by necessity their settlements evolved into fortified towns and this was the germ from which the Classical city-states and ancient Greece as we think of it, grew. Alphabetic writing also appeared in their time, as did Greek colonies in Asia Minor, the idea of the gods on Mount Olympus and Homer, who came at the height of a great tradition of storytelling.

MYCENAEAN POWER (c1500–1125 BC) The people who took control of Crete from the Minoans and who attempted to control trade in the Aegean, as legend tells us King Minos did, came from Mycenae, a town in the northern Peloponnese, north of the Saronic island of Spétses. It was during this era that many of the events that inspired Greece's epic poets took place.

THE BASIS OF GREEK ARCHITECTURE The roots of Greek architecture can be traced to the Mycenaeans. A great Minoan palace, such as Knosós, rambled over the hillside with its hundreds of chambers, but the Mycenaeans favoured a controlled symmetry. The main component of their palaces was a *mégaron*,

THE ARCHAIC ERA The period loosely called Archaic saw important changes to the society of the islands. There were significant shifts of population as colonies were founded

Archaic sculptures were often a strange interpretation of foreign, mainly Egyptian, statues

across the Mediterranean. As Greek culture spread, so did the influence of Greek ideas, of poetry, philosophy and architecture. The most important change was undoubtedly the rise of the city-state (*polis*). Greece was divided into about 1,500 of these. Notable city-states on Crete included Górtys (the most powerful), Polyrriniá, Lató and Praísos.

There had never been anything like the *pólis* before. For the first time, ordinary people had a part to play in the running of their community. Regarding themselves as independent political and military units, city-states fostered their individual identities in times of peace but formed leagues or alliances with others when it was expedient. The most powerful cities to emerge were Sparta and Athens, usually bitter rivals.

A row of magnificent Mycenaean lions guards the waters of the Sacred Lake in Dílos

❏ According to Homer, among the men who followed Agamemnon and Achilles to Troy, 'Euboea [Évvoia] sent the fiery Abantes, the men of Chalcis, Eiretria and Histiasa, rich in vines...Those from Dulichium and the sacred Echinean Islands... Odysseus next, leading the proud Cephallenians, masters of Ithaka' (*Iliad* Book II).

From Homer's list it is clear that during the Mycenaean period the islands all had separate and recognisable identities, each with a number of ships, a leader, a band of warriors and a community at home to which they hoped to return one day. ❏

At the height of the Classical period, around the 5th century BC, Athens achieved the glory for which she is still renowned. In poetry and sculpture, in warfare and politics, the Greeks and particularly the Athenians shone. By the time of Alexander the Great (336–323 BC), the vitality of Athens was exhausted, but her achievements have not been lost.

CLASSICAL GREEKS United at the beginning of the 5th century BC by a common enemy in the form of the Persians, who threatened the Delian league (effectively Athens's empire), the people of Athens and her colonies emerged with a common identity and with artists and poets to question and refine it.

THE GLORY OF ATHENS Much that we admire about ancient Greece – the Parthenon, lifelike statues, moving drama, the political force of democracy or the wisdom embodied in treatises such as Plato's *Republic* – was conceived or already flourishing during the Classical period. The power

Top: Pericles, Athens's great statesman. Below: Alexander the Great in battle at Issus in 333 BC

and wealth that ensued after Athens had fought off the Persians and taken control of most of the Cyclades and Dodecanese was shared among the Greek people.

Although not all classes were entitled to vote – women and slaves were prohibited – those who could had a more active hand in the administration of power than the average voter of today: for example Pericles, the most famous Athenian general, was voted out of office by an electorate he had temporarily angered, shortly before his death in 429 BC.

THE PELOPONNESIAN WARS Athens was not the only great city-state. Corinth and Sparta were her rivals for trade in the eastern Mediterranean. Although they had all banded together to face the Persian threat, they

An early 5th-century amphora

were also suspicious of each other. From 460 to 445 BC Athens fought against the Peloponnesian League but it was Corinth, not Sparta, who was at the forefront of the conflict. Athens was victorious in that she had her maritime empire acknowledged in the peace treaty – though only at the cost of handing back territory gained on the mainland. After a mere 14 years they were fighting again: Athens lost the Second Peloponnesian War (431–404 BC), but all parties were so weakened by the conflict that they were unable to prevent the rise of the Macedonians (Philip II and Alexander the Great) in the 4th century BC.

ALEXANDER THE GREAT In 338 BC, Philip II of Macedonia defeated the Athenians and Thebans, in his single-minded attempt to unite the diverse and widely scattered city-states under his control. Two years later Philip was succeeded by his son, Alexander III, the Great. The 5th-century BC Greek historian Herodotus identified *hellen-ikón*, Greekness, as 'shared blood, shared language, shared religion and shared customs'. The remarkable Alexander lost no time and showed little mercy, in extending the concept: having conquered the Persians (334–327 BC) and taken control of the land between Greece and Afghanistan, he hoped his culture would provide a common bond between the diverse people of his empire that would allow them to trade and thrive.

THE HELLENISTIC IDEAL Alexander was said to have founded over 70 new cities (though it was really many

fewer). The generals who divided up the empire on his death, at the age of only 33, carried on where he had left off. These cities were the perfect vehicle for spreading Greek culture and, in the process, for Hellenising conquered people by introducing Greek institutions, constitutions and language. This was an attempt not so much to convert new subjects to Greek ways as to establish Greek colonies to rule over new territories: 300 years after the founding of Seleucia in Persia, for example, the only people with Greek names were those who actually had Greek fathers.

With new cities came new rulers and new courts, all wishing to emulate the cultural achievements of Athens. Alexandria, with her library and her great thinkers and writers, did this so successfully that Athens was eclipsed as the cultural centre of the Hellenistic world. This set a precedent that the emerging Romans were only too happy to follow: Rome annexed Greece more than a century before Cleopatra committed suicide and Alexandria was taken. Even under Roman rule, however, Greek remained the common language of the lands conquered by Alexander.

❏ The Greek alphabet, from which ours has evolved, was adopted from the Phoenicians in the 8th century BC. By the Classical period, it was taken for granted that a man of wealth could read. In Athens during this period, at least half of the male population was literate. ❏

The Romans regarded themselves as the inheritors of the achievements of ancient Greece and were more tolerant of the Greeks than of many other subjects. With the decline of the Western Empire and the move of the Emperor Constantine to Constantinople, the Greeks found themselves part of a glorious civilisation – that of Byzantium.

ROME'S EMPIRE The Roman conquest of Greece started in 215 BC. The Macedonians, under Perseus, were defeated in 168 BC when Athens was taken. Corinth fell in 146 BC. Under Roman rule, the city-states survived, with Corinth, as the principal city and Athens, as the artistic and spiritual centre, attracting special favour. In Greece, the Romans stressed continuity, while the hallmarks of Roman presence – the security of the *Pax Romana* and the building of roads and of aqueducts and other irrigation works – brought wealth and an increase in population.

The Byzantine icon of the Virgin and Child from Skiádi on Rhodes

❑ Religious subjects dominated Byzantine art, but in the 8th century, differences of belief led to what is known as the Iconoclastic Controversy. While Iconoduli worshiped icons (religious images), Iconoclasts wanted them banned and they were until the Empress Theodora had them legalised in AD 843. ❑

IMPERIAL GREECE The Romans loved Greece and many emperors made the journey from Rome. Nero is said to have competed in the Olympic Games and danced and sung at the Temple of Zeus at Kassiópi, on Corfu. In AD 122, the Emperor Hadrian visited Athens, having been deified by the Greeks and calling himself Olympian Zeus. He rebuilt the city, added the suburb of Adrianopolis (approached through Hadrian's Arch), built his library and completed the Temple of Olympian Zeus.

CHRISTIANITY St Paul is credited with bringing Christianity to Greece and in the mid-1st century he visited the great mainland cities, as well as several islands. The Greeks took to Christianity with a passion, converting pagan temples into churches and some local deities into saints. In those early years, they also provided martyrs, including the Ágioi Déka (Holy Ten) of Crete, who were killed by the Romans for their faith.

BYZANTIUM In the 4th century AD, the Emperor Constantine had a vision of a cross on which was written *Hoc vinces* ('By this you shall win'). It was a defining moment in history:

Byzantine church near El Greco's birth-place in Fódele

in AD 330, having made Christianity the state religion, he moved his capital to Byzantium, which he renamed Constantinople (now Istanbul). After 65 years the empire split into two. The Eastern (Byzantine) Empire – the more vital – was based on Greek culture, Roman regulations, Christian morality and the wealth of the eastern Mediterranean.

In AD 476 the Western Empire was overrun by 'barbarians,' but under the Emperor Justinian (AD 527–65), Byzantine fortunes revived, lost provinces were restored, the entire imperial law was codified and the empire's defenses were strengthened; it was at this time that many of the islands' *kástri* were built.

BYZANTINE ARTS AND ARCHITEC-TURE As well as the *kástri*, the Byzantines built glorious churches and cathedrals throughout the empire. Many have survived on the Greek Islands. Byzantine art and architecture blended Greek and oriental elements into a new form. Literature was written in a form of Greek that was increasingly removed from the spoken language. Drama and poetry were ignored, while writers concentrated on theology, history and philosophy. Byzantine painting,

The Temple of Olympian Zeus in Athens, built by the Emperor Hadrian on earlier foundations, is the largest temple in Greece

also blending eastern and western elements, made rich use of colours, particularly gold.

THE END OF BYZANTIUM The Byzantine Empire had to fight for its existence from the very beginning. Persians, Arabs, Egyptians, Seljuks, Turks and Venetians all sought to undermine it, but in the end the very brilliance of Constantinople and the jealousy of the provinces in its power, were its downfall. The fatal blow was struck not by unbelievers, but by Christians – Crusaders – who sacked the city in 1204.

In the 11th century Byzantium gave Venice trading rights in Greece in return for protection against the Normans. Before long Byzantium needed to counter Venetian power by encouraging the Genoese. But in 1204 the Venetians deported the Crusader army that sacked Constantinople and ushered in a period of diverse foreign rule.

THE CRUSADERS When the Seljuk Turks captured Asia Minor and Jerusalem, some Christian kings, seeing commercial and political advantage behind religious justification, sailed east to recover the Christian holy places from Muslim control. Christian power bases were established in the region, some of them taken from the Byzantines – Cyprus, for instance, was taken by England's Richard I during the Third Crusade. The Fourth Crusade (1202–4), undertaken with the blessing of the Latin Pope, saw the sack of

The Knights of Rhodes defeated the Turks in the naval battle of Embro

Constantinople and the creation of a Latin Empire of Romania. In the dismemberment of the Byzantine Empire, the Greek mainland was divided among Flemish, French and German barons, owing only nominal allegiance to the new Latin emperor.

VENETIAN MIGHT The power of Venice was based on its navy. The dominant sea power of the eastern Mediterranean, rich from carrying trade between eastern ports and Europe's capitals, Venice had been the obvious choice to provide a shipping service for the Crusading armies, both for the strength of its navy and for the rapacious ambition it shared

with the Christian knights. Part of the payoff was Venetian control of most of the Aegean, which helped Venice to secure the shipping routes to Alexandretta and the Black Sea as well as to Alexandria. The Venetian aristocracy controlled the republic's new possessions, most noticeably the Orsini family in Kefalloniá and the Sanudi, who became the dukes of Náxos and thus effectively controlled the Cyclades.

CHANGING TIMES The Venetians continued to add to their possessions in the Aegean: in 1204 they acquired Crete, valued for its grain and sugar; they held the island until it was captured by the Turks in 1669. Évvoia was bought in 1209 and, until its capture in 1470, served as an excellent maritime base. The Venetians faced increasing competition from their commercial rivals the Genoese, who had been enlisted by the Byzantines in 1261 to help bring down the Latin emperor in Constantinople. When that succeeded they were given control of the islands of Chíos, with its lucrative mastic trade and Lésvos, while in 1267 the Genoese occupied the Golden Horn at Constantinople and controlled trade to and from the Black Sea.

WANING POWER Some time around 1354 a new and irresistible force appeared in Europe for the first time: within 200 years the Ottoman Turks

The Turks in Rhodes: Prince Zizim is served food on board ship by the Knights Hospitalers

❏ Crusaders on their way to the Holy Land showed little interest in Greece and her islands. The most influential Crusader presence appeared only after the collapse of the Eighth and final Crusade (1270–2) when the Christians were forced to flee the Holy Land: the Knights Hospitalers of St John, an order founded to care for sick pilgrims in Jerusalem, arrived on Rhodes in 1309 and, until their defeat by the Turks in 1522, were a significant force in the islands and in eastern Mediterranean trade (see pages 168–9). ❏

had seized control of much of the eastern Mediterranean. At the time, the Venetian Republic was still adding to its strategic possessions: Tínos and Mýkonos were taken in 1390 and four years later Venice even had control of Athens, which it held until 1402. But in 1453, only two years after the Venetians took Aígina, both Venetians and Genoese failed to respond in time to prevent the Turks capturing Constantinople. In September 1453, rather belatedly, the Pope issued a Bull calling for another Crusade, but there was no response. The Genoese ceded control of the Black Sea trade, the Knights of St John were forced out of Rhodes in 1522 and one by one the heavily fortified Venetian posts fell to the Turks, although Tínos held out until 1715.

Greece was too close a neighbour for the Ottoman Turks to leave in foreign hands. But the sultan in Constantinople (Istanbul) had little interest in this newly acquired territory. Having been treated as the private property of European rulers, the Greeks found themselves neglected by the Ottomans (1453–1827).

The Turkish fleet attacks Rhodes in 1480

SECURING NEW TERRITORIES

After setting up their capital in Constantinople, the Turks took more than two centuries to capture all the Greek islands. One legacy of this period is the islands' ruined fortresses, many of them sacked by Kheir-ed-Din Barbarossa. Born and brought up on Lésvos, Barbarossa made his reputation raiding European ships and establishing, under Turkish sovereignty, the kingdom of Algiers. In 1535, Sultan Suleiman (the Magnificent) appointed Barbarossa High Admiral of the Ottoman fleet. Within three years, Barbarossa's notoriously ruthless tactics had ensured Turkish domination of islands and sea in the golden age of the Ottoman empire. He died in triumph in Constantinople in 1546.

OLD WAYS PRESERVED

The Ottomans were generally negligent in their occupation of Greece. They regarded the Greeks and other Christians as lesser beings, from whom they required obedience, particularly concerning taxes. At the time of the Ottoman conquest, Patriarch Gennadius guaranteed obedience and regular taxes in return for self-government. Although in this way the Church became an instrument of foreign rule, it also had an important role to play in creating the national identity by preserving Greek and Byzantine traditions.

THE BITTER YEARS

The British ambassador to Constantinople in 1622 complained that Turkish rule was so hard that he had to ride for three or four days in Greece to find food for himself or his horse. Taxation had its effect, as had the taking of children to be trained as Janissaries (imperial soldiers), a practice that was stopped later in the 17th century because it affected people's ability to pay taxes.

❑ The Orthodox Church still commemorates 28 May each year, remembering that Tuesday in 1453 when Constantinople, centre of the Eastern Empire and of the Orthodox Church, fell to the Ottoman Turks. ❑

THE PHANARIOTES Not all Greeks suffered. In the 17th century, some official posts became available to them. In 1669, Panagiotaki, a Greek Christian from Chíos, was appointed Dragoman to the Porte, in effect a secretary of state to the sultan. Other Greeks were appointed to govern territories, or as assistants to senior officials. Most lived near the Patriarchate, beside Constantinople's lighthouse – the *Phanar* – and were known as Phanariotes.

❑ As Orthodox Christians, the Greeks found support in the 18th century from Russia, particularly under Catherine the Great. In 1783 she took the Crimea and forced the Sultan to allow Greek ships to trade under the Russian flag. This new status gave a boost to the fortunes of Greek traders while depriving the Turks of mercantile support. ❑

THE TURKISH LEGACY Considering how long the Turks occupied Greece, very little has survived from the occupation, mostly as a result of a backlash against Turkish institutions and property after independence. Notable exceptions include the mosques and houses in old towns such as Rhodes, Chaniá on Crete and Myrína on Límnos.

Monuments of the Turkish legacy, like the Defterdar Mosque on Kós, are often neglected in Greece

The French Revolution; the weakening of the Ottoman Empire; the conviction of Western aristocrats that Greece must rediscover her glory; rebellions and atrocities within the Greek territories; and growing opposition to the Turkish occupation by sympathisers elsewhere in Europe – all these factors helped create the circumstances that brought about Greek independence.

THE ORIGINS OF THE STRUGGLE

Although in some places (particularly on the islands previously held by the Venetians) there was initial relief when the Ottoman Turks arrived as the new masters, from the beginning of the Turkish occupation Greeks had fought for their independence. Not for a Greek nation – there had not been one for so long that most would not have understood the concept – but at least for freedom from what was, for many people, in effect slavery. In the last decades of the 18th century, Catherine the Great of Russia promoted the cause of Greek Christians, but events took a more significant turn when Napoleon

Bonaparte took the Ionian Islands from Venice in 1797. Two years later a combined Russo-Turkish force captured them and created the autonomous Septinsular Republic and for the first time in 350 years the islanders had at least the pretence of governing themselves.

CULTURAL SIGNALS The movement toward independence had interesting cultural indicators. While Smyrna-born scholar Adamántios Koräis was working in Paris on reviving classical Greek, groups in Europe were raising awareness of Greek aspirations. They included the *Filikí Etaireía*, founded in 1814 in Odessa by three Greek merchants and the Philomuse Society in Vienna which numbered the Bavarian king and the Russian czar among its supporters. The British poet Lord

A wreath on Byron's statue in London commemorates the cause that was dear to him as well as to many other foreigners

44

Byron, who first visited Greece in 1807, was one of many classically educated foreigners who sympathised with the Greek cause, while the arrival in European capitals of Greek antiquities did much to win over the western public.

ACTION The Metropolitan of Pátra raised the Greek flag on 25 March 1821, a date still celebrated as Greece's national day. Nothing that occurred in the ensuing struggle for independence was as simple. European governments condemned the move, but public opinion was for Greek independence. Early Greek successes led to a power struggle between rival groups. In April 1824 the death of Lord Byron at Messolóngi increased international support for the cause and when Messolóngi fell to the Turks in 1826, British, French and Russian fleets were sent to pressure the Turkish sultan. It ended in conflict, with the Turkish and Egyptian navies being destroyed at Navarino in October 1827, ending the long period of Turkish control of the Greek seas and paving the way for independence.

THE CONTINUING STRUGGLE It took the Greeks until the middle of the 20th century to take possession of the land they regard as their own. During the reign of King George I of Greece (1863–1913) the British relinquished the Ionians (1864) and Crete was finally won in 1913, following the Balkan Wars. In 1897 Greece went to war against the Turks and was defeated. The resultant upheavals saw the advent of one of the country's most able and best-loved rulers, Elefthérios Venizélos, who took Greece into another conflict with Turkey (1912–13), this time to emerge with considerable territorial gains, including the eastern Aegean islands.

In 1921, having supported the Allies during World War I to their advantage, the Greeks again went to war with Turkey. Turkey had undergone considerable changes of its own under the leadership of

Ioánnis Kapodístrias, Greece's first president after independence

❏ Count Ioannis Capo d'Istria (later spelt Kapodístrias) from Corfu was one of the most powerful Greek politicians during the independence struggle. With the Treaty of Adrianople (1829), Greece won its autonomy. Kapodístrias had already been elected governor and when the new state was created he became its first president. He provoked strong opposition by ignoring the constitution and in October 1831 he was assassinated. As a result, the European powers imposed a monarchy on the country. ❏

Kemal Ataturk and the Greeks were crushingly defeated. The consequences were catastrophic: around a million and a half Greek refugees were forced out of Turkey, back to their homeland. It took Greece until the 1950s to recover from their arrival.

45

Greece emerged from World War II in a state of crisis and immediately slid into civil war. Since then it has been ruled by monarchs, military dictatorships and socialist governments. Only now is it enjoying an extended period of stability for the first time.

ÓCHI! In August 1940 the Italians tried to provoke the Greeks into joining World War II by sinking one of their battleships in Tínos harbour. They failed. Two months later they demanded the right to march Italian troops across Greek soil, to which the head of Greece's government, General Metaxas, gave his famous response – 'Ochi!' (No!) – still commemorated with a public holiday. Early victories against the Italians in Albania led to a German occupation of Greece in 1941. With the help of British commandos a bitter resistance

❑ The Dictatorship of the Colonels from 1967 to 1974, led by Colonel George Papadópoulos, marked the low point in modern Greek history. Executions, mass imprisonment, the hounding of public figures (even the beloved Melína Merkoúri) and inept administration were typical of the junta. In 1974 the Colonels were forced from power and a referendum also brought an end to the monarchy. ❑

The actress Melína Merkoúri was a strong opponent of the Junta

campaign was waged and in 1944 most of Greece was liberated from the rule of the Germans.

CIVIL WAR Even during the German occupation, rival resistance groups had begun fighting each other. From December 1944, after the government returned from exile, Greece became an ideological battleground. It was by now surrounded by Communist regimes in Albania, Bulgaria and Yugoslavia. After right-wing parties won the 1946 elections, the United States offered massive financial and military aid. Although internal Greek politics were polarised, the country came under increasing American influence, joining NATO in 1951. Continued American backing created the climate (and some say gave instructions) for the 1967 military coup that stopped George Papandréou's Centre Union Party from taking power.

THE EUROPEAN IDEAL Since the downfall of the Colonels and the monarch, Greece has been a republic keen to measure itself by European standards. Democracy was encouraged and living standards improved under Constantine Karamanlís, a hard-line conservative who also lobbied for entry into the European Union. Greece became a member of the EU in 1981, the year of her first socialist government, led by Andréas Papandréou, son of the former Centre Union Party leader.

PASOK The major force in recent Greek politics has been Papandréou's PASOK (Panhellenic Socialist Movement). With a decisive majority, it ruled from 1981 until its scandal-ridden government was brought down in 1989 by a bizarre coalition of left- and right-wing parties. In 1990 the right-wing New Democracy Party was voted in with a small majority, but although its austerity plans seemed to be approved, humiliation over the creation of an independent Macedonian state brought back Papandréou's PASOK with a large majority in 1993. Ill health forced Papandréou to step down in 1995 and he died the following year.

THE PRICE TO PAY Despite the image of wealthy shipping families, Greece is not a rich country. There has been extraordinary economic and social change since World War II, with growth in housing, education and health care (although the last still

The multi-millionaire shipping magnate Aristotle Onassis was as internationally renowned as Zorba the Greek

cannot be taken for granted). At the same time there has been hardship, a move away from the countryside and islands to towns where living conditions for many remain poor.

Andréas Papandréou at the height of his powers

❏ 'Macedonia...is Greek – always has been, always will be.' So says one particularly plain-speaking sticker that has appeared all over Greece. In 1991, one of the provinces of the former Yugoslavia proclaimed independence under the name of Macedonia. As part of northeastern Greece is also called Macedonia (and only passed from Turkey to Greece in 1913), Greece vigorously opposed the new state using the name, fearing that in time it will call for the unification of Macedonian lands. As a strange compromise, both the UN and the European Union recognised the new state under the name of The Former Yugoslav Republic of Macedonia (FYROM). ❏

'Don't mention the Turks'... Greeks are still bitter about the Turkish occupation of their country. The proximity of the two countries, and recent events, have ensured that Greeks remain suspicious of Turkish intentions.

WHEN TURKS WERE MASTERS There are obvious historical reasons for Greek mistrust of Turkey. From a religious point of view, it was the Turks who brought an end to the Greeks' spiritual centre, the Orthodox capital of Constantinople. Politically, the centuries of Turkish rule have also left bitter memories. The Greek state was built upon the rejection of Turkey, independence coming only after Greeks had taken up arms. While Greeks wrapped their actions in the cloak of romance, the Turks were always seen as barbarians: no one mentions Greek atrocities in the War of Independence but the Turkish massacre of the islanders of Chíos caused international outrage.

A NEW ERA The last islands were handed back to Greece in the 1940s, but that has not eased fears about Turkish expansionist policies. Independent Greece is as uneasy as ever about its neighbour. There are few Ottoman buildings left intact in Greek towns, few mosques left unconverted and Turkish artifacts are conspicuous by their absence in Greek museums, but despite all the Greek efforts to

On a clear day the coast of Turkey is easily visible from the beach in Kós

erase traces of the occupation, the Turks still loom large. Nor will the rest of the European Union adopt Greece's attitude of condemning Turkey since they fear alienating a strategically valuable ally (Turkey's stand during the 1991 Gulf War was evidence of this strategic value).

CYPRUS In 1974, the Greek military junta, headed by former secret police chief General Ioannídes, attempted to stage a coup in Cyprus to overthrow the independent Cypriot leader Archbishop Makários. The coup failed to dislodge the archbishop but still provoked an aggressive Turkish response: some 30,000 Turkish troops helped Turkish Cypriots divide the island into two separate entities, taking at least a third of the land even though Turks accounted only for some 18 per cent of Cyprus's population. The Greeks attempted to fight back and for a few days a full-scale war between the two enemies looked likely, until international diplomacy defused the situation. Although only

The Archbishop Makários waving at a crowd of Greek Cypriot supporters

49

Turkey has recognised Turkish Cyprus as an independent state and has, apparently, settled mainland Turks on the northern part of the island, enforcing their position with a considerable garrison, the international community has held back from implementing the anti-Turkish measures that Greece has demanded for the simple reason that Turkey is too valuable an ally to alienate. A status quo now appears to be observed, giving Greece justification for blocking Turkey's application for membership of the European Union.

TROUBLE IN THE 'GREEK LAKE'

Greek islands fringe the western coast of Turkey and sit on the vital shipping lane from the Bosphorus to the Mediterranean. The Turks complain of having to sail through what has become a 'Greek lake', while the Greeks watch Turkish movements with alarm. The isolated positions of some Greek islands make the situation even more difficult: there is a story circulating in the Dodecanese, for instance, that if the population of Kastellórizo drops below 200 the island will revert to Turkey. Greek officials deny this as vigorously as they protest invasion of Greek air space by the Turkish air force: Greek jets are scrambled periodically in response to these aerial 'invasions'. From its side, Turkey protests at the heavy Greek military presence on the island of Límnos, so close to the Turkish mainland.

THE FUTURE As the futility and trauma of the exchange of Greek and Turkish populations showed in the 1920s, there are no quick solutions to this crisis between neighbours. Differences in religion, history and self-image, in economies and military standing, will always remain.

A negotiated settlement, an easing of tension and, especially, a solution to the Cyprus problem will have to come about before relations will begin to improve – more easily said than done. Mutual suspicion is inevitable, in view of the long history of conflict.

Turkish tombstones dumped outside the Archaeological Museum in Irákleio, Crete

The famous porch of the Eréchtheion, supported by Caryatids, thought to be aristocratic maidens in the service of Athena

There is no escape from the ancient Greeks, even in modern day Athens

ATHÍNA (ATHENS) Greece's capital city has such a reputation for traffic and pollution problems that many visitors who arrive at its airport on their way to the islands prefer to head straight for their destination. But the capital's sights and the atmosphere in some areas of the city make it a wonderful place to spend a few days, especially out of season. The Acropolis, of course, is essential viewing, despite the crowds and several of the city's museums complement visits to the islands by their displays of island artifacts and antiquities, which bring the islands' history vividly to life.

ANCIENT BEGINNINGS Athens has grown enormously in the past few decades, but its centre remains clustered around the Acropolis and Areopagus hills, where the first settlement grew, around 3000 BC. Athens played her part in the Mycenaean and Dorian periods but did not really shine until the 8th century BC, when, under the protection

of the goddess Athena, the city dominated the Greek world, its wealth and power attracting intellectuals and artists still influential today.

ATHENIAN GLORY The Persian King Darius attacked the rising city-states of Athens, Sparta and Corinth in 490 BC, but his formidable army was defeated by a smaller Athenian force at Marathon. Ten years later the Persians returned under King Xerxes with the largest army ever seen. The Athenians were strongest at sea: after Athens was destroyed, the Greek navy outmanouvered the Persians at Salamis and forced them to withdraw. The glorious city that attracts us today – the city of the Parthenón, the Eréchtheion and the Temple of Athína Nike, of Phidias's famous statue of Athína, Herodotus's histories, Socrates's philosophy and Sophocles's and Aristophanes's dramas – rose out of the 5th-century BC reconstruction of the city.

▶▶▶ CITY HIGHLIGHTS

Acropolis
see pages 54–5

Museum of Cycladic and Ancient Greek Art
see pages 58–9

National Archaeological Museum
see pages 56–8

USEFUL NUMBERS
Olympic Airways
(Odós Syngrou 96)
tel: 01 926 9111
Hertz Rent-a-Car
tel: 01 922 0102
Airport (western terminal
flight information)
tel: 01 936 9111
Airport (eastern terminal
flight information)
tel: 01 969 4111

FOREIGN RULE Athens's power was already waning when the Macedonians – Philip and his son Alexander the Great – sought her help with their eastern ambitions. Alexandria and Pergamon began to challenge her cultural supremacy, though even after the Roman conquest (146 BC) Athens was revered for her achievements. Roman emperors, especially Hadrian, added to her beauty, while shipping treasures off to Rome and later to Constantinople. By the 3rd century AD they were unable to defend her and the city was sacked by barbarians.

THE MODERN CITY Fifteen hundred years of foreign rule – Byzantine, Catalan, Neapolitan, Venetian, and Turkish – eventually left Athens a heap of derelict housing crouching around the Acropolis. For the capital of the newly

52

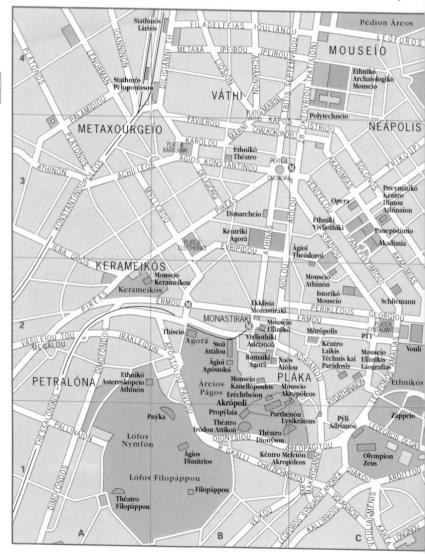

independent Greek state, King Otto I (1833–62) planned new districts along neoclassical lines, their broad avenues now forming the centre of the modern city. In the 20th century, the population of Athens has been swelled with returning nationals and with islanders attracted to the new metropolis. The plain between the Athenian hills and the port of Pireas has now been filled with apartment houses.

ISLAND DREAMING More and more people dream of leaving Athens and returning to the islands of their birth or parentage. Those who stay in the city flee to the islands in the summer, so if you want to see Athens in full swing, visit in spring or fall: winter is cold and can be wet, summer is hot and many shops and restaurants are closed.

TOURIST INFORMATION
The Greek National Tourism Organisation (EOT) has its adminis-trative headquarters at Amerikis 2 in central Athens (tel: 01 331 0561), where there is also a public information office (open from 11–1 Mon–Fri). The Athens Municipality also has an information booth on the corner of Syntagma and Ermou. There is an information desk at the airport's east terminal (tel: 01 969 4500) and at Marina Zeas in Piraeus (tel: 01 428 4100). In summer the GNTO. opens an office at Stadiou 4 (tel: 01 322 1459) for dealing with the Athens Festival.

53

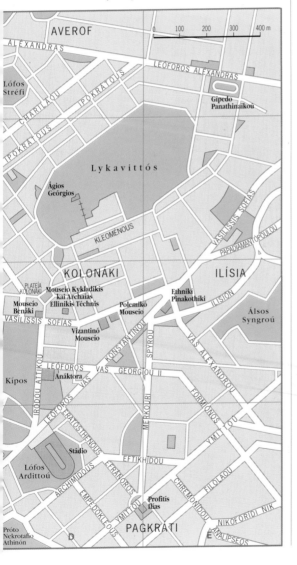

The picturesque streets of old Athens are a reminder of the simple village life on the islands

Athína (Athens)

A STROLL THROUGH THE AGORÁ

After visiting the Acropolis it is a pleasant stroll down to the Agorá and the area of Monastiráki via the hill of Áreios Págos (Areopagus). Just below the entrance to the Acropolis, stairs ascend to the site of Areopagus, with various ancient and Roman foundations and good views over the entire area. From here it is possible to continue to the southern entrance of the Agorá.

SON ET LUMIÈRE AT THE ACROPOLIS

Shows in several languages take place daily. Tickets can be bought at the entrance or at the Athens Festival Office (tel: 01 322 1459). For information about times and prices, tel: 01 322 6210.

The Acropolis is still the heart of Athens, often visible from wherever you are when the smog clears

▶▶▶ Akrópoli (Acropolis)   52B2

(Tel: 01 321 0219)

Open: summer, Mon–Fri 8–6.30, Sat and Sun 8–2.30; winter Mon–Fri 8.30–2.30, Sat and Sun 8.30–2.30 (hours change frequently). Admission charge, free Sun and public holidays Metro: Monastiráki

The Ancient Greeks always built their acropoli on high places, a safer bet and also a step closer to the gods. The Athens Acropolis was already a cult place when the Athenians erected their magnificent temples and buildings here in the 7th century BC. After the Persians set fire to Athens and sacked the Acropolis in 480 BC, the ruins were at first kept as a reminder, but 50 years later Pericles rebuilt the city in all its splendour. The remaining buildings are still a testimony to the magnificent achievements of Greece's Golden Age. The weathered stone glows in the sun, seductive to our modern eye but looking rather different from the original buildings, painted in bright colours and with dressed-up statues covered in golden trinkets.

Even before it was finished, the massive gateway or **Propýlaia**, constructed in 437–432 BC by the architect Mnesikles, was considered as great an achievement as the Parthenon. The graceful **Naós Apteroú Níkis (Temple of Athena Nike)**, built in 427–424 BC by Kallikrates, was surrounded by a marble wall sculpted with war scenes and figures of the winged Victory. According to legend, this is where Aegeus waited for the return of his son Theseus from Crete, and where he jumped to his death after Theseus forgot his promise to signal victory over the Minotaur by hoisting a white sail. Today the site, as the city itself, is dominated by the **Parthenón**, but in classical times the temple, less important than the Eréchtheion, was mostly hidden by other buildings. Hundreds of books have been written about the perfection and optical illusions of the vast Doric temple, but a simple wink of the eye reveals its magnificence and harmonious proportions. It was built in Pentelic marble between 447 and 438 BC by the architects Iktinos and Kallikrates. Phidias completed the sculptures in 432 BC, including the 10m high

bronze statue of Athena which stood in front of the temple and was visible from Cape Sounion. The statue was taken to Constantinople and later lost. Most of the Parthenón sculpture is in the British Museum in London, some in the Louvre in Paris and the rest in the Acropolis Museum. Over the years the Parthenón has been put to many uses, from Greek and Roman temple to Byzantine church, Frankish cathedral and Ottoman mosque.

The last great monument on the Acropolis is the complex **Eréchtheion**, built on an older sanctuary and dedicated to Poseidon, whose spring provided the temple's inhabitants with water, and to Athena, whose sacred olive tree grew on this site. The famous southern Porch of the Caryatids or Maidens was used for rituals. Four of the original caryatids are displayed in the **Mouseío Akropóleos (Acropolis Museum)** (*Open* Tue–Sun 8.30–3, Mon 11–2.30), which houses some magnificent sculpture from the Acropolis including fragments of the Parthenón frieze and the unique 6th-century BC *korai* – statues of young maidens attending Athena.

The **ancient Agorá** (*Open* Tue–Sun 8–2.30. *Admission charge*), northwest of the Acropolis, was the market place and the centre of Athens's political and social life. Its buildings cover a large area and date from the 5th century BC to late Byzantium, making the site difficult to understand. Among the ruins is the 5th-century BC **Thiseío (Theseum)**, the best-preserved ancient building in Greece. It was in fact a temple to Athena and Hephaistos, though the adventures of Theseus are depicted on its frieze. The museum, housed in the **Stoá Attálou (Stoa of Attalos)** (2nd century BC, reconstructed 1953–6), has 6th- to 4th-century BC pottery and fine red-figure dishes.

BEST VIEWS OF THE ACROPOLIS
There is a good view of the Acropolis from Odós Aiólou, where the rock rises up at the end of the street, and from the area around the Naós Aiólou (Tower of the Winds) at night when the site is illuminated. The views from the nearby pine-wooded hills of Arditóu, Filopáppou and Lykavittós are excellent, and make for the ultimate picnic with a view. One of the most pleasant tavernas with excellent *mezédes* and a view is Strofi, Odós R Gálli 25 (tel: 01 921 4130).

55

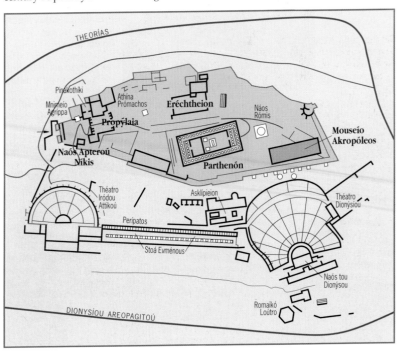

Athína (Athens)

MOUSEIO BENAKI (BENAKI MUSEUM)

The Benáki Museum (corner of Odós Koumbári and Vasílissis Sofías; tel: 01 361 1617) houses the wonderful collection of the Egyptian Greek, Antoine Benáki. The museum contains Egyptian antiquities and Ottoman manuscripts, a superb collection of folk costumes and crafts from the Ionian islands as well as several paintings by the Cretan-born El Greco.

Many of the best archaeological pieces from the islands are in the National Archaeological Museum, including these vases from Santorini

FOLK ART FROM THE ISLANDS

The Mouseío Elliníkis Laografías (Museum of Greek Folklore), (Odós Kydathinaíon 17, Pláka; tel: 01 321 3018. *Open* Tue–Sun 10–2. *Admission charge*) is a must for anyone interested in the fast-vanishing traditions of most of the islands. It houses an important collection of folk art from the mainland and the islands, including ceramics, shadow puppets, embroideries, jewels, and costumes, as well as a series of murals by the primitive artist Theophilos (1873–1934) who came from Lésvos.

►►► Ethnikó Archaiologikó Mouseío (National Archaeological Museum)   52C4

Odós Patissíon 44 (tel: 01 821 7717)
Open: Mon 12.30–7, Tue–Fri 8–7 (earlier closing in winter), Sat, Sun and public holidays 8.30–3. Admission charge Trolley buses: Nos 2, 3, 4, 5, 12 from Síndagma or Omónia

Although ancient Greek works star in foreign museums and the exhibits here are often badly labelled and poorly displayed, this astounding collection of the world's finest Cycladic, Minoan, Mycenaean and Classical Greek art deserves several visits. The best finds from the islands have made their way here, some of them as the prize exhibits, so a visit is essential to get a complete picture of the archaeological sites on the islands.

The visit starts with three prehistoric rooms, the first of which (room 4) often renders visitors speechless as it is packed with the rich treasures discovered by the archaeologist Heinrich Schliemann in the chamber tombs at Mycenae (see pages 86–7). Most famous of all is the **Funerary Mask of Agamemnon** (No 624), named by Schliemann for its supposed connection with the words from the *Iliad*: 'He was the King of Men... distinguished among many and outstanding among heroes.' There is the silver **bull's head with golden horns** (No 384) and the earliest known depiction in Europe of a historical event, on the silver **Siege Rhyton** (No 481). Almost every case contains objects of extraordinary refinement, including gold seals with hunting scenes

(Nos 33–5) and a delicate duck-shaped vase in rock crystal (No 8638). To the left of the central gallery, in the pre-Mycenaean room (room 5) are neolithic figurines, pottery and jewellery from the Thessalian plain. In the **Cycladic room** (room 6), on the central gallery, the finds are arranged island by island. The largest female figurine (No 3978) and a beautiful large head (No 3909) were discovered on Amorgós, while the amazing harpist and flute-player (Nos 3908 and 3910) come from Kéros, near Amorgós. The excellent marble figurines (6195, 6140.21 and 6140.22) come from Náxos, as do the finely decorated vases, some in the shape of animals.

Most of the remainder of the ground floor is devoted to sculpture, arranged chronologically and showing clearly the developments from immobile stylised statues of the early Archaic period to the free and more naturalistic masterpieces of the Classical period. Rooms 7–13 are devoted to Archaic sculpture from the 7th to the 5th centuries BC. Room 7 has the first statue listed in the museum's catalogue, the **Artemis of Nikandra** (No 1), discovered on

Dílos. Rooms 8–13 contain many *kouroi* and steles, of which the best examples are the **kouros from Mílos** (room 9, No 1558), the exquisite **Stele of Marathonomachos** (No 29) and the strong, graceful **Kroisos** (No 3851) from around 530 BC. The extraordinary bronze **Poseidon of Artemision** (room 15), found in the sea near Évvoia, has the perfectly balanced body of an athlete, muscles tensed as he prepares to throw his trident. The impressive **Eleusinian relief** (No 126) in the same room shows Demeter and Persephone with the young Triptolemos, from about 430 BC.

Among the Classical steles from 5th-century BC graves in rooms 16–17, note the delightful **relief of the actors** (room 17, No 1500), where Dionysos, lying on the bed, is worshiped by an actor holding a mask and by two drummers. The exquisitely carved funerary **Stele of Hegeso** (room 18, No 3624) expresses sorrow and a kind of despair in a very subtle and dignified way. Quite poignant for anyone from the islands today is the **Stele of Demokleides** (room 18, No 752), showing a man sitting on a rock, his head resting in sorrow, with his prow and high waves in front of him, suggesting that he died far from home.

Room 20 has a small Roman copy of Phidias's Athena (No 129), the cult statue from the Parthenón. Does the 'jockey' belong with the jumping horse (room 21, No 15,177)? The question continues to divide experts, but most people who see the 2nd-century BC bronze statue tend to marvel at the passion and the tension of the boy and the racing horse. It is hard to imagine what else the boy might have been designed for.

In the middle of room 28 stands the **Youth from Antikýthira** (No 13,396), a large bronze statue from about 340 BC, discovered in many pieces near Antikýthira. The statue is a masterful portrait of a relaxed, confident and

57

The magnificent statue of Poseidon was found on the same shipwreck as the Little Jockey in room 21

The vivid Hellenistic portrait of the unnamed philosopher was found off the coast of Antikýthira

58

totally harmonious youth. Room 30 has another treasure from Antikýthira, the Hellenistic **Head of the Philosopher** (No 13,400), which shows the man, wrinkles and all. This is in direct contrast to the earlier Classical **Head of the Boxer** (room 28, No 6439). The 2nd-century BC **Poseidon** (No 235) supported by a dolphin, dominating the room, once adorned the Poseidon Temple in Mílos. The 1st-century BC **Man from Dílos** (No 14,612) looks anxiously towards the future (as well he might – Greece was a Roman province by then), while in the **Group with Aphrodite and Pan**, made around 100 BC and also from Dílos, Pan is held back by Eros while seducing the naked and bashful Aphrodite. Rooms 41–3 contain Roman sculpture, including some pieces that come from the islands.

On the upper floor, rooms 49–56 house the **Vase Collection** with amazing pottery from the Geometric period, black-figure and red-figure vases and white *lekythoi* (containers for oil or perfume), many of which came from Eretria on Évvoia. In room 48, the **Thíra Exhibition** contains various finds from excavations on Thíra (Santoríni), including pottery, bronze objects and the famous frescos from Akrotíri, remarkably well preserved having been covered by volcanic pumice for so long. These wall paintings have provided much essential information about life on Thíra at the end of the 16th century BC. The best-preserved frescos are the **wall-painting of the fisherman**, where a naked young man holds two bunches of fishes and the strange **wall-painting of Spring**, which shows a Thiran landscape before the volcanic eruption, with swallows and flowers.

►► Monastiráki   52B2

Monastiráki, the area between the Agorá and Syntágma, is famous for its weekend flea market and also for its restaurants and budget hotels. Monastiráki metro stop is useful for the area around Syntágma and Pláka.

►►► Mouseío Kykladikís kai Archaías Elliníkis Téchnis (Museum of Cycladic and Ancient Greek Art)   53D2

Odós Neofítou Douká 4, Kolonáki (tel: 01 724 9706)
Open: Mon and Wed–Fri 10–4, Sat 10–3. Admission: charge
All buses for Plateía Syntágmatos (Syntagma Square)
Sometimes also referred to as the Goulandrís Museum, this fine collection was amassed by a wealthy shipping magnate who was a keen patron of the arts. The Nikolas P. Goulandrís Foundation opened the museum in 1986, with astonishing displays of Cycladic art, as well as Minoan and Mycenaean sculpture and pottery.

Unlike many other museums in Greece, it exhibits and labels every object perfectly, allowing even the most casual visitor to understand the intricacies of Cycladic art

JUST A BIT OF TORSO

'There remains only a fragment of the torso, just the two breasts, from the base of the neck to above the navel. One of the breasts is draped, the other uncovered. What breasts! Good God! What a breast! It is apple-round, full, abundant, widely spaced from the other; you can feel the weight in your hand. Its fecund maternity and its lovesweetness make you swoon. The rain and sun have turned the white marble yellow, a tawny colour, almost like flesh...How one would have rolled on it, weeping! How one would have fallen on one's knees before it, hands joined!... A little more and I'd have prayed'. The French writer Flaubert describing a statue in the Archaeological Museum, from *The Letters of Gustave Flaubert, 1830–57*, edited and translated by Francis Steegmuller (London, 1954).

GREEK MUSEUMS

'The least expert haunter of such places must surely feel the difference between other museums and those of Athens, which contain hardly anything but masterpieces exhumed on or near the spot where they took life. You may not be a connoisseur, but in presence of original marbles undishonoured by the proximity of even excellent copies, your eyes become cleansed and sharpened and you see as you never saw before'. Ethel Smyth, *A Three-Legged Tour in Greece* (London, 1925)

59

(see page 31). In the basement are a café and a shop with expensive copies of the figurines on display. The first floor is mainly devoted to exquisite Cycladic marble figurines (3200–2000 BC). The stylised 'violin' figurines (case 3) are among the most common types of early Cycladic sculpture, with a long stem for the neck and two symmetrical shapes for the chest and the voluptuous hips. In case 5, the more intricate Plastira type of early Cycladic figurines have facial details and well-formed buttocks. The majority of these statues are female, but there are a few rare examples of male torsos, such as the one with a folded arm in case 9. Cases 22 and (especially) 26 hold some of the best and most impressive figurines, where it seems the artists were more confident and more masterful in handling of the marble.

Some of the works have an astonishingly modern feel to them – perhaps because the smooth, simple lines of Cycladic sculpture have inspired some famous 20th-century artists, including Modigliani and Henry Moore. The entire second floor of the museum has been dedicated to Ancient Greek art including Minoan and Mycenaean ceramics, Geometric pottery, Archaic art, bronze vessels and some lovely Tanagra, female terracotta figurines (4th century BC, displayed in case 40).

Go through a lovely cool courtyard (with cafeteria) to reach the adjacent neoclassical Stathatos mansion. This was the former home of the 19th-century German architect Ernst Ziller, designer of the Olympic Stadium and the Presidential Palace. This is now the sumptuous annex of the museum, used for those exhibitions and other displays of a temporary nature.

These exquisite marble figurines inspired many 20th-century artists

Athína (Athens)

Monastiráki has few of its original market stalls left, but a flea-market fan can still discover a bargain or two

ETHNIKOS KIPOS (NATIONAL GARDENS)
The National Gardens offer welcome shade to both Athenians and visitors. They were formerly the private palace gardens, stocked with plants shipped from all over the world in the 1840s by Queen Amalia. There is still an amazing variety of trees and shrubs. On the southern side can be found the Záppeio, a grand exhibition hall and some elegant café terraces.

NAÓS AIÓLOU (TOWER OF THE WINDS)
The Syrian astronomer Andronikos of Kyrrhos designed this octagonal tower in the 1st century BC as a water clock, compass, weather vane and sundial. Each side represents one of the eight winds, each personified by a different figure flying through the air. Underneath each figure was a sundial.

▶▶ Pláka   52C2

The Pláka is definitely the most atmospheric part of Athens. Its pedestrian streets wind steeply up the hill towards the Acropolis, lined with lovely neoclassical houses, flower-filled balconies, café terraces, Roman ruins and stunning views of the Parthenón. Part of it is now very touristy, with mediocre but expensive tavernas, tacky souvenir shops and endless crowds in the evening.

Stroll off the main streets of the city in search of the quieter squares, the little museums and the archaeological sites to enjoy its beauty. The **Monument of Lysikrátous**▶▶ (Odós Lysikrátous) is an elegant marble structure from 335 BC and nearby are the **Sanctuary of Olympian Zeus**▶▶ (*Open* Tue–Sun 8.30–3. *Admission charge*), the largest temple in Greece and **Pýli Adrianoú (Hadrian's Arch)**▶▶. The **Naós Aiólou (Tower of the Winds)**▶▶▶ is easily the loveliest and best-preserved building in the **Romaïkí Agorá (Roman Forum**, Odós Aiólou. (*Open* Tue–Sun 8.30–3. *Admission charge*).

▶ Plateía Omonoías (Omonia Square)   52B3

All roads in Athens seem to lead here. The whole district surrounding the square has a somewhat run-down air but the lively **meat and vegetable markets**▶▶, the 'bazaar' area, and the nearby National Archaeological Museum (see pages 56–8) make it a useful stop.

▶▶ Plateía Syntágmatos (Syntagma Square)   52C2

This is the centre of government, business and tourism in the capital: the best area to look for banks, as well as tourist and travel offices. Up the hill are the **Greek National Parliament (Voulí)** and the **Tomb of the Unknown Soldier**, guarded by the Evzónes, soldiers in traditional mountain costume. Across the street stands another Athens institution, the Hotel Grande Bretagne, the capital's grandest hotel. Political demonstrations frequently take place in the square, also adding to the traffic chaos.

Getting around Athens and Piréas

Airports Athens's Ellinikón Airport has two separate terminals. The western terminal handles all Olympic Airways flights, both international and domestic. All other airlines leave from the eastern terminal. A shuttle bus covers the five-minute drive between the two at least every hour between 8.30am and 8.30pm.

Buses and Metro Athens has an extensive network of buses and trolley buses, running from 5 am to midnight. Tickets are inexpensive, but must be bought in advance from kiosks, individually or by the ten and cancelled on the bus. Buses are crowded and often interrupted by strikes or other problems. The one-line Metro runs from Piréas to Monastiráki, Omónia and Kifissiá in the north. A second line is being built.

Taxis Athenian taxis are inexpensive by European standards, but make sure the meter is switched on and that the display is on zero when you get in. As elsewhere, unsuspecting tourists are often overcharged, especially on the run from the airport or the harbour. The legal surcharges – for luggage, Christmas and Easter bonuses and double fare after midnight – are displayed in English in every taxi. A tip of 10–15 per cent is customary. Any other charges are robbery.

Ferries Travel agents and tourist offices give approximate ferry schedules, but these are subject to change. There is no need to buy ferry tickets in advance, except for a cabin or if taking a car. Most shipping agents in Piréas have offices around the Metro or on Plateía Karaïskáki. Prices for all trips are standard, but lines often differ in travelling times and levels of comfort. There are fixed quays for departures to each group of islands – ask if you cannot find your way.

Hydrofoils Direct hydrofoils to Aígina leave from the main harbour (see above). All other hydrofoils leave from the Zéa Marina, about a 20-minute walk from the Metro. Tickets are on sale one hour before departure from the office on the quay, but in season it is best to book well in advance through a travel agency in Athens or Piréas.

Piréas, a port since antiquity, has now grown into a city in its own right

LEAVING THE AIRPORT

From the western terminal only there is a regular Olympic Airways bus (6.30am–10.30pm) to Syntágma (only for Olympic passengers). There are also several express airport buses: Nos. 90 and 91 to Syntágma- Omónia and No. 19 to Piréas; stop at Plateía Karaïskáki for the main harbour, at Telonío for Zéa. Taxis are obviously easier and quicker and inexpensive compared to a similar ride in other European capitals (but insist that the meter is switched on).

ATHENS-PIRÉAS- ZÉA MARINA

The easiest and the fastest way to get from Piréas to Athens is by Metro, which runs every 10 minutes and stops at Monastiráki and Omónia. Bus No. 40 leaves Odós Filellínon, just off Syntágma, every 15 minutes and goes near the ferry docks. From the street next to the Piréas Metro station bus No 905 goes to Zéa Marína.

Most foreigners visit Piréas to catch one of the island-bound ferries

Kríti (Crete)

Kríti (Crete)

KRÍTI (CRETE) The most southerly of Greece's major islands has been getting a bad press for insensitive tourist development and much of it is deserved. Away from the resorts, however, it is still 'the Great Island', rich in history and tradition, important historical sites and excellent museums, beautiful landscapes, an incomparable variety of flora and still a few idyllic, out-of-the-way beaches.

IN THE BEGINNING: MYTH AND FACT Most people arriving in Crete have heard of Minos, the legendary king who already belonged to ancient history when the Athenians built the Parthenón. Minos's wife, Pasiphae, gave birth to the Minotaur, half-man, half-bull, who was contained in a great labyrinth beneath King Minos's palace. There is no proof for any of this, but great palace complexes have been found across the island, dating from 2000 to 1450 BC. For want of any more accurate name, the people who built them have been called Minoans, after the legendary king. Enthusiasm for the splendours of this civilisation is often tempered by a sneaking suspicion that the Minoans sacrificed humans. The sudden demise of the Minoan era,

Kríti (Crete)

Page 62, top: Lasithiou Plateau
Right: some coastal towns, like Ágios Nikólaos, have kept their charm despite rapid development

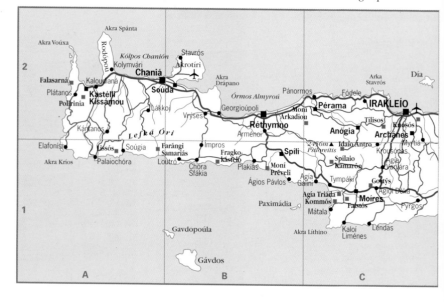

when the palaces are thought to have been destroyed by an earthquake or a tidal wave, remains a mystery. However, it heralded the end of Crete's golden age and by the time Athens was enjoying her glory, the island had become a backwater.

ROME AND CHRISTIANITY Crete, an important prize for anyone wanting to control the eastern Mediterranean, was always hard-won: the Romans attempted invasions in 71 BC and again in 69 BC, but only succeeded in controlling Crete until 67 BC by getting Cretan to fight with Cretan. From the Roman era to the Byzantine, the island flourished economically, though there was little social advancement. Christianity spread through the island: St Paul is believed to have visited Crete around AD 50, the famous Ágioi Déka (ten martyrs) were put to death at Górtys and after the conversion of the empire to Christianity many splendid churches and chapels were decorated with extraordinary frescoes.

VENETIAN AND TURK Venetian nobles won control of Crete after the sack of Constantinople (1204). They encouraged farming, stripped for timber for their shipyards and used the excellent harbours as way stations for east-west trade. When the Turks took Constantinople in 1453 many Byzantine scholars fled to Crete, stimulating a period of

64

artistic excellence, the Cretan renaissance. The Venetians built magnificent fortifications to fight off the Turks, but by 1649 the island was lost.

INDEPENDENT IDENTITY Turkish rule was negligent at best and the memory of the occupation is still bitter. The Cretans fought regularly for their independence, which was not won until 1913. In May 1941, Nazi Germany invaded the island, Allied defenses crumbled and the Cretans found themselves fighting again. For four years they suffered great brutality, but by the start of 1945 Cretan partisans and Allied intelligence officers had penned the Germans into Chaniá and were in control of most of the island.

THE NATURAL WORLD While Crete's capital and main towns are all along the coast, Cretan tradition is an agricultural one. The island's history and the character of its people are shaped by the geology of the country, which is dominated by mountains. Zeus, the father of ancient gods, was born in the Cretan mountains, great Minoan cities were built in them and resistance to Nazi Germany was centred up there. It is in the mountains that Crete's age-old traditions have been best maintained and where its spectacular catalogue of rare flora and fauna finds refuge.

ARTISTIC HERITAGE Crete is known for its legacy of painters and writers, from El Greco to Níkos Kazantzákis, creator of Zorba the Greek. There is also a strong tradition of folk music, of *mantinádes* (improvised poems, accompanied by the lyre), of songs glorifying history, songs for the table and songs for the road. Equally strong is the tradition of dances: one is said to represent the legendary hero Theseus leading his companions out of the Labyrinth. It is often performed for tourists in tavernas, the leader guiding his companions with his handkerchief.

THE CRETAN CHARACTER
'The Cretan character – warlike, proud, compulsively generous to a friend or stranger in need, ferociously unforgiving to an enemy or traitor, frugal day-by-day but prodigal in celebration – was, of course, strongly influenced by the landscape of dramatic contrasts in which the islanders lived...From sub-tropical vegetation with banana trees, carobs and orange groves, a mountain village, only 15 kilometres away as the crow flew, but probably sixty on foot, seemed to exist in a different world and a different climate.' Anthony Beever, *Crete: The Battle and the Resistance* (1991)

65

MODERN THREATS
In the 1960s much of Crete was underdeveloped and many Cretans were extremely poor. This has changed, in part because tourism has brought cash and work to the island, but at a price. Large tracts of the north coast have been spoiled by sudden, unplanned development. In some places the situation is so bad that hoteliers have been known to wish for an earthquake of Minoan proportions to bring it all down and give them a chance to do it differently. Tourists preferring to go elsewhere, as they are beginning to do now, may have the same effect. But the greater part of the island has been relatively untouched by this development and the further you go from main roads, the more likely you are to see something of the individual customs and character that Cretans have fought so bitterly and so often to defend.

Kríti (Crete)

WHAT'S IN A NAME
The capital of Crete was
known as Irákleio in antiquity, when it served as a
minor harbour for Knosós.
The Saracens, in the 9th
century, built a stronghold
(near the old Venetian
fort) which they called
Rabdh al-Khandah, the
Fortress with a Moat. The
Greeks then turned the
Turkish word for moat –
khendek – into
Khandákos, which was
further corrupted in sev-
eral European languages
into Candia, by which the
whole of Crete was then
known. During the 19th-
century Hellenist
movement, the ancient
name of Irakleío was
revived and in 1923 the
capital officially changed
its name.

*The square in front of the
Ágios Minás cathedral is
quieter and more typical
than busy Plateía
Venizeloú*

▶▶▶ Irákleio (Iráklion)   64C2

Irákleio, the capital of Crete, has a reputation for being
charmless and crowded – true, perhaps, but Irákleio is a
fascinating city nonetheless. A visit is sure to be rewarding, even if it is only long enough to see the superb Minoan
artifacts in the Archaeological Museum and Irákleio's
Venetian monuments – not to mention the important
Minoan site of Knosós nearby (see pages 83–5). As to the
living city, the market and the pedestrian streets around it
have plenty of local colour and character.

On the **Plateía Venizélou▶** stands the fine **Morazíni
Fountain** (see panel opposite), surrounded by restaurants,
car-rental offices and shipping agencies. On 25
Avgoústou (the street leading from the square to the
port), **Ágios Márkos▶** was the first church built by the
Venetians and is now an exhibition centre (*Admission free*).
The elegant Venetian **Loggia** is nearby. Further down,
10th-century **Ágios Títos▶** (*Admission free*) has been
reconstructed several times, lastly in the 1800s. It contains
the relics of the saint who first brought Christianity to
Crete. Seat of the Orthodox Archbishopric in Byzantine
times, of the Roman Catholic Archbishopric under the
Venetians and of the mosque during the Ottoman period,
it was reconsecrated in 1925 and is an interesting architectural hybrid.

The **Church of Agía Aikateríni▶▶** (Plateía Ag Aikaterínis. *Open* Mon–Sun 10–1, also Tue, Thu, Fri 4–6. *Admission charge*) is a beautiful old building in the shadow of the imposing **Ágios Miná Cathedral** (*Open* daily 7 am– 8 pm. *Admission free*). Connected to the monastery of St Catherine in Sinai, Egypt, it contains a wonderful collection of icons, the most famous being a series by the near-contemporary (and maybe even teacher) of El Greco, Mikhális Damaskinós.

The magnificent **city walls▶** (*Admission free*) withstood the 21-year-long Ottoman siege of the city, during which 30,000 Christians and 117,000 Turks died, but which ended with the city falling in 1669. Only a small stretch is accessible: from the bastion of St Antonio it is possible to walk on the 16th-century Venetian walls (4km long and 60m wide in places) to the Martinengo Bastion and the **Táfos Kazantzáki (tomb of Kazantzákis)▶** (see page 91). The epitaph on his simple tomb reads, 'I believe in nothing, I hope for nothing, I am free.' More Venetian fortifications can be seen near the port: the **Koúles▶** (*Open* Mon–Sat 8–6, Sun 10–3. *Admission charge*), a well-preserved 16th-century fortress with a Lion of St Mark guarding the doorway; and the boat sheds known as the **Arsenali▶** (*Admission free*), both recently restored. Up from the harbour, the **Istorikó Mouseío Krítis (Historical**

(see page 91).

THE MORAZINI FOUNTAIN
The fountain is Irákleío's most important legacy from the Venetian period. It was ordered in 1628 by the Venetian Governor Francesco Morazíni. The basin is decorated with a relief of sea gods from Greek mythology. Water spouts from the mouths of four lions. Once upon a time a giant Poseidon rose up from the upper pool, but the colossus went missing during the Turkish occupation.

67

Kríti (Crete)

UNDERSTANDING THE MINOANS
To get a better understanding of Knosós and the various Minoan sites all over the island, as well as of the fascinating Minoan civilisation in general, it makes sense to visit Irákleio's Archaeological Museum at least once before and once after visiting the rest of the island.

Museum of Crete)▶▶ (Odós Kalokairinoú 7. *Open* Mon–Sat 9–2 and Mon also 5–8. *Admission charge*) contains an excellent collection of Byzantine, Venetian and Ottoman art, Cretan folk art, the books and furniture of Níkos Kazantzákis and the only El Greco painting on Crete, the *View of Mount Sinai and the Monastery of St Catherine* (c1570).

The **Archaiologikó Mouseío (Archaeological Museum)** ▶▶▶ (Odós Xantoudídou. *Open* Tue–Sun 8 am–6 pm, Mon 12.30–6; winter closing 5 pm. *Admission charge*) houses the world's greatest collection of Minoan art: most local finds have been kept on the island. Ground-floor exhibits are arranged chronologically from Neolithic and Minoan through the Post-Minoan, Classical, Hellenistic and Roman periods. A magnificent collection of frescoes from the Minoan palaces is on the upper floor.

Some fascinating Neolithic finds (room I) came from the Cave of Eileithyia (see below), such as the **fertility goddess** (No 2716). Also of interest here is the **Vassilikí pottery** (case 6). Room II has a collection of finds from the Protopalatial period (2000–1700 BC), mainly from Knosós and various mountain sanctuaries dedicated to Zeus. Most exceptional are the early **Kamáres vases** (see cases 26–9) and the **faience** (case 25), which represent detailed façades of a Minoan town. Room III holds more superb **Kamáres ware**, mainly from

The wonderful murals confirm the sophistication of Minoan Crete

Faistós, especially the fruit bowl (No 105,800) and the krater with flowers (No 10578). The star item of this room, however, is the undeciphered **Faistós Disk**, the earliest known example of printing. The New Palace period (1700–1450 BC) represented the peak of the Minoan civilisation, proved by the exhibits in room IV: the **lily vases** from Knosós (case 45), the **jug of reeds** (case 49), the **bull's head rhyton** (case 51) and the astounding bare-breasted **snake goddess** (case 50). One of the most amazing objects is the **checker board** (case 57), made of ivory, gold leaf and rock crystal, from Knosós. Room V shows the decline of the New Palace period (1450–1400 BC) with the Mycenaean influence discernible in most of the exhibits. The large number of **Egyptian objects** suggests a flourishing trade between Crete and Egypt, while the clay house from Archánes (case 70a) looks very much like Cretan houses today. The finest **jewellery** is on display in room VI, as well as two superb **helmets** (case 82), one of boar's tusks. Finds from smaller sites and villas (room VII) from throughout the Palace period show the richness and abundance of the Minoan life. Note especially the **pendant of two bees** (case 101). Room VIII has magnificent

A TROUBLED ODYSSEUS
'He [Odysseus] also was on his way to Troy, but the force of the wind drove him out of course past Malea to Crete. He escaped the storm with difficulty and managed to get into the dangerous harbour of Amnisos, where is the cave of Eileithyia'.
Homer, *Odyssey* Book XIX

THE CAVE OF EILEITHYIA
The Neolithic Cave of Eileithyia (Cave of the Nymphs) is one of the oldest shrines in Crete. Eileithyia, daughter of Zeus and Hera, the goddess of childbirth, was worshiped here from before 3000 BC until Christian times. The goddess was the midwife who helped Leto give birth to twins Apollo and Artemis on the island of Dílos. Pregnant women rubbed themselves against a stalagmite looking like a pregnant belly with a navel, to ensure a safe delivery. Some of the other stalagmites look like a mother and a child.

ANCIENT VOTIVE OFFERINGS
Greeks today hang aluminum votive offerings in the shape of a baby or of some part of the body by icons in churches and chapels in the hope of being cured of an ailment. This is nothing new, as the votive offerings in the Archaeological Museum show. In room II of the museum, in the case situated against the back wall, are displayed ancient representations of several parts of the body, found at mountain shrines. They look much like the *ex votos* found in Classical shrines of Asclepius, the healing god and are definitely the predecessors of today's aluminum versions.

items from Zákros, including the **rock-crystal rhyton** and the **jug with the Argonauts** (cases 109 and 111). The naturalistic terracotta statues (room IX, case 123) give a clear idea of what Minoans looked like, while the large collection of fine seal stones portrays scenes from daily life. Room X shows merely a repetition of former glory with strong Mycenean influences and rooms XI and XII show the later Dorian and Egyptian influences. Room XIII is filled with sarcophagi and bathtubs.

The upper-floor rooms (XIV–XVI) display tiny fragments of frescoes mounted on a painted background. Most of these superb wall paintings are from the New Palace period of Knosós.

Around Irákleio Amnisos▶, one of the closest beaches to Irákleio, was important in Minoan times as the main harbour for Knosós. The fresco of the lilies, now in the Irákleio Archaeological Museum, was found in a villa here. Nearby is **Neiradaspílios** or the **Cave of Eileithyia▶▶**, noted for its large stalagmites. The cave is closed, but it is sometimes possible to get a key from the guardian on the site of Nirou Hani in Háni Kokkíni, 7km further east (not on Mondays).

Fódele▶ is a lovely village surrounded by a fertile valley. It has Byzantine chapels and a church, but its biggest claim to fame is as the supposed birthplace, in 1541, of Doménico Theotokópoulos, better known as the greatest of Cretan painters, El Greco (see page 70). There is nothing to support the claim, but the memorial with his bust on the main square (offered in 1934 by the Spanish University of Valladolid) and the so-called **El Greco House** across the river seem enough to attract visitors.

For **Knosós▶▶▶** see pages 83–5.

Crete fell to Venice after Constantinople was sacked in 1204. Some 250 years later, when Constantinople fell to the Turks, the island offered refuge to Byzantine artists. Out of this mixing of influences came a school of painting that was essentially Cretan.

A 14th-century fresco in the church of St Cristos Kakodiki, Crete

The Byzantine inheritance After the Turks captured Constantinople on 28 May 1453, refugee Byzantine painters moved to Irákleio, reviving what was becoming a stagnant tradition and bringing to it a new elegance, seen in the frescoes that survive in a number of churches from the second half of the 15th century.

The Cretan School Fresco painting in Crete quite suddenly stopped at the end of the 15th century as the artists moved to the mainland. In their place came icon painters, some of whom travelled to Venice and returned suitably impressed with the ideas of the Renaissance. The most famous of these was Michális Damaskinós. Having worked in Venice, Damaskinós returned to Irákleio and began working on large-scale pictures that fuse elements from Byzantine tradition with new Venetian ideas and which epitomise what is known as the 'Cretan School'.

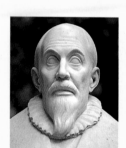

There is a statue of El Greco (above) in the park named after him in Irákleio. Below right: his View of Mount Sinai and the Monastery of St Catherine

El Greco The village of Fódele makes the loudest claim to be the birthplace of Doménico Theotokópoulos. The painter later known as El Greco (1541–1614) spent very little time on Crete, travelling to Italy and settling in Toledo, Spain by 1577. His paintings developed out of the Cretan School, initially adhering to its traditions of religious subjects, spiritual intensity and richness of colour, adding credibility to the theory that he studied in the school of the monastery of Agía Aikateríni in Irákleio.

WHERE TO SEE THE PICTURES IN CRETE
For early 15th-century work, see the frescoes in churches at Varsamónero, at Apáno Sími (near Viannos) and at Agía Paraskeví in the Amári valley. As to Michális Damaskinós's work, six of his larger paintings hang in the Church of Agía Aikateríni, Irákleio and others in the Istorikó Mouseío Krítis (Historical Museum of Crete) (see page 68). The only El Greco painting on display in Crete is his *View of Mount Sinai and the Monastery of St Catherine*, also in the Historical Museum.

Drive

Réthymno to Irákleio

This drive between two of Crete's largest towns crosses the island's rural heart, passing ancient and Byzantine ruins and farming villages. (Allow six to seven hours; 125km. Be sure to allow time to get off the winding mountain roads by nightfall.)

Leave Réthymno eastwards, following signs for Arkádi (22km). In Plátanias, turn right at the sign for Arkádi, cross under the new road and climb up through olive groves towards Mount Psiloreítis. In Amnátos look out for the **Sacred Church of Panagíos Merkoúri** (right) and continue to the monastery of **Arkádi (Moní Arkadíou)**▶▶, a national monument (*Open* daily 8am–8pm. *Admission charge*). Founded in the 11th century, the monastery was a focus for the Cretan rebellion against Turkish rule. The 16th-century church, a unique example of Cretan rococo, has a simple, double-vaulted interior. The adjacent **museum** has a collection of religious artifacts (*Open* daily. *Admission charge*).

Leave Arkádi on the track past the cafeteria, to Eléftherna (7.5km and continue through the village to see the post-Minoan settlement of **Archaía (Ancient) Eléftherna**▶. Return to Old Eléftherna and turn left for Margarítes (4km), famous for ceramics. Some 5km beyond Margarítes, a right turn leads to Pérama and on to the **Melidóni cave**▶▶ (*Open* daily.

Admission free), where some 300 Greeks, mostly women and children, were killed by the Turks in 1824. Back

Arkádi is a shrine for the victims of the Cretan rebellion

at Melidóni village, take the left turn off the square, which leads after 5km to a junction. Turn left along the fertile Mylopótamos Valley through Garazó to Axós, high on the mountain. The 8th-century BC acropolis of **Ancient Axós**▶ (*Open* daily. *Admission free*) is signposted.

From Axós, continue past Anógia to the junction with signs to the right for **Idaío Ántro (the Idean Cave)** (see page 92) and left for Irákleio. After 14km the road winds down past the site of **ancient Tílisos** (see page 95) to Irákleio.

71

Kríti (Crete)

**TOURIST INFORMATION
(ÁGIOS NIKOLAOS)**
The staff at the EOT
Tourist Office in Ágios
Nikólaos are extremely
helpful and will provide
information not only about
the Lasíthiou area but
about the whole of the
island. They also have a
free town map. The office
is by the canal, between
the lake and the port
(tel: 0841 22357. *Open*
8.30am–9.45pm during
the summer).

ESSENTIAL READING
John Freely, *Crete*
(London, 1988)
Adam Hopkins, *Crete, its
Past, Present and People*
(London, 1977). An infor-
mative account of the
island then and now.

*Fishing nets laid out to
dry in the sun at Ágios
Nikólaos*

▶▶ Archánes   64C2

Surrounded by vineyards, the villages of Káto Archánes
and Páno Archánes produce much of Crete's table wine.
Páno Archánes, a quiet town of narrow streets at the foot
of Mount Ioúhtas, was built over the site of a larger
Minoan town. The remains of four people, discovered in
1979 in the **Temple of Anemospília▶**, led to the controversial suggestion that when the temple was struck by an
earthquake the Minoans were practicing human sacrifice.
Neither this nor the other Minoan sites in the area (a villa
in the centre and the burial ground in nearby Foúrni) are
open to the public, but there is a small **archaeological
collection▶** (centre of the modern town. *Open* Wed–Mon
8.30–2.30. *Admission charge*) with finds from the area.
About 8km higher up into the hills, tiny **Vathípetro** has
wide views over the green valleys. The remains of a large
Minoan villa▶ (*Open* Mon–Sat 8.30–2; ask in museum in
Archánes), built around 1580–1550 BC, were found with
rooms filled with household objects and agricultural
equipment. Southeast of Archánes at **Trapsanóu▶** potters
still make *pithoi*, the large urns seen on Minoan sites. One
workshop, just outside the village, is Paradosiakí
Keramikí, which also makes other excellent objects.

▶▶ Ágios Nikólaos   65D2

One of the prettiest port-towns on Crete, Ágios Nikólaos
has over the last decades developed into a resort of international renown, often compared to St Tropez in France. It
is certainly not the place to go in search of the 'old Crete',
but it has managed to retain some of its charm. Most
attractive of all is its setting on the Gulf of Mirabéllo and
its harbour, connected by a small canal to the deep
Voulisméni lake. Catching the early-evening breeze on
one of the many lakeside terraces is one of the more pleasant occupations the town has to offer. The town's name
comes from the early Byzantine church on the peninsula of
Liména, the **church of Ágios Nikólaos▶**, notable for fine
frescoes from the 8th, 10th and 11th centuries. Crete's second finest collection of antiquities is housed in the

THE MYSTERY OF THE LAKE
Many stories are told about the lake in Ágios Nikólaos. It is said to be about 70m deep, but natives believe it to be bottomless and the home of spirits. Some people believe it is connected with Thíra: one of the stories told as proof of this is that after the 1956 earthquake on Thíra, all the fish in the lake died.

Chaniá, with the snow-capped White Mountains in the background, is one of the most frequently photographed views on Crete

Archaeological Museum▶▶ (Odós Palaiológou. *Open* Tue–Sun 8.30–3. *Admission charge)*, which has a wealth of finds from the nearby sites of Agía Fotiá near Siteía, Mochlós, Kritsá and Mýrtos. In the same building as the Tourist Office there is a tiny **Museum of Folklore Art▶** (*Open* Sun–Fri 10.30–3. *Admission* inexpensive). The **church of Panagía Vrefotrófou▶**, near the bus station on Odós Meletíou, dates from the 12th century.

Around Ágios Nikólaos The road to **Eloúnta▶▶** is lined with mostly luxurious hotel complexes, so it comes as no surprise that the pretty fishing hamlet of Eloúnta gets quite crowded in the season. On days when the water is calm and clear it is possible to get a glimpse of the under-water ancient site of Oloús. Boats can be rented for the excursion to the peninsula of **Spinalógka▶▶**, where the Venetians built an impregnable fortress and, in 1579, made it an island by cutting a canal. Later – until as recently as the 1950s – there was a leper colony here. Another popular day trip is to the villages of **Krítsa and Lató▶▶▶** (see page 88) and the **Lasíthiou Plateau▶▶▶** (see pages 88–9).

▶▶▶ Chaniá 64A2

The historic centre of the city of Chaniá is the most pic-turesque and beautiful in all Crete. Elsewhere, Chaniá, the island's capital until 1971, feels like a bustling modern town. Package tourism has spread to the new town and to nearby beaches, but the area around the Venetian harbour remains as attractive as ever. With the usually snow-capped White Mountains looming over it, Chaniá is the perfect base to use for exploring the more remote parts of western Crete.

The harbour is especially lively during the evening *volta*, when young and old stroll along the waterfront. The huge dome of the 17th-century **Mosque of the Janissarie**s▶, near Plateía Sindriváni, gives the waterfront an Oriental flavour. **Kastélli▶▶** is a Byzantine fortress later fortified by the Venetians.

USEFUL NUMBERS (CHANIA)
Olympic Airways tel: 0821 57701 and 57702
Tourist information EOT (Odós Kriári 40, 4th floor, tel: 0821 26426. *Open* Mon–Fri 7.30–2.30)
Hertz Rent-a-Car tel: 0821 40366
Minoan Lines (for ferry information and tickets) tel: 0821 23939.

LOVELY CHANIA
'The appearance of the town was striking, as its irregular wooden buildings rose up the hill sides from the sea, interspersed with palm-trees, mosques and minarets. There was no mistaking that we were in Turkey. The whole place is surrounded by a Venetian wall of great massiveness and the harbour is enclosed by extensive moles'.
Henry Fanshawe Tozer, *The Islands of the Aegean* (1890)

ROOMS WITH A VIEW
Several Venetian mansions on and around Chaniá's waterfront have been converted into guest houses and hotels, all with splendid views. There is something for every budget, from the elegant Casa Delfino to the much cheaper Stella Pension near the Naval Museum.

ST JOHN THE HERMIT
St John the Hermit is thought to have lived and died in a cave near the Katholikó monastery on the Akrotíri peninsula. Every 7 October a *paiyíri* is held in his honour: the previous day busloads of pilgrims walk from Agía Triáda monastery to Gouvernéto to attend all-night services. The next morning they walk to the cave, where an emotional service is held. At the point where the saint died, the water which collects in the cistern is believed to be holy.

One of the pleasures of old Chaniá is a stroll along the paralía *in search of that perfect setting for a sunset drink*

The scant remains of the ancient **acropolis of Cydonia**, one of the three most important Minoan towns on Crete, have been excavated on Odós Kandanoléon. In the yacht harbour, at the bottom of Kastélli, look for the 16th-century Venetian **Arsenáli** (boat sheds) and walk along to the lighthouse at the end of the harbour wall. A tower on the other side of the **outer harbour** houses the **Naval Museum▶** (*Open* daily 10–4. *Admission charge*), where Chaniá's long and exciting seafaring past is brought to life.

The **Archaeological Museum▶**, housed in the Venetian church of San Francesco (Odós Chálidon. *Open* Mon 12.30–7, Tue–Fri 8–7, Sat–Sun 8.30–3. *Admission charge*), includes a considerable collection of Minoan pottery, lovely 3rd-century Roman mosaics and tablets inscribed with Linear A and Linear B, the Minoan and Mycenaean scripts. Past the museum lies the cathedral and Odós Skridlóf, a tourist bazaar where leather-workers still sell traditional footwear. Nearby is the pleasant central market, a huge, crowded hall whose colourful stalls are piled with fresh local produce.

Around Chaniá Akrotíri▶, the peninsula north of Chaniá, is developing into a wealthy suburb. On top of the Profítis Ilías hill, the **tomb of Elefthérios Venizélos**, father of modern Crete and his son, stands in the middle of a pleasant garden that has wonderful views. Further inland, **Agía Triáda▶ ▶**, one of the most famous monasteries in Greece, was founded by a Venetian family in 1634. Some 4km away are the fortress-like **monastery of Gouvernéto▶** and the **Katholikó monastery▶**, where a cave contains the tomb of St John the Hermit.

West of Chaniá on the mountainous **Rodópou peninsula▶**, stands the **monastery of Goniá▶** (*Open* daily 9–2 and 5–7. *Admission free*) commanding spectacular views. Its monks are proud to show their small collection of 17th- and 18th-century icons as well as the remains of a Turkish shell which is incorporated in the eastern wall of the monastery.

Walk

Old Chaniá

There is more to Chaniá than waterside cafés and souvenir shops. Not far away, beautiful old houses and atmospheric streets are a reminder of the port's long and illustrious past. (Allow three hours, including breaks.)

Starting at Plateía Sindriváni, walk up Odós Kanenáro, the main street of the Venetian town of La Canae. Some noble mansions can be seen on Odós Lithínon (first left), quite a few now turned into guest houses. At the top of this street is the **Venetian Archives and Financial Exchange▶▶**, from 1623. Going back down Lithínon, Odós Psaromiligón on the left leads past the remains of **Minoan Cydonia** (no access). Returning to Kanenáro, turn left and then take the first left (Odós Ágios Márkos) past the **ruins of a monastery▶** to Plateía Ágios Títos, with wonderful views over the harbour and coast. Steps from the plateía lead to the imposing and elegant ruins of the **Palace of the Rector▶▶**, the centre of government for western Crete during the Venetian period and down to the waterfront. Turn right, past the **Arsenáli▶** (Venetian boat sheds) and walk along the breakwater to the minaret-like **lighthouse▶**, pausing to enjoy the views.

Returning to the Arsenáli, continue along the waterfront to Plateía Sindriváni. Odós Zambelioú leads off the square into the picturesque **Jewish Quarter** of the Venetian town, which has many narrow houses. Odós Kondiláki (first left), another fine Venetian street, leads to Odós F Portoú. Turn right, with the city wall and bastion on your left and then right into Odós

Doúka, which leads back to Zambelioú and turn left. Just past a row of medieval houses, Odós Moshón, a passageway of steps with the only surviving **Venetian chapel** (15th-century), leads to Odós Theofanoú and the **Casa Delfino** (17th-century). Climb up the hill, turn right into Odós Zambelioú and then first right into Odós Theotokópoulos, with Turkish houses (wooden upper stories) towards the bottom. Turn right onto one of the old town's most beautiful streets, Odós Angeloú, which brings you back to the waterfront.

Chaniá's lighthouse stands on the harbour breakwater

▶ Chóra Sfákia   64B1

The small harbour of Chóra Sfákia, on the south coast, comes alive only during late afternoon, when crowds of tired hikers return from the Samariá Gorge (see page 93) to catch a bus from here to Chaniá or Réthymno. Most of the portside *kafeneía* cater only to tourists, but the calm and beauty of the place are restored once the buses leave around 7 pm. Nearby **Loutró▶**, accessible by boat or road, is a quieter option in this region; it has a small beach overlooked by a Turkish castle. East of Chóra Sfákia is **Fragko Kástelo▶▶**, an isolated, crumbling Venetian fortress (see panel). The beach below is superb.

▶▶▶ Faistós   64C1

Open: daily 8–6. Admission charge; free Sun
Several buses daily from Irákleio

The setting of Faistós is magnificent, with sweeping views over the Messára plain and both Mount Díkti and the twin peaks of Mount Psiloreítis. This was the second most important Minoan city and the capital of Messára, with two harbours, Mátala and Kómmos. The site, like most other Minoan cities, was inhabited during the neolithic era, but what remains today are the ruins of the grand New Palace built around 1700 BC, incorporating some of the foundations of the Old Palace, built around 2000 BC and destroyed in an earthquake 300 years later. The New Palace was destroyed by the same disaster that brought down the other Minoan palaces in 1450–1400 BC. Faistós

The most superbly set of all Minoan sites, Faistós overlooks the fertile Messára plain

was inhabited afterwards and remained an autonomous state until the end of the 3rd century BC when it was again destroyed, during a war with Gortýna.

Unlike Knosós, the site has not been reconstructed, leaving scope for the imagination to fill in the gaps. The Palace is approached from a **Grand Stairway**, past the remains of the first palace and the **Theatral Area**. Beyond the storage rooms is the Central Court with the remains of what was a grand façade. A corridor to the north leads to the **Royal Apartments** with the large **Peristyle Hall** and the **Lustral Basin**. Across the Central Court are the **Prince's Rooms** with a small peristyle hall and beside it the workshops in which perhaps the oldest metal forges in the world were found.

These giant píthoi, *still in place in the magazines, were used for storing grain, olive oil and wine*

77

It is thought that about 50,000 people lived near the palace and the ruins of their villages are scattered all over the Messára plain. A 45-minute walk or a short drive away from Faistós, **Agía Triáda▶▶** (*Open daily 8.30–3. Admission charge*) is a Minoan villa complex, perhaps the summer residence of the king of Faistós. The nearby village of Agía Triáda was abandoned in 1897 after the Turks killed most of the inhabitants. The villa or palace dates from around 1550 BC and some of the finest Minoan artworks discovered here are now in the Irákleio Archaeological Museum.

THE FAISTOS DISK
The famous clay disk, dated to 1700–1600 BC, (see illustration on page 31) was stamped with seals on both sides, with hieroglyphics spiralling from the middle. The hieroglyphics represent persons, body parts, tools, flowers, animals and ships. So far the disk has not been deciphered but it is thought that these hieroglyphics were typical of Minoan Crete.

Greece in the summer is all sun and scorched earth, but in spring and autumn it is a different place, full of flowers and the scent of blossoms. With more than 2,000 species of plants – 160 not seen anywhere else in the world – Crete, even more than most of the islands, is a botanist's dream.

The seasons Summer visitors to the Aegean could be forgiven for thinking that the flora is nothing but olive trees and geraniums. The usual pattern of hot dry weather means that by July, most flowers are reduced to brown sticks by the roadside. In spring, however, even the most barren islands are likely to have a burst of flowers. The ruins at sacred Dîlos are scattered with red poppies, the olive groves of Paxoí are luminous with white blooms, while Zákynthos lives up to the nickname the Venetians gave it – the flower of the Levant – with its fields full of wild flowers.

Spring arrives in different places at different times: mid to late February in southern Crete and perhaps as late as May or early June in the more mountainous regions. This is the season to walk in the islands, when the days are warmer, the air rich with the scent of aromatic foliage. While the Aegean summer has the same effect on plants as the northern winter, in cooler, higher places there are still flowers to be found. After the summer season, there are other rewards as certain species of cyclamen and crocus bloom between October and December.

Flowers of Crete Nowhere on the Greek islands is there such an abundance of flowers as on Crete. Its 8,311 sq km provide a variety of terrains, each of which is suited to different species and subspecies of plants. Of the 700 species of plants endemic to Greece, at least 160 are found on Crete and nowhere else.

Crete's coastal strip is only a few metres wide in some places and, because of tourist development, much at risk. Plants that thrive on the salty terrain include sea daffodils and lilies, stonecrops, various species of convolvulus as well as tamarisk and jujube trees. In autumn, crocuses and sea squills bloom on the shore.

The lowland plain covers the area from the littoral across the hills and lowest mountain slopes, up to approximately 300m. As this is intensively cultivated, in many places wild flowers have simply disappeared, but survivors may include poppies, Cretan ebony, lupins, chrysanthemums, gladioli, species of ranunculus and euphorbia and many other unexpected treasures.

Higher ground – between 300m and 800m, including the Omalós, Lasíthiou and Nída plains – is the place to find brilliant brooms and wild orchids, asphodels,

PLANTS IN DANGER

Of the species endemic to Crete, six are in danger of immediate extinction as their habitat is systematically destroyed. Fifteen more are threatened and 78 others are rare. (These figures are taken from George Sfikas's excellent handbook – see the panel opposite.)

*Top: wild cistus
Below: islanders often have colourful displays of flowers in their gardens and balconies*

cyclamens, anemones and convolvulus, thyme, clematis and several types of cistus and phlomis. Of the trees, the pink blossoms of the Judas trees are especially dramatic.

The mountainous regions of Crete used to be differentiated by whether or not they had trees, but deforestation has robbed even the subalpine regions of its forests. Clumps of trees have survived here and there, like the small forest near Mourniés, in eastern Crete. In areas ranging in height from 800 to 1,800m, look in the summer for several unique tulips, including the delicate pink-tinged Tulipa bakeri, endemic to western Crete. Crocuses, anemones, saxifrages, alyssums and species of centaury can also be found. Higher up, trees disappear altogether and plants are mostly herbaceous or bulbous, with some shrubs that can survive in the cold. Here may be found rock-cress (flowering in June), vetches, alkanets and violets.

Cretan ebony is one of many flowers endemic to Crete

Crete's other distinct botanical habitat is its gorges, most famous of which are the Samariás, Imriotico and Coutraliotico. Usually running north-south, from the uplands to the sea, they are a particularly good place to look for rock plants, including several campanulas, endemic *Symphyandra cretica*, certain types of flax, also endemic to Crete and *Scabiosa minoana*, which has two subspecies endemic to specific regions of the island – subsp. *minoana* to the Mount Díkti gorges, subsp. *asterusica* to Mount Cofinas.

Every year more fields with rare and endemic flowers are cleared for the rapid development of the tourist industry

FLOWER BOOKS
If you want more information about plant life on Crete, the following books will be of interest:
Anthony Huxley and William Taylor, *Flowers of Greece* (London, 1977)
Paul and Jenne Davies and Anthony Huxley, *Wild Orchids of Britain and Europe* (London, 1983)
George Sfikas, *Wild Flowers of Crete* (Athens, 1987), David Burnie, *Flowers of the Mediterranean* (London, 1995).

79

The ancient town of Gourniá must have looked much like the large mountain villages of Crete today, with small houses clustered around a few cobbled streets

▶▶ Gávdos   64B1

The isolated island of Gávdos, some 40km off the southern coast of Crete, is Europe's southernmost point. Locals believe that theirs was the island of Calypso, visited by Odysseus and known in Roman times as Clauda. Ferries dock at Karabé, from where it is an hour's walk to the capital, Kastrí. Today it is hard to believe that Kastrí had 8,000 inhabitants in the Middle Ages. Now, only five families remain amid the crumbling houses. There are good beaches, but food and water are in short supply. The island gets incredibly hot in summer, when small ferries make twice weekly trips from Palaiochóra via Sóugia, as well as twice weekly from Chóra Sfákia. Out of season there are only erratic connections.

▶▶▶ Gortýs   64C1

The remains of **ancient Gortýna**▶▶▶ (*Open* daily 8.30–3. *Admission charge, free* Sun) are scattered over the whole area of Ágioi Déka and modern Gortýs. The site was inhabited from the neolithic period, but Gortýna only became an important commercial power in the 8th century BC. In the 3rd century BC Gortýna conquered Faistós and its harbour Mátala. After it sided with Quintus Metellus against Knosós, the Romans made it the capital of the Province of Crete and Cyrenaica (North Africa and Egypt) in 67 BC. The island's first centre of Christianity after St Paul appointed Titus as bishop in AD 67, Gortýna remained the capital during the Byzantine era until the Saracens sacked it in AD 824.

The site is important for its excellent remains from several periods. One of the most prominent, by the entrance, is the ruins of the 6th-century three-aisled **basilica of Ágios Títos**, still revered as one of Crete's most important Christian monuments, as the shrine inside shows. Behind the basilica is the *agora* (marketplace) and the Roman **Odeion** with the famous **Law Code**, a series of huge stones engraved around 500 BC with laws and rulings. They are written in a Doric Cretan dialect, in a system called *boustrophedon*, 'as the ox ploughs', meaning that one line must be read from left to right and the next from right to left (see panel). Across the river are the remains of a Hellenistic theatre, built over the acropolis of ancient Gortýna. Fragments of the walls remain, probably the ones Homer meant when he mentioned the 'walled city of Gortýna' in the *Iliad*. On the other side of the main road are the remains of the **Praetorium** (governor's house) and a Nymphaeum among many other ruins.

Nearby is the village of **Ágioi Déka▶▶▶**, or the Holy Ten, named after ten early Christians martyred for their faith around AD 250 by the Romans. A chapel was built over a crypt which supposedly contains their remains. These 'Holy Ten' are among the most important Cretan saints: martyrs not just for their faith but also for their island against a foreign occupation.

▶▶▶ Gourniá 65D1

Open: Tue–Sun 8.30–3. Admission charge

Ancient Gourniá is the best preserved of the Minoan towns, set beautifully against hills and overlooking the sea. Little visited today, it is extremely pleasant to stroll around and gives a rare insight into how ordinary Minoans liked to live. The narrow cobbled alleys between Gourniá's small houses are not so very different from the old mountain villages of Crete today.

The site was inhabited from the early second millennium BC, but what remains today is from the New Palace period (*c*1500 BC). The town was destroyed in 1450 BC by the same unknown disaster that struck Knosós and other Minoan palaces. In the centre of the site is the so-called palace (probably the governor's house) and an open courtyard believed to have been the *agora*. In the houses a large number of tools and objects from different trades were found, showing that the people of Gourniá were engaged in carpentry, fishing, pottery and weaving.

81

Kríti (Crete)

A GOOD DRIVE
Most people take the quick coastal road from Irákleio to Ágios Nikólaos or the Lasíthiou Plateau. The inland roads may be more winding and slower, but the drive is much more pleasurable. The hilly countryside is beautiful and the villages and tiny churches are a far cry from the coastal resorts.

VISITING CHURCHES
Many of the old churches in the interior of the island are often closed – disappointing for visitors who have come to see their famous frescoes. The dedicated traveller can always try to find the keeper of the key. Start by asking at the nearest *kafeneío*: news travels fast in these villages and there is a good chance that the key will appear.

▶ Ierápetra 65D1

The centre of a thriving agricultural industry, Ierápetra is a modern, unattractive city. Most visitors come here for the sandy beaches nearby, but also worth visiting is the small **Archaeological Museum** (*Open* Tue–Sat 8.30–3. *Admission charge*) and the Venetian fort. In summer excursion boats make the trip to the nearby Hryssí islet, which has excellent beaches. The southern coast of Crete boasts the warmest climate in Europe and close to **Árvi▶**, west of Ierápetra, there is a lovely gorge surrounded by banana and pineapple groves.

▶ Kastélli Kissámou 64A2

To distinguish itself from the many Venetian castles called *Kastélli*, the town still uses its ancient name Kíssamos, a legacy from the days when it was the port of the powerful inland town of Polyrrinía. The area behind the health centre, where there are lovely Roman mosaics, is to be opened to the public. The foundations of the 6th-century BC **acropolis of Polyrrinía▶** can be visited from nearby Palaiókastro.

▶▶ Kastélli Pediádos 65D2

Kastélli is the main village in the middle of the picturesque and little-visited farming region known as the Pediáda. The Venetian castle after which the village was named has disappeared, but Kastélli is pleasant enough, with a few taverns and *kafeneía*. More rewarding would be a drive through the lovely surrounding countryside, through tiny old villages where there are some amazing medieval churches. Near Pigí is the site of **Ágios Pandeleímon▶▶**, where parts of a 10th-century basilica, built over a spring, are incorporated in the 13th-century church, which boasts some very early frescoes. Two Byzantine churches, **Ágios Nikólaos** and the frescoed **Ágios Giórgios▶**, stand at the foot of Mount Díkti, near Xidás. Above Kastélli to the east is the site of the once-important **ancient city of Lýttos▶**, once a rival of Knosós, but very little remains. The **Moní Agárathou▶**, near Sabás, one of Crete's oldest monasteries, was built to house the sacred icon of the Assumption of the Blessed Virgin, found nearby. The 15th-century church **Isódia Theótokon▶▶**, near Sklaverochóri, has 15th- and 16th-century frescoes.

82

Not all traditions are lost: the old men still watch the world go by from the kafeneío or barbershop

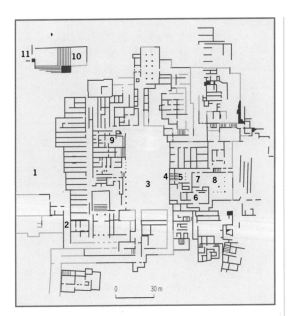

1 West Court
2 Corridor of the
  Procession
3 Central Court
4 Grand Staircase
5 Hall of Colonnades
6 Queen's Apartments
7 King's Apartments
8 Hall of Double Axes
9 Throne Room
10 Theatral Area
11 Royal Road

▶▶▶ Knosós   64C2

Open: Apr–Sep, daily 8–6; Oct–Mar, daily 8.30–3.
Admission charge
Bus: No 2 from opposite the Loggia, Av 25 Avgoústou, Irákleio.
Visit at opening time, or at midday with hat and water, to
avoid the worst crowds.

The palace of Knosós, with its 1,300 rooms and alabaster
throne, exerts a magical attraction. This may have something to do with the fact that, until a century ago, Knosós
was no more than a legend – the place where King Minos
was said to have lived, where his wife gave birth to
the Minotaur, for whom the Labyrinth was constructed
and where human sacrifices are believed to have been
made in ancient times.

Knosós was built some time after 1950 BC and damaged
in an earthquake around 1700 BC. Much of what we see
now – the foundations of the Royal Palace, the Little
Palace, a caravansary and other buildings, covering more
than 2 hectares – belongs to the reconstruction in the New
Palace period; at this high point in Minoan civilisation, the
palace and the city around it would have held as many as
100,000 people. Around 1450 BC all the Minoan buildings
except Knosós were destroyed. It is still unclear what happened – perhaps an earthquake or a war, or a tidal wave
caused by the massive volcanic eruption that blew Thíra
apart. Knosós survived, albeit under Mycenaean control;
Homer mentions King Idomeneus of Knosós joining the
war against Troy.

In 1380 BC Knosós too was destroyed by fire. Its remains
lay buried under a growing mound until they were discovered by Sir Arthur Evans at the beginning of this
century (see pages 86–7). Much of Evans's reconstruction
of the palace was enlightened guesswork and while it has
protected many of the ruins from the elements and perhaps made the site easier for us to understand, it has
certainly intruded upon the ancient ruins.

EVANS'S RECONSTRUCTION

As Sir Arthur Evans uncovered the great palace of
Knosós, he was faced
with an increasingly urgent
problem. Because of the
bad state of preservation
of much of the palace,
because it was a several-
storey building on a
hillside and because the
Cretan winter is cold and
wet, he had to protect the
site as best he could.
Evans, who had paid for
the site with his own
money and obviously felt
he had proprietorial rights,
decided on a reconstruc-
tion. While the Throne
Room was roofed over to
preserve the floor and the
throne itself, in other
places Evans took what
some consider
unwarranted liberties, in
particular with the Grand
Staircase and the upper
rooms. Much of his recon-
struction is based on pure
guesswork. In our own
time, when archaeology
has become such an
exact science, Evans's
actions are being increasingly criticised, for while
most of today's visitors to
Knosós come to see the
Minoan ruins, much of
what they actually see is a
20th-century concrete
rebuilding by Evans.

Kríti (Crete)

KNOSÓS TREASURES

The treasures found at Knosós and now on display in the Archaeological Museum in Irákleio include (room II) remains from the Old Palace such as faïence plaques showing two- and three-storey buildings and clay models of people, bulls and ships, with which the Minoans made their fortune. From the New Palace period (room IV) there are two masterful faïence snake goddesses, which give a good idea of the dress of the period, a gaming board and a soapstone libation vessel in the shape of a bull's head, with rock-crystal eyes, mother-of-pearl nostrils and horns that would have been of gilded wood. Room XIV contains the frescoes from Knosós including the Procession, the Prince of the Lilies, the Ladies in Blue, the Dolphins and the woman known as 'La Parisienne'.

Long, narrow storage rooms still contain the huge píthoi *or storage jars*

The story of the Labyrinth may have been based on fact, for Knosós is hard to negotiate in any particular order. Try wandering around to get a sense of the ground plan, then return to look again. Knosós needs imagination as well as patience, for much of it is either very ruined, heavily reconstructed or under restoration.

The site is entered through the **West Court (1)**, leading into the **Corridor of the Procession (2)**, named after its frescoes (now, like all the others, in the Archaeological Museum in Irákleio). Follow the inevitable crowds to the **Central Court (3)**, which divides the site in two and which would have been enclosed by the walls of the surrounding buildings. On the west side of the court are the ceremonial chambers, to the east the royal apartments.

The royal apartments are reached via the **Grand Staircase (4)▶▶**, one of the great architectural achievements of prehistory, which originally continued for another two stories above the Central Court. The part that still exists leads down from the court to the **Hall of Colonnades (5)** and would have continued, around a light well, further down the hillside. Off the Hall of Colonnades lie the **Queen's Apartments (6)▶▶▶**, which archaeologists believe would have been brightly decorated and comfortable – qualities that were as important to the Minoans as to us. Beyond are the bathrooms, one with a clay bath and another with a toilet. The main attraction here is the drainage system, a series of terracotta pipes which appear to have carried off not just dirty water but also sewage. The queen, it seems, used a flushing toilet.

Pipework has been found all over the palace, forming a drainage system which not only brought fresh water from Mount Juktas but could also have coped with even the worst storms. It was unparalleled in the world until

The original frescoes at Knosós have been replaced by reproductions, while the originals are shown in Irákleio's Archaeological Museum

THE MINOTAUR
Among the treasures that survived at Knosós there were bull's-head libation vessels, shrines in the shape of bulls' horns and a wonderfully preserved fresco showing a group of men and women involved in bull-leaping, one man having gripped the bull by its horns and leapt over its head. This striking image calls to mind the myth of the Minotaur, the beast said to inhabit the Labyrinth at Knosós, to whom young men and women from Athens were offered as sacrifice.

ARIADNE'S DANCING FLOOR
Homer, describing the god Hephaistos decorating the shield of Achilles, gives a vivid impression of celebrations at Knosós – perhaps on the dancing floor in the theatral area: 'Youths and marriageable maidens were dancing on it with their hands on one another's wrists, the girls in fine linen with lovely garlands on their heads and the men in closely woven tunics showing the faint gleam of oil and with daggers of gold hanging from their silver belts. Here they ran tightly round, circling smoothly on their accomplished feet...and there they ran in lines to meet each other. A large crowd stood round enjoying the delightful dance, with a minstrel among them singing divinely to the lyre, while a couple of acrobats, keeping time with his music, threw cart wheels in and out among the people'. Homer, *Iliad* Book XVIII

Roman times. Back up the Grand Staircase, above the Queen's Apartments, are the so-called **King's Apartments (7)**. These are a series of rooms connected by double doors, leading to the **Hall of Double Axes (8)**, named after the motif carved into its blocks.

Across the Central Court lie the palace's most intriguing and atmospheric chambers, starting with the **Throne Room (9)**. This has stone benches and an alabaster throne, one of the oldest in the world, though archaeologists are divided over its date (was it Minoan or later Mycenaean?) and its function (was it for a king or a priest?). Beside it is a chamber with a sunken floor, clearly used for ritual cleansing. Its place beside the throne room suggests the close relationship between religion and state in Minoan times and perhaps the possibility of there having been a priest-king. Stairs lead up to chambers reconstructed by Evans. Their functions, however, are not known.

Reproduction **frescoes** have replaced several of the originals, some of which are now on display in the Archaeological Museum in Irákleio (see panel opposite). A priest-king looks over the Central Court, dolphins adorn the Royal Apartments and a bull charges at the northern portico. Beyond the entrance, past the gatehouse and lustral bath, also used for ritual purification, lies the **Theatral Area (10)**, whose stone platform is surrounded by amphitheatral stone seating for about 500 people, clearly an area for ceremony or entertainment. Leading away from the Theatral Area is the **Royal Road (11)**, a paved road which runs as far as the present main road to Irákleio, towering above you.

The old road is thought to have run right across the island. It has been excavated on the other side of the modern road and runs past a couple of reconstructed town houses to the Small Palace, which, along with the caravansary, a Roman villa, the so-called Royal Villa and a royal tomb-chapel, is closed to the public.

As late as the mid-19th century, when excavations had already revealed so much about ancient Rome and Egypt, many of the antiquities of ancient Greece lay waiting to be uncovered. With the advent of an inspired amateur in the 1870s, all this began to change, but many questions still remain to be answered.

Heinrich Schliemann, the excavator of Troy, arrived on Crete with his copy of Homer in hand, hoping to uncover a major Minoan palace, but didn't get permission to excavate

Heinrich Schliemann (1822–90) In the 1870s, Greek archaeology was transformed by the arrival of a wealthy German called Heinrich Schliemann. Having made a fortune as a trader, he retired from business to fulfil his ambition of proving the truth behind Homer's epics. He started on the coast of Asia Minor by uncovering the site of Troy. In 1876, with Homer still as his guide, he uncovered the remains of an extraordinary warrior civilisation at Mycenae. And in 1878, on Itháki, he identified what he believed to be Odysseus's palace.

The critics Not everyone greeted Schliemann's discoveries with enthusiasm, least of all the professional archaeologists whom he had upstaged. His methods, certainly far from scientific, were called into question and many of his claims ridiculed. While he certainly made mistakes – most obviously with the so-called 'jewels of Helen', which turned out to be from another Trojan period – he was clearly vindicated for his belief in Homer's historical accuracy. In 1878, perhaps spurred on by Schliemann's Mycenaean discoveries, a Cretan antiquarian called, appropriately, Mínos Kalokairinós, began to dig near Irákleio and uncovered storerooms full of large pottery jars. Could these be the remains of the great city of Knosós, also mentioned by Homer? Schliemann was soon on the site, but was unable to acquire the rights to work on it.

The Palace of Knossos, as it was found, bears no resemblance to Evans's later controversial reconstruction

Sir Arthur Evans (1851–1941) Oxford-educated Evans, formerly keeper of Oxford's Ashmolean Museum, arrived in Athens in 1893 to study Schliemann's Mycenaean seals. He saw similar seals in an Athens antiques shop, whose owner said they came from Crete, where women used them as charms to help with breast-feeding. In 1898 the Turks lost control of Crete and two years later Evans had bought the mound called Kefala, where the large pottery jars had been found and was ready to start excavating. Within a very short time it became clear that this was to be a major discovery: the Knosós that Homer mentioned, but belonging to a civilisation much older than that of the Mycenaeans and Achaians. As nothing was found to give a name to the period or the people who inhabited Knosós, Evans felt free to invent. Remembering that mythology credited King Minos, son of Zeus and Europa, with building the city of Knosós, Evans called the people and their age, Minoan.

Halbherr at Faistós While Evans was excavating Knosós, an Italian enthusiast was at work on another site on the island. Federico Halbherr had been working on Crete for some years, excavating more recent sites, but at the turn of the century he was digging at Faistós. He was just as surprised as Evans when his excavation of the palace shed more crucial light on the Minoans. Schliemann had caused a sensation by proving that the heroic age depicted by Homer had actually existed. Between them, Evans and Halbherr provided proof for the period that preceded the Homeric age.

The continuing challenge It is almost 100 years since Evans discovered Knosós, yet despite the wealth of architectural details, it is still not known who the Minoans were, what language they spoke, nor what they believed in. However, there are still many sites to be excavated on Crete and these may provide the answers. In the meantime we remain ambivalent, attracted by the beauty of Minoan buildings and artifacts, horrified by the idea that they might have made human sacrifices.

Schliemann was convinced of the historical truth behind Homer's epics and proved his point by discovering Agamemnon's citadel at Mycenae in 1874

87

FURTHER READING
Leonard Cottrell, *The Bull of Minos* (London, 1953). A dated account of the early excavations on Crete.
Arthur Evans, *The Palace of Minos* (London, 1921). His own account.
Dilys Powell, *The Villa Ariadne* (London, 1973). On archaeology and modern Crete.
Jacquetta Hawkes, *Dawn of the Gods* (London, 1968). A vividly written study of the Minoan and Mycenaean civilisations.
Brian M. Fagan (ed.), *Eyewitness to Discovery* (Oxford, 1996). First-person archaeological accounts, includes Evans and Schliemann.

▶▶▶ Krítsa and Lató   65D1

Krítsa, one of Crete's largest villages, is set dramatically against hills and surrounded by olive and carob groves. Although it is one of the most popular day-trip destinations from Ágios Nikólaos, Krítsa has maintained much of its character as well as its weaving traditions. The **church of Ágios Geórgios Kavousiótis**▶ has early 14th-century frescoes. A signposted path to the right on the road into town leads to the finest Byzantine church on Crete, **Panagía Kerá**▶▶▶ (Our All-Holy Lady. *Open* Mon–Sat 9–3, Sun 9–2. *Admission charge*). Believed to have been founded in the 13th century, with 14th-century additions, it is particularly worth visiting for its extraordinary and well-preserved frescoes. The church has three aisles: the central one – the oldest – is dedicated to the Assumption of the Virgin, the south to St Anne, the Virgin's mother and the newer north to St Anthony. Together, they show clearly the artistic flourish of the late Byzantine empire.

Past Panagía Kerá, the right turn leads to the ruins of **Lató Etera** (*Open* Tue–Sun 8.30–3. *Admission free*). The setting is dramatic, covering two neighbouring hilltops and the saddle between them, with fine views over the Krítsa plain and the Gulf of Mirabéllo. Lató Etera, the region's most important city in the Archaic period, was built around the 7th century BC, about 800 years after the great Minoan palaces were destroyed and yet it shows strong Minoan influences. The best-preserved part is the **agora**, or marketplace, surrounded by a town hall, *stoas* (roofed colonnades) and a sanctuary.

▶▶▶ Lasíthiou   65D1

The Lasíthiou Plateau, a basin set into Mount Díkti (2147m), is famous for its 10,000 windmills, traditionally used to pump water to the fields or as grain mills, most of which no longer work. The soil here has always been very fertile – every possible strip of land is cultivated – and it was heavily populated even in antiquity. A circular road connects the villages along the plateau starting from **Tzermiádo▶**. (The drive alone is worth the trip.) Nearby is the oldest inhabited site, the **Cave of Trápeza▶▶**, where 7,000-year-old neolithic tombs were discovered, like miniature houses (*Open* at all times; torch essential). Uphill is the 11th-century BC site of **Karfí**, where statuettes of fertility goddesses were found (now in the Irákleio Archaeological Museum). Ágios Giórgios has a tiny **folk museum▶** (*Open* Jun–Aug daily 10–4. *Admission charge*) in a farmhouse, which explains the daily life of a farmer. Most people make the trip to **Psichró▶** and the nearby **Diktaío Ántro (Diktean Cave)▶▶** (*Open* daily 8–6.45). The latter is one of several places which are claimed as birthplaces of Zeus. Nearby, off the circular road before Krási, the 12th-century **convent of Panagía Kardiótissa▶▶** has some superb well-restored frescoes from the 14th century, that were undiscovered until the 1960s.

THE DIKTEAN CAVE
Legend has it that this cave was where the goddess Rhea gave birth to Zeus. Zeus's father Kronos feared that he would lose his throne to a son, so in an attempt to prevent the prophecy from being fulfiled, he ate all his children. At the birth of Zeus, however, Rhea fooled Kronos into eating a stone instead and hid her son in this cave. Whatever the truth, the cave must have been a cult centre for the Mother Goddess and for Zeus, since offerings were discovered going back to Classical times.
  When visiting the cave, take a torch and nonslip shoes. If you want to miss the crowds, visit in the early morning.

89

One of the most popular excursions from Ágios Nikólaos is a drive through the beautiful Lasíthiou countryside. The Lasíthiou Plateau is often called the Valley of the Windmills, though most are no longer functioning

▶ Mália   65D2

Modern Mália is a rather ugly beach resort with a dwindling old town. Its main interest lies in the nearby **Palace of Mália▶▶▶** (3km east of Mália. *Open* Tue–Sun 8.30–3. *Admission charge*). The site has a fine setting – near the sea and with the Lasíthiou mountains in the background – and resembles Knosós without the reconstructions and without the usual crowds. The site has the same history and ground plan as the two more important Minoan cities, Faistós and Knosós, but is much easier to grasp than either of them.

Excavations have uncovered remains of the second palace to occupy this site, built soon after the first palace was destroyed in about 1700 BC and inhabited until it too was destroyed around 1450 BC. As at Knosós, there is a vast Central Court in which it is believed bull-games were held, surrounded by royal apartments, cult rooms and granaries. Recent excavations outside the palace area have revealed houses – probably part of a large Minoan town.

THE JEWELS FROM MÁLIA
A rectangular mausoleum called Chryssolákos (Golden Pit) was found near the Minoan palace at Mália. The burial chambers, which seem to date to the Old Palace period, were filled with gold objects. Some of these treasures – like the famous gold amulet in the form of a couple of bees holding on to a drop of honey (illustrated on page 33) – are in the Irákleio Archaeological Museum, but a large number are exhibited in the Aegina Collection in London's British Museum.

Kríti (Crete)

The extraordinary caves at Mátala are no longer inhabited, but they continue to fascinate busloads of tourists

ROADSIDE SHRINES
All over Crete and the rest of Greece, there are small roadside shrines. Many visitors believe that they were built for someone who died there in an accident, but that is not completely true. These shrines are sometimes built by the victim of an accident or his family in honour of their favourite saint, in thanksgiving for allowing their survival. At other times they are erected as a simple act of devotion or piety. Inside there is usually a picture of the saint, an oil lamp, small bottles of oil and matches. The people who put up the shrine in the first place may take responsibility for maintaining it, cleaning and lighting the lamp. Passers-by will often leave coins to help with the maintenance of the shrine.

THE OLD ROAD
A new highway connects Kolymvári on the north coast with Palaiochóra. It saves time, of course, but the old road from Kaloudianá makes for an even more spectacular drive. There are some quiet villages on the way, mostly untouched by package tourism and enjoying wonderful views across the mountains.

PALAIOCHORA IN LITERATURE
In *The Last Lemon Grove* (London, 1977) Jackson Webb gives a wonderful description of how an American survived his lonely stay in Palaiochóra.

▶▶ Mátala
64C1

Mátala, on the southern coast, may no longer be the 'hippie' beach it once was, but it is still one of the island's most beautiful. The man-made caves cut into the cliffs, probably ancient tombs inhabited by early Christians, were famous for their foreign hippie community in the 1960s and 1970s. The place has now been cleaned up and although the caves still attract crowds, they are now locked at night. The underwater remains of **ancient Mátala**, an important harbour under the Romans, can be seen from the cliffs on the northern side of the cove. On the other side of Ákra Líthino (Cape Líthinon) is **Kaloí Liménes**, a big harbour for oil tankers. A small chapel marks the spot where, according to tradition, St Paul first landed on Crete.

▶▶ Myrtiá
64C2

Lost among olive groves and vineyards, the picturesque village of Myrtiá has a single attraction for visitors, as a sign in a dozen languages makes clear: it was the home of the family of the writer Níkos Kazantzákis. The **Kazantzákis House▶**, the town's most imposing villa (next door to Zorba's *kafeneío*) has been turned into a museum containing memorabilia of the writer and his family (*Open* Mar–Oct, Mon, Wed, Sat, Sun 9–1 and 4–8; Tue, Fri 9–1; Nov–Feb, Sun 9–2. *Admission charge*). A 20-minute video in four languages tells the story of the author's life and work.

▶ Palaiochóra
64A1

Palaiochóra, once a remote fishing hamlet with a crumbling castle, was recently brought to life by the laying of a new north-south highway from Kolymvári. In summer, daily excursion boats leave the harbour for the site of **ancient Lissós▶**, but walking there is also possible. The site contains the remains of a healing temple or Asklepion, a theatre and some houses.

Further on, Soúgia is a small hamlet near **ancient Syia▶**, a former port whose remarkable 6th-century basilica contains a fine mosaic pavement depicting deer and peacocks surrounded by vines.

Of all modern Greek writers, none is as familiar to non-Greeks as Níkos Kazantzákis. As might be expected of someone who has been several times nominated for the Nobel Prize for Literature, there is more to Kazantzákis's work than Zorba the Greek.

Before Zorba Born in Irákleio in February 1883 and educated at the University of Athens and at the Sorbonne, Níkos Kazantzákis began his career by writing books describing his travels in foreign countries. He went on to write 22 plays, nine film scenarios, a history of Russian literature (he had lived in Russia for two years), articles for newspapers and journals and an epic poem, *The Odyssey*. Among his other activities, he held the post of minister without portfolio in 1945. But it is on his novels that his reputation rests, in particular *The Last Temptation of Christ* and *Zorba the Greek*.

Alexis Zorba Kazantzákis's best-known novel, set in Crete, tells the story of Alexis Zorba, a 'free spirit' who gives his all to pleasure as to work and shows the English narrator of the story how to stop worrying and start living. The narrator also witnesses the growing relationship between Zorba and Madame Hortense, an old woman down on her luck – 'a sort of blonde walrus who had been cast up, half-rotting, on this sandy shore', as Kazantzákis describes her in his typical, overblown style. In the background, Crete before the days of tourism comes memorably to life.

The Zorba effect Not even in his wildest dreams (or nightmares?) could Kazantzákis have predicted the success of *Zorba*. In 1964, seven years after Kazantzákis's death, the film of the novel was released with Anthony Quinn as Zorba. To foreign audiences, Quinn's vital hero epitomised the spirit of modern Greece, just as Míkis Theodorákis's *bouzoúki* music characterised its sound. As a result, the name 'Zorba' has been widely adopted by Greek hotels and restaurants and Theodorákis's soundtrack remains the anthem for the island way of life.

FREEDOM AND DEATH

This was perhaps Kazantzákis's most powerful work. Setting his story in the time of the 1878 Cretan revolt against Turkish rule, he brilliantly catchest the spirit of the time, particularly the terror and the belief in sacrifice that drove the Cretans in their determined fight for independence.

91

KAZANTZÁKIS'S MEMORIAL

Celebrated now as one of the most important Greek writers of the century, Kazantzákis was less appreciated by his countrymen during his lifetime. Because of his freely expressed thoughts on politics and history and his much publicised doubts about Christianity, he spent most of the later part of his life abroad, banned from returning to Greece and excommunicated by the Orthodox Church. One explanation of why he was buried on Irákleio's city ramparts and not in a cemetery was because the Church authorities denied him burial, a decision that must, to them, have seemed fully justified after his story *The Last Temptation of Christ* was filmed in 1988.

Above left: Many hotels put on Greek dancing, in an attempt to convey Zorba's joie-de-vivre
Left: Níkos Kazantzákis is often overlooked by the tourist

THE IDEAN CAVE
According to legend, the *Kuretes* (young warriors) danced around in the cave and beat their bronze shields so that the crying of baby Zeus would not be heard. One of the first things archaeologists found upon excavating the cave were votive offerings in the shape of bronze shields, one of which is now in the Irákleio Archaeological Museum. It is thought that the ceremonial was re-enacted here at celebrations of Zeus's birthday.

MOUNTAIN CLIMBING
The path up Mount Ida is marked with red dots but, whether experienced or not, climbers should consult the Mountaineering Club in Irákleio (Odós Dhikeosínis 53, tel: 081 227 609) before ascending.

The monastery of Préveli is dedicated to St John the Theologian, whose ancient Byzantine icon is preserved in the church

▶▶ Psiloreítis 64C1

Mount Ida (2,456m), the peak of the Psiloreítis range, is the highest in Crete. At the end of a rough road from Anógia, above the beautiful Nida Plateau, is the **Idaío Ántro (Idean Cave)▶▶** (closed at the time of writing), which claims, along with the Diktaío Ántro (Diktean Cave; see page 89), to be where Rhea gave birth to Zeus and hid him from his father Kronos. A cult place probably before the Minoan period, it remained the most sacred cave until well into Roman times, mentioned often by ancient writers. There is an altar in front of the cave and a labyrinthine corridor leads to the 60m-high main cavern.

The ascent to the summit starts either behind the cave or at the **Spílaio Kamarón (Kamáres Cave)▶**, where the first Kamáres pottery (now in the Irákleio Archaeological Museum) was discovered.

▶▶ Réthymno 64B2

Réthymno, Crete's third largest town and an important harbour, has preserved its historical centre from Turkish and Venetian times remarkably well; a new resort area sprawls along a beautiful beach to the east of the old town. Out of season it is a rewarding place to stroll and an excellent base for exploring the nearby mountain ranges. Seen from the sea, a 16th-century **Fortress▶▶** dominates the town (*Open* Tue–Sun 8–8; earlier closing in winter. *Admission charge*). It claims to be the largest Venetian castle ever built. Much of it is ruined, but at sunset, the views are great and there is a pretty, domed mosque with a fine

USEFUL NUMBERS (RÉTHYMNO)
Port Authority tel: 0831 22276
Tourist information (Odós Venizélou. *Open* Mon–Fri 8–8, Sat and Sun 8.30–2) tel: 0831 24143 and 29148
Olympic Airways tel: 0831 24333, 22257 and 27353
Hertz Rent-a-Car tel: 0831 26286

*Behind the inner harbour
and lighthouse lies the
most atmospheric part of
Réthymno*

mihrab, indicating the direction to Mecca. Opposite the entrance is the **Archaeological Museum▶** (*Open* Tue–Sun 8.30–3. *Admission charge*), which includes a collection of Roman finds. The **Historical and Folk Museum▶** (Odós Mesolongíou. *Open* daily 9–1, Mon and Tue also 6–8 pm. *Admission charge*) gives a good insight into rural life and traditions. In the heart of town near the 17th-century **Venetian loggia**, now a library, is the 17th-century **Rimondi fountain**, adorned with spouting lion heads. Nearby is the **Nerandzes Mosque▶** (closed for renovation). Enjoy the views over the town from its minaret.

Places to visit from Réthymno include the **monastery of Arkádi** (see page 71). Also within easy reach are the pretty village of **Spíli▶ ▶**, with its old alleys and extraordinary lions'-head fountain and, further south, the monastery of **Préveli▶ ▶**, a centre of Cretan resistance against Ottoman rule and, later, during World War II, against occupation by Germany.

▶ ▶ ▶ Farángi Samariás (Samariá Gorge) 64A1

*Open: May–Oct, daily 6 am–sunset (conditions permitting)
Admission charge*

The spectacular Samariá Gorge, an 17km-long canyon running from Omalós down to the beach at Agía Rouméli, offers a popular but strenuous downhill hike, suitable for anyone who is used to long walks and is reasonably fit. The trail starts from **xilóskalo** (literally 'wooden stairs') and drops down about 1000m in the first 2km. After that it becomes flatter, with a wealth of wild flowers, especially in spring. The gorge is named after the 14th-century **church of Óssia María▶** in Samariá (almost halfway) which was abandoned after the villagers were relocated in 1962. Beyond the church, the path follows the river and becomes even more spectacular as it gets closed in by steep cliff walls, reaching what are popularly known as the **sidiróportes** (iron gates), where it is almost possible to touch both sides of the gorge. The valley soon widens and, a little further on, reaches the gate of the White Mountains National Park. From here it is about another half-hour's walk to the beach. Lucky walkers might just spot the famous *kri-kri*, the rare Cretan wild goat, which is protected here in the National Park.

PRACTICALITIES FOR THE SAMARIÁ GORGE
The easiest (and often the *only*) way to do the hike in a day is to buy a day trip from a travel agent. If you prefer to walk by yourself, or to stay on the south coast, early morning public buses from Chaniá go to the top of the gorge near Omalós (1½ hours). The first buses from Réthymno and Irákleio to Chaniá continue straight to Omalós. The walk takes 4–5 hours to Agía Rouméli, from where several boats a day leave for Chóra Sfákia. From there, several buses daily, especially in the late afternoon, return to Chaniá and one to Réthymno. Wear good walking shoes, take a picnic and enough to drink, a hat, sunscreen and, in summer, swimsuits for the beach at the end.

93

THE WHITE MOUNTAINS
'The high mountains had the austerity, the extravagance and sometimes the melancholy of the backgrounds of primitive religious paintings in Italy (though not the softness) or the vertigo of those insane and toppling crags – steel grey on purple, or ice blue on asbestos white – that surround the saints and martyrs on the ikons of Byzantium'. Patrick Leigh Fermor, in his introduction to George Psychoundákis, *The Cretan Runner* (1955)

USEFUL NUMBERS (SITEIA)
Port Authority
tel: 0843 22310
Olympic Airways
tel: 0843 22270
Tourist Police
tel: 0843 24200

LINEAR A AND LINEAR B
The term 'linear' differentiates these early scripts from the even earlier hieroglyphic ideograms also used by the Minoans; instead of pictures they use abstract groups of lines. Linear A, which has never been deciphered, was a new script used from the beginning of the New Palace period (*c*1700 BC). Although it is not known which language it is, there are suggestions that it is related to the pre-Hellenic languages of western Anatolia, where the Minoans originally came from. Linear B, a modification of Linear A, is known to have been used at Knosós for palace inventories from 1450 BC. It has been deciphered as Mycenaean Greek and is therefore regarded as the first Hellenic language.

Tóplou monastery was built as a fortress against the Turks who destroyed the original building

▶ **Siteía** 65E2

A harbour town and the capital of Crete's eastern province, Siteía struggles to compete with the beauty of the surrounding hills. The modern town has preserved few reminders of its long history, but still has some of its old sleepy charm. Modern Siteía is built on the site of **ancient Iteía**, an important Minoan port and the supposed birthplace of Mysonas, one of the seven sages of ancient Greece. East of the town, at Pétra, this partly excavated Minoan settlement has yielded what was probably a palace and storage rooms. Siteía flourished under the Venetians, the much-restored **fortress** above the town being one of the few reminders of this period. First devastated by an earthquake in 1508, it was then sacked by the Turkish admiral Kheir-ed-Din Barbarossa.

The excellent **Archaeological Museum▶▶** on the Ierápetra road (*Open* Tue–Sun 8.30–3. *Admission charge*) has finds from the nearby excavations, mainly from Zákros (see below) and some evidence that a post-Minoan culture did exist in this area after the destruction of the Minoan palaces around 1450 BC. Among the treasures is a collection of rare Linear A tablets. The charming **Museum of Folklore▶** (Odós Arkadíou. *Open* Tue–Sun 9.30–2.30, Wed–Thu also 6–8 pm. *Admission charge*) contains local costumes and embroideries. The waterfront has several restaurants, good *zacharoplasteía* (pastry shops) and an extrovert pelican.

Around Siteía Many visitors to Siteía travel on eastwards to the famous palm-fringed beach of **Váï▶▶** (see page 97). On the way, near **Agía Fotiá** (where the largest early Minoan cemetery was found), is the fortified **Moní Tóplou▶▶**, one of the richest monasteries in Greece. After the stark exterior, the interior is remarkably beautiful and contains the amazing 18th-century **icon of the Greatness of the Lord▶▶**, by Ioánnis Kornáros, one of the masterpieces of Cretan art. Set into the exterior wall is the historic **Tóplou inscription▶▶**, an appeal by the people of Ítanos to the Egyptian King Ptolemy VI, made in 146 BC, asking for

help against their enemies from Ierápytna (Ierápetra). **Ítanos►**, on the most northeasterly tip of the island, has the scattered remains of both a Minoan and a Roman Acropolis. At nearby **Palaíokastro►►** is the largest Minoan town so far found. Visitors can wander through the remains of streets and houses half lost among the olive trees. On the other side of Siteía, **Móchlos►►** is a charming and quiet little fishing harbour, a reminder of how most of Crete used to be not so long ago. An important archaeological site has been discovered on rocky Psíra island in front of the harbour, containing a Minoan settlement from after the 1450 BC disaster.

►► Tílisos
64C2

At the edge of the village of the same name is **ancient Tílisos►** (*Open* daily 9–3. *Admission charge*), whose three Minoan villas from the Neopalatial period (c1700 BC) are still surrounded by rich farmland. The remains of House A suggest an elegant construction with a colonnaded court. House B is less well preserved, while the refined House C has evidence of a drainage system and a cult room. Both A and C have stairways, indicating that they had at least one more floor.

►► Zákros
65E1

From Áno Zákros, a sleepy town surrounded by lush vegetation, a memorable two-hour walk (see panel) is an alternative to the bus ride to the lovely fishing harbour of Káto Zákros. The **Palace of Zákros►►** here is Crete's fourth largest Minoan palace (*Open* Tue–Sun 8–2.30. *Admission charge*). Although it is much smaller than Knosós, Faistós and Mália, much of the town that surrounds it has been preserved. Zákros was most probably an important trading port with Egypt and the Levant. The new palace was built around 1600 BC and destroyed in the 1450 BC disaster, perhaps by tidal waves caused by Thíra's volcano (a lot of pumice was found at the site).

Quiet Zákros is believed to have been a major Minoan seaport, which traded with Egypt and other countries in the Middle East

GORGE OF THE DEAD
The 11km walk from Áno Zákros to the Minoan site near Káto Zákros passes through a magnificent ravine known as the Gorge of the Dead. Follow the road towards Káto Zákros for the first half hour, until a path to the left goes up to the ravine. Getting down into the gorge can be tricky, but once down by the riverbed the path is marked with red. Surrounded by wild vegetation and high cliff walls, you start to understand how the place got its name: the Minoans buried their dead in caves in the cliffs. From the end of the gorge, make your way back on to the road that leads to Káto Zákros and the palace.

Kríti (Crete)

One of the undeveloped and wonderful beaches in southern Crete, near Ierápetra

BEACHES ON CRETE
There is very little happy news to report on Cretan beaches. Package tourism has spoiled many of the once-famous splendours, like Váï and Mátala and even where land access is difficult – as, for instance, to the most remote beaches on the south and west coasts – crowds of day trippers arrive by boat in summer. So even if you find that beach of your dreams – with white sand, good swimming, hills or greenery behind and no development – you won't be alone. And since these out-of-the-way beaches have no facilities or services, when visitors leave their trash behind them, it stays there...

INTERNATIONAL FERRIES
There are ferries in summer from Irákleio to Ancona, Haifa (Israel), Çesme (Turkey) and Cyprus, although not all of these operate regularly.

SUNKEN TREASURES
Many historic treasures still lie on the sea bed near the coasts of the islands. This is the main reason why scuba diving is not permitted in most Greek water – a rare exception is Mýkonos. The Greek government is still hoping to recover these treasures one day.

Beaches
Irákleio There are no great beaches around the capital. Amnísos, to the east, is the cleanest, but has continuous noise from aircraft. The coast further east is one built-up resort after the other, each with a thin strip of pebbly beach. Beaches are better along the Gulf of Mália, but most have been developed. The beach near the Minoan palace at Mália is pleasant for a swim. Of the overdeveloped beaches west of Irákleio the best (but near a power station) is Amoudári. More up-market Agía Pelagía, with a good beach and clear water, is often less crowded.

Agía Galíni This popular package resort on the south coast has only a small beach, but boats go to beaches further west. Ágios Geórgios is the most popular cove, but the better one is Ágios Pávlos. Mátala beach, overlooked by the cliff, remains truly spectacular, even if it is completely overrun in summer. Léndas's long beach is popular with nudists and the former crowd from Mátala.

Ágios Nikólaos The best near the town are the sandy, clean beach of Almýros and some pretty sandy coves near Istro. Eastwards towards Gourniá and Pachiá Ámmos the beaches are often dirty and polluted. Móchlos is cleaner.

Chaniá The town beach and Akrotíri beaches, Stavrós especially, are usually crowded. Westwards, the best are Chryssí Aktí or Golden Beach, increasingly built up but good and Kalamáki, which has excellent swimming. From Chaniá to Kolymvári the coast is one long line of development and the beaches are not very clean. Falasarná, near Plátanos, is a long and isolated stretch of fine sand.

Chóra Sfákia Chóra Sfákia is a popular resort with a tiny beach. Boats run to the tranquil beaches of Gávdos island, Sweetwater Beach with cool springs and Mármara with

CONNECTIONS
Ferries run from Irákleio to Piréad, Íos, Mýkonos, Páros, Skíathos, Tínos, Thíra, Náxos, Thessaloníki, Kárpathos, Kásos, Rhodes, Sýros, Amorgós, Kálymnos, Chálki, Milos and Pátmos. There are also excursion boats in summer to Thíra and the major Cyclades. From Ágios Nikólaos and Siteía there are links with Thíra, Kýthnos, Mílos, Piréas, Sérifos, Sífnos, Sými, Kárpathos, Kásos, Chálki, Rhodes, Folégandros and Síkinos. Chaniá and Réthymno offer services to Piréas, while from Kastelli Kissámou there are ferries to Antikýthira, Kýthira and Piréas.

rock formations. Agía Rouméli has a pebble beach, Plákias is still good but development is coming fast. Nearby are smaller secluded coves such as Damnóni, Amoúdi and Palm Beach, but they too are far from empty.

Ierápetra Near Ierápetra is Long Beach, a good stretch of sand. Agía Fotiá is an attractive beach set in a green valley, but Makrýgialos, once a magnificent beach, is now getting increasingly developed. Westwards the beach at Mýrtos, a small white resort, is a better option.

Palaiochóra Palaiochóra has a superb sandy beach, which so far is not too crowded and more unspoiled beaches are within walking distance. Daily boats go to the wonderful, almost tropical beach of Elafonísi (no longer a secret), with white sands and warm turquoise waters. Elafonísi island can be reached by wading through the shallow water. One of Crete's best beaches.

Réthymno The wide, sandy beach in town is packed, but the water is cleaner away from the harbour. The coast east-wards has fine beaches near Balí, but most of it has given in to serious development. There are sandy beaches towards the Georgioúpoli resort, but the currents can be dangerous.

Much of Mália has been overrun by package tourism and space is short on its beach

Siteía Palm-fringed Váï is still a magnificent and exotic beach, even if the palm trees are now fenced in. If the crowds in summer get too overwhelming, there are emptier beaches 1.5km away near Ítanos. There are excellent sandy beaches south of Palaíkastro and a small pebble beach near Káto Zákros. Further south, dirt paths lead to deserted sandy beaches near Xerókampos.

The Cyclades match everyone's dream of the perfect Greek island

THE CYCLADES Perhaps more than the other island groups, the Cyclades fulfil most visitors' expectations of how Greek islands should look. And yet, as the largest island group, they offer a great variety of landscape and character, from the dramatic cliffs of Thíra (Santoríni) to the lush valleys of Náxos. The Cyclades are the peaks of a mountain range beneath the Aegean, a fact most easily appreciated when looking at the volcanic caldera of Thíra.

FIRST CULTURE In an age when sea travel was constantly hazardous, the relative proximity of the Cyclades to each other allowed islanders to trade among themselves earlier than elsewhere; from this sprang the enigmatic Cycladic civilisation of the period around 3000 BC (see page 31). The remarkable artifacts attributed to this culture appeal to modern taste, particularly the carved figures with their clean lines and restrained movement.

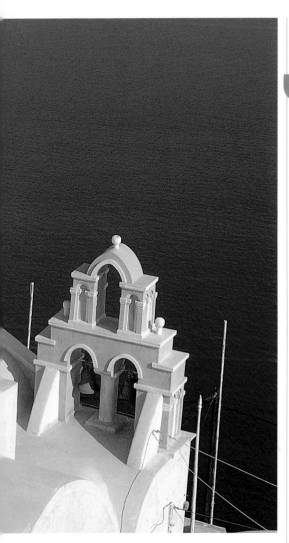

EARLY POWER The name 'Cyclades' is derived from the Greek word for circle or ring: at the centre of the ring of islands lies Dílos (Delos), long respected as a place of both religious and political importance. In the 5th century BC, the creation of the Delian League brought cohesion to the islands. Subsequent Athenian Confederacies also kept the islands together, but they were no match for the powers that swept through the Aegean in the coming centuries: Egyptians and Romans, Vandals and Goths.

FOREIGN RULE AND INDEPENDENCE The Cyclades were nominally held by the Byzantines until the sack of Constantinople in 1204, after which they were ceded to Venice, which divided them among the adventuring sons of her aristocracy. The Venetian Sanudos, who claimed the title of Dukes of Náxos, were the most powerful of these families, but not even they held out against the Turks, who

The Cyclades

Amorgós (ΑΜΟΡΓΟΣ)
Anáfi (ΑΝΑΦΗ)
Ándros (ΑΝΔΡΟΣ)
Dílos (ΔΗΛΟΣ)
Folégandros
    (ΦΟΛΕΓΑΝΔΡΟΣ)
Íos (ΙΟΣ)
Kéa (ΚΕΑ)
Kímolos (ΚΙΜΩΛΟΣ)
Kýthnos (ΚΨΘΝΟΣ)
Mílos (ΜΗΛΟΣ)
Mýkonos
    (ΜΨΚΟΝΟΣ)
Náxos (ΝΑΞΟΣ)
Páros (ΠΑΡΟΣ) and
    Antíparos
    (ΑΝΤΙΠΑΡΟΣ)
Sérifos (ΣΕΡΙΦΟΣ)
Sífnos (ΣΙΦΝΟΣ)
Síkinos (ΣΙΚΙΝΟΣ)
Sýros (ΣΨΡΟΣ)
Thíra (Santoríni)
    (ΘΗΡΑ)
    (ΣΑΝΤΟΡΙΝΙΗ)
Tínos (ΤΗΝΟΣ)

Cyclades

BEST BEACHES
● Mylopótamos (Íos), for its summer 'scene'
● Paradise and Super Paradise (Mýkonos)
● Chrysí Aktí (Páros)
● Pláka (Náxos)
● Roúkounas and tamarisk-lined Klisídi (Anáfi)

then controlled the archipelago until Greek independence. The importance of the Cyclades to the independent Greek state was immediately apparent: the port of Ermoúpoli on Sýros became its principal commercial and shipping centre and one of the eastern Mediterranean's main coaling stations. It remains a busy port and is still the administrative capital of the Cyclades.

LANDSCAPES AND LIFE Surrounded by a dramatic landscape of rock and olive trees, of green terraces, golden sand and brilliant blue sea, the islanders have created an architecture of simple lines and smooth surfaces, painted white

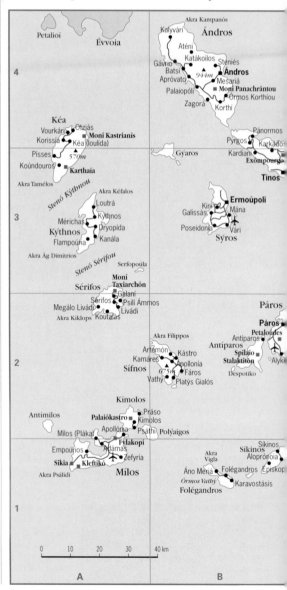

and blue – the colours of the Greek flag – which has much in common with the art of their Early Cycladic ancestors.

The islands within easy reach of Piréas were among the first to be developed. But even on Mýkonos, famous (some would say notorious) the world over for its nightlife, much of the island's original character remains intact. While, in summer, some of the islands can seem to have sold their soul to tourism, in winter, with the high sea crashing on the beaches and ferry arrivals limited, island life is the same as it ever was. Visit some of the smaller villages, stop and talk to a farmer or a fisherman and experience the Cycladic inheritance firsthand.

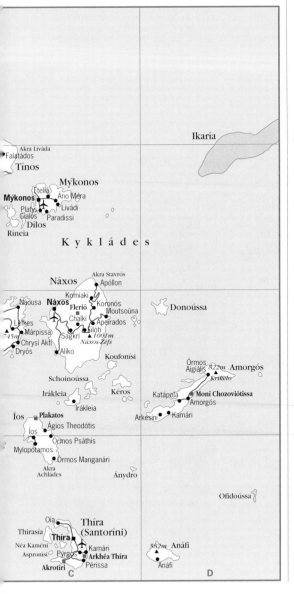

Religion takes inspiration from the beauty and isolation of remote places

Cyclades

USEFUL NUMBERS
Port Authority (Amorgós)
tel: 0285 71259
Tourist information
(Amorgós) tel: 0285
71278, on the quay
Port Authority (Anáfi)
tel: 0286 61216
Port Authority (Ándros)
tel: 0282 22250
Tourist information
(Ándros: Gávrio. *Open*
Jun–Sep) tel: 0282 71785

102

CONNECTIONS
Amorgós has ferry links
with Náxos, Páros, Piréas,
Schoinoússa, Sýros,
Donoússa, Mýkonos,
Astypálaia, Rafína, Tínos
and Crete (Irákleio).
Hydrofoils run to Ándros,
Íos, Rafína, Mýkonos,
Náxos, Páros, Tínos,
Sýros, Koufonísi, Thíra
and Schoinoússa.
Excursion boats operate
to Rafína, Páros, Náxos,
Sýros and Tínos.

AMORGÓS

Amorgós, the dramatically rugged island that starred in Luc Besson's film *The Big Blue*, is still a low-key place, though more visitors head this way each summer.

▶ Amorgós Town (Chóra)　　　　101D2

The island's capital, built around a 13th-century Venetian castle, has more than 40 chapels and churches, including the smallest one in Greece, **Ágios Fanoúrios**, which can hold a congregation of three. Outside the town a path leads towards the striking white **monastery of Chozoviótissa▶▶** (*Open* daily 8–1 and 5–7 pm. *Admission donation*), founded around a miraculous 11th-century icon of the Virgin. Downhill is the harbour, Katápola and a track leading past **ancient Minoa▶**, with the remains of a temple of Apollo, to the site of **ancient Arkesíni▶**, with a burial site and some houses.

▶ Órmos Aigiális (Eyiáli)　　　　101D2

This harbour in the northern part of the island is a good base for the nearby beaches and walks to the villages of Tholária, Langáda and Potámos or a climb up the peak of Kríkelo (780m), with its splendid 5th-century **church of Theológos▶▶**.

Beaches
The only sandy beach on the island is near Órmos Aigiális, though further north there are a few pleasant coves. From Amorgós Town a trail goes down to the pleasant pebble beaches and coves of Agía Ánna. Near Kamári there are fine secluded beaches at Moúros, Notiná and Poulopódi, all with good swimming.

The Chóra in Amorgós has more than 40 churches, including the smallest one in Greece

ANÁFI

According to legend, Anáfi, a small and idyllic island, was pulled up from the sea by Apollo to give refuge to the Argonauts. Today it offers refuge to people escaping nearby Thíra, though there are no paved roads, few tourist facilities and food can be scarce.

▶ Anáfi Town (Chóra)   *101D1*

The island's 300 inhabitants live in Anáfi Town or the port of Ágios Nikólaos. At first sight, the former looks like a windswept ghost town, but closer inspection reveals friendly *kafeneía* and sheltered terraces.

The island's main attraction is the **monastery of Panagía Kalamiótissa▶▶**, three hours' walk away from Anáfi Town, less from Kálamos, reached by daily boats. The path up to the little monastery offers spectacular views.

Beaches

Klisídi is a lovely tamarisk-lined beach near the harbour. An hour's walk away is the island's best beach, Roúkounas, with sandy dunes and shade under the trees. Further down are some superb coves and the secluded Kálamos beach.

ÁNDROS

Green, pine-forested Ándros has long been a favourite holiday destination for Greek families. Other Europeans are slowly arriving, attracted by the cosmopolitan atmosphere combined with traditional village life.

▶▶▶ Ándros Town (Chóra)   *100B4*

The oldest part of the island's capital is built on a rocky tongue of land, while a later addition was built on the hillside. It is a charming place with marble pavements, elegant squares and grand 19th-century mansions. A 13th-century Venetian **kástro▶** sits on a rocky islet reached by an arched bridge. The modern galleries of the excellent **Archaeological Museum▶▶▶** (*Open* Tue–Sun 8.30–3. *Admission charge*) contain a fine statue of Hermes, Byzantine and Venetian marbles and finds from the

CONNECTIONS
Anáfi is linked by ferry with Thíra, Píreas, Íos, Náxos, Astypálaia, Sikinos, Folégandros, Páros and Sýros. Hydrofoils serve Mýkonos, Náxos, Páros, Thíra, Íos, Tínos and Sýros.

THE GOULANDRÍS FAMILY
The extremely wealthy and famous Goulandrís shipping magnates, originating from Ándros, put their island on the map of the art world when they opened two museums in Ándros Town. The Archaeological Museum contains the beautiful statue of Hermes of Ándros, on display until 1981 in the National Museum in Athens. The Museum of Modern Art has wonderful collections of contemporary Greek and European work. After all that, it comes as no surprise that both the square at the heart of the Ándros Town and its main street carry the Goulandrís name.

GREEN ÁNDROS

The countryside of Ándros is perfect for hiking. The strong prevailing winds keep it cooler than most islands, even in summer, and freshwater springs are abundant. The countryside is dotted with lovely Venetian dovecotes and there is an interesting system of dry-stone walling around many fields and orchards. The Andriots, noted for their hospitality, are always proud to show off the beauty of their island.

CONNECTIONS

Ferries from Ándros serve Rafína, Tínos, Mýkonos, Sýros, Kós, and Thíra. A summer hydrofoil service operates to Tínos, Mýkonos, Páros, Náxos, Schoinoússa, Koufonísi, Irákleio, Íos, and Amorgós.

Panachrántou, the most ancient of Ándros's monasteries, has recently celebrated its 1,000th birthday

ancient fortified town of Zagorá. Close by, the equally modern **Museum of Modern Art**►►► (*Open* daily Wed–Mon 10–2 and in summer also 6–9 pm. *Admission charge*) has a remarkable collection by modern artists including Picasso, and a fine sculpture garden.

► Batsí   100B4

Ándros's main resort, Batsí, has a fine fishing harbour and a beautiful but crowded beach. The walk up the mountain to the picturesque villages of Káto and Áno Katákolos, Aténi and Arní is rewarding. Further along the coast is the 7th-century BC site of **Palaiopólis**►. Most of the once-grand former capital has now disappeared.

► Gávrio   100B4

Gávrio is the island's main harbour, on the more sheltered west coast. A short walk away is **Ágios Pétros**►►, a 20m-high Hellenic round tower – perhaps once a royal tomb, later converted into a watchtower.

►► Korthí   100B4

Korthí village is isolated from the rest of the island by a high ridge. The nearby convent of **Zoödóchou Pigís**►► (*Open* mornings) is a Byzantine school, converted into a monastery during the 14th century and into a convent in the 1920s. The convent, which takes its name from the miraculous spring next door, has a finely embroidered icon. North of Korthí is Palaiókastro, which has a crumbling Venetian castle.

►►► Mesariá   100B4

Mesariá is a picturesque medieval village near the **monastery of Panachrántou**►►, the finest on the island. It was probably built in the 10th century and is still surrounded by impressive defensive walls.

► Zagorá   100B4

Most of the finds from this ancient fortified town are in the Ándros Archaeological Museum. This site, which was never built over, is spectacular, with steep cliffs on three sides.

Beaches

Beaches near Ándros Town can suffer from a strong *meltemi* wind, while the beach near Gávrio is usually full of ducks and litter. If Batsí is too crowded, head south for the more secluded Káto Apróvato.

More important in the calendar than Christmas, Easter in Greece is a magical time of traditions, prayers and, later, of treats as well. It is also a time when many quiet island villages are suddenly filled with celebrating Athenians. If you are lucky enough to be on the islands for the festival, prepare to rejoice.

The tradition Greeks take their celebrations seriously and none more than Easter, a time of celebration rather than mourning. It is usual for people to return to their place of origin and both ferries and hotels fill up at this time of year. The islands of Ýdra, Pátmos, Sýros and Tínos are particularly noted for their Easter festivities. On Good Friday, after church bells have tolled, the *Epitáfios*, a symbolic bed for Jesus, decorated with flowers, is carried through the streets.

Easter celebrations are intense

The rising In keeping with a religion that emphasises joy, the main event of Orthodox Easter takes place at midnight on Easter Saturday: the bells toll again, lights are dimmed in churches and a priest calling *Christós Anésti* (Christ has risen) offers a lighted candle to the community. People light their own candles from the priest's, make the sign of the cross in smoke on the threshold of their houses and then leave the candle to burn down while they eat. The traditional late-night dish is *mayarítsa*, a soup of tripe and rice.

The Easter slaughter Few restaurants serve dinner on Easter Saturday as islanders are saving their appetite for the following day's Easter feast. During the previous day or two, a great slaughter will have taken place and on Easter Sunday every family that can afford to do so will roast a lamb. The summer barbecue is often brought out for the first time after winter in order to roast it. On the Thursday before Easter, there is also a tradition of painting hard-boiled eggs red. Some are used in *tsouréki* (see panel) while others are saved for a typically Greek holiday game: the eggs are knocked together two at a time and the holder of the last unbroken egg is considered the lucky one.

FASTING
Patience Gray wrote in her wonderful book *Honey from a Weed* (London, 1986): 'From Advent until Christmas Eve and from Ash Wednesday until midnight on Easter Saturday the diet is reduced to the consumption of dried beans, lentils, rice, spaghetti and weeds. The normal standbys – goat, lamb, pork, fresh cheese, eggs and often fish, as well as olive oil, are eliminated. As the diet of island Greeks was already restricted, one marvelled at their ability to deprive themselves still further'.

EASTER BREAD
Of all the traditional Easter fare on the Greek islands, the most common is *tsouréki*, a sweet twist-bread, usually flavoured with mastic from Chíos. A red-painted egg is usually inserted into the dough and baked into the bread as it cooks.

Lamb on a spit for the Easter feast

Three of the lions from the stunning Lion Terrace are now in the Arsenale in Venice

GETTING THERE
The entire island of Dílos is an archaeological museum and can only to be visited as a day trip. Boats leave Mýkonos harbour daily around 9 am for the 40-minute ride, returning around 1.30pm. This allows visitors three hours on the site – enough for most people. Tickets for guided or non-guided trips are best bought in advance from the booths on the quay, rather than from a travel agent. Note that most tickets sold on Mýkonos do not include the (expensive) admission to the site (which, incidentally, is closed on Mondays).

THE DELIAN GAMES
In antiquity, the Delian Games were as famous as the Olympics. Both were religious festivals held in honour of the gods, who were believed to be delighted to see humans enjoying themselves on their account. Homer confirmed this in his *Hymn to Apollo*: 'But it was on Dílos, Phoibos, that your heart especially took delight, Where the long-robed Ionians gathered together With their children and wives on your sacred street; There in boxing and dancing and singing They think of you and rejoice, when they hold your contest'.

DÍLOS (DELOS)

▶▶▶ Ancient Dílos   *101C3*

Open: Tue–Sun 8.30–3

Leto, the pregnant mistress of Zeus, was pursued all over the world by his jealous wife Hera, until the winds brought her to Dílos. Poseidon struck the island with his trident and anchored it with four columns of diamond, while Leto gave birth to Artemis on the nearby island of Ríneia and to Apollo under a date palm on Dílos's Mount Kinthos. The dry, barren island, which immediately started to flourish, was to become one of the most sacred places in Greece.

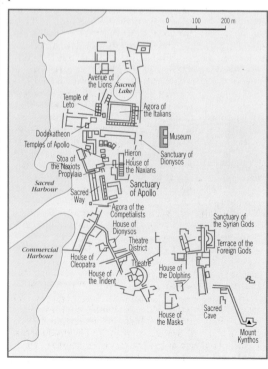

The Ionians, who considered Apollo the father of Ion, the founder of their race, made Dílos their religious capital. The rising Athenians became increasingly jealous of Dílos's power and tried everything in their might to diminish it. The Athenians tricked the oracle in Delphi into ordering a purification of Dílos: in 426 BC, they went as far as forbidding all births and deaths on the island! The island flourished again in the 3rd and 2nd centuries BC as one of the great trading centres of the eastern Mediterranean, especially after the Romans declared it a free port. Mithridates and his pirates plundered the island twice, in 88 and 69 BC, killing more than 20,000 people – a blow from which Dílos never recovered.

Excavations on the island started in 1872 and continue today. The site is large, but easy to visit as everything is clearly labelled. The **Sacred Way**, once lined with grand statues, leads to the **Sanctuary of Apollo** and the **House of the Naxians**, originally fronted by a huge statue of Apollo. There are three subsequent **temples of Apollo**. Towards the museum is the **Sanctuary of Dionysos** with the often-photographed marble phalluses on pedestals. The **Agora of the Italians** leads to the 6th-century BC **Temple of Leto** and the **Dodekatheon**, dedicated to the 12 Olympian gods. Beyond lies the dried-up **Sacred Lake** and beside it the impressive 7th-century **Avenue of the Lions**. The **museum** has some fine Hellenistic and Archaic sculpture, mosaics, murals and daily objects from private houses. A path leads up to the **Terrace of the Foreign Gods**, with the 1st-century BC **Sanctuary of the Syrian Gods** and several temples dedicated to the Egyptian gods Serapis and Isis. Further up is the **Sacred Cave**, site of the oracle of Apollo and **Óros Kynthos (Mount Kinthos)** (110m), with excellent panoramic views over the entire island. At the foot of Mount Kinthos, in the **Theatre District**, well-preserved private houses and streets give a good feel of what life on Dílos must have been like. The 2nd-century BC **Theatre** once seated 5,500 people, but is now ruined. The houses date from the Hellenistic and Roman period, some still decorated with exquisite mosaics. In the **House of Dionysos** there is a superb mosaic of Dionysos seated on a panther. The **House of the Dolphins**, the **House of the Masks** and the **House of the Trident** also have fine mosaics.

One of several giant phalluses on Dionysian pedestals near the Sanctuary of Dionysos

The Greeks had no word for religion – that came with the Romans – nor did they have sacred texts. Ancient Greeks had their own ways of establishing relationships with the gods.

READING THE SIGNS

'... if the bird flying from right to left disappears from view the omen is favourable; if it raises its left wing, flies away and disappears the omen is unfavourable; if flying from left to right it disappears on a straight course the omen is unfavourable; but if after raising its right wing, it flies away and disappears the omen is favourable...'
6th-century BC divination from Ephesus, quoted in F Sokolowski, *Lois sacrés de l'Asie mineure* (1955)

GREEK GODS

The 5th-century BC historian Herodotus wrote, 'Not till the day before yesterday, so to speak, did the Greeks know the origin of each of the gods, or whether they had all existed always and what they were like in appearance... It was Homer and Hesiod who created a theogony for the Greeks, gave the gods their epithets, divided out offices and functions among them and described their appearance'. (*The Histories*)

ANCIENT AND MODERN

It was common practice in ancient Greece to make offerings at times of illness at the shrines of gods or heroes associated with healing (notably Asklepius). Offerings were often clay effigies of the part of the body that was affected, a habit that modern Greeks continue by bedecking holy icons with metal effigies of their afflicted parts.

The ritual of pouring a libation to the gods is depicted on a black-figured vase

Of gods and men Greeks had a very clear view of who their gods were. They were mostly related to each other, but each was associated with a specific area of human experience. The primary gods lived on Olympus and also in the world of men, sometimes associated with certain cities. However, gods and men were not on equal terms: men needed to do their utmost to keep the gods happy – all of them, because to ignore one particular god was to risk being cut off from a sphere of human interest or activity.

Understanding the will of the gods Greeks knew about the gods from mythology – from Homer and Hesiod, in particular. Although there were priests and priestesses, there was no unifying religious institution. Instead, Greeks relied on what they believed was a more direct and personal relationship with the gods. The most direct way to understand the will of the gods was via the oracles, the most famous being at Delphi, Olympia, Siwa (in Egypt) and Dîlos. Seers did not speak the will of the gods, like the oracles, but they knew how to interpret signs (see panel).

How to make your god happy The gods were happy when humans remembered them in their prayers and paid their respects by observing daily rituals and making offerings to temples and cult shrines. This observance ran throughout Greek society: fathers made sacrifices for the household, while priests and civil leaders did so for the people. There was a calendar of dates on which sacrifice was due to certain gods. Sacrificial offerings were either animals, slaughtered on site, or dry offerings, like grain or fruit. The most common form of sacrifice was for the thigh bones of a slaughtered animal to be wrapped in fat and burned on an altar. The meat could then be eaten by the mortals. To give thanks to a god, one might make a donation to the temple or cult centre.

Fun and games The gods loved fun and games and activities held in their honour had to reflect this. Greeks sang, danced, recited poetry, enacted dramas and held carnivals to delight the gods. Competing in athletics was also acceptable to the gods. The Olympics were the most prestigious of several athletics meetings held to honour them – games held on Dílos were similarly famous. Not only did these observances encourage a common Greek identity, they also allowed Greeks to feel they had a relationship with the gods: humans sacrificed and prayed and in return the gods granted wealth, health and happiness.

Mysteries and afterlife The dead in Homer's epic stories are mere shades of themselves, left to wander aimlessly in the underworld, with the occasional taste of heaven or hell. However, there were secret rites – the mysteries – that might just improve things in the afterlife. Initiation was via a long and extraordinary ritual. The most important mysteries were those connected to Demeter and Persephone at Eleusis, near Athens, but the mysteries connected to the great gods at Samothráki were still sufficiently important for Roman emperors to make the long journey to the island after the start of the Christian era.

One of the finest temples on the islands, the Temple of Aphaia on Aígina is associated with women, wisdom and light

GREEK ATHEISM
The power of the Greek religion lay not in texts but in its universality: people paid their respects to the gods and observed the necessary rituals. But in the 5th century BC there was a religious crisis in Athens as philosophers and scientists began to question the nature and the very existence of the gods. 'About the gods I cannot declare whether they exist or not', stated the intellectual Protagoras. Soon after, it seems, the common good or the common will exerted itself and there was a backlash against such thinkers: one of the charges levelled at Socrates, whom the oracle at Delphi had called the world's wisest man, was that he did not recognise 'the gods that the city recognises' and that he searched 'into things under the earth and above the heaven'. He was sentenced to death for his thoughts in 399 BC.

USEFUL NUMBERS
Port Authority
(Folégandros) tel:
0286 41249
Port Authority (Íos)
tel: 0286 91264
Tourist information (near
bus stop in Íos Town.
Open daily in summer
8 am–9 pm; also sells
ferry tickets) tel:
0286 91028

CONNECTIONS
Ferry services from
Folégandros operate to
Piréas, Thíra, Íos, Síkinos,
Sífnos, Mílos, Kímolos,
Kýthnos, Náxos, Páros,
Sérifos and Sýros. There
are additional summer
services to Mýkonos,
Crete, Kásos, Kárpathos,
Chálki, Sými and Rhodes.
Daily boats run to Íos
during the summer.
From Íos, ferries run to
Piréas, Náxos, Páros,
Thíra, Sýros, Síkinos,
Folégandros, Anáfi,
Sífnos, Kímolos, Kýthnos,
Mílos, Skiathos,
Kárpathos, Thessaloniki,
Sérifos and (summer only)
Mýkonos and Crete.
Hydrofoils serve Mýkonos,
Náxos, Páros, Thíra,
Tínos, Sýros, Anáfi,
Irákleia, Schoinoússa,
Koufonísi and Amorgós.

HOMER ON ÍOS
One story has it that
Homer's ship, on a trip
from Sámos to Athens,
was forced to call at Íos
and that while in port the
poet died. Another tradi-
tion claims that Homer's
mother was from the
island and that the poet
chose to return to this
place to die.

*Opposite: The blue-
domed Byzantine
churches of the Chóra are
a little oasis away from
the nightlife crowds*

FOLÉGANDROS

The high barren cliffs of Folégandros always deterred
eager invaders, until recent years. Now tourists have discovered this peaceful and quiet island.

▶▶ Folégandros Town (Chóra)   100B1

The island's capital, perched on a cliff high above
the harbour of Karavostásis, is a delightful village with
pretty squares, tree-shaded *kafeneía* and a 13th-century
Venetian **kástro** surrounded by solid two-storey houses.
A steep path leads to the **church of Koímisis Theotókou**
with spectacular views and, beneath it, the stalactite cave
of **Chrissospiliá**, accessible only to experienced climbers.

Beaches

The beaches near Karavostásis are average, but there is a
superb small-gravel beach at Katergó, reached by boat or
after a hard walk. Buses from Folégandros Town pass
close to the various beaches on the southwest coast of the
island: Angáli is the busiest, while nudism is tolerated on
Firá and sandy Ágios Nikólaos. From Áno Meriá a path
leads to the more secluded beach of Vígla.

ÍOS

Íos, one of the prettiest Cycladic islands, has a reputation
for good beaches and an even better nightlife. For these
reasons it attracts a particularly large number of tourists.
Depending on your idea of fun, you will either love it or
loathe it!

▶ Íos Town (Chóra)   101C1

A pretty, whitewashed village with a host of Byzantine
churches, the island's capital bursts with life at night when
music blares from countless bars and discos. The nearby
port of Gialós has excellent fish tavernas. Two to three
hours' walk away, above Ágios Theodótis, the Venetian
fortress of Palaiokástro overlooks the site of ancient
Aigina and a Byzantine church. A longer walk or a trip by
boat gets you to the ancient town of Plakatos, at the northern end of the island, where a tomb is believed to be that of
Homer, who is said to have died on Íos. Every year on 15
May, there is a Homer festival, when the villagers carry a
flame from the harbour to the grave.

Beaches

Good beaches and an easy lifestyle are what Íos is really
about. Gialós beach is nothing special; better is Koumbára,
20 minutes away, less crowded and mostly nudist.
Mylopótamos is a superb but very popular sandy beach.
For more secluded beaches walk, or take a bus or boat, to
Órmos Manganári, in the south, or to Ágios Theodótis or
Psáthis on the east coast.

Note that, although sleeping on the beach was always
the thing to do on Íos, these days it is better not to. With a
growing number of people looking for a good time,
reports of theft and violent crime have increased dramatically. The police, in response, have become really tough.
They will try to convince people to make use of the official
campsites and can be very unfriendly towards those who
do not take their advice.

Cyclades

USEFUL NUMBERS
Port Authority (Kéa)
tel: 0288 21344
Tourist Police (Kéa)
tel: 0288 21100
Port Authority (Mílos)
tel: 0287 22100
Tourist information (Mílos,
on the quay in Adamas)
tel: 0287 22445
Olympic Airways (Mílos)
tel: 0287 22380

112

CONNECTIONS
From Kéa, ferries operate
to Lávrio (mainland), Kýth-
nos and Sýros. There are
hydrofoil links with Piréas
and (summer only)
Kýthnos, Mílos, Sérifos,
Sífnos, Kímolos and
Rafína.
Ferries from Kímolos serve
Piréas, Mílos, Kýthnos,
Sífnos, Sérifos,
Folégandros, Íos, Páros,
Thíra, Síkinos and Sýros.
There is a summer hydro-
foil service to Mílos,
Sífnos, Sérifos, Kýthnos,
Kéa and Rafína.
Boats operate to Mílos in
summer.
Ferries operate from Kýth-
nos to Piréas, Sérifos,
Sífnos, Kímolos, Mílos,
Kéa, Thíra, Folégandros,
Íos, Síkinos, Crete,
Kárpathos, Sýros and
Lávrio. In the summer
hydrofoils serve Kéa,
Sérifos, Sífnos, Kímolos,
Mílos and Rafína.

KÉA

The closest Cycladic island to the capital, Kéa has long
been a favourite weekend escape for Athenians.

▶▶▶ Kéa Town/Ioulída (Chóra)   *100A4*

Red-tiled houses are set tight against the hills. The crum-
bling Venetian **kástro** was built on the acropolis of ancient
Ioulis; a few stones from the Apollo Temple remain. The
Archaeological Museum▶ (*Open* Tue–Sun 8.30–3.
Admission free) has finds from local sites, but the best are in
Athens. East of the town, the striking 6th-century BC **Lion of
Kéa▶▶▶** was chiselled out of rock. A pleasant walk leads
to the 18th-century **monastery of Panagía Kastrianís▶**,
famed for its miracle-working icon. Kaíki go south to
ancient Karthaía and its remains of a Temple of Apollo.

Beaches

The best beach near the harbour, Korissía, is Yialiskári,
lined with eucalyptus trees. Písses has a large beach with
tavernas. Koúndouros has several sandy coves but is more
developed. Otziás is a popular resort.

KÍMOLOS

Known in antiquity for sea urchins and to the Venetians
for silver, the unspoiled volcanic island of Kímolos long
survived on the export of chalk (*kimolía* in Greek).

▶▶ Kímolos Town (Chóra)   *100A2*

The gleaming white houses of the capital, perched on the
ridge above the working windmills, are overlooked by a
wonderful Venetian **kástro▶** and the beautiful 14th-
century **church of Chrisostómos▶▶**. All boats arrive in
the tiny harbour of Psáthi.

Beaches

Práso has a good beach and hot springs, with several
shady secluded coves nearby. Elliniká's coarse sand, overlooked by capes, is the island's best.

KÝTHNOS (THERMIÁ)

Older Greeks come here to soak in the thermal spas and to
enjoy the company of friendly islanders.

▶ Kýthnos Town (Chóra)   *100A3*

The inland capital has little action and few attractions
beyond its interesting churches, particularly 17th-century
Ágios Saba. Boats dock at Mérichas, where most tourists
stay. Some 3km away is the island's 19th-century spa of
Loutrá with mostly modern buildings. Further north, on
Akra (Cape) Kéfalos, stands the medieval **Palaiokástro▶**.
From Kýthnos Town, a fine 1½-hour walk leads south to
the lovely **Dryopída**, the former capital and the nearby
cave of Katafíki.

Beaches

The nearest beach to Mérichas is unexceptional Episkopí.
Towards the south, Flampoúria is the better beach. Loutrá
has an adequate beach with tavernas and there are several
secluded coves around Kanála.

MÍLOS

The island that is best known for a world-famous statue has fertile, rolling countryside, but is scarred by a long (and continuing) tradition of quarrying.

▶ Mílos Town/Pláka   100A2

This is an attractive capital but more modern than those on other islands. The **Archaeological Museum▶** (*Open Tue–Sun 8.30–3. Admission charge*) has mainly finds from ancient Fylakopí, the oldest site on the island. Inhabited from the third millennium BC, Fylakopí has revealed evidence of both Minoan and Mycenaean settlement. The museum also has a plaster cast of the Venus de Milo. The original – now in the Louvre in Paris – was found in 1820 by a local farmer, in a cave near the theatre of ancient Melos. The **Folklore museum▶▶** situated in the old quarter (*Open Tue–Sat 10–2 and 6–9 pm, Sun 10–2; shorter hours in winter. Admission charge*) has a fine collection of Milian costumes and old photographs.

Above the town there are breathtaking views over the Aegean from the Venetian **kástro▶▶** and the chapel of Panagía Thalassítra. Between the town and the harbour, Adámas, are 1st-century AD **Christian catacombs▶▶** (*Open Tue–Sun 8.45–2. Admission free*), where thousands of bodies were buried in rock-cut corridors. Below the town lie the extensive remains of **ancient Melos▶▶**, including a huge temple podium and a well-preserved theatre. Below it is the lovely fishing harbour of **Klíma**.

Beaches

Adámas is popular but mediocre. The island's second resort, Apollónia, has a sandy (though often windy) beach. Tree-lined Plathiéna is the first choice near Mílos Town, but the island's best beach is the remote sandy Palaiochóri.

Photogenic Klíma with the typical boat houses on the waterfront

THE VENUS DE MILO
After its discovery in 1820, the statue was apparently given to the French for safe-keeping from the Turks, but the two arms broke off in transit. Safe-keeping, however, has turned into ownership: it was given to Louis XVIII, who put it on display in the Louvre, where it remains one of the star attractions.

CONNECTIONS
Mílos is linked by ferry with Piréas, Kímolos, Kýthnos, Sérifos, Sífnos, Náxos, Amorgós, Náfphio, Chálki, Sými, Thíra, Folégandros, Crete, Íos, Páros, Síkinos, Sýros, Kárpathos, Kásos and Rhodes. Hydrofoils run in summer to Kéa, Kímolos, Kýthnos, Rafína, Sífnos and Sérifos.

MÝKONOS

Mýkonos was originally a stopover for those en route to the nearby island of Dílos (Delos, see pages 106–7), so it has a long tradition in the service of tourism. Although dry, windy and barren, it is one of the most visited of all the Greek islands and its famous windmills are one of the most photographed sights in Greece. In spite of this, Mýkonos has managed to maintain its postcard-like beauty *and* a cosmopolitan flair, although few of its Greek traditions survive. It may no longer be *the* gay resort of the Med, but it still attracts its share of 'beautiful' people.

Now the most popular of the Cycladic islands, Mýkonos was originally only visited as a stop on the way to Dílos

A NIGHT ON THE TOWN
The legendary nightlife of Mýkonos Town still throbs, but is becoming increasingly expensive. At sunset head for the terraces of Le Caprice or the long-established Kastro bar in Little Venice. Pierro's on the main street is a long-time favourite of the Mýkonos *beau monde*. The Remezzo is one of the oldest discos, but it still swings. The newer Anchor club has good music after midnight. The Factory is the disco of the moment, with a very mixed crowd and drag shows after 1am in summer.

▶▶▶ **Mýkonos Town (Chóra)**   *101C3*

Ferries arrive at the big new harbour, but the heart of the town still beats around the old fishing port, its waterfront lined with elegant terraces from which to see and be seen. Its maze of streets was intended to confuse pirates; now full of designer boutiques and trendy bars, they still bemuse visitors. Cars are forbidden, so the only way to explore the town is by walking and getting lost. The cubist whitewashed houses are well looked after, decorated with the traditional bright blue woodwork, masses of flower-pots and, often, with a cat asleep on the stairway.

Just past the Dílos jetty is the bizarre asymmetrical church of **Panagía Paraportianí**▶▶ and the **Folklore Museum**▶ (*Open* Mon–Sat 5.30–8.30, Sun 6.30–8.30. *Admission free*), which has a vast collection of para-phernalia relating to the island. Further along is **Alefkándra**▶▶▶, the most picturesque and the trendiest quarter of the capital. It is known as 'Little Venice' because of its tall Venetian houses, built right on the water's edge. Here and elsewhere in the town, visitors may be surprised to encounter one of the resident Mýkonos pelicans which roam the streets and pose vainly for photographs. On the rise beyond Alefkándra, whitewashed windmills complete the picture. Inland from here is the **Maritime Museum**▶▶ (Odós Évoplon Dynaméon. *Open* Tue–Sun 8.30–3. *Admission charge*), which has fine model ships and other nautical items. Next door is the **Traditional House of Helena** (*Open* daily in summer 7–9 pm. *Admission free*). Here, a typical 19th-century house, complete with its orig-inal furnishings and equipment, has been turned into a lovely museum. The **Archaeological Museum** (*Open Tue–Sat 9.30–3, Sun 9.30–2.30. Admission charge*) has a few artifacts from Dílos, but the best finds are in Athens.

Elsewhere on the island, the village of Áno Méra offers the most traditional atmosphere and its 16th-century **monastery of Panagía Tourlianí▶** (*Open daily 9–3. Admission free*) has Cretan frescoes and lovely baroque woodcarvings. Nearby stands another monastery, **Palaiokástro**, set in an oasis on a barren hill (*Open daily 9–2. Admission free*).

Beaches

Mýkonos has magnificent beaches and coves, nudism is widely allowed and scuba-diving is legal, unlike in most other places in Greece. An excellent network of buses serves most of the beaches, as do daily boats from Mýkonos Town's harbour and Ornos Bay. The good beaches near the capital – Megáli Amnos in town, popular but average Ornos and more pleasant Ágios Stéfanos – all have developments. Ágios Ioánnis is more secluded and has a little chapel on its pebble beach.

The south coast has excellent beaches, but as this is what most people come to find on Mýkonos, even these can get crowded, with boats arriving all the time in summer. Plat‹s Gialós is a fine family beach, Psárou is a delightful sandy bay with paths to the fashionable, mainly nudist, Paradise Beach (Paradíssi) and, in the next bay, Super Paradise, once only gay but now a mixed nudist beach. The island's longest and probably finest beach is Elía. If that is still too busy, head for the superb beaches of Agrári, Livádi and Lía Ammóudia in the next bays. The north coast beaches often get strong winds; Mýkonos is notorious for the unpredictable *meltemi*. Ftelía, on Panórmos Bay, is the best for windsurfing.

Some of the picturesque windmills near Little Venice are now up for rent

The lovely narrow streets in the Chóra become more colourful every year, as tourism increases

CONNECTIONS
Mýkonos has ferry links with Ándros, Piréas, Rafína, Sýros, Tínos, Amorgós, Crete, Ikaría, Schoinoússa, Kýthnos, Kéa, Pátmos, Leipsoi, Léros, Nisyros,Koufonísi, Astypálaia, Sífnos, Skíathos, Thessaloníki, Donoússa, Kós, Rhodes, Síkinos, Sérifos, Folégandros and (summer only) Íos, Páros, Náxos and Thíra. Hydrofoils run in summer to Tínos, Páros, Náxos, Ráfina, Íos, Thíra and also to Anáfi.

Greek civilisation grew up alongside the water. Both the nature of the country, with its scattered islands and its position astride a major sea route have ensured that navigation remains important to Greeks, whose shipping magnates, such as Onassis and Niarchos, have become wrapped in legend.

ANCIENT JOURNEYS

It was not only trade that led people in ancient Greece to hoist their sails. The holy isle of Dílos, the sanctuary of the Great Gods at Samothráki and the health spa and hospital on Kós were but three of many centres that could be reached only by boat. Today, when it is possible to fly to so many islands, it is often those islands that can still be reached only by boat that make the greatest impression on the visitor.

THE SHIPPING NEWS

Shipping is still so important a business in Greece that a daily shipping newspaper is published in Athens. Called *Naftemborikí*, it lists the following seven days' domestic sailings from Piréas and other important Greek ports, as well as international arrivals and departures. Up-to-date information on sailings from the islands is available from local Port Authorities, whose telephone numbers are listed beside many of the A-Z entries in this book. In Athens, the day's sailings from Piréas can be heard on a recorded message by telephoning 143.

Early shipping It was the readiness of Greek ships, so Homer tells us, that allowed Agamemnon to collect the army that sacked Troy. That should come as no surprise. The early civilisations of the Greek world – the Minoans and Mycenaeans and Phoenicians – were primarily naval powers, their success based on an ability to move people and goods across the water. The power of Antony and Cleopatra collapsed when their fleets were defeated by Octavian just off Lefkáda.

Without maps or navigational aids, without motors or rows of oarsmen, early sailors needed to stay close to land. This was easy in the Greek islands, many of which were close enough for a sailor to see his destination before setting sail.

A long tradition Romans and Byzantines, Venetians and Turks – the foreign powers that controlled the islands – often came to rely on the skill of local sailors. Most famously, Kheir-ed-Din 'Barbarossa', the 16th-century corsair, born on Lésvos, ended his life as grand admiral of the Turkish fleet. After independence, the Greeks were quick to build up their fleet and Ermoúpoli on Sýros, the new nation's main port, was the most important coaling station in the eastern Mediterranean.

Modern fleets Greek shipping magnates such as Onassis and Niarchos made their fortunes building oil tankers and after the glorious days of the 1970s there were more than 4,000 registered Greek ships. Oil crises, fear of a socialist government (elected in 1981) and stiff competition from Asian shipping corporations brought a sharp reversal of fortunes for the Greek tycoons. But for as long as her islands are surrounded by sea, Greece will remain a seafaring nation.

Proving an ancient tradition, Greek sailing ships on an altar cup from Vulai, c520 BC

NÁXOS

Náxos, the largest and highest of the Cyclades, is also the most fertile, with an abundance of cultivated valleys and orchards. The island – centre of the Cycladic group – is just as rich in historical remains, having been continuously inhabited for some 5,000 years. It is equally blessed with amazing, often deserted beaches. Perhaps surprisingly, tourism has only just begun to develop on a larger scale on Náxos, but the new airport is sure to speed up this process. Nevertheless, the island's size and its viable farming economy, mean that tourism is unlikely to take over completely. (For a map of Náxos, see page 122.)

▶▶▶ Náxos Town (Chóra)   101C2

The island's harbour has plenty of charm and is surprisingly laid back for the capital of such a large island. Behind

USEFUL NUMBERS
Port Authority
tel: 0285 22300
Airport tel: 0285 23292
Tourist information (near
the ferry landing) tel:
0285 24358/25201
Tourist Police tel:
0285 22100

The long causeway connecting Náxos Town with its symbol, the gateway on the islet of Palátia

the waterfront (and most of the town's restaurants and bars) lies the old town, a maze of narrow alleys and low arches, intended to keep invaders out. The lower part is known as the Bourgos, where Greeks lived in two-story houses with gardens full of almond trees and bougainvillea, while higher up is the well-preserved 13th-century **kástro▶▶**, where Marco Sanudo – the Duke of Náxos – and other members of the Venetian aristocracy resided. The outer walls of the kástro have disappeared, but the inner walls and one of the original seven towers or **pýrgoi** remain.

Many large mansions here – several of which still bear their Venetian coats of arms – are still inhabited by the descendants of Venetians, others by local artists. On the square stands the 13th-century **Catholic Cathedral▶**, restored in the 1950s. In 1627 the Ottomans founded a French school where Nikós Kazantzákis studied for a while. It is now the **Archaeological Museum▶▶▶** (*Open Tue–Sun 8.30–3. Admission charge*), housing a large and interesting collection of Cycladic figurines, Mycenaean pottery, Roman glass and a famous mosaic of Europa. To the north of the port, an ancient causeway connects the town with the islet of Palátia, where Ariadne was abandoned. The 6th-century BC **Temple of Apollo▶** was never finished and only the monumental gateway, a symbol for Náxos, is still standing.

ARIADNE'S ISLAND
According to mythology Náxos was the island where the Minoan princess Ariadne was abandoned by her husband-to-be Theseus, on their return from Knosós, where he had killed the Minotaur. The god Dionysos found her and married her and, as he was the god of wine and the good life, they lived happily ever after. Some believe that this story illustrated the decline of Crete and the rise of the Cycladic culture, although archaeologists dispute the dates. Whatever the truth, it inspired many artists over the years, including the composer Richard Strauss, who took the story as the theme for his opera *Ariadne auf Naxos*.

Filóti and its pretty Cycladic houses with red-tiled roofs and colourful shutters

VENETIAN HOMES
Pirgi or fortified Venetian manor houses, built between the 14th and 18th centuries, are typical of Náxos. As the island was the seat of Venetian dukes, many of the Italian nobility were given land according to the feudal system. Every aristocratic family had a house in the *kástro* in Náxos Town as well as a *pirgos* to keep their possessions safe from pirate raids. Some 30 of these buildings have survived and it may be possible to rent a few of them.

▶▶▶ Apeírados (Apíranthos)   *101C2*

Arguably the most beautiful village on Náxos, Apeírados, with its un-whitewashed houses and balconies, clearly shows a Cretan influence. The winding streets are paved with marble while the core of the village is built around a Venetian *pirgos* or fortified tower. On the *plateía* at the entrance is the village church of Koímisis tis Theotókou, with an unusual three-tiered bell tower and further inward the small **museum▶▶** (if closed ask for the guard). Near Apeírados are the only emery mines in Greece. The emery was shipped from the nearby tiny harbour of **Moutsoúna**.

▶▶ Apóllon   *101C3*

The pretty fishing village of Apóllon has become too commercialised for its own good, as it tries to make the most of the daily arrivals of tour buses. However, the scenery along the road to it is magnificent. The star attraction lies in a nearby ancient marble quarry, home to a **kouros▶** (statue of a naked young man) which would have stood over 10m tall. The unfinished 7th-century BC statue was probably a representation of the god Dionysos; at over 30 tonnes, it is the largest but not the finest *kouros* on the island.

Nearby is delightful **Komiakí▶▶**, the island's highest village, where *kitron* liqueur was first distilled. From here a mountain trail leads to the ridge and on to an amazing marble staircase which goes steeply down to the lush village of **Myrísis▶**.

▶ Chalkí   *101C2*

The small town of Chalkí has several fine churches, one of the oldest and the most beautiful being the church of **Panagía Protóthronis▶▶** (*Open* mornings only. *Admission free*), with a 6th-century apse and remarkable 9th- and 13th-century frescoes. The church is overlooked by the imposing and remarkably well-preserved **Pýrgos Grazia (Frangopoulos)**, a fortified Venetian villa set amid olive trees and orchards. A pleasant walking path leads up to the village of **Moní▶** with wonderful views over the

Tragéa valley. This beautiful and fertile area, rich in interesting villages, little churches and historical sites, is one of the best places to explore unspoiled Náxos (see the Drive on page 122). Just before Moní is the 6th-century **church of Panagía Drosianí►►** (*Open* most of the time), which has marvellous frescoes.

►► Filóti
101C2

The pleasant town of Filóti lies on the slopes of **Náxos-Zéfs** (**Mount Zas**) (1,001m), the highest peak in the Cycladic islands and one of several places contesting the honour of being the birthplace of the god Zeus. A path leads to the summit of the mountain, offering spectacular views (allow two or three hours and be sure to check directions before you go because the path is not always easy to follow). To the south of the peak, another trail leads to a fortified 15th-century monastery, **Moní Fotódotou**, built on a rise and looking more like a castle than a religious centre. The ground-floor church is well preserved.

►► Flerió (Melanés)
101C2

One of several Naxian quarries used in antiquity, the Flerió quarry, covering a considerable area, contains two 6th-century BC *kouroi*, presumably abandoned because of flaws in the stone. The more accessible statue, lying in an orchard, is in a good state of repair.

► Sagkrí
101C2

Káto Sagkrí► is a small village with the remains of a Venetian villa standing on a barren hill. The area around **Áno Sagkrí►** is dotted with Byzantine chapels and churches. From the village, a path leads southward to the tiny Byzantine **chapel of Ágios Ioánnis Gýroulas**, built on the foundations of a classical 6th-century BC temple of Demeter (now closed for excavations).

Satellite islands near Náxos

The small islands between Náxos and Amorgós, home to peaceful, traditional communities, are becoming increasingly popular, especially with young Greeks. Facilities tend to be basic, where they exist at all, but there are some good beaches to be found. There are, especially in summer, frequent ferries to Piréas, Náxos, Páros, Sýros and Sérifos, as well as a daily boat to Náxos and a hydrofoil from Amorgós and the other Cyclades. **Kéros►** is the

THE LAND OF DIONYSOS
The main deity on Náxos was Dionysos, the god of wine and ecstasy and at one time in its history the island was even called Dionysia. Dionysos was eternally young from drinking wine and after marrying him Ariadne soon forgot her sorrows. Ever since then, Naxian wine has been considered an efficient remedy for love-sickness. The only problem is that it is now hard to find. During the Dionysian festival, held on the island during the first week in August, is probably one of the only opportunities to taste this legendary product.

119

The cultivated valleys of Náxos often come as a surprise to visitors used to the barren landscapes of the other Cyclades

WALKING COUNTRY
The Náxos countryside has countless good walking trails. For walks other than the one described opposite, look out for the excellent German-published book *Walking Tours on Náxos* by Christian Ucke, available in Náxos Town.

CONNECTIONS
Náxos has ferry links with Piréas, Páros, Sýros, Thíra, Íos, Amorgós, Koufonísi, Schoinoússa, Crete, Donoússa, Kárpathos, Rhodes, Sámos, Anáfi, Astypálaia, Irákleio, Ikariá, Kásos, Síkinos, Chálki, Folégandros, Foúrnoi, Kastellórizo, Pátmos, Leípsoi, Léros, Kálymnos, Kós, Nísyros, Tílos, Sými and (in summer) Mýkonos. There is a summer hydrofoil service to Ándros, Mýkonos, Páros, Tínos, Sýros, Íos, Rafína, Amorgós, Thíra and Anáfi.

One of the island's best beaches, Agía Ánna, on a quiet day

important site of ancient Karos, but the island is now uninhabited. Tiny **Áno Koufonísi**►► has only one village and lovely beaches such as Fínikas and Bóri with underwater caves to explore. **Káto Koufonísi** is barely inhabited, apart from its goat herds, but it has some fine secluded beaches. On **Schoinoússa**►► it is only a short walk from Mirsíni, the harbour, to the capital with its medieval fortress. The nearest beach to the capital is Tsigourí. Mesaría is a small resort on the north coast.

Irákleia►►► is an idyllic islet with a fishing harbour (Ágios Geórgios) and a village up in the hills. The large sandy beach at Livádi is excellent but Fínikas beach is even better, with trees and bushes along the shore and clear turquoise water. **Donoússa**►►, even more remote, is the island of silence with one village, about 50 houses and fine sandy beaches nearby. It can also be the island of hunger – fresh food and water are sometimes scarce.

Beaches

The best beaches on the island are south of Náxos Town, easily accessible by bus, daily boat, or walking. Ágios Giórgios and Ágios Prokópios are long sandy bays with a few hotels and campsites, while Agía Ánna is the island's busiest beach with facilities and a nudist beach nearby. Further south is the excellent 5km-long beach of Pláka with fine sand, popular with campers, but usually almost empty at its southern end. Even better and easier to reach by road, are Mikrí Vígla and Kastráki, which has brilliant water and pure white sand – an ideal beach for children. The last stop on the bus route is Pyrgakía, not as beautiful but more remote.

The beaches near Moutsoúna – little bays fringed with trees and here and there a little chapel on a rock – are usually completely deserted. Apóllon on the northern tip of the island has a good beach and there are other pretty beaches nearby, but the *meltemi* winds can make life unpleasant. Avram Beach is magnificent and has a lovely taverna; Amýti and Pachiá Ámnos are more deserted, like most of the beaches in this part of the island.

Walk

Ágioi Apóstoloi and Potamiá

A walk through some of the most fertile land on Náxos, taking in some famous but quite hidden sights, including a *kouros* in someone's orchard and the 9th-century church of Ágios Mámas (8–10km; allow about 5–6 hours).

Regular buses from Náxos Town pass the village of Ágioi Apóstoloi (see the map on page 122). From the church at Ágioi Apóstoloi continue 200m southwards, where a path goes along the slope overlooking the Melanés valley. As the path becomes more unclear, follow the red markers in a wide arc around the hillside, looking out for a white chapel in the south.

At a crossroads, 300m further on, follow the path to the east, cross the stream and continue to a cemented street, which leads from the main street to the *kouros*. At the end of the street, turn left under the trees and look for a sign to a garden, where a family will show you the well-preserved,

Lovely old churches like the Ágioi Apóstoloi are scattered all over the peaceful Tragéa region

6th-century BC **kouros▶**. There is another one near-by, both probably left in the quarry because they became broken before they were finished.

Return to the cement road where a red-marked path leads uphill, with views of **Náxos-Zéfs** (Mount Zas) and a Venetian fortress. Follow the red markings to the cemetery and **church of Ágios Ioánnis** in Potamiá, then continue to Áno Potamiá, where there is a pleasant taverna, Pigis. Take Odós Ágios Ioánnis Theológou and then Odós Protopapadáki. At the end of the village, turn eastward and head downhill, to the river. Across the river, a paved path leads along the slope to Káto Potamiá.

In the village, by the church of Panagía, Odós Nikodimu descends back to the river. Cross the river and follow the green arrows, crossing another river towards the **church of Ágios Mámas▶**, set among orange trees. Pause to look at the frescoes here before continuing up above the church to a farm, once the summer residence of a Catholic bishop. Beyond the farm, behind a wall, there is a clearly marked path: follow it westward to the asphalt road, along which pass buses for Náxos Town.

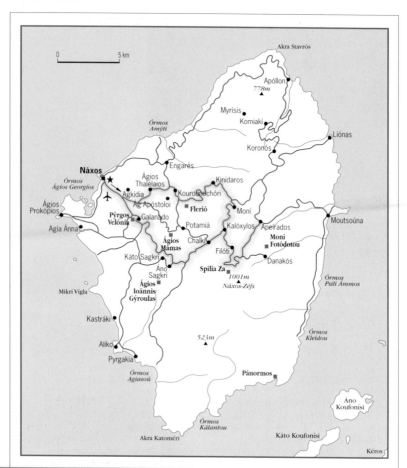

Drive

The Tragéa valley

Roads on Náxos are good and even remote places can be reached by car (about 60km; allow 5–6 hours).

Leave Náxos Town by the Apóllon road. After a kilometre turn right and later left to Galanádo. Further on, to the left, is the lovely church of **Ágios Mámas**▶ (see page 121). A while later, to the right, are Káto and Áno Sagkrí (see page 119), beyond which the road descends into the Tragéa valley and to Chalkí (see page 118).

Follow the sign to Filóti (right), turning left after another 300m for the village of Kalóxylos, known for its pretty **church of Agía Triáda**▶. Return to the main road and continue to Filóti (see page 119). Pass the little chapel and the sign on the right to **Spiliá Za (Cave Zas)**▶, reputedly the cave where Zeus was born.

After 6km Apeírados offers the possibility of lunch with a view (see page 118). Return to Filóti and beyond it, by a war memorial, turn right to Moní. Before Moní, on the right, is the **church of Panagía Drosianí**▶▶ (see page 119). Go through Moní to Kinídaros, where there are spectacular marble quarries and good views out to sea. At Ágios Thalélaios follow the sign to the right and at the junction make another right turn for Náxos Town.

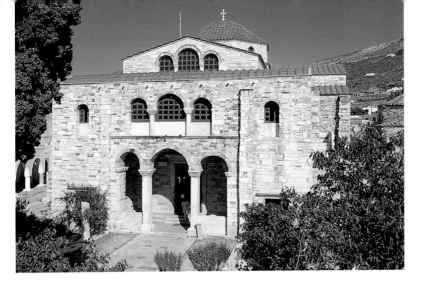

PÁROS

Panagiá Ekatondapilianí

Páros provided the marble for some of the most beautiful classical statues, including the Venus de Mílo and the Winged Victory of Samothráki. It is also one of the most attractive Cycladic islands; towns like Páros, Náousa and Léfkes have managed to preserve their character despite attracting increasing numbers of tourists.

▶▶▶ Páros Town (Parikiá)   100B2

Beyond the busy commercial waterfront lies the well-preserved Cycladic old town. The narrow streets, lined with bars and shops, are completely overrun by visitors in summer but remain pretty and quiet for the rest of the year. Just beyond the centre is the interesting Byzantine cathedral of **Panagía Ekatondapilianí**▶▶▶ (*Open* daily 8–1 and 4–9. *Admission free*). Originally built in the 6th century, the church, whose name means 'Our Lady of the Hundred Doors', was rebuilt in the 10th century using fine Parian marble. Behind it is the small **Archaeological Museum**▶▶ (*Open* Tue–Sun 8.30–2.30. *Admission charge*). Its exhibits include a good collection of sculpture and a fragment of the Parian Chronicle, which lists important political and social events in Greek history from the 16th to the 3rd centuries BC. It is through this document that we know the year of Homer's birth. South of the windmill are the remains of the 13th-century Venetian **kastro**▶▶. Marble fragments from ancient temples were used to build its fortified walls. On top of the *kástro* are the two superb churches of Ágios Konstandínos and Agía Eléni.

About an hour's walk from the town is the **monastery of Ágioi Anárgyroi**▶, a popular picnic spot for islanders. A two-hour walk will bring you to **Petaloúdes**▶▶, the 'Valley of the Butterflies' (*Open* Jun–Sep, daily 9 am–8 pm. *Admission charge*). As on Rhodes (see page 171), millions of Jersey moths descend every summer on this walled oasis in the middle of a barren landscape. The route to Petaloúdes passes the 18th-century **convent of Christoú Dásos**▶. Men are not permitted inside, even though the convent contains the grave of the island's second patron saint, Ágios Arsénios.

USEFUL NUMBERS
Port Authority
tel: 0284 21841
Airport tel: 0284 91256
Tourist information (near the windmill on the harbour) tel: 0284 24528

OUR LADY OF THE HUNDRED DOORS
The cathedral was built in the 6th century by Isidore of Miletus and his pupil Ignatius. When it was finished it was of such beauty that, according to one story, the two architects started to fight on the roof. Both fell to their deaths. Another legend has it that there are only 99 doors and that the hundredth one referred to in the name will be found only when the Turks return Constantinople to the Christians – so it may never be found!

Náousa harbour has some of the best and most atmospheric ouzeris on the island

UNUSUAL SHOPPING ON PÁROS
Among the many chic boutiques in Páros Town there is a totally different shop called The Teapot, just off the *agora* or main street, opposite the Levantis Tea Room. This small shop is filled with the dried herbs and spices you may have encountered on your country walks, as well as pot pourris of local wild-flowers. In O Dromos, a small shop in the centre of Léfkes, the friendly Athenian artist Dimitris sells old and new traditional jewellery and the best of Greek craftwork. His dream of returning to live and work on his mother's island has come true and he is quite happy to chat the afternoon away with a glass of *mavro*, the local wine.

►► **Antíparos**   *100B2*

The island of Antíparos was once connected to Páros by a natural causeway, but visitors now have to take one of the many boats making day trips to the island to visit its beaches or famous cave. Many former devotees of relaxed Páros now stay on Antíparos which, despite the summer day trippers, is still a quiet backwater. Most of the 500 islanders live in the pleasant Cycladic village on the northern side of the island beneath a small Venetian **kástro►**. There are several good beaches: Psaralidáki is a nudist beach just outside the village, but the small coves in Ágios Giórgios are far more pleasant and secluded. **Spílaio Stalaktitón►►** (*Open* daily 10.45–3.45. *Admission charge*), the island's well-known cave, was known for its stalactites more than 2,000 years ago and has been attracting people to Antíparos ever since. Two buses daily from the port). There is electric lighting now and cement steps instead of ropes, but the 70m-deep cave still retains its grandeur and some of its mystery.

►►► **Léfkes**   *101C2*

Léfkes, the medieval capital where the population hid from raiding pirates, is still one of the most untouched towns on Páros. The lovely houses are set against the hill and the narrow marbled and cobblestoned streets are immaculately kept. There are a few traditional *kafeneía* and life here still seems very peaceful indeed. In nearby **Maráthi** are the ancient underground marble quarries from where marble was exported all over Europe: it was last used for Napoleon's tomb. **Prodrómos**, a charming farming village, formerly walled and still entered through a gateway, is named after the 17th-century **church of Ágios Ioánnis Prodrómos►**. An equally attractive village, inland but not far from the resort of Píso Livádi, is **Márpissa**, its narrow alleys bordered by balconies full of flowers. Above stands a Venetian castle now occupied by the **monastery of Ágios Andónios**.

► **Náousa**   *101C2*

Náousa may have succumbed to mass tourism in recent years, but its tiny, colourful fishing harbour is still a won-derfully picturesque place, with a choice of bars and tavernas for an early evening *oúzo* and a helping of freshly caught seafood *mezédes*. Near the harbour is a mostly

PARIAN MARBLE
Parian marble, used in so many classical statues, was particularly prized for its grainy, translucent quality. It is the closest of Greek marbles to the quality of Carrara marble. In some Athenian temples it was used for roof tiles in order to let in the light. It is unusual for quarries to be underground, but here the marble was hacked out of the mountain and brought up to the light by slaves. In the 19th century the French reopened the quarries to get marble for Napoleon's tomb, but today they are abandoned: the remaining marble is of poorer quality and the vein too deep to be economically viable.

submerged Venetian castle. Náousa's other 'sight' is the **Byzantine Museum▶** (*Open* daily 9–1.30, 7–9. *Admission free*) in the church of Ágios Nikólaos Mostratos, which has a good collection of icons.

Beaches

The best beaches near Páros Town are towards the south. Paraspóros is known for the remains of an Asklepion (therapy centre), while the better, sandy Agía Iríni has a taverna. Further south, Poúnda, with all facilities, is very popular, while the large sandy cove and fishing harbour of Alykí is also fast becoming a major resort. From Alykí a dirt track leading to Dryós goes along several secluded and pleasant sandy coves, although Dryós is just a small pebble-stone beach overlooked by a modern tourist village. The beaches north of here are exposed to the strong *meltemi* winds, sometimes making them unpopular with sandcastle builders but a first choice for windsurfers. Chrysí Aktí, or Golden Beach, lives up to its name but is becoming more developed, while the once quiet Píso Livádi has become a full-blown resort. The island's best beaches, however, are on the north coast near Náousa. Kolimbítres, to the west, has beautiful sand, clear azure water and a lunar landscape with strange rock formations. Just a little further along is the mainly nudist beach of Monastíri. To the north are found the clearest waters and good windsurfing. Langéri Beach is popular, but the trendiest beach is definitely Sánta María.

CONNECTIONS
Páros has ferry links with Antíparos, Piréas, Náxos, Thíra, Sýros, Tinos, Thessaloniki, Mýkonos, Sífnos, Sérifos, Amorgós, Crete, Rhodes, Ikaría, Sámos, Síkinos, Kós, Anáfi, Kárpathos, Koufonísi, Schoinoússa, Chálki, Donoússa, Folégandros, Fournoi, Irákleia, Kásos, Kastellórizo, Astypálaia, Skíathos, Pátmos, Leipsoi, Léros, Kálymnos, Nísyros, Tílos and Sými. In summer there are hydrofoil services to Mýkonos, Tínos, Ándros, Náxos, Rafína, Thíra, Íos, Sýros, Irákleia, Schoinoússa, Koufonísi and Anáfi.

There is still much of Páros that has escaped the effects of mass tourism

The Greeks loved both continuity and variety in art as elsewhere, so while Greek artists absorbed new ideas and influences, they also preserved all that was best in their tradition. The result is an extraordinary legacy that continues to fascinate and inspire.

*Above: a fine plate made in Athens c520–510 BC
Below: a beautiful depiction of a lyre-player on a black-figure vase*

126

Regional beginnings The first art in Greece was localised. In the 3rd millennium BC, the appearance in the Cyclades of idols of soft marble – elegant figures with minimal detail – coincided with the development of the trade in metal. As the power of the Cyclades declined, so their artistic style gave way to that of the Minoans from Crete, who took control of the Aegean around 1600 BC. Frescoes, particularly those from Thíra, are among the most powerful Minoan creations, their everyday subjects – people, animals, leaves – animated and joyful. Great treasures have been found from the Mycenaeans who succeeded the Minoans, including jewellery, weapons, vases, pots and copper tripods, all of which suggest a shift in the attitude of their creators: where the Minoans were playful and celebratory, life for the Mycenaeans was clearly a struggle against nature.

Ceramic art The end of Mycenaean civilisation brought another shift: Archaic art concentrated on terracotta vases and *kraters* (drinking vessels), with a new geometric style (900–700 BC) evolving in which images on stone and terracotta were contained within geometric patterns. In the 7th century bc, exotic creatures and plants from Egypt and the Near East appeared on vase decoration. Around this time, when the finest ceramics came from Corinth and mythological stories were the usual source for decoration, the technique of putting black figures against orange backgrounds was perfected. Late in the 6th century the tradition was turned on its head: the backgrounds became black, the figures were red and Greek artists revelled in their new freedom. A few decades later, new techniques allowed artists to paint against a white background and made naturalism possible.

WORLD WONDER
One of the Seven Wonders of the Ancient World, Phidias's statue of Zeus for the temple at Olympia is believed to have been about 12m high. Sitting on a throne of ebony, ivory, gold and precious stones, it suffered from the Olympian climate; the ivory cracked in the 2nd century BC; the statue was struck by lightning during Julius Caesar's reign and was reported to have been taken later to Constantinople, where it was destroyed by fire in AD 475.

Kouros in Vathí Museum, Sámos

Sculpture When the Greeks started building big temples in the 7th century BC, the need for statues in their sanctuaries gave a boost to large-scale marble sculpture. In the 6th century BC, two Samian artists – Rhoikos and Theodorus – learned to make hollow bronze statues. Whether stone, wood or metal, most art remained religious in function until the 4th century.

The finest sculptures from the Archaic period were *kouroi*, carvings of naked youths which show, in their increasing attention to detail, a growing understanding of human anatomy.

Kouroi were placed in sanctuaries to delight the gods or as funerary offerings. A rare series of female figures, *korai*, were dedicated to Athena at her temple on the Acropolis. Notable *kouroi* can be seen in the National Archaeological Museum in Athens, in the museum of Vathí on Sámos and in the quarry near Apóllon on Náxos.

Classical masters Some of the finest sculptures ever executed belong to the Classical period, whose artists created works that perfectly expressed both the grandeur and spirituality of the gods and, in breathtaking detail, the reality of the human form. Among the masters were Polykleitos and Phidias, the latter the creator of the chryselephantine statues of Olympian Zeus (one of the Wonders of the Ancient World) and of Athena in the Parthenón – both now lost – as well as of the Parthenón frieze. In the 4th century BC, artists such as Praxiteles concentrated increasingly on the expression of the moods and character of humans, making their sculpture less stylised and more lifelike.

Hellenism After Alexander the Great's conquest of the known world, the Greek market became increasingly cosmopolitan and Greek artists found themselves expected to satisfy demands for a variety of forms and styles, trends and influences and also found a new and very mixed market for their work. The tastes of the period were clearly different, more theatrical, with artists looking to thrill or charm the spectator. The 2nd-century BC Horse and Jockey of Artemision (National Archaeological Museum, Athens) exactly expresses the mood of the period in its dramatic sense of movement and in its perfectly executed forms of horse and boy rider (who is certainly not a native Greek).

The Parthenón has some of the finest art of classical times

AGES OF GREEK SCULPTURE
Cycladic; Minoan; Mycenaean; Archaic; Classical; Hellenistic; Roman-Greek

NO SCUBA HERE
The Aegean looks so inviting in summer that it would seem to be a perfect place for scuba diving. Too perfect, in fact, as the number of sculptures and other treasures recovered from the Aegean and now on display in Greek museums testifies. To stop people helping themselves to antiquities, the Greek government banned the use of scuba equipment in Greek waters (there are a few exceptions). Among the many masterpieces in the National Archaeological Museum in Athens that were recovered from the sea are the Boy of Marathon, the Poseidon of Artemision and the Youth from Antikýthira.

SÉRIFOS

Nothing ever seems to happen on Sérifos, which is what attracts more Athenians and foreigners every summer. Most islanders, meanwhile, remain hard at work on their farms and want little to do with visitors.

Sífnos is one of the best-kept secrets in the Cyclades

USEFUL NUMBERS
Port Authority (Sérifos)
tel: 0281 51470
Port Authority (Sífnos)
tel: 0284 31617
Tourist information
(Sífnos) tel: 0284 31977
Aegean Thesaurus Travel
and Tourism (Sífnos) for
excellent information on
the island, all tickets and
accommodations tel:
0284 33151

A GOOD WALK ON SÉRIFOS
A path leads from Sérifos Town to Kállitsos (allow at least an hour), from where it is another 3km to the striking monastery of Taxiarchón. This beautiful place is inhabited by a lone, happy man, Makarios. An asphalt road leads back to the town, via the lovely villages of Galaní and Panagía, where you will find a 10th-century church.

▶▶▶ Sérifos Town (Chóra)   *100A2*

The island's capital, clinging to its rock, looks particularly spectacular when seen from the harbour. At the top of the ruinous **kástro▶**, a gleaming white church sticks to it like a melted ice-cream.

▶ Livádi   *100A2*

The harbour of Livádi, where most visitors stay, is set in an oasis of fields and orchards. An old long stairway, hand-hewn into the rock, goes up to Sérifos Town.

Beaches

Psilí Ámmos has a superb sandy beach with two popular tavernas. Nearer to Livádi is the beach of Livadáki, with fine sand, and the smaller (partly nudist) Karávi beach. West of Livádi is the old mining village of Koutalás, a small sandy beach at Ganema and, beyond, the peaceful beach of Megálo Livádi.

SÍFNOS

Sífnos, a favourite with young Greeks wanting to avoid the crowds on the other Cyclades, is one of the prettiest islands. Delightful walks meander through a landscape dotted with windmills, Venetian dovecotes and hundreds of chapels.

▶▶▶ Apollonía   *100B2*

Apollonía is an idyllic village, with lovely squares, belfries and flowers everywhere. On the main square is the **Folk Museum▶** (a notice on the door explains where to find the guardian). The church of **Panagía Ouranoforía▶** was built over (and incorporates fragments of) the 7th-century BC Temple of Apollo. Nearby **Artemón▶▶** has elegant mansions and fine churches. The 17th-century **church of Ágios**

Geórgios▶ has a collection of icons while the multi-domed **church of Kochí**▶▶ was built over a temple of Artemis. The harbour of Kamáres, down below, is where most of the visitor facilities are.

▶▶ Kástro   100B2

Kástro, the ancient and medieval capital, has maintained its character and its picturesque streets with old houses and 17th-century churches. Higher up in the village is a small **archaeological museum**▶ (*Open* Tue–Sat 9–3, Sun 11–2. *Admission free*).

▶▶ Vathý   100B2

Although remote, Vathý is an excellent base for beaches and walks to the nearby monasteries of Firágia, Ágios Andréas, Chrysopigí, and Panayía Vounoú. There is even a tiny monastery of the Archangel Gabriel on the quay.

Beaches

Platýs Gialós is a long stretch of fine sand, clear calm water and sunbathers. Fáros is quieter with excellent beaches nearby, including naturist Glifó and Chrysopigí where the monastery rents out cells.

SÍKINOS

Síkinos is a sleepy island with only one town, from where you can walk (or take a mule) to most beaches.

▶▶ Síkinos Town (Kástro-Chóra)   100A1

Boats go to the harbour of Aloprónoia. From there an erratic bus service goes up to Síkinos Town, which consists of the simple village (Chóra) and the medieval *kástro*, its 18th-century houses still packed within the fortified walls. The town is overlooked by the ruins of the **Monastery of Zoödóchou Pigís**. An hour's walk away at **Episkopí**, an ancient temple or Roman tomb was incorporated in a 7th-century church known as the **Iroön**▶▶. **Palaiokástro**▶ is the site of an ancient fortress.

Beaches

Ágios Pandelímonas is easily the nicest and certainly the most sheltered beach, an hour's walk from the harbour. Towards the north are the beaches of Ágios Nikólaos and Ágios Geórgios.

CONNECTIONS
From Sérifos and Sífnos ferries operate to Piréas, Páros, Kýthnos, Kímolos, Mílos, Folégandros, Síkinos, Íos, Thíra, Mýkonos, Sýros, Crete, Kárpathos, Kásos, Rhodes and Chálki. There are hydrofoil links in summer with most of the other Cyclades.
Ferries from Síkinos serve Piréas, Folégandros, Íos, Páros, Thíra, Sérifos, Sífnos, Náxos, Kímolos, Sýros, Kýthnos, Mílos and in summer also Crete, Kásos, Kárpathos, Chálki, Rhodes and Mýkonos.

129

THE SIFNOS CUISINE
Sífnos is known for producing the best olive oil and the best chefs in Greece. The chefs are in such demand that most of them leave the island, but happily there is still some good food to be had. The island's most famous dish is *revithada*, a simple stew made with chick peas, olive oil and bay leaves, baked in the oven. Sífnos also produces some unique cheeses including fresh *xinomizithra*, similar to a ricotta and *gilomeno*, a hard, mature goat's cheese with a strong taste.

FAMOUS POTTERY
As if good cooking were not enough, Sífnos is also famous throughout Greece for its ceramics. There are still several workshops making simple, inexpensive grey and red clay pottery for daily use, although some do more elaborate work with folk motifs.

Almost every single corner of Sífnos is pleasing to the eye

*Below the Catholic
Cathedral of Ágios
Giórgos is the intricate
and fascinating medieval
quarter of Áno Sýros*

SÝROS

Sýros, the administrative capital of the Cyclades, sees relatively few foreign tourists apart from ferry travellers in the process of changing boats in its busy port. Without a tourist economy, the island has remained very Greek, supporting itself from its traditional businesses of shipping, agriculture and the production of *loukoúmia* (Turkish delight). Sýros is as good a place as any in the Cyclades for visitors who want to experience the flavour of workaday Greek life. Buses and cycle-rental outlets make this an easy island to explore. Distances are manageable, with nowhere very far from the sea and the scenery is mountainous in the north, gentler and fertile in the south.

▶▶▶ Ermoúpoli and Áno Sýros 100B3

Either by day in the dazzling sunlight or at night when wonderfully illuminated, the twin cities of Ermoúpoli and Áno Sýros, built on neighbouring hills, entrance the visitor upon entering the harbour. Ermoúpoli, 'City of Hermes', founded by refugees in 1824, quickly became the most important harbour in Greece after the War of Independence. These refugees were Eastern Orthodox while most of the islanders were Roman Catholic, but the two communities lived – and continue to live – side by side, each on its own hill: to the left, as you sail in, Catholic Áno Sýros and to the right, Orthodox Vrondádo.

Ferries and hydrofoils dock at the busy waterfront of Ermoúpoli, where the large neoclassical mansions are slowly crumbling. Just inland is the grand Plateía Miaoúli, paved with marble, where islanders drink their coffee or early evening *oúzo* on elegant terraces under palm trees. This is a good place to sit and watch the nightly *volta*, where locals stroll up and down, often dressed up, meeting friends and enjoying the cool of the evening. The square is dominated by the imposing, neoclassical **Town Hall**. To its left is the **Archaeological Museum▶▶** (*Open Tue–Sun 8.30–3. Admission free*), which has a small collection of early Cycladic, Hellenistic and Roman sculpture. Beyond the museum is the **Apollon Theatre▶**, a

SYRIAN DELIGHTS
On the quayside and even
on the ferries, various
hawkers sell *loukoúmia*
(Turkish delight) and delicious *chalvadópita* (a
sugary confection), for
which the island is
famous. *Loukoúmia*
comes in different
flavours: mastic, almond,
rosewater and mint.

19th-century scaled-down copy of the famous La Scala in Milan. The next square up has the world's first **Monument to an Unknown Warrior**, by the 19th-century sculptor Vitalis and the large **church of Ágios Nikólaos▶**, which has a finely carved iconostasis by the same sculptor. This is the heart of Vaporía, where wealthy shipowners built mansions in a French style. Uphill from the Platea Miaoúli, stairs climb to the Orthodox quarter of **Vrondádo▶▶**, topped by the delightful church of **Anástasi▶▶**.

Áno Sýros▶▶▶, on the taller hill, was Sýros's medieval capital, founded by the Venetians. There are several Catholic churches below the **Cathedral of Ágios Giórgios▶**, one of the oldest Catholic churches on Sýros, founded in the early 13th century and rebuilt in the 1830s. Nearby is the 16th-century **monastery of the Capuchins▶▶** with magnificent views over Ermoúpoli and the island. Áno Sýros can be reached by a steep stairway from Ermoúpoli or by bus. South of Ermoúpoli are the *tarsanás* or shipyards, the biggest of which is Neórion, which constructs vessels up to 80,000 tonnes. Like many such shipyards today, they have an uncertain future.

▶ Poseidonía   *100B3*

Poseidonía, also known under its Venetian name Dellagrazia, is the favourite summer resort of the Syrians. It still has some flamboyant neoclassical villas surrounded by beautiful gardens, now often up for rent. The exclusive Possidonia Club established itself here in 1913. The entire southern part of the island is taken up by vineyards and by greenhouses producing vegetables for export to Athens.

Beaches

Few beaches on the more accessible Greek Islands have escaped development and Sýros is no exception. However, it has escaped the worst excesses of the tourist boom and there are still pleasant bays and coves to be found.

Kiní is a developed resort with summer villas and a good beach. For more isolation head further north to the lovely sandy beaches of Delfíni, Varvaroússa and Grámmata, surrounded by rocks. South of Kiní is the bay of Galissás, whose great beach is becoming increasingly popular. Nearby is the more solitary nudist beach of Arméos. Within walking distance of Poseidonía are some good sandy beaches; Agatopés, empty Komitó and lovely Ambéla. Mégas Gialós has a long narrow beach with pebbles.

CONNECTIONS
Sýros has ferry links with Piréas, Tínos, Mýkonos, Náxos, Páros, Íos, Amorgós, Astypálaia, Thíra, Koufonísi, Rhodes, Schoinoússa, Sámos, Chálki, Crete, Donoússa, Irákleia, Kárpathos, Kásos, Kéa, Kímolos, Kós, Kýthnos, Mílos, Rafína, Sérifos, Sífnos, Ándros, Folégandros, Ikaría, Kastellórizo, Síkinos, Patmos, Leípsoi, Léros, Nísyros, Tílos and Sými. Hydrofoils operate in summer to Rafína, Páros, Mýkonos, Tínos, Náxos, Íos, Thira, Amorgós and some of the other Cyclades.

131

The grand buildings in Ermoúpoli are a reminder of its days as an important port

Wine has been produced in Greece for over 4,000 years – a considerable tradition – and yet most visitors expect to find only retsina and Demestica. Reasons for this lie in recent history, but a remedy has already been applied: winemaking has been transformed and Greek wines are now worthy of their tradition.

132

WINE CLASSIFICATIONS

Under Greek legislation, the following categories apply to wine and are on labels:

OPAP (VQPRD): Vin de qualité produit région determinée – *appellation* of proven, superior quality. These wines are then distinguished, according to the time they have been aged, into Reserve (red and white, two years) and Grande Reserve (red, four years; white, three years).

Topikós Oínos: Vin de Pays, mostly made from local grape varieties.

Epitrapézios Oínos: Table wine

Cava: Table wine that has been aged: the red for at least three years; the white for two years.

THE RETSINA TASTE

Retsina owes its distinctive flavour to the addition of resin. This was first practised by the Chinese, but the Greeks have long used resin to seal their wine jars. The amount of resin that can now be added to white wine is governed by law. Like other Greek wines, retsinas have recently improved in quality. The most popular brand is Kourtakis, whose up-market 'Yellow Label' deserves its following. Boutari's retsina lives up to its new-wave reputation, but as always the best retsina is – very occasionally – found in tavernas and wine shops, sold by the litre served young and cool in aluminium cans.

From Homer to home-leavers Anyone who has read Homer's epics will know how central winemaking was to ancient Greek culture. A meal was not complete without wine, with drops being poured as a libation to the gods. At Vathípetro on Crete a wine press has been found dating back to the 16th century BC, while the Archaeological Museum of Thásos holds several 4th-century BC artifacts from winemakers, including *appellation* stamps and a tablet laying out winemaking laws. Winemaking was a profitable business under the Byzantines, but the Turks did not encourage it and only the Greek Orthodox Church kept the traditions alive. Wines can only be as good as their grapes and the movement of Greek people in the 1950s away from countryside and vineyards, to cities or overseas, led to a drop in the quality of wine.

New Greek wines The situation improved in the late 1960s and in 1971 *appellation* laws were brought into force. Ten years later, when Greece joined the EU, subsidies helped to modernise wineries. At the same time, Australian and American winemakers were forcing growers in places like Bordeaux and Burgundy to change their style; Greek winemakers have now brought in a number of overseas oenologists to help them blend their wines. As a result of these measures a variety of good-quality wines is now available.

Choosing Greek wine The only way to get to know Greek wines is to drink them. From the islands, Nico Manessis, in his *Greek Wine Guide* (Corfu, 1995), particularly recommends white wines from Thíra (Boutari and Sigalas; see panel on page 137), Kefalloniá (Calligas and Gentilini) and Zákynthos (Comoutos). For sparkling white try Emery, from Rhodes, while the sweet wines of Sámos and Vatis's white wines from Sýros, are also recommended.

THÍRA (SANTORÍNI)

Thíra, also known as Devil's Island, offers one of the most appealing natural spectacles in the entire Mediterranean. Visitors arriving by boat sail into the flooded crater (caldera) of its volcano to find two dazzling white Cycladic towns dramatically perched high on the rim. The island is unique, but as most visitors list it as one of their favourites, it has also become heavily developed and in season gets very crowded.

►►► Thíra (Fíra)   101C1

Painstakingly rebuilt after the serious 1956 earthquake, the island's capital, in its spectacular setting, never fails to impress. However, the toll that tourism has taken on the town is easily felt. Many terraces with views over the caldera have been turned into bars or *kafeneía*, but a drink to watch the sunset over the caldera is far from cheap. The 'old town' has kept little of its Greek character: gone are the tavernas, little grocery shops and old barbers. Instead, the narrow streets are taken over by expensive jewellery shops, trendy boutiques and bars playing Euro-pop. A young crowd is being attracted to Thíra in increasing numbers and nightlife is getting livelier. Some of the old atmosphere can be detected in the quieter area past the **Archaeological Museum►►** (*Open* Tue–Sun 8.30–3. *Admission charge; free* Sun), which has stunning and free views of the amazing caldera. The museum has an interesting collection, mainly artifacts from Akrotíri though not the superb frescos, which are still drawing the crowds in the National Archaeological Museum in Athens. Nearby is the **Megaron Gyzi Museum►►** (*Open* Mon–Sat 10.30–1.30 and 5–8 pm, Sun 10.30–4.30. *Admission charge*), in a lovely 17th-century mansion, with old maps, costumes and photographs of a Thíra which is no more. Most ferries dock at Athiniós, south of Thíra, while excursion boats and cruise ships usually call at Skála Thirás from where some 600 steps climb steeply up to the sparkling white capital. Wealthy ship-owner Evángelos Nomikós has donated a cable-car, which makes the two-minute ascent every 15 minutes.

Continued on pages 136–7.

If you are looking for peace and quiet on Thíra, head straight for Oía, on the northern tip of the island

USEFUL NUMBERS
Port Authority
tel: 0286 22239
Airport tel: 0286 31523
Theoskepasti Travel (for ferry information and tickets) tel: 0286 22256
Hertz Rent-a-Car,
tel: 0286 22221

EARLY EVENING STROLL
To escape the sunset madness of Thíra's bars, head north along the footpath on the island's spine to Imerovígli, the old Catholic quarter. The views over Thíra and the volcano are stunning and some of the houses have been elegantly restored. The last sunlight softens up this hard landscape and adds to its appeal and its sense of mystery. Take a flashlight for returning after dark, since the edge of the cliff is surprisingly nearby and it's a very long way down to the bottom.

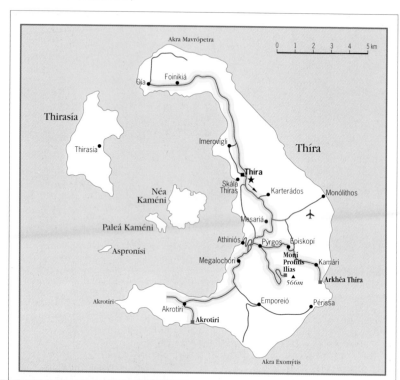

134

Drive

Thíra in a day

Thíra is a small island with good roads. The countryside, with its vineyards and magnificent views over the caldera, offers a welcome change from the over-commercialised capital (about 50km; allow 6–8 hours).

Drive out of Thíra following signs for the airport and after 5km follow signs to Akrotíri and go through **Megalochóri▶▶**. Beyond it, on the right, is a signpost for the **Boutari Winery** (see panel on page 137). About 2km on, follow the sign to the right for Akrotíri. From this part of the road the views over the **caldera** and Thíra island are simply marvellous. Continue through the village of Akrotíri, then follow signs to the archaeological site of ancient

Akrotíri▶▶▶ (see page 136). Just down the road from the site is a small beach of red, white and black pebbles, pleasant for a swim.

Return through Megalochóri, then follow the road to the right to the beautiful village of **Pýrgos▶▶** (see page 137). From the main square in Pýrgos you can make a detour to the **monastery of Profítis Ilías▶** (see page 137), the road winding up the hill with wonderful views. Return to Pýrgos and follow the signs for Episkopí, continuing through Episkopí and Kamári, then following signs to (ancient) **Archaía Thíra** (see page 136).

Return to Thíra by the same route. Drive through the main street in Thíra, take a left at **Imerovígli▶▶** to enjoy the views and return to the main road. The road further north is the best part of the drive, with the caldera on one side and a fertile valley down below on the other side.

Be sure to get to **Oía** (see pages 136–7) before sunset and have a well-deserved drink on one of the cliffside terraces before returning by the same route to Thíra.

'Larger than Libya and Asia put together...the island of Atlantis...was swallowed up by the sea and disappeared.' So wrote the Greek philosopher Plato (c428–347 BC), lamenting the loss of an island and the passing of a golden age. Since then, there has been much speculation as to where this magical place might have been.

The legend of Atlantis Plato describes Atlantis as a rich, sophisticated place which had been given to Poseidon, god of the sea, at the sharing out of the Earth. At the centre of the city of Atlantis there was a palace and a temple dedicated to Poseidon, decorated with silver and surrounded by a golden wall. Atlantis, initially a utopia, became corrupt and aggressive and finally disappeared into the sea, reclaimed by Poseidon.

The search for Atlantis Ever since Plato's description of the place, scholars and adventurers have speculated on the whereabouts of this lost realm. When Columbus reached the Americas, some people believed that he had found Atlantis. Since then, Atlantis has been variously identified with Sweden, Brazil, a submerged landmass near the Bahamas and the Atlantic Ocean off Africa.

PLATO'S SOURCE
Plato, the first author to write about the legend, claimed that the story of Atlantis was true and had been told to Solon by priests of Saïs, in Egypt. Since Plato published his account, more than 2,000 books have been written on the subject, most accepting his statements as true.

135

The legend of Atlantis continues to fascinate the world: a clip from the film The Warlords of Atlantis

Thíra's claim Frescoes, pots and other artifacts have proved the connection between Thíra and Minoan Crete and obvious parallels can be drawn between the Minoans and the inhabitants of Atlantis. Both were wealthy and sophisticated and both worshipped the bull, sacred to Poseidon. According to Plato's account of the matter, the Egyptian priests told Solon (c640–c559 BC), the Athenian poet and ruler, that Atlantis was destroyed 9,000 years before their time. Some scholars believe that they meant 900 years; if so, the destruction of Atlantis would have occurred around 1450–1550 BC – the time of the disastrous volcanic eruption on Thíra. Crete's Minoan civilisation collapsed at around the same time. So could Thíra, or even Crete, be Atlantis?

Plato is explicit that Atlantis lay *beyond* the Pillars of Hercules – the Straits of Gibraltar – and therefore out in the Atlantic Ocean. This seems to favour the New World theories of Atlantis's whereabouts – but (fortunately, perhaps) the mystery seems likely to remain unsolved.

THE GARDENS OF THE HESPERIDES
The Gardens of the Hesperides were, according to Greek mythology, the home of the Hesperides, a group of nymphs. The gardens were to be found on an island in the ocean far to the west and on them grew a tree which belonged to the goddess Hera and bore golden apples. The nymphs, aided by a dragon called Ladon, were responsible for the tree. The eleventh labour of Hercules was to kill the dragon and take the apples, which he did. Was this magic isle part of Atlantis, perhaps?

Cyclades

Continued from page 133.

CONNECTIONS

Thira has ferry links with Piréas, Páros, Íos, Náxos, Crete (Irákleio), Folégandros Mílos, Síkinos, Sýros, Thessaloniki, Anáfi, Kárpathos, Kásos, Kýthnos, Rhodes, Sérifos, Sífnos, Kímolos, Ándros, Chálki and in summer also with Mýkonos and Skíathos. Hydrofoils operate to Amorgós, Koufonísi, Rafína, Schoinoússa and in summer also to Mýkonos, Páros, Íos, Náxos, Tínos and Sýros. In the summer excursion boats also run to Crete and Thirasía.

▶▶▶ Akrotíri   101C1

Open: Tue–Sun 8.30–3. Admission charge
Regular buses from Thíra

Professor Spyridon Marinatos started excavating this site in 1967, hoping to find that the eruption of Thíra's volcano precipitated the downfall of Minoan civilisation on Crete. Instead he discovered a large and well-preserved Minoan city, destroyed by a massive volcanic eruption in 1625 BC. The area of 1 hectare has now been roofed and is one of the most exciting archaeological sites in the Cyclades. The superb frescoes from the two- and three-storey houses are in the National Archaeological Museum in Athens and much of the Cretan pottery is in Thíra's museum. However, walking around Akrotíri's streets, lined with *píthoi* (huge storage pots), it is easy to visualise what life in this town must have been like. Peering through windows into houses, one almost expects to find women preparing dinner for the family.

Walking the streets of Minoan Akrotíri

THE ATTRACTION OF THIRA

'I found it a fantastic spot. Picturesque, or romantic, is too mild a term; the cliff-scenery and the colours of the sea and land made one catch one's breath. Under a bleak northern sky it would be a horrific kind of place; drenched in the glittering light of May it was fabulously beautiful... Santorin is surely a vision which can disappoint nobody.'
Norman Douglas, *Looking Back* (1933)

▶▶ Archaía Thíra (Ancient Thíra)   101C1

Open: Tue–Sun 9–3. Admission charge
Regular buses from Thíra to Périssa, then a steep walk, expensive taxi or a donkey ride up to the site

Arkhéa Thíra was the island's ancient capital, inhabited from the 9th century BC onwards. Most of the ruins visible today are Ptolemaic, with temples dedicated to Egyptian gods and to Dionysos and Apollo. The impressive remains of the *agora* and the theatre command dazzling views of the sea straight below. Some houses and temples have kept their mosaics.

▶▶▶ Oía (Ía)   101C1

Although it is well known as the most beautiful place on the island, Oía has preserved most of its character and its peacefulness. Its white houses, built virtually on top of each other, appear to hang on to the cliff; some of them are even built into it. Although there are many rooms and cave dwellings for rent, the place rarely feels overrun, except sometimes towards the end of the day when

busloads from Thíra and Kamári come to watch the sunset. On the little headland is a ruined fort and below it the remains of a basilica. In the other direction, a rough footpath towards Imerovígli offers some of the island's most memorable views (especially on the way back towards Oía). About 200 steps lead down from Oía to the tiny fishing harbour of Ammoúdi, which has two pleasant tavernas and some good bathing nearby. Some ferries dock at Arméni, the other beach near Oía. There is also a winery at Oía (see panel).

▶▶ Pýrgos 101C1

Pýrgos is one of the oldest villages on Thíra, with a cluster of traditional houses, a Venetian fort and Byzantine walls. A small road leads to the island's highest point (566m), where the 18th-century **monastery of Profítis Ilías**▶ shares the remote hilltop with several large communications antennas. The monastery, set in a lovely garden, has a small museum of religious objects and folklore items (*Open* daily, but check opening hours locally first).

▶▶ Thirasía 101C1

An excursion to the dark islets opposite Thíra gives a clearer idea of the volcano. Like Thíra itself, they form the edges of the now mostly submerged crater. Thirasía, which was part of Thíra until the 3rd century BC, has three small hamlets with a few tavernas and plenty of peace and quiet. The nearby islets of Paleá and Néa Kaméni are still volcanically active.

Beaches

Thíra is not the best place in the Cyclades to look for a secluded beach. Buses from Thíra bus station pass close to most of the island's beaches, so that wherever you go you are unlikely to be alone. The volcanic black sand gets unbearably hot on summer afternoons, so beach footwear is recommended.

The nearest beach to Thíra is Monólithos, but Kamári has a longer and cleaner beach, although it is now a package-tour resort. Périssa beach is a little less crowded but also less well kept. Oía has two small but average beaches, Ammoúdi, with a small harbour and Arméni, which has a fish taverna.

Kamári's black pebble beach was long ago discovered by package tourism. It is Thíra's most popular destination

GOOD WINE ON THIRA
Thíra has always been renowned for its wines, especially its rather sweet white wine. The volcanic soil is good for growing grapes, but the vines are kept short and basket-shaped to protect them from strong winds and the dry climate. Boutari, one of Greece's biggest wine producers, has a winery just outside Megalochóri, producing several excellent white wines and offering daily tastings. For a more specialised tasting, islander Paris Sigalas has set up a small winery in Oía, using only grapes from the northern part of the island, which produce a different kind of wine.

There are two great earthquake 'belts' in the world: one in the Pacific Ocean, another in the Mediterranean, running through the Greek Islands into Asia Minor. Even since 1900 parts of Greece have been shattered by earthquakes.

KOS'S DOUBLE BLOW
There is a certain satisfaction in the history of earthquakes on Kós for, while the ancient city was brought down by an earthquake in AD 554, the earthquake that devastated the medieval and modern city in 1933 allowed archaeologists to expose the ancient site, which is still visible in the centre of the rebuilt town today.

138

SEEING IS BELIEVING
If you want more evidence of the extent of the 1953 earthquake that ripped the Ionian islands apart, visit Kefalloniá's Historical and Cultural Museum (see page 184). On Zákynthos, visit the Solomós Museum (see page 198) where you can buy N.A. Varviani's book with photographs of Zákynthos before, during and after the quake.

Pýrgos, one of the oldest settlements on the islands, is still scarred by the 1956 earthquake

Recent earthquakes When Thíra was levelled around 1450 BC, the ancients thought it was the work of the god 'Earth-Shaker'. Nowadays we know differently, but that does not stop it from happening. In September 1986, the mainland town of Kalamáta was destroyed and many of its 42,000 inhabitants lost their homes and their livelihood. In the summer of 1995, another earthquake on the mainland brought down more buildings and claimed many lives.

The islands The Greek islands have been just as vulnerable as the mainland and almost everywhere you go, you are likely to find evidence of a long history of earthquakes. Archaeologists have confirmed that on several occasions the Minoans on Crete suffered from earthquakes. The Colossus of Rhodes, one of the Seven Wonders of the Ancient World, stood for only 65 years before being brought to its knees by an earthquake in 225 BC. In this century, even little Kastellórizo was shattered by an earthquake in 1927.

The Ionian tragedy The Ionian islands seem particularly susceptible to earthquakes. Archaeologists hoping to uncover traces of Odysseus's palace on Itháki are hindered by the damage from previous quakes which has shuffled the stones around beneath the earth. In this century, a quake in 1948 destroyed Lefkáda Town. When it was rebuilt, the bell towers were made of iron, which is more likely to withstand another earthquake (and less likely to cause damage if they fall) and houses were mostly limited to two storeys, the upper ones being built of corrugated iron or wood. The most damaging earthquake of modern times happened across the Ionian Islands in August 1953: most of the towns on Zákynthos and Kefalloniá were levelled by it.

The elaborate Tinian dovecotes are strewn all over the island's striking countryside

USEFUL NUMBERS
Port Authority
tel: 0283 22220
Tourist information
tel: 0283 23780
Windmills Travel (on the quay) tel: 0283 23398

TÍNOS

Tínos is often characterised as the island of pilgrimage, but many visitors come for the beauty of its countryside – a rolling, fertile land filled with 60 villages, 1,200 white chapels and about 600 typical Tinian dovecotes. This is an ideal island for hikers.

▶▶ Tínos Town
100B3

The island capital is dominated by the neoclassical **church of Panagía Evangelístria**▶▶ (*Open* daily 8–8), the main attraction for thousands of pilgrims. Streets leading up to it from the harbour are lined with stalls of religious paraphernalia. A huge staircase leads to the atmospheric marble church, which has several galleries and a famous icon of the Virgin, covered in gold offerings. Found in 1823 by a local nun, whose dream of a buried icon turned out to be true, the icon is the focus of special celebrations on 25 March and 15 August, when sick people from all over Greece make pilgrimages to Tínos in the hope of a miraculous cure. Also worth a visit in Tínos Town is the **Archaeological Museum**▶ (*Open* Tue–Sun 8.30–3. *Admission charge*), which houses finds from the Sanctuary of Poseidon and Amphitrite.

▶▶▶ Exómpourgo
100B3

Both the ancient acropolis and the medieval capital were on the summit of Mount Exóbourgo, now best reached from the steps in nearby **Xínara**. Xínara is the seat of the Roman Catholic Bishopric and, apart from Tripótamos which is deeply Orthodox (and has very striking buildings), most of the neighbouring villages are Catholic. The area offers plenty of opportunities for long walks to remote villages and monasteries, of which there are many.

CONNECTIONS
Tínos is connected by ferry with Piréas, Rafína, Mýkonos, Sýros, Ándros; Páros, Crete, Skíathos, Thessaloníki, Amorgós, Kós and Rhodes. Summer hydrofoil services run to Mýkonos, Náxos, Páros, Thíra, Sýros, Rafína, Íos and Amorgós.

139

▶▶▶ Pýrgos
100B4

The artisans of this beautiful village are famous for their fine marble work. Sculptors can still be seen at work here and local marble is much in evidence, paving the streets as well as embellishing buildings. There is an 18th-century cemetery with ornate marble tombs and a small museum of the 19th-century sculptor Halepas. Below Pýrgos, the harbour of Pánormos has a crowded beach, while the nearby Kardianí village has one of the island's most striking settings.

Pýrgos's artisans are known throughout Greece for their intricate marble ornamentation

Beaches

Northwest of Tínos town is Kiónia, site of the Sanctuary of Poseidon and Amphitrite. Eastwards, Pórto has two sandy beaches while Lychnaftía is usually less crowded than Ágios Fókas and Livádi nearer to town.

Reminders of religious life are never far away in Greece. All over the islands, inhospitable hilltops and secluded valleys provide often spectacular settings for monasteries. Priests mingle with villagers in kafeneía and on buses. In times of need, Greeks make pilgrimages to pray before specific icons or shrines.

THE ANCIENTS LIVE ON

It is tempting to see the Greek reverence for icons as a continuing of pagan practices, where offerings were made to images of the gods. In some cases it is more than tempting: after the last pagan temples were shut down in AD 392, the image of the goddess Demeter at Eleusis was replaced by that of a Christian saint, Dimitra. The saint's story was very similar to that of the ancient goddess – both lost a daughter and, after much searching, had her restored.

Right: the walls of even the most derelict churches and monasteries are often covered in stunning frescoes
Below: all Greek monks belong to the same order

140

An everyday religion Religion lies at the heart of Greeks. When fleets go out to fish or the olives are ready to harvest, prayers are offered and a procession may be gathered together. When something in life requires exceptional intercession, Greeks make a pilgrimage.

Saints, icons and relics In ancient Greece every settlement had its shrine and every city its grand temples. Today every modern Greek community has its icons and shrines. Icons often miraculously appear or, as on Tínos (see page 139), are found by a pious person, guided by a dream. Greek Orthodox worshippers believe that during Communion saints inhabit their icons: it is to icons and relics of particular fame that people will turn in times of need.

The Greek Orthodox Church has a wealth of relics. Some are kept hidden, like the part of the nail from the Holy

Cross, formerly kept at Mount Athos, which was miraculously transported to Archangélou monastery on Thásos by the Archangel Michael. Others become the focus of public celebrations, like the relics of St Spiridon which are paraded through the streets of Corfu Town four times a year to commemorate the saint saving the city from the threat of plague or war.

Miraculous powers The icon of the Virgin at Tínos (see page 139) is held to have the power to heal and throughout Greece, individual saints are credited with the skill to deal with specific problems. A typical case is that of the icon of St John the Theologian on Mílos: when the community was threatened by pirates and took refuge in the church, the saint protected them by turning the church door into impenetrable iron.

The monastic order Greek monasticism traces its origins to the 4th century when, after periods of persecution under Decius and under the Emperor Diocletian, Christians responded by leaving the community to live in remote places. Greeks have no different monastic orders: monks all wear the same habit, recite the same liturgy and follow a single tradition. Monks are laymen, not clerics, their main goals being not to teach, to convert, or to do good work in the community, but to remove themselves from the community, to escape the trials and temptations of society and to come closer to God. Still, there are differences in the way they go about this. Some monks are *cœnobitic*, living in a community, under an abbot, sharing work, meals and services; others are *idiorrhythmic*, literally 'going their own way', living apart from each other during the week, coming together as a community only on Sundays and holidays. The most extreme monastics are anchorites, who take the idea of living apart literally and will not see other humans for weeks, months, or even years at a time.

Greece's monastic centres The remote peninsula of Mount Athos, on the northern mainland, towers both literally and metaphorically over all other monasteries in Greece. An autonomous republic within Greece, this haven of the reclusive life includes 20 monasteries.

Throughout the islands there are monasteries of great age and importance. The monasteries and convents of St John on Pátmos (1088), Néa Moní on Chíos (1042), Archangélou on Thásos (1974) and Tóplou (1365) and Arkádi (11th century) both on Crete, are all highly respected on the islands.

TRADITION OF PILGRIMAGE
There is a long tradition in Greece of making pilgrimages to places with sacred connections. One of the most important centres of pilgrimage in antiquity was the supposed birthplace of Zeus in the Idean Cave. Among the rich and famous who made the journey, Pythagoras visited the cave and Plato wrote about the pilgrimage route in *The Laws*.

141

Every year the Panagía Evangelístria in Tínos draws thousands of pilgrims, many of whom crawl up the long flight of steps on their knees

Somehow the island of Pátmos has managed to resist the damage done by package tourism, even though it is very welcoming to all visitors

THE DODECANESE The furthest-flung of Greece's islands, the Dodecanese cling to the Turkish coast and were only officially united with Greece in 1948. For most of their recorded history, the islands have had to face up to invasion. As a result, their archaeology and architecture are as varied as the landscape.

THE ANCIENT ISLANDS Early and lucrative trading links existed between the Dodecanese and the nearby coast of Asia Minor. In the era of city-states, both Rhodes and Kós enjoyed prominence. When the Persian threat disappeared, after the Persians' defeat at the Battle of Salamis (480 BC), the Dodecanese flourished. Such was their prestige that Ptolemy I claimed them on the death of Alexander the Great. By 164 BC, Rhodes was sufficiently powerful to negotiate an independent treaty with Rome.

A SPECIAL PLACE FOR CHRISTIANS St Paul is believed to have visited the Dodecanese and, according to tradition,

the islands had another part to play in the spread of Christianity when St John the Theologian was exiled from Asia Minor to Pátmos, where he received his Revelation. The founding in 1088 of a monastery in honour of St John has ensured that the island is still treated with reverence.

CENTURIES OF OCCUPATION Their remoteness made the Dodecanese a suitable stopping place for Crusaders on their way to the Holy Land and several of the islands experienced the Christian form of savagery which led, in 1204, to the sacking of Constantinople by Crusaders. The islands then became the war booty of the Genoese nobility, one of whom traded Rhodes to the Knights Hospitalers of St John after the Holy Land fell to the Turks at the end of the 13th century. But as the Turks' power in the region grew, so did their hold over the islands and by the time the Knights of St John finally abandoned Rhodes in 1522, all the Dodecanese were under the Sultan's control.

The Dodecanese
Astypálaia
  (ΑΣΤΥΠΑΛΑΙΑ)
Chálki (ΧΑΛΚΗ)
Kálymnos
  (ΚΑΛΥΜΝΟΣ)
Kárpathos
  (ΚΑΡΠΑΘΟΣ)
Kastellórizo (Megisti)
  (ΜΕΓΙΣΤΗ)
Kós (ΚΩΣ)
Léros (ΛΕΡΟΣ)
Leipsoí (ΛΕΙΨΟΙ)
Nísyros (ΝΙΣΥΡΟΣ)
Pátmos (ΠΑΤΜΟΣ)
Ródos (Rhodes)
  (ΡΟΔΟΣ)
Sými (ΣΥΜΗ)
Tílos (ΤΙΛΟΣ)

Dodecanese

144

ITALIAN OCCUPATION The Turks held the Dodecanese for almost four centuries but eventually lost them in the Italo-Turkish war (1911–12). Italy cherished these possessions and Mussolini ordered the construction of grand public buildings throughout the Dodecanese (most obviously in Rhodes Town) as well as the excavation and sometimes the reconstruction of buildings from earlier periods. But while this civic activity was welcome after more than a century of Turkish neglect, the accompanying cultural scheme, whereby the islanders were forbidden to speak Greek or follow the Orthodox rites, made the occupation particularly bitter. The British fought the Italians out of the

The old traditions still prevail in some mountain villages on Kárpathos

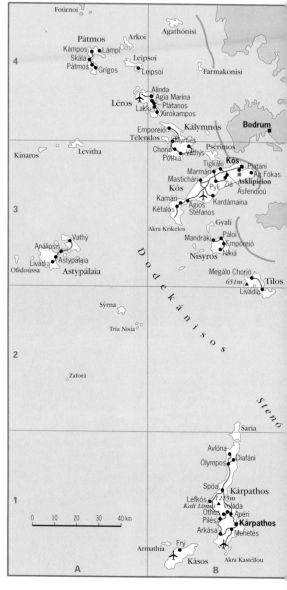

islands during 1944 and 1945 and on 7 March 1948, they were formally returned to Greece.

LOCAL CHARACTERISTICS If the islands share a history and a geographical location close to Turkey, they differ widely in their landscapes. Pátmos is rocky with volcanic soil, Léros's valleys are abundantly fertile, while Rhodes is blessed with a great variety of landscape, flora and fauna. Some of the Dodecanese have undergone extraordinary changes in the past few decades as mass tourism, particularly on Kós and Rhodes, has changed the look of some islands as well as the customs of their inhabitants.

A MISNOMER
'Dodeca' means 'twelve' but there are in fact 16 inhabited islands in the group. They were given their name in 1908, when 11 of them – along with Ikária – protested when the Turkish government took away privileges, including tax exemptions granted by the 16th-century Sultan Suleiman.

BEST BEACHES
● The sandy cove beneath Líndos (Rhodes) – out of season!
● Tsampíka (Rhodes east coast)
● Psili Ammos (southern Pátmos)
● Kéfalos (southern Kós)

145

The villagers of Ólympos on Kárpathos were only recently introduced to the idea of mass tourism

CONNECTIONS

Ferries operate from Astypálaia to Piréas, Sýros, Amorgós, Kálymnos, Irákleia, Koufonísi, Náxos, Nísyros, Tílos, Rhodes, Kós, Páros and Schoinoússa. In summer, hydrofoils serve Kálymnos and kaíki run to Kós and Kálymnos.

From Chálki ferries go to Kárpathos, Kós, Rhodes, Crete, Kásos, Náxos, Mílos, Sými, Piréas, Thíra, Sérifos, Sífnos and Síkinos. Kaíki run daily to Rhodes in summer.

USEFUL NUMBERS

Port Authority (Astypálaia)
tel: 0243 61208
Tourist information
(Kálymnos – behind the Olympic Hotel, *open* Mon–Fri 7–2.30)
tel: 0243 29310
Port Authority (Kálymnos)
tel: 0243 24444
Olympic Airways (Kálymnos)
tel: 0243 29265

WALK FROM ASTYPALAIA TOWN

From the windmills a path (keep to the left) leads to Arménohori and Messariá. From there another path through the rocks leads to the monastery of Ágios Ioánnis, surrounded by orchards. From the monastery, a rougher path leads down the valley to a tiny, pretty pebble beach where waterfalls plunge down into clear pools, great for a swim.

ASTYPÁLAIA

This most westerly island of the Dodecanese is shaped like a butterfly, with a narrow isthmus a mere 100m wide connecting its two wings.

►►► Astypálaia Town (Chóra)   144A3

Ferries dock at the harbour of Gialós with its Italianate waterfront. As the steep road goes up to the capital, the whitewashed, Cycladic-looking houses become older and more derelict. The town is crowned by an impressive 14th-century **kástro**, built on the site of the old acropolis by the Venetian Quirini family, whose arms are on display above the entrance. Still called the Palazzo Quirini-Stampalia, the fortress contains a fine collection of Venetian art. Two churches survive inside the ruined shell and views from the hilltop site are superb.

► Análipsis (Maltezána)   144A3

Análipsis is a small fishing harbour surrounded by olive groves. Nearby are some well-preserved Roman baths with fine mosaic floors.

►► Vathý   144A3

In winter, ferries dock in the attractive harbour of this remote and peaceful fishing village if the winds are too strong at Gialós.

Beaches

Livádia's beach is adequate; nearby Tzanáki is a quieter nudist beach and Ágios Konstantínos is a lovely cove surrounded by orchards. On the isthmus Sténo offers the best bathing. The beaches round Análipsis are fine and often empty.

CHÁLKI

Only about 300 people remain on this tiny island, most of the population having moved to nearby Rhodes or emigrated abroad. Designated by UNESCO as the 'isle of peace and friendship', it still offers a relaxing escape from Rhodes, although tourism is developing slowly.

►► Chálki Town (Emporeió)   145C2

In 1983 Chálki was chosen as the seat for the annual UNESCO youth conference. The plan did not work out, but old houses had already been restored for this purpose and locals and tour operators were quick to exploit the possibilities offered by the pretty town, so it is now difficult to find hotels without a reservation. The comings and goings of fishing boats are the main activity along the waterfront. Several tavernas and bars are hidden among the elegant neoclassical buildings that make up much of the town.

Beaches

Chálki's only sandy beach is Póndamos, west of Emborió. For superb views, walk from here to the deserted village of Chorió, with its hilltop Crusader castle and church, Ágios Nikólaos, which has Byzantine frescos. Elsewhere on the island are many peaceful shingle coves – reached either by boat or on foot.

KÁLYMNOS

To compensate for the decline of the natural sponge industry (see page 148), Kalymniots have built up Greece's largest fishing fleet and recently opened their doors to tourism.

▶ Póthia   144B3

Most islanders live in Póthia, a lively and sometimes extremely noisy commercial centre. The houses are bright and colourful, a symbol of the resistance against the Italian occupation. The **Museum of Kálymnos▶▶** (*Open* Tue–Sun 10–2. *Admission charge,* Guided tours only), a stunning mansion owned by a local sponge magnate, has a strange collection of archeological finds and personal memorabilia. The **Astor Sponge Workshop▶▶** (*Open* daily in summer, 10–6) is one of the better sponge factories, which shows every stage in the preparation of sponges.

▶▶ Chorió   144B3

The old capital is watched over by two ruined castles, which offer fine views over the island. There is a group of Hellenistic graves and the remains of a temple of Apollo in the nearby village of Dámos. The church of Christos of Jerusalem was built with stones that came originally from a Hellenistic temple.

▶▶ Vathýs   144B3

A long, narrow and sheltered inlet of the sea reaches into this long, lush valley of fruit trees, making for pleasant walking country dotted with well-kept villages and several early churches.

Beaches

The beaches at Myrtiés and Massoúri are often very crowded, but from Myrtiés frequent boats cross to the islet of Télendos, which has a castle, a monastery and good beaches. Emporeió's fine beaches, in the far north-west, are seldom overrun. South of Póthia, Vliháda Bay has an attractive sandy beach; boats go to the beautiful caves of Skaliá and Kéfalos.

The imposing Castle of the Knights of St John over-looking the old capital of Chorió, Kálymnos

THE CUBES OF KALYMNOS
'In Kálymnos the infant's paint-box has been at work again on the milky slopes of the mountain. Carefully, laboriously it has squared in a church-yard, a monastery and lower down repeated the motif: a church, a monastery, a town; then, simply for the sake of appropriateness, a harbour with a shelf of bright craft at anchor and the most brilliant, the most devastatingly brilliant houses.'
Lawrence Durrell, *Reflections on a Marine Venus* (1953)

CONNECTIONS
Kálymnos has ferry links with Kós, Léros, Pátmos, Rhodes, Piréas, Sámos, Nísyros, Tílos, Astypálaia, Kastellórizo, Sými, Agathónisi, Leipsoí, Crete, Kásos and Kárpathos. Summer hydrofoil services go to Kós, Rhodes, Pátmos, Sámos, Léros, Leipsoí and Sými.

Earlier this century sponges were one of Greece's most sought-after commodities, but growing demand and sudden blight has led to the catastrophic depletion of sponge beds around the islands. The remaining sponges will need very careful management indeed if the industry is to survive.

LIBYAN SPONGES
When the beds near Kálymnos failed to satisfy demand for natural sponges, divers began looking elsewhere in the region. As sponges thrive in clean water, the search in the Mediterranean became increasingly frantic. The sea off Libya was the exception and Kalymniot divers regularly sailed south until Libya's Colonel Qaddafi banned them a few years ago.

THE LAST DIVE
'The younger generation, they won't see sponges; all of them are dying in the shallow waters of Greece, Turkey and Egypt.'
Lefteris Kampourakis, Kalymniot sponge diver.

SPONGES IN HOMER
The Ancient Greeks knew the properties of sponges. Homer provides useful insights: in the *Iliad*, the god Hephaistos cleans himself with a sponge, while in the *Odyssey*, servants in the palace of Odysseus use sponges to wipe tables. As ancient shields have shown, sponges were also used by warriors to make shields more comfortable.

Few natural sponges come from Kálymnos now

148

The life of a sponge Sponges are multicelled living organisms, shaped like vases and supported by tiny spines. Growing together in beds, in large colonies, sponges survive on organisms carried in the water that is filtered through their porous walls. When dried and with the living matter removed, sponges remain malleable, absorbent and tough, making them sought after for both domestic and industrial use.

From the sea to the bathroom Sponges need treatment to reach the state in which we like to use them in our bathrooms. Black when first brought from the seabed, they are purged of impurities and rinsed in saltwater tanks. Sponges for home use are then bleached to lighter shades which many foreign users seem to prefer.

The two most sought-after varieties of sponge are the honeycomb, mainly used for the bath and the cup, preferred for industrial use. The cheaper unbleached sponges are for cleaning while the smooth ones with fine pores are for cosmetic use.

Sponge divers Of all the islands, it was Kálymnos that grew rich from sponges: from the 1880s its economy was dominated by the trade. The sponge trade peaked in the 1950s, when Kálymnos exported over 5 million sponges a year, but by 1985, the whole of Greece produced only 2.5 million sponges. By 1988 the number had fallen to one million as a blight decimated eastern Mediterranean sponge beds. They have not recovered and little more than 100 Kalymniots now dive, the others having changed profession or moved abroad.

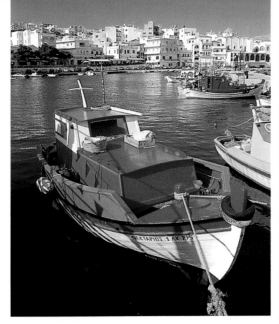

Pigádia's colourful fishing harbour is surrounded by lively cafés and places with rooms for rent

KÁRPATHOS

Isolated Kárpathos, a large and mountainous island, fiercely guarded its age-old traditions and its peace and quiet. That was until recently, but now the island is changing. Lawrence Durrell called it 'an ideal hideaway' and American Karpathians who have been returning each summer agreed. Increasingly, their influence is being felt as new roads are laid, charter flights land more frequently and new hotels appear. The visitor looking for unspoiled village life may be disappointed, but the natural beauty of the interior remains – thanks largely to the island's rugged terrain and often hair-raising roads, especially in the remoter north.

▶ Kárpathos Town (Pigádia) 144B1

Almost completely modern, Kárpathos Town has no 'sights', but its small sleepy fishing harbour is a pleasant enough place to while away an evening. The town beyond the waterfront has many bars and restaurants. One of the older surviving houses, beside the church, is now a traditional *kafeneío* with good live music in the evening.

▶▶▶ Apéri 144B1

Apéri is the largest of a series of attractive villages dramatically set in the hills of central Kárpathos. The others are Voláda, Pilés and, prettiest of all, Óthos.

▶▶ Arkása 144B1

Arkása has been developed for package tourism in recent years and has lost a lot of its charm, but it has retained some Venetian buildings. Near the town are the remains of the ancient capital **Arkessia▶**, where mosaic floors from several Byzantine churches can be seen. From **Finíki▶**, 2km away, a small fishing harbour with a tiny beach, it is a steep climb to the striking village of **Menetés▶▶**, which contains some old houses and a small folklore museum.

USEFUL NUMBERS
Olympic Airways
tel: 0245 22150
Port Authority
tel: 0245 22227

KASOS
The 1,500 inhabitants left on the barren neighbouring island of Kásos mostly live in the five villages clustered on the north side of the island. From Emborió, the port, it is a 10-minute walk to the capital, Frý. The place has little to offer the visitor apart from small but good beaches, total peace and rural calm in the many groves and gardens.
   In 1824 the Egyptian troops of Ibrahim Pasha killed most of the men on the island and enslaved the women and their children. Strangely enough there was later a voluntary emigration to Egypt where Kasiots helped to build the Suez Canal.

Dodecanese

TRADITIONS IN ÓLYMPOS
Ólympos was always isolated and even now some people who live there have never been to Kárpathos Town. The older inhabitants speak a kind of Dorian Greek. Two of the medieval windmills are still working and the bread is baked by the women in communal ovens. The older women still wear heavily embroidered clothes and two shoemakers at the entrance to the village make the leather boots worn by the older people. The houses consist of one divided room, built around a central pillar and heavily decorated. People sleep on mattresses that are on a raised platform.

CONNECTIONS
Kárpathos has ferry links with Piréas, Chálki, Rhodes, Crete, Thíra, Páros, Náxos, Kásos, Sými, Mílos, Sífnos, Sérifos and Kýthnos.

Apéri is the wealthiest of the hillside villages: nearly everyone has spent some time in North America to make money

►► **Lefkós (Paralía Lefkoú)**   *144B1*

Lefkós, a beautifully situated resort on the west coast with excellent beaches, is still quite unspoiled. The only problem is getting there: buses are few and far between and it is a long way by bicycle.

►►► **Ólympos**   *144B1*

The traditional village of Ólympos is one of the most popular day trips from Kárpathos Town; however, the road to it is so rough that most people prefer to take a boat to the harbour of Diafáni and from there take a bus or walk (see page 151). There are some hotels and rooms to rent if you wish to stay overnight. The influx of visitors has already taken its toll on Ólympos and a lot of the traditions are being kept for the sake of the holiday-makers, but it remains a lovely village, clinging to its steep hilltop site and offering breathtaking views. A family runs a small cafeteria near their windmill, where they grind the flour they use to make excellent *loukoumádes* (honey puffs) and cheese and spinach pastries. Nearby is a small folklore museum, which is just a traditionally furnished room.

Beaches
Most of Kárpathos's splendid beaches are accessible only by boat from Kárpathos Town. To the north of the town, within easy walking distance, is Vrontis Bay, a long stretch of white sand. Amopí, 8km south, has a fine sandy beach, crowded at times and a more secluded pebbly beach, the only place on the island where nudism is unofficially allowed. There are several beautiful beaches in Lefkós, but they can be crowded. Boats go every morning to Apélla, a fine beach with clear water and a rocky background. It can also be reached by road. Kýra Panagía is a lovely sand and pebble beach overlooked by the village of Mertonas and surrounded by pine forest. Also on the east coast is the fine sandy beach of Ágios Nikólaos.

Walk

Diafáni to Ólympos

Every travel agent in Kárpathos Town advertises the boat trip to Diafáni and a visit by bus to Ólympos. The bus ride is an experience, but the walk through the village of Avlóna is unforgettable. If you do not like climbing, take the bus up and walk back downhill, taking enough to drink. Wear a hat and good walking shoes (about 11km; allow 4 hours).

Boats leave Kárpathos Town at 8.30am and return at 4.30pm from Diafáni. The walk starts at Diafáni waterfront; walk northwards and then follow the path between the houses. Ignore the signpost after a few metres to Vanandá (right) and stay in the valley, passing Hotel Sunrise. Walk through the wood and, after 500m, veer left, uphill, with good views over Diafáni. About 3km from Diafáni continue straight where a dirt track goes right to Vanandá. Approximately 700m from here, turn right onto an old road with red markings. There is a final view of Diafáni and Vanandá and then there are only mountains and the serpentine road ahead of you.

After another 2km, in a valley with fields surrounded by old walls, a donkey track comes in from the right, from Vanandá. Ignore this, taking instead the left-hand path which leads to **Avlóna**, an age-old agricultural community, hardly touched by the modern world. Heading southeast at the edge of the village, a small road runs through the fields and, after 600m, makes a sharp bend to the right. Walk straight on to join the old road again.

About 1.5km from Avlóna, a paved donkey path leads to the pretty church

Ólympos is run by women as most of the men emigrate to work outside the village, only returning on holidays

of **Ágios Konstantínos**. Suddenly the village of Ólympos comes into sight; the road from here is one of the island's most beautiful.

Some 50m beyond the church turn left and look out for a small winding path on the right that goes down into the valley, joining the road. Follow the road southwards through the valley, amid lovely fields and gardens, towards the delightful old village of **Ólympos►►►** (see page 150).

CONNECTIONS
Kastellórizo has ferry links with Rhodes, Kálymnos, Páros, Náxos, Nísyros, Tílos, Sýros and Piréas. Day trips operate from Kaş in nearby Turkey.

The Turkish coast looms over Kastellórizo's harbour

USEFUL NUMBERS
Airport (Kastellórizo)
tel: 0241 49241
Port Authority
(Kastellórizo)
tel: 0241 49270
Olympic Airways (Kós)
tel: 0242 28331
Port Authority (Kós)
tel: 0242 26594
Airport (Kós)
tel: 0242 51255
Hertz Rent-a-Car (Kós)
tel: 0242 28002

KASTELLÓRIZO (MEGÍSTI)

Kastellórizo, one of the smallest of the Dodecanese islands, is far closer to the Turkish mainland town of Kaşthan to its nearest Greek neighbour, the island of Rhodes, which is more than 100km away. Less than 100 years ago there were over 16,000 inhabitants, but today the permanent population is down to about 200 people. Emigration has been largely responsible: there are now over 30,000 Australians of 'Kassie' descent.

▶▶▶ Kastellórizo Town   145D1

Kastellórizo thrived by transporting goods between the Turkish mainland and Greece, but the trade went into decline when the Italians captured the island in 1912 and stopped completely after Anatolian Greeks were expelled in 1923. In 1943 it was occupied by the British, who blew up more than 2,000 houses when they were forced by the Germans to leave.

Most people live in Kastellórizo Town, which feels distinctively Asian. The attractive waterfront – still much visited by passing yachts – has red-tile roofed mansions with balconies and coloured doors, but just beyond this, the houses look desolate and abandoned.

The **museum▶** (*Open* Tue–Sun 7.30–2.30. *Admission free*) in the ruined Castle of the Knights has an eclectic collection of Byzantine ephemera and frescos from local churches. The mosque has now been turned into a folklore museum. Restaurants lining the quay serve excellent seafood. A short walk up from the port lie the remains of the Doric city of Palaiokástro; the views from here are truly stunning.

Beaches

Kastellórizo has no beaches and the sea near the town is often infested with sea urchins. Boats make excursions to Perastá to visit the astonishing 'blue grotto', which is hung with stalactites.

KÓS

Kós has to be the number one choice in the Dodecanese for sun, beaches, nightlife and fun. Avoid it if you long for the Greece of quiet individual experiences – although there are still some lovely corners on the island and Kós's friendly people make it well worth a short visit.

▶▶▶ Kós Town

144B3

Kós Town is a strange mixture. Beach tourism, complete with a lively nightlife, shares the town centre with Hellenistic and Roman archaeological sites. To escape the crowds in summer, wake early and explore while others recover from their long night on the town.

Approaching Kós harbour, the first striking sight is the imposing 15th-century **Castle of the Knights▶▶** (*Open* Tue–Sun 8.30–3. *Admission charge; free* Sun). A walk on the walls offers splendid views over the town, and the interior is littered with fragments of ancient columns and statues. The 18th-century Turkish **Mosque of Hatzi Hasan** in Plateía Lózia is under restoration, while in Plateía Eleftherías is the **Defterdar mosque**. The old Turkish bazaar, now filled with tacky souvenir shops, lacks authenticity. The **Archaeological Museum▶▶** (Plateía Eleftherías. *Open* Tue–Sun 8.30–3. *Admission charge; free* Sun) has lovely mosaic floors and elegant statues from Roman town houses. The **Agora▶** has a 4th-century stoa and the ruins of a Temple of Aphrodite. The **Casa Romana▶▶** (Odós Grigouriou. *Open* Tue–Sun 8.30–3. *Admission charge; free* Sun) is a complete Roman villa restored by the Italians in the 1930s.

Further down the road at the well-kept Roman **Odeum▶**, a statue thought to be of Hippocrates was found. Across the road is the site known as the **Western Excavation▶▶**, whose ruins include a **Nymphaeum** with superb mosaic floors, the colonnade of a gymnasium, and some Roman and early Christian houses, the best of which is the **House of Europa**.

Most visitors to Kós prefer the vibrant nightlife to the ancient sites

Cycle ride

The island of Kós is dedicated to its ancient son, Hippocrates, even though there is little evidence of his existence. The healthiest and most pleasant way to get around Kós is to cycle. Bicycles can be rented in town. This trip (approximately 25km) will take most of a day, with time left for a swim. In summer take sunscreen, hat and water. (Note that the optional detour to Asfendioú demands fitness and a mountain bike – see below.)

Start from the **Hippocrates Tree▶** (see panel on page 153) in Platía Lózia, between the Castle and the Roman Agora. Turn right along Aktí Miaoúli and right again at the tourist office into Odós Ippokrátous, passing the modern Hippocrates Hospital (No 32). In the **Archaeological Museum▶▶** on Plateía Eleftherías (see page 153) is the so-called statue of Hippocrates and a well-preserved

In the footsteps of Hippocrates

The tree may not have been around in Hippocrates's time, but its maturity certainly demands respect

mosaic depicting him welcoming Asklepios to Kós. Take Odós Vassiléos Pávlou, then at the end of the street turn right into Odós Grigoriou and continue to the circle with flags where a signpost shows the direction (right) to the Asklepion (Asklípieio; about 4km). Continue under pine and fig trees to the village of **Platáni▶** (see page 157). Beyond the village, the road climbs gently. At the little traffic island with trees, continue straight ahead along the lane that leads to the **Asklepion▶▶▶** where Hippocrates's techniques were applied (see page 156). From here you can try out his recommendation of fresh clean air by biking a further 10km through lovely pine forests to the villages of **Asfendioú▶▶▶** (see page 156). (The road is steep; try it only if you have a mountain bike and are fit.) Alternatively, return to Platáni where a road to the left leads to the main coastal road and beyond it to the beautiful beaches just past **Tigkáki** (about 12km). Reward yourself with a cooling swim before riding back to Kós Town.

The priest-doctors of the Ancient Egyptians claimed to have invented medicine and that may be true, but it was from Hippocrates and the priests of the Asklepion that western medicine and its code of practice evolved.

Asklepios The Greeks believed that Asklepios, god of medicine, was a son of Apollo and Coronis. His daughter, quite logically, was Hygieia, goddess of health. Asklepios's main cult centre and temple was in the Peloponnese, at Epídavros, where patients initially received prescriptions in the form of a dream, as they slept in the temple. Those who were cured later offered a sacrifice at the temple, traditionally a cockerel. The god is often shown as a bearded man, with a stick around which was curled a snake, a symbol now sometimes used to denote a pharmacy.

Hippocrates Born on Kós around 460 BC, Hippocrates became the most famous physician of antiquity. Many surviving texts on medical subjects are credited to him, but there is some doubt over the authorship of most of them. Certainly, he classified the medical knowledge of his time. Unlike priests at the Asklepion in Epidáuros, Hippocrates sought to treat the sick by using drugs, infusions and other therapies and he understood the importance of diet, climate and living conditions in maintaining good health. He believed that most diseases were carried in the four fluids or humours of the body: blood, phlegm, black bile and yellow bile. How much of this was his own thinking and how much was wisdom imported from Egypt or elsewhere is unknown. The practice was carried on by hereditary temple priests, called Asklepiadai, who claimed descent from the god himself.

After Hippocrates The riches of the Asklepion on Kós and the Sanctuary at Epidáuros suggest that the cult continued to grow after Hippocrates's death, reaching its peak during Ptolemaic and Roman times, when both sites functioned as spas for the healthy and sanitariums for the sick. The reputation of Asklepios and of Hippocrates was such that when Rome was suffering from a particularly savage epidemic in 293 BC, Asklepios's serpent was sent for to work a cure.

THE HIPPOCRATIC OATH
Although many of the great number of writings ascribed to Hippocrates are disputed, the Hippocratic Oath is usually credited to him. In it, he expresses the ethical doctrine of physicians which remains in use today. Part of the oath states: 'I will use treatment or help the sick according to my ability and judgement, but never with a view to injury and wrong-doing. Neither will I administer a poison to anybody when asked to do so. Similarly I will not give to a woman a pessary to cause abortion. Into whatever houses I enter, I will enter to help the sick and I will abstain from all intentional wrong-doing or harm. And whatever I shall see or hear in the course of my profession in my intercourse with men, if it be what should not be published abroad, I will never divulge'.

155

A CURE TOO MANY
According to mythology, Asklepios went too far with his cures and brought a man back from the dead. For daring the gods, Zeus struck him down with a thunderbolt and Apollo turned him into a constellation, the Serpentaria.

Hippocrates, the Father of Medicine, who established a medical code still in use today

The temple dedicated to Apollo the Healer in the Asklipeío

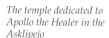

CONNECTIONS
Kós is well served by inter-island ferries. There are links with Rhodes, Kálymnos, Nísyros, Léros, Pátmos, Piréas, Sými, Tílos, Kastellórizo, Náxos, Páros, Leipsoí, Astypálaia, Thessaloníki, Chálki, Kárpathos, Crete, Sýros, Mýkonos, Tínos, Ándros, Rafina and Cyprus.
In summer there are frequent hydrofoils to Rhodes, Pátmos, Nísyros, Kálymnos, Léros, Sámos and Bodrum (Turkey).

►► Asfendioú   144B3

The villages clustered on the slopes of Mount Díkeos, known as the Asfendioú, offer a welcome cooling breeze in summer. This is definitely the most Greek part of Kós – though some of the more accessible villages see their fair share of visitors. Buses go to Pylí, from where a dirt track crosses the island's only forest to the other villages. A steep walk away from Pylí is the old town **Palaiopíli►►**, where an amazing ruined castle sits on top of a rocky pinnacle. Crumbling stone walls and little abandoned churches stand among drifts of wild plants and the views over mountain and sea are magnificent. **Evangelístria►** has lovely houses and a good taverna while nearby **Asómati** has picturesque whitewashed houses. **Ziá►►**, more developed with a few tavernas, is a spectacular place to watch the sunset.

►►► Asklipeío (The Asklepion)   144B3

4km from Kós Town, past Platáni. Open Tue–Sun 8.30–3.
Admission charge; free Sun
Bus No 3 from Kós Town at least every hour

The Asklepion was a religious centre, with temples dedicated to Apollo the Healer and his son Asklepios and also a medical resort with a medical school, a treatment centre and a museum of anatomy and pathology. Although the Asklepion was built after Hippocrates's death, it was undoubtedly based on his theories and methods. The three wide terraces seen at the Asklepion today were built after the 4th century BC and most of the buildings are Hellenistic or Roman. The lowest terrace, just beyond the Roman baths, was once the medical school, the museum and the hospital. The middle terrace has an altar dedicated to Apollo the Healer, with an elegant 4th-century BC Ionic temple to the right and a less impressive Roman-Corinthian version to the left. An imposing ceremonial stairway leads to the highest terrace, crowned with the huge 2nd-century BC Doric Temple of Asklepios, where the Hippocratic Oath is still sworn today. Along the exterior wall there are two subterranean chambers with a statue of Venus, where it was believed that venereal diseases were treated.

▶ Kamári   144B3

This fishing harbour boasts some good beaches and is rapidly developing into a package-tour resort. Nearby, at **Ágios Stéfanos ▶ ▶**, are two very early Byzantine churches with well-preserved mosaic floors and some columns, probably built on the site of a classical temple.

▶ Kardámaina   144B3

A stone's throw from the airport, Kardámaina is the second largest and fastest growing resort on Kós. There is nothing left of the old fishing village, but a beach packed during the day (and often at night) and continuous nightlife attract young people from all over Europe.

▶ ▶ Kéfalos   144B3

Kéfalos, at the end of the bus line on Kós's southwestern peninsula, has its fair share of bungalows and summer houses but still tends to be less hectic than the other resorts. Nearby, the remains of a Hellenistic temple and a theatre were probably part of ancient Astypálaia, the earliest capital of Kós.

▶ Mastichári   144B3

Another fishing village recently turned resort, Mastichári is more relaxed than Kardámaina. Boats leave from here for the islands of Psérimos and Kálymnos.

▶ Platáni   144B3

Platáni is a bi-ethnic village where Greek Orthodox seem to live rather peacefully among a Muslim minority of Turkish descent. It is a popular lunch stop on the way back from the Asklepion and, apart from some Turkish-style houses and an Ottoman fountain, its main attractions are the Turkish–Greek restaurants under the plane trees.

▶ Psérimos   144B3

Almost equidistant between Kós and Kálymnos is the small island of Psérimos. Day trips from both islands are popular and a few lucky visitors can stay overnight in one of Psérimos's guest houses. There are no cars on this idyllic island and the main settlement consists of a mere 30 or so houses. The main sandy beach is just in front of the village and there are other, pebbly, beaches nearby.

Beaches

Most people visit Kós for its superb beaches even though these become very crowded in summer. The beaches nearest Kós Town are narrow and absolutely packed. To the west are Lámpi and, 9km on, Tigkáki, equally crowded, while Marmári is slightly calmer, with good windsurfing. Eastwards, the good pebble and sand beaches are lined with big beach hotels. Brós Thermá, 5km past the last bus stop at Ágios Fókas, is more isolated and has black sand and hot springs. Mastichári, on the north coast, is a fast-developing resort with sandy beaches. The fine beaches at Kardámaina, in the

Most independent travellers avoid Kós as there is not much left to discover

157

It has no superb beaches, but Léros is becoming increasingly popular

EXCURSIONS TO TURKEY
In summer there are usually daily boats to Bodrum from Kós Town. Contact the Tourist Police on Odós Aktí Miaoúli (tel: 0242 26666) for the latest information on boats and regulations, which change frequently.

CONNECTIONS
There are ferries from Léros to Kós, Rhodes, Piréas, Kálymnos, Tínos, Pátmos, Agathónisi, Leipsoí, Sámos, Tílos, Sými, Páros, Sýros and Náxos. In summer, hydrofoils go to Kós, Pátmos, Kálymnos, Sámos, Ikaría and Leipsoí and boats serve Leipsoí and Kálymnos.
From Leipsoí, ferries go to Patmos, Agathónisi, Kálymnos, Léros, Piréas, Sámos, Kós, Páros, Mýkonos, Náxos, Sýros, Rhodes, Tínos, Sými and Tílos. There are hydrofoil services to Léros, Kálymnos, Kós, Pátmos, Sámos and Ikaría and summer boats to Pátmos and Léros.

south, are lined with hotel complexes. The most beautiful beaches on the island are Paradise Beach (an often crowded stretch of sand between dramatic cliffs), Ágios Stéfanos (the site of a Club Med complex) and Kamári. There are still deserted beaches on the southern tip of the island, beyond Kéfalos, but it can be quite an adventure to reach them.

LÉROS

Léros, with its deeply indented coastline, somehow still feels more Italian than Greek. The island has quite a reputation among Greeks, to whom it is best known for its prisons and mental hospitals. Mussolini made it a hospital island for the mentally ill and even today the most serious psychiatric cases are sent to Léros.

▶▶ Plátanos 144B4

The inland capital of the island is a busy market town with some attractive 19th-century mansions. Above the town towers the *kástro*, built by the Byzantines, restored by the Knights of St John and later by the Venetians. The small museum of local finds and craft items, in the main square, is worth a visit (*Open* daily 8.30–12.30 and Wed, Sat and Sun 4–8 pm. *Admission charge*).

▶▶ Lakkí 144B4

Lakkí, the main harbour, is a surreal sight with crumbling fascist art-deco buildings and empty broad avenues. Boats usually arrive in Xirókampos, a little fishing port nearby.

Beaches

The main resort, Alínda, has a good gravel beach, which gets crowded in summer. Vromólithos is nicer, with a sand and gravel beach and forested hills behind. The nearest beach to Plátanos is Agía Marína, which has tavernas open in season.

LEIPSOÍ

Leipsoí gets more visitors now than ever, since it recently became a port of call for ferries between the Cyclades and the Dodecanese, but it is still a good place to do nothing more than swim, walk, eat and relax.

A blue-domed church is part of Leipsoí's charm

▶▶▶ Leipsoí   144A4

Leipsoí, the only village on the island, has cube-shaped houses painted in bright colours and is crowned by a blue-domed church. There are several good tavernas, rooms for rent and lively *kafeneía* on the fine harbour front. As there are few cars there is often little to do other than walk, but it takes only two hours to cross the island.

Beaches

To the west of the town is Liéndou, but Katsadía is more pleasant, with sandy coves and an excellent taverna in summer. Less than an hour's walk away is Platýs Gialós, a sheltered sandy bay on the north coast.

USEFUL NUMBERS
Port Authority (Léros)
tel: 0247 22224
Airport (Léros)
tel: 0247 22277
Tourist information
(Leipsoí) tel: 0247 41250

ROBINSON CRUSOE ISLANDS
There are a few tiny islands near Leipsoí which can sometimes be reached from there, or more often by boat from Pátmos. Arkoí has about 25 inhabitants and a few rooms for rent. Maráthi has some lovely empty beaches and tavernas rent rooms here, but boats are very erratic. Agathónisi has two villages and a guest house providing lunch and dinner. The population makes a living from goat herding and fishing.

The sheltered and undeveloped bay at Platýs Gialós

Dodecanese

The sunken crater of Nísyros volcano is like a dramatic grey and brown moonscape

USEFUL NUMBERS
Tourist Information
(Pátmos waterfront, *open* daily in summer
7.30 am–9.30 pm)
tel: 0247 31666
Enetikon Travel (Nísyros; for information and map of walking trails)
tel: 0242 31180
Port Authority (Nísyros)
tel: 0242 31222

ST JOHN THE DIVINE
The Roman emperor Domitian, who banished John the Theologian to Pátmos in AD 95, made the island famous forever. The only mention in the Book of Revelation of the saint's stay on Pátmos is: 'I dwelled in an island which is called Pátmos, as to preach the word of God and have faith in the martyrdom suffered by Jesus Christ.' A writer named Prochorus, who claimed to have been St John's disciple but is now considered to have lived a few centuries later, wrote the eventful *Travels and Miracles of St John*, both filled with fantastic stories and adventures.

CONNECTIONS
Nísyros has ferry links with Kós, Rhodes, Kálymnos, Sými, Kastellórizo, Tílos, Piréas, Astypálaia, Páros, Náxos, Sýros, Léros and Leipsoí. A summer hydrofoil service runs to Kós, Rhodes, Tílos and Sými and another to Kálymnos.

NÍSYROS

Day-trippers from Kós invade the island to visit its volcano, but drinking water is scarce, so Nísyros cannot support large numbers of visitors. However, it manages very well without the dubious benefits of mass tourism, deriving its prosperity from its rich volcanic soil and from the quarrying of pumice and gypsum on the neighbouring islet of Gyalí.

▶▶▶ Mandráki   144B3
Mandráki is a jewel of a harbour with fine whitewashed houses and brightly coloured wooden balconies. The narrow streets are overlooked by two castles: the highest, **Palaíokastro▶▶** is a stunning 6th-century BC Doric bastion with thick Cyclopean walls. Below it, the Knights' Castle contains the **monastery of Panagía Spilianí▶▶**, its much-venerated icon of the Virgin usually covered with gold and silver offerings. A house nearby has been converted into the **Historical and Popular Museum▶**.

▶▶▶ Nikiá   144B3
Nikiá is set dramatically on the rim of the volcanic crater, while the nearby **monastery of Ágios Ioánnis Theológos▶** offers another spectacular angle. Neighbouring Emporeió was abandoned until foreigners and Athenians started restoring the old houses. From Nikiá a path descends to the crater floor, where there is still volcanic activity – occasional bubbles are seen and the sulphurous smell is often overpowering. Subterranean rumbling noises, according to legend, are the groans of the giant Polyvotis, who was crushed when Poseidon threw at him a huge lump of rock wrenched from the island of Kós.

Beaches
The town beach is not very pleasant, but nearby Hohláki beach, covered in volcanic stones, has clear water. Further east, the spa of Loutrá has hot mineral springs which are reputed to have healing properties for sufferers from rheumatism and arthritis. Just beyond it, White Beach is often crowded with guests from the adjoining hotel. The best beach is Páloi which has the advantage of a wonderful taverna.

CONVENTS
In addition to the monasteries, the Chóra has over 40 churches and convents in and around the town. Try to see the 17th-century Convent of Zoodóchos Pigí, which is usually open in the mornings and early evening and has some excellent frescos. The Convent of the Evangelismos is signposted to the west of the town and is open daily 9–11am.

CONNECTIONS
Ferry services from Pátmos operate to Piréas, Léros, Kálymnos, Leipsoí, Rhodes, Sámos, Kós, Léros, Ikaría, Agathónisi, Lésvos, Thessaloníki, Crete, Sými, Tílos and Rafína. Hydrofoils go to Ikaría, Léros, Kálymnos, Kós, Sámos and Leipsoí in summer, when excursion boats also serve Sámos, Leipsoí, Kós, Arkoí and Maráthi.

161

PÁTMOS

This unique and beautiful island has managed to keep a happy balance between maintaining its old religious and monastic traditions and welcoming the 'right' kind of visitor. It is a sacred island where, according to tradition, St John the Divine had the revelation described in the Bible's Book of Revelation. Its other attractions are beautiful beaches and a lively social scene.

▶▶▶ Pátmos Town (Chóra)   144A4

The houses and monasteries of the island capital loom dramatically from their steep cliff over Skála, the harbour. A bus travels between the two several times a day but the walk up is much more spectacular, either along the road or up the old cobbled path. Many of the wonderful old houses in Pátmos Town have been restored by residents, who fiercely guard the tranquillity of the place. The town looks compact but contains no fewer than 40 churches and monasteries in its narrow alleys. The most famous is undoubtedly the **monastery of St John**▶▶▶ (*Open* Wed, Fri, Sat 8–2; Mon, Tue, Thu, Sun 8–2 and 4–6. *Admission free*, moderate entrance fee for museum/treasury). Founded in 1088 by the monk Christodoulos, the monastery was built as a fortress to protect it from pirates. Although much of it is closed to the public, there is still plenty to see. The outer narthex has striking 17th-century frescoes depicting the life of St John. The refectory has a long stone table with spaces for storing plates and cutlery and there is a bakery, part of the original building. The museum/treasury dis-

The Treasury of the Monastery of St John contains the most important monastic collection in Greece after the one at Mount Áthos

plays only part of the monastery's rich collection of icons, manuscripts and religious artifacts. Halfway between Skála and Pátmos Town, the **monastery of the Apocalypse**▶▶ (*Open* Mon, Wed, Fri 8–2 and 4–6, Tue, Thu, Sat, Sun 8–2. *Admission free*) is built around the cave where the saint is said to have heard God's voice, which caused a triple fissure in the rock.

USEFUL NUMBERS

Port Authority tel: 0241 28888
Airport information tel: 0241 83214/83200
Hertz Rent-a-Car (Rhodes Town) tel: 0241 21819; (Rhodes Airport) tel: 0241 92902; (Líndos) tel: 0244 31347
Tourist information: EoT/National Tourist Organisation of Greece (information on hotels and private accommodations; corner of Odós Makariou and Papagoú; *open* Mon–Fri 8–3) tel: 0241 23255
City of Rhodes Tourist Office, (information about tours, buses, ferries, hotels, etc. Plateía Rimíni; *open* Mon–Fri, 9–6, Sat 9–12) tel: 0241 35945
Tourist Police (next to EoT) tel: 0241 27423
Many countries have a consul or honorary consul on Rhodes; check with the tourist office for phone numbers and addresses.

THE COLOSSAL LEGEND

The Colossus – the legendary bronze statue, more than 30m high, which was one of the Seven Wonders of the Ancient World – was a symbol of Rhodes's wealth and power. The sculptor Chares is said to have worked on it for 12 years before killing himself in despair after discovering that some of his calculations were wrong. The work was completed around 292 BC by another sculptor, Laches. The statue stood in place for only 65 years before it was brought down by an earthquake. The pieces lay on the ground for hundreds of years before they were taken away to Syria where they were probably melted down. At the harbour entrance two columns with a stag and a doe mark the place where the Colossus is believed to have stood.

▶▶ **Skála**   *144A4*

Unlike Pátmos Town, hanging above the harbour halfway to heaven, Skála, Pátmos's port of arrival, seems to be devoted to the more worldly of pleasures. In July and August the town is overrun by scantily dressed day-trippers, but for the rest of the year an air of sophistication pervades the simple waterfront cafés, where well-heeled visitors and long-time residents sip coffee. Most visitors head for the beaches or make their way to the monastery.

Beaches

Pátmos has excellent beaches. The town beach is sandy but unexceptional and boats go to the better beaches further away. Méloi, the next beach along (15 minutes' walk), has a good taverna and is pleasant but quite crowded. More secluded is the sandy cove of Agriolivádo, while its neighbour, Kámpos Beach, is the most developed on the island. Lámpi in the north is one of the most beautiful beaches, famous for its multicolored stones. On the other side of Skála, Grígos, reached by bus, gets crowded, but from there a 30-minute walk crosses the island to Psilí Ámmos, a splendid sandy beach which has an area where nudism is tolerated. Many residents prefer the (often windy) beaches of Léfkes, in the northwest, for their isolation and rough beauty.

RÓDOS (RHODES)

Excellent beaches, rich history and a wonderful climate have made Rhodes one of the most popular Greek islands. Most visitors come for the sea and the sun, but the historic monuments reward close inspection and the countryside inland, away from the often commercialised resorts, can be truly entrancing.

▶▶▶ **Rhodes Town**   *163C4*

Rhodes Town is divided into two main areas, the Old and the New Town. The much bigger New Town, which surrounds the medieval town, is a mainly residential area with many hotels, especially near the town beach and the yacht harbour, Mantráki, whose entrance was famously (but briefly) spanned by the enormous Colossus of Rhodes (see panel). **Monte Smith▶**, to the southwest of the New Town, is the site of the 5th-century BC Hellenistic acropolis. Little remains on the hill (which was renamed after a British admiral) apart from a restored theatre, a stadium and a few columns of the Temple of Apollo, but it is a popular place for joggers. On the northern tip of the island is the **Aquarium▶** (*Open* daily 9–9. *Admission charge*), which offers an interesting display of Mediterranean marine life.

The most exciting sights are in the Old Town, an historic monument in its own right and designated by UNESCO as a World Heritage site. The easiest way to enter this medieval maze for the first time is from Mantráki Harbour through **Pýli Eleftherías** (**Liberty Gate**), which leads to **Plateía Sýmis**.

The excellent **Mouseío Archaiologikó** (**Archaeological Museum**)▶▶ (Plateía Mouseío. *Open* Tue–Fri 8–7, Sat–Sun 8–3, Mon 12.30–7. *Admission charge*) offers a chance to see the Knights' Hospital, in which it is housed. The collection consists mainly of Hellenistic sculpture

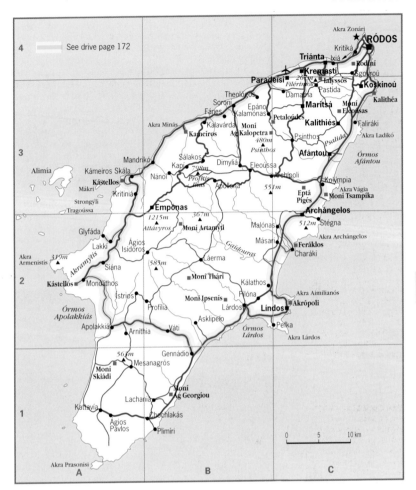

including a striking statue of Aphrodite, some fine funeral steles and 5th- and 6th-century pottery. Close by, in Plateía Argyrokástrou, is the **Decorative Arts Collection▶** (*Open* Tue–Sun 8.30–3. *Admission charge*), which displays woodwork, furniture and tiles saved from old houses. The **Mouseío Vizantinó (Byzantine Museum)▶▶** (Plateía Mouseío. *Open* Tue–Sun 8.30–3. *Admission charge*), housed in the grand 11th-century Knights' Cathedral, has a superb collection of icons from the 5th to the 18th centuries; evocative medieval religious music is played in the background.

The heavily restored **Odós Ippotón (Street of the Knights)▶▶▶** leads from **Plateía Mouseío (Museum Square)** to the Palace. This lovely cobbled street is lined with the Inns of the medieval Order of the Knights of St John which functioned as clubs and meeting places and were divided by languages ('Tongues') or countries (see panel).

On top of the hill is the **Paláti Ippotón (Palace of the Grand Masters)▶▶▶** (*Open* Tue–Fri 8–7, Sat–Sun 8–3, Mon 12.30–7. *Admission charge; free* Sun). The original 14th-century palace, a wonder of medieval architecture, stood

ODOS IPPOTON (STREET OF THE KNIGHTS)
Starting from Plateía Mouseío, the inn next to the museum shop was the Spanish House. Beyond it stands the 16th-century Inn of the Order of the Tongue of Italy. Opposite was the Inn of England, destroyed and rebuilt several times. The French Language Institute is housed in the Inn of France, built in 1492. Past the arch over the street, on the right, is the Inn of the Tongue of Provence, while facing opposite is the Inn of the Tongue of Spain.

WALK ON THE WALLS
Access to Rhodes Town's magnificent fortified walls can only be gained by taking an organised walking tour. These depart from the entrance to the Paláti Ippotón (Palace of the Grand Masters) on Tuesdays and Saturdays at 2.30. The walls are 5km long, but the walk is only 1.5km and takes about 90 minutes. The Knights worked on these walls for many years and in some places they are 12m thick. Each stretch was called a curtain and it was up to every different Tongue (see page 163) to defend its curtain.

One of the most picturesque streets in Rhodes Old Town, the beautifully restored Street of the Knights

SON ET LUMIÈRE
The history of Rhodes at the time of the Knights is told in an interesting '*Íchos kai Fos*' (sound and light) show which takes place in the Municipal Park on Plateía Riminí. The show, in several languages, has two or three performances nightly from April to October. For more information check the board outside or call the box office (tel: 0241 36795).

until the 19th century, when it was first damaged by the earthquake in 1851 and, five years later, ruined by an explosion. The Italians started to restore it in 1939 as a summer palace for Mussolini and King Victor Emmanuel III, but not without removing most of its character. The first floor, a series of rather dull state rooms, contains fine mosaics from Kós and some good Renaissance furniture. The superb ground-floor exhibits explain the importance of Rhodes throughout its 2,400 years of history.

There is evidence all over the Old Town of the Ottoman occupation, which started in 1522 and lasted over 300 years. **Odós Sokrátous**, now very much geared to the souvenir shopper, formed the heart of the Turkish bazaar. No 76 is still a lovely Turkish-style coffee-house where men play *tavli* (backgammon).

At the end of Sokrátous is the stripy **Tzamí Suleïman** (**Suleiman Mosque**) with, opposite, the **Tourkikí Vivliothíki** (**Turkish Library**). There are mosques and masjids all over town (see Walk opposite), some of them still used by the Turkish-speaking minority.

The 16th-century **Bánio (Turkish Bath)▶▶** (Plateía Ariónos. *Open* Tue–Fri 11–7, Sat 8–6 but check times for men/women. *Admission charge*. Take your own soap and towels) was once considered one of the finest in the East. Damaged during World War II, it has been restored and is now in use again. The eastern part of the Old Town once had a flourishing **Jewish Quarter▶▶**, with a fine **Synagogue▶▶** just off Plateía Martyrón Evraïön (Square of the Jewish Martyrs).

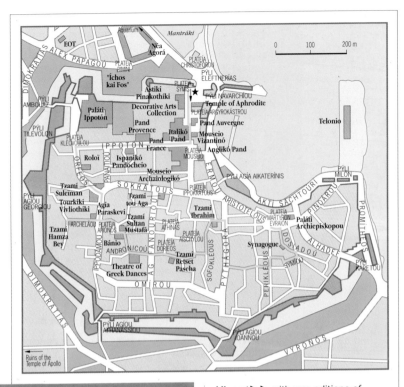

Walk

Rhodes Old Town

This walk meanders through narrow arched lanes and past attractive squares with little chapels, mosques and even a synagogue. Although not all the monuments will be open, the best time to do the walk is late afternoon, when the light softens the colours and a breeze cools the town (allow two to three hours).

Walk south from Plateía Sýmis and turn right onto **Odós Ippotón** (**Street of the Knights**)▶▶▶. Walk up past the **Paláti Ippotón** (**Palace of the Grand Masters**)▶▶▶ into the bazaar area and turn left onto the tree-lined Odós Orféos. To the left is the **Roloï**▶ (Clock Tower) and to the right, at No. 44, is the interesting 18th-century **Tourkikí Vivliothíki** (**Turkish Library**)▶▶ with rare editions of the Koran and finely illustrated manuscripts. Just past the library, by the pink **mosque, Tzamí Suleïman**▶, turn right onto Odós Ippodámou. Turn right again after the 15th-century **church of Agía Paraskeví**▶ (on the right), to see the elegant minaret of the mosque **Tzamí Hamza Bey**▶. Return to Ippodámou and go straight ahead via Odós Archeláou to Plateía Ariónos and another mosque. Turn left onto Odós Androníkou, then right at Taverna Nisyros and into the alleyway, immediately left, going to Plateía Dorioús. Past the fountain turn left onto Plateía Aíschylou and left again between two tavernas towards the **mosque, Tzamí Ibrahim**▶. To the right Odós Pythagorá goes under a beautiful arch, then turns left past walled gardens and vines. At Odós Perikléous turn left, follow the bend in the street to Odós Symíou, then turn left again onto Odós Dosiádou with the **Synagogue**▶▶ on the left. At the end of the street turn left towards Plateía Martyrón Evraïón.

RHODIAN SPECIALITIES
Rhodes is definitely the gastronomic centre of the Dodecanese, with a cuisine that has always been influenced by the East. Franks, Turks, Jews and Armenians all made an impact and Rhodian food often seems closer to Middle Eastern cuisine than to the Greek kitchen. Among the island's specialities are fish baked with *tahini* (sesame paste) sauce and a *pilaf* with seafood. A few restaurants serve a wide variety of fresh seafood: molluscs, mussels and even oysters, especially those from Kastellórizo.

► Archángelos 163C2

This large, pleasant village, overlooked by a crumbling fortress, was until recently hidden by its citrus orchards; it now risks disappearing under the weight of package tourism. The two churches of Archángelos Gavriél and Archángelos Michaíl are beautiful and the church of **Ágios Theodóros** has 14th-century frescos. Nearby are **Charáki**, a quieter fishing harbour and the ruins of **Feráklos**, once one of the strongest castles on Rhodes.

►► Asklipeío 163B2

This hill village once had a school for the followers of Asklepios, but there are no classical remains. Instead, the 11th-century **church of Koímisis Theotókou►►** contains some remarkable and well-preserved 17th-century frescos, unusual in that they are like cartoon-strip versions of Old Testament stories, extending all over the church.

►► Eleoússa 163B3

The monastery of Eleoússa, on the slopes of the Profítis Ilías ridge, has been taken over by the military, but happily the nearby **church of Ágios Nikólaos Fountoúki►►** (St Nicholas of the Hazelnuts) is still open to the public. This Byzantine church, in the shape of a perfect Greek cross, has fine Cretan-style frescos from the 13th to the 15th centuries. Surrounded by lovely pine woods and commanding great views, it is a favourite weekend picnic spot for locals. Several dirt tracks lead to the summit of Profítis Ilías, where an almost-abandoned Italian summer station lies hidden in the forest. It is possible to stay at the chalet hotel Elafos – about as close as you can get to Switzerland in the islands.

►► Empónas 163B3

Empónas is a quiet traditional village in the heart of the wine-producing region of western Rhodes. A two-hour trail leads to the summit of the island's highest peak, Mount Attávyros (1,215m), from where the views stretch (on a clear day) as far as Crete. The village is also known for its fine folk dances: in summer, daily folk-dance tours arrive from Rhodes Town.

►►► Eptá Pigés (Seven Springs) 163C3

Open: Apr–Nov daily 9–6. Admission charge
Buses: Rhodes Town–Kolýmpia, several daily
This lovely oasis, one of the island's most popular beauty spots, can be reached by a fine 3km walk from Kolýmpia. There is a small man-made lake for a cool swim and a good taverna overlooking the stream.

► Faliráki 163C3

Faliráki has what many people want from Rhodes: a long sandy beach, every imaginable watersport facility and a nonstop exuberant nightlife. It is consequently very popular with the younger crowds. An unusual alternative to the beach is the **Faliráki Snake House►** (*Open daily 11 am– 11 pm, but closed during lunchtime. Admission charge*). Nostalgics will find nearby **Kalithéa►** more to their taste. The Italians built this spa town in the 1920s in pure Hollywood style. Today it is dilapidated and almost completely abandoned.

The Monastery of Filérimos, used by Suleïman the Magnificent as his base for the take-over of the island

▶▶ Ialyssós 163C3

Tourist developments on the approach to Ialyssós do little to honour the past of this once important city – one of the three powerful city-states (with Líndos and Kameíros) which together founded, in 408 BC, a new common capital, Rhodes. Very little remains of the classical site at Ialyssós, but the view over Rhodes harbour and the sea to the north, south and west explains its strategic importance. The Knights, who began their invasion of the island here, built the Church of Our Lady of Filérimos as a military bastion, beside and on top of the vestiges of a 3rd-century BC **Temple of Athena▶**. On the walk down from the temple there is a fine 4th-century BC fountain. The Italians built their **monastery of Filérimos▶** (*Open* Tue–Sun 8.30–5. *Admission charge*) on the same site.

Kameíros (below) united in the 5th century BC with Líndos and Ialyssós to found the powerful state of Rhodes

▶▶▶ Kameíros 163B3

Open: Tue–Sun 8.30–5. Admission charge, free Sun
Two morning buses from West Side Bus Station, Rhodes Town
One of the best-preserved classical Greek towns, set on a beautiful hillside above the sea, Kameíros lay forgotten under the dust until it was rediscovered in 1859. Once a large and important city, tracing its origins back into pre-historic times, the site was inhabited until the 4th century, when it was abandoned; this has undoubtedly contributed to its remarkable state of preservation.

The upper part of the site was probably used for religious rituals and the two water basins which supplied the city are still visible. The lower valley has clearly distinguishable foundations of houses, streets, temples and an *agora*, which give a good impression of what the city must have looked like.

Finds from Kameíros are on display in the Archaeological Museum in Rhodes Town (see page 162) and also in London's British Museum.

WINE ON RHODES
The house of Emery, one of the leading winemakers on Rhodes, produce their much appreciated Villare wine in Empónas, the island's main wine-growing area. Most vineyards are exclusively planted with the Athiri grape, which is indigenous to the area and has proved difficult to transplant. The Emery Winery at Empónas offers free tasting as well as an opportunity to purchase direct from the producer (tel: 0246 41208. *Open* Mon–Fri until 3pm).

For 200 years, the Knights of St John ruled Rhodes as their private domain, making its name famous throughout the Mediterranean for the strength of its defenses and the advancement of its society, and making its harbour one of the most important gateways to the East.

Right: the shields on the walls of the Castle of the Knights of St John

168

MAINTAINING ORDER
Five years after losing Rhodes to the Turks, the Knights were given Malta by the Emperor Charles V. When Malta was taken by Napoleon Bonaparte in 1798, the Knights practically ceased to exist. They have, however, survived in Rome in much reduced circumstances and in Britain, mainly as the St John Ambulance Association which has a charter to carry out ambulance and other charitable work, not so very different from the original hospital duties the Knights carried out in 11th-century Jerusalem.

The Order of St John In 1099, when the Crusaders captured Jerusalem from the Seljuk Turks, the Knights Hospitalers of St John, originally a militaristic, religious order, became responsible for running the city's hospital for sick Christian pilgrims. In 1290, after 200 turbulent years, the Crusaders were finally forced out of the Holy Land. The Knights Hospitalers fought to the end but when Acre fell to the Mamluks from Cairo, even the Knights were obliged to flee. In 1309 they captured the city of Rhodes and, soon after, some neighbouring islands. Until 1522 they controlled what was, to all intents and purposes, an independent state.

The order of the Order The most obvious characteristic of the Order was its rigid hierarchy. Members of the lowest level of the Order were known as sergeants. The sons of freemen, they helped the Knights to run and defend their small empire and to look after the sick and needy. Above them were the Chaplains – the priests of the Order – and higher still were the Knights, drawn from the ranks of Europe's aristocracy and responsible for all administrative and military matters.

One of the gates into the walled medieval city of Rhodes

The Knights' Tongues Members of the Order were divided according to nationality as well as rank. There were seven 'Tongues' (referring to the languages spoken) at the outset: Provence, Auvergne, France, Italy, Aragon, England and Germany. Castile was admitted in the 15th century. The leaders of the Tongues sat on the Council, headed by the Grand Master. As supreme ruler of Rhodes, elected for life, he held great power, for the Order controlled not only Rhodes and most of the Dodecanese but also large estates across Europe.

Life on Rhodes Under the Knights, Rhodes became rich, shipping and trading imported perfumes, spices, wool and silk, oil and wine as well the island's products – mostly

sugar and soap. As well as commodities, the Knights also looked after transport and their fleet protected the sea passages as well as carrying merchandise. Rhodes under the Knights was also an important conduit for knowledge and culture: everything from the study of history to the painting of icons was encouraged.

The siege Rhodes thrived for as long as the Knights controlled the sea passages essential for trade, but throughout the 15th century the shadow of the Turks grew longer. After 1453, when Constantinople fell to the Turks, the Knights hurriedly strengthened their own fortifications. After many smaller skirmishes and attacks, on 23 May 1480, a Turkish fleet of 170 ships sailed to Rhodes, 100,000 soldiers disembarked and the city was besieged. After many fights, some within the fortifications, the Knights inflicted such losses on the Turks that the siege was lifted on 17 August and for some years the Knights were left alone. On 26 June 1522, a Turkish army of 100,000 again besieged the city. This time the Knights were less prepared: inside the town were fewer than 7,500 soldiers, only 290 of them Knights. The fighting was lengthy and bloody, but the Knights finally admitted defeat and negotiated a surrender with the Turkish Sultan Suleïman. On 1 January 1523, the Grand Master, the Knights and up to 5,000 islanders sailed out of Rhodes and into history.

The Knights' legacy There is no escaping the Knights' legacy, either in Rhodes Town or elsewhere on the island: the great stone forts, churches and palaces are reminders of one of the island's most glorious periods. In the museums, collections of icons, manuscripts and other objects, both for daily use and for special rituals, are an equally eloquent testimony to the Knights' cultural legacy.

The splendid courtyard in the Palace of the Grand Masters, reconstructed by the Italians as a summer home for Mussolini

THE KNIGHTS AND THE JEWS
Whatever social benefits the Order brought to Rhodes (and there were many), justice for minorities was not one of them. Subjugated from the beginning of the reign of the Knights, Jews were always considered a problem and on 9 January 1502 an edict was issued by the Order to provide a solution: Jews must either be baptised or leave the island within 40 days.

CHOOSING THE MASTER
When a Grand Master died, a commander was chosen by the Order. He had the right to name 13 electors, who then met to choose the new Grand Master.

Damp has damaged the 14th- and 15th-century frescoes in the monastery of Láerma, but they are still exquisite

ANCIENT LÍNDOS
Archaeologists have found remains showing that Líndos was already inhabited in the 3rd millennium BC. The city's importance grew as it became richer from its many colonies, the most important of which were Parthenope (Naples) and Gela in Sicily, founded in the 7th century BC. It was the only city on Rhodes with natural twin harbours. Cleobulos, its 6th-century BC ruler, was so enlightened that he was considered to be one of the Seven Sages, respected by all Greeks. After Rhodes Town gained importance, Líndos remained a religious centre and St Paul is said to have stopped here on his way to Rome.

▶▶ **Kritiniá**   *163A3*

Near the quiet village of Kritiniá, founded by Cretans, towers an impressive fortress built by the Knights. On closer inspection, the **kástro** is only a shell but still worth a visit as its masonry is quite intact and the fantastic views explain its strategic importance. Not far away is the striking village of **Siána** in the middle of the forest, famous for its local alcoholic brew called *souma* and for its sage honey. **Monólithos**, the main village in the area, takes its name from the 250m-high single rock on which a Crusader castle is dramatically perched.

▶▶ **Láerma**   *163B2*

The **church of Ágios Giórgios▶** in Láerma has some 14th-century frescos, but it is for the **Thári monastery▶▶** that most visitors make their way here. This is the oldest monastery on the island, although its community was only recently reestablished, by a few monks from Pátmos. The fine frescos can be hard to make out, but they date from the 14th and 15th centuries. The monastery is said to have been founded after a princess, who had been kidnapped by pirates, had a visitation from the Archangel Gabriel. The princess promised the archangel that if he helped her out of her predicament, she would build as many monasteries in his honour as her gold ring, thrown from her hand, would make circles. As the princess lost her ring soon after being freed, her family built only this one monastery.

▶▶▶ **Líndos**   *163C2*

Líndos, Rhodes's second tourist attraction and the jewel in its crown, offers a unique view into the island's long history. Although the town's stunning beauty is protected as a National Monument, a lot of its atmosphere has been lost to commercialism – in summer it gets very crowded. The town has a Byzantine **church of Panagía Líndou**▶▶, with fine 18th-century frescos and elegant well-preserved merchants' houses from the 15th to the 18th centuries, many of them restored out for renting out to tourists.

Líndos was the most important of the three ancient cities of Rhodes and visitors still head first for the ancient **acropolis**▶▶▶ and the **Knights' castle**▶▶▶ (*Open* Mon 2.30–6.40, Tue–Fri 8–6.40, Sat–Sun 8.30–2.40. *Admission charge; free* Sun). All castles should surely look exactly like this – imposing and impregnable, perched on a perfect rock and dwarfing the town in its shadow. The path leading up to the castle is now lined with souvenir stalls and women selling handicrafts, but near the top is a podium carved in the rock which once supported a statue of a priest of Poseidon.

Further on is a stoa of Athena Lindia, the patroness of the ancient city. Higher up, inside the fortress, the small 4th-century BC **Temple of Athena** is under scaffolding. The Knights recognised the excellent strategic position of the acropolis and built their citadel over it.

▶▶ Petaloúdes (Valley of the Butterflies)   *163C3*

Open: Jun–Sep daily 9–6. Admission charge
Morning buses from West Side bus station, Rhodes New Town
Visitors continue to flock to this thickly forested gorge covered with pine and storax trees. The resin of the storax tree, which smells like vanilla and is used to make frankincense, attracts millions of Quadrina 'butterflies' – actually Jersey tiger moths – to the valley in summer. The population of these black-and-white moths has seriously declined in recent years: the poor creatures are continually disturbed by hordes of visitors clapping their hands to make them fly up in a cloud, so they can take that special souvenir photograph.

REFLECTIONS ON RHODES
'In Rhodes the days drop as softly as fruit from trees. Some belong to the dazzling ages of Cleobolus and the tyrants, some to the gloomy Tiberius, some to the Crusaders. They follow each other in scales and modes too quickly almost to be captured in the nets of form.'
Lawrence Durrell, *Reflections on a Marine Venus* (London, 1953)

Petaloúdes is a popular family excursion and often nicknamed 'the Valley of the Tour Buses'

Drive

The stunning view over the Castle of Monólithos and the bay

The Knights' castles

This is a drive from Rhodes Town along the less-visited west coast to sites mostly associated with the Knights of St John. The route offers great coastal views, spectacular inland scenery and several opportunities for bathing and sightseeing. (See the map on page 163. Up to around 200km; allow a whole day.)

Leave Rhodes Town from Mantráki harbour and head south for **Ialyssós▶▶** (9km, see page 167). Follow signs left to **Filérimos▶** (5km), a hilltop (267m) with wonderful views, ancient ruins, a Knights' church and a monastery, restored in 1931. Return to Ialyssós and turn left, following the coast for 25km to Kameíros. Turn left at the sign for **Ancient Kameíros▶▶▶** (see page 167). Heading south for 13km, the road passes several exposed gravel beaches. Ignore the sign for 'Johnny's to the Beach' to reach the new access road to **Kritiniá Castle▶▶** (see page 170), a fine ruin with excellent views of land and sea. Continue on the main road to Kritiniá (3.5km) and follow signs for Empónas, then (3.5km) for Siána on an older road through pine-clad hills. Some 5km later, a sign to **Glyfáda** beach gives no warning that it is 6km away, mostly on dirt track. The beach is minimal, but there is a 13th-century tower and an old-style taverna offering garden produce, home-made wine and *souma*, a clear, powerful spirit.

From the main road, continue to **Siána** (7km), a quiet hill village noted for its sage honey (available by the roadside) and then to **Monólithos▶** (5km), whose ruined castle is built on a rock high above the sea, with views, on a clear day, to Chálki.

From here, either retrace the coast road back to Rhodes Town or continue south to Apolakkiá and cross to the east coast, making time to visit **Líndos▶▶▶** (see pages 170–1), **Archángelos▶** and Feráklos (see page 166).

▶ Tsampíka
163C3

The beach at Tsampíka is wonderful, but Greek visitors usually come here for the **Tsampíka monastery▶**. The small white Byzantine church comes alive on 8 September when women climb up to it, barefoot or on their knees, to pray for fertility. If their prayers are answered, the child may be called Tsambíkos or Tsambíka.

Beaches
Rhodes has excellent beaches and clean water. The sheltered east coast is the most popular, while the west offers good windsurfing. Between Rhodes Town and Líndos the coast is well developed and often crowded; most beaches are easily accessible by car or moped and often also by bus from either town. The beach of Rhodes Town is a large sandy stretch but becomes completely packed in the summer months, as does the beach in Faliráki, which draws a younger crowd. The best spot to swim near here is Ladikó, with its pebble beach. Tsampíka has an excellent beach which draws a lot of sunbathers but has no development going on. Agía Agáthi beach near Charáki is a small, secluded sandy beach which is lovely even in summer.

The sandy beach at Líndos always seems crowded and even the nearby coves, which are generally more pleasant, attract crowds. The coast south of Líndos might belong to a different island, its beaches more deserted, wilder and more beautiful. Gennádio is a long pebble beach with deserted stretches, while Plimíri is an attractive sheltered sandy bay. Ágios Geórgios has excellent bathing and fine sand but is difficult to reach. Akra (Cape) Prasonísi, practically an island, is a paradise for windsurfers and a lovely spot to camp.

There are fewer beaches on the west coast and they are usually very windy, with rocks rather than sand. The villages west of Rhodes Town were the first to be developed for package tourism: the coast here is completely built up and tends to attract an older clientele than the other resorts on the island. Monólithos and Apolakkiá, in the south, have good and secluded pebble beaches but the sea can often get rough.

Go early if you want to be sure of a towel space on the long and sandy Rhodes Town beach

173

CONNECTIONS
Rhodes has ferry services to Piréas, Kós, Kálymnos, Sými, Pátmos, Léros, Nísyros, Páros, Náxos, Tílos, Sýros, Crete, Kárpathos, Kásos, Kasteilórizo, Thíra, Chálki, Astypálaia, Mílos, Mýkonos, Folégandros, Tínos, Sífnos, Sérifos, Leipsoí, Síkinos, Thessaloníki, Cyprus and Haifa (Israel). Excursion boats go to Sými and Marmaris (Turkey) and in summer there are hydrofoil services to Kós, Kálymnos, Sými, Nísyros and Tílos.

USEFUL NUMBERS
Port Authority (Sými)
tel: 0241 71205
Sými Tours/Olympic Airways (for information on the island and tickets)
tel: 0241 71307
Port Authority (Tílos)
tel: 0241 44350

POSTCARD SÝMI
The traditional well-kept houses of Sými are featured on many Greek postcards. The Sýmians are proud of their many ornate churches and grand mansions, proof of the island's prosperity at the end of the 19th century. Sými is under the same archaeological decree as Pátmos and Líndos, by which the restoration of old buildings and the construction of new ones is carefully regulated. Developers, together with foreign tour operators, have restored some old houses and the island is now popular with wealthy Athenians and smaller tour groups trying to avoid the crowds.

SÝMI

This small and rugged island just off the Turkish coast has a lot to offer individual travellers: well-preserved villages, good beaches and, most of all, a peaceful countryside with good walking trails.

►► Sými Town   145C3

The island's capital is, like many other port towns, divided in two: Gialós, the harbour and port of arrival and Chorió, the older town on top of the hill. Once the excursion boats have left Gialós the town becomes a tranquil place again, with several beautiful neoclassical mansions and a few shipbuilding yards – reminders of Sými's illustrious past, as a prosperous trading and sponge-fishing port. The conflicts and changing times of the 20th century brought depopulation and neglect, but recent years have seen many buildings restored and a thriving tourist industry established.

Two huge stairways, the Kalí Stráta and Kataráktes, go up to Chorió, whose attractive houses are almost Cycladic in style. The **museum**►► (*Open* Tue–Sun 10–2. *Admission charge*), housed in one of the old mansions, has good exhibits from medieval Sými and frescos from local churches. On top of the village is the **Castle of the Knights**►, built over the ancient acropolis and the lovely **church of the Panagía**►► (*Open* only during services, 7–8am daily and Sun morning), which has the best frescos on the island.

►►► Taxiárchis Michaíl
Panormítis Monastery   145C3

The principal 'sight' for visitors to Sými (and usually the first stop for excursion boats) is the vast **Panormítis monastery**► (*Open* daily 10–12.30). Very few of its treasures survived the pillaging of World War II, but the courtyard, a galleried cloister, is the most appealing part. Rooms are available for those who want to stay overnight

Until the beginning of this century, when the Kalymniots took over the sponge diving, Sými Town was wealthier and bigger than Rhodes Town

ELEPHANTS ON AN ISLAND

Archaeologists working on Tílos found a burial pit near Livádia containing the bones of what is believed to have been a herd of small mammoths. Local historians find in this the proof that all of these small Dodecanese islands were attached to the Anatolian mainland in prehistory.

WALKS ON SÝMI

There are lots of lovely walks on Sými: the one from Gialós to Kefálos passes five monasteries. A dirt road past the monastery of Panormítis leads to the monastery of Ágioi Anárgyroi and then past a hill to Ágios Ioánnis Theológos. From there a path goes to Ágios Filomónos and on to Ágios Emiliános near Kefálos (allow 6 hours to walk there and back).

An English guide organises walking tours locally. For more information contact Sými Tours (see USEFUL NUMBERS, opposite).

(only one monk is now in residence). The small museum has an eclectic collection of exhibits, from a stuffed koala bear to models of ships.

Beaches

The nearest swimming to Sými Town is at the rocky beach of Nós or, slightly further away but more attractive, the pebble beach of Emporeió. On the other side of the town is Sými's only sandy beach, at Ágios Nikólaos, which has a taverna. More secluded but beautiful coves in the south, like Maratoúnda, Nanoú and Ágios Giórgios Dissálona, can only be reached by taxi-boats or after a serious hike. The best beach, accessible only on foot, is Ágios Vassílios.

TÍLOS

Tílos, the least visited of the Dodecanese, is a small, remote and delightful island – the perfect place to get away from it all. The fertile landscape, crisscrossed by many old mule tracks, makes Tílos a pleasure for walkers.

▶ Livádia   144B2

Livádia, Tílos's minuscule harbour, has a few tavernas, hotels and rooms for rent. The only road on the island leads from here to Megálo Chorió, 7km away, but the bus is erratic. The road passes **Mikró Chorió**, the remains of a ghost village abandoned in the 1950s.

Megálo Chorió   144B3

Megálo Chorió, the island's second village, has the interesting **church of Taxiárchi Michaílis**, preserving a wall of the classical temple over which it was built. A Venetian castle looms very high on a rock over the town.

Beaches

Livádia has a long rocky beach; also good are Erestos, lost in orchards and gardens and the isolated Pláka.

CONNECTIONS

Sými and Tílos have ferry links with each other and also with Rhodes, Kós, Kálymnos, Nísyros, Kastellórizo, Léros, Pátmos, Leipsoí, Páros and Piréas. In addition, Sými has ferries to Crete, Sámos and Arkói, while Tílos is linked with Sýros and Náxos. In summer, hydrofoil services operate between the two islands and going from both to Rhodes, Kálymnos, Kós and Nísyros.

THE IONIAN ISLANDS The Ionian Islands run down the western coast of Greece with Corfu (Kérkyra), in the north, facing Albania, and Kýthira, the most southerly, some distance away from the others, off the Peloponnese. Known to Greeks as the Eptanísi (seven islands), after the principal islands (Corfu, Paxoí, Lefkáda, Kefalloniá, Itháki, Zákynthos, and Kýthira), the Ionians – with the exception of Kýthira – are united by a common history and culture. Since they stand in the southern Adriatic, in many of their towns everything from architecture to food has been influenced by the Italians. Heavier rainfall makes the islands green and fertile, and agriculture still plays its part in island life, along with fishing and transport. Tourism, of course, has an increasingly large role; several islands, most noticeably Corfu and Zákynthos, have become major international tourist destinations.

MYTHOLOGY AND EARLY HISTORY The Ionian Islands have a rich history, with early Kefallonian remains dating back to prehistoric times. The islands' earliest chronicle is

The Ionian Islands
Itháki (ΙΘΑΚΗ)
Kefalloniá
 (ΚΕΦΑΛΟΝΙΑ)
Kérkyra (Corfu)
 (ΚΕΡΚΨΡΑ)
Kýthira (ΚΥΘΗΡΑ)
Lefkáda (ΛΕΦΚΑΔΑ)
Paxoí (ΠΑΞΟΙ) and
 Antipaxoí
 (ΑΝΤΙΠΑΞΟΙ)
Zákynthos (Zánte)
 (ΖΑΚΨΝΘΟΣ)

Ionian Islands

BEST BEACHES
● Cove below the Arethoúsa Fountain (Itháki)
● Mírtos (Kefalloniá)
● Myrtiótissa (Corfu)
● Porto Katsíki (Lefkáda)
● Porto Róma (Zákynthos)
● Antipaxoí

178

INTER-ISLAND CONNECTIONS
Because so many visitors arrive on direct charter flights or on ferries from Italy, it can be frustratingly difficult to move between the islands, so island hopping, especially out of season, often involves delays and doubling-back or travelling via a mainland port.

Pages 176–7 the pure transparent water and the secluded bays of Palaiokastrítsa on Corfu are as attractive as ever
Page 176: Kýthira's unspoiled beauty and Greek atmosphere are enough of a reason for a visit

Right: a tiny islet near Corfu's airport

Homer's *Odyssey*, based on the life of Odysseus, a 12th-century BC ruler of Itháki. Odysseus, according to the poet, went to fight against Troy with men from Itháki and Kefalloniá. Corfu was the home of the renowned King Alcinoös, while Kýthira is claimed as the place where the goddess of love, Aphrodite, rose from the waves. There are remains from the Mycenaean (Bronze Age) period (c1600–1100 BC) at sites and in museums scattered throughout the islands.

The Ionians' next prominent moment came in 664 BC, when galleys from Corinth and Corfu fought the first recorded sea battle. In the 5th century BC, fighting that started between these two adversaries spread to include Athens and Sparta in the Peloponnesian Wars, at the end of which Athens's power was fatally diminished. In 31 BC the islanders witnessed another great moment in history, when Octavian (thereafter the Emperor Augustus) defeated the fleets of Mark Antony and Cleopatra at Actium, just north of Lefkáda.

The rule of Venice From the end of the Roman era to the 13th century AD, the Ionian Islands fell under Byzantine rule. When Constantinople fell to the Fourth Crusaders, the islands came under Venetian control, although the Italian Orsini family initially held only the islands of Kefalloniá, Lefkáda, Itháki, and Zákynthos, while Corfu suffered under the Greek Despots of Epirus until 1386, when the Venetians took the island by force. The Venetians remained in control of the Eptanísi for more than four centuries and made a vital contribution to the character of the islands. The fact that they were only briefly under Turkish control also distinguishes the Ionians from other islands in the Greek seas.

The Ionian state At the beginning of the 19th century the three 'Great Powers' – Britain, France, and Russia – took an interest in the Ionian Islands. Napoleon Bonaparte assumed control of them when he conquered Venice in 1797, and a treaty between Russia and Turkey bundled the islands into a short-lived republic in 1799. By 1815 the British had captured all of the islands and created an independent state under British protection and 'guided' by a British High Commissioner, based in Corfu Town. As much of the rest of Greece won its independence, so the

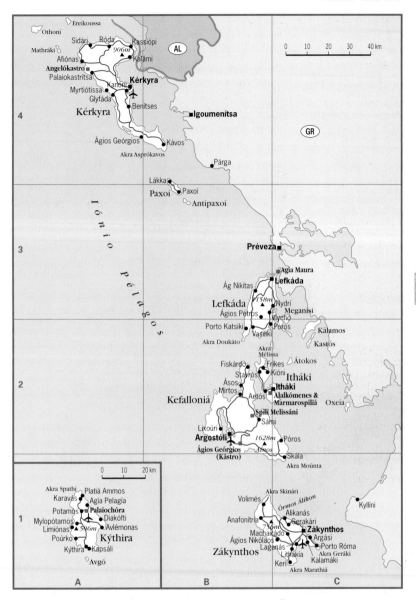

Ionian islanders struggled to be free. In 1864 the British finally agreed to unite the islands with the Greek state.

An Ionian character Of all the features that set the Ionian Islands apart from the rest of Greece, the landscape and architecture are probably the most noticeable. The lushness of the islands and their abundance of olives, fruits and flowers contrasts with many islands in the Aegean. Within the region, the music of Zákynthos, in particular its ballads or *arékias*, the earthquake-proof houses of Lefkáda, the Homeric traditions of the Ithakans and the cosmopolitan inheritance of Corfu are all distinctive.

THE IONIAN INHERITANCE
The word 'Ionian' has many applications. It is applied to one of the three orders of Greek architecture; to a mode in ancient Greek music regarded as soft or gentle; to a school of philosophy, founded by Thales of Miletus; and to a measure in poetic verse.

USEFUL NUMBER
Port Authority (Itháki
Town) tel: 0674 32909

WHERE HAVE ALL THE PEOPLE GONE?
In 1939, over 15,000 people lived on Itháki; there are now around 3,000. Mass emigration, particularly after the war and the 1953 earthquake, has left some villages, like Exoghí and Anoghí, almost abandoned. But Ithakan exiles (12,000 in Melbourne, 2,500 in Johannesburg) maintain an interest in their homeland and send money to keep up houses and churches.

ITHAKI
'... Keep Ithaka always in your mind.
Arriving there is what you're destined for.
But don't hurry the journey at all.
Better if it lasts for years, so you're old by the time you reach the island,
wealthy with all you've gained on the way,
not expecting Ithaka to make you rich.
Ithaka gave you the marvellous journey.
Without her you wouldn't have set out.
She has nothing left to give you now.
And if you find her poor, Ithaka won't have fooled you.
Wise as you will have become, so full of experience,
you'll have understood by then what these Ithakas mean.'
From Constantine Cavafy, 'Ithaka' (1911).

CONNECTIONS
Itháki has ferry links with Kefalloniá and Pátra (from Itháki Town) and with Lefkáda and Kefalloniá (from Fríkes and Píso Aetrós respectively).

ITHÁKI

Rocky severe Itháki, Homer called it. The probable homeland of the hero Odysseus is a rugged island of two distinct peninsulas joined by a narrow, hilly isthmus. Some visitors come here in search of Odysseus and yachtsmen arrive to seek out its many coves and harbours, but Itháki has been spared the worst excesses of the tourist industry, as seen on nearby Zákynthos.

►► Itháki Town (Váthi)   179C2
Badly damaged in the 1953 earthquake, the island's capital has retained few mementos of its past, but it is splendidly sited on a huge, sheltered bay entirely enclosed by hills and is still a place of some elegance. Of most interest is the **Archaeological Museum►►** (Odós Kallinikó 30. *Open* Tue–Sun 8.30–2. *Admission free*), where finds from local digs include items from Epáno Aetós and Polí Bay. Odysseus-seekers should look at item number 814, a bronze statue of the heroic wanderer.

►► Alalkómenes   179B2
The famous 19th-century German archaeologist Heinrich Schliemann (see pages 86–7) came to the slopes of Mount Aetós after finding Troy and believed this to be the site of Odysseus's palace, but the British School in Athens dug in the 1930s and could find nothing to support the theory. Archaeologists resumed digging in 1984 and have since found evidence of an important settlement going back to 1400 BC, but none of the 250,000 artifacts so far uncovered mention Odysseus.

► Marmarospiliá (Cave of the Nymphs)   179B2
Open: Tue–Sun irregular hours, usually approx 7–7
Admission charge
Local legend claims this cave, half an hour's walk from the capital, was the hiding place for Odysseus's treasure. It was certainly an ancient shrine, as suggested by the 60cm-high base on which a cult statue once stood and by the hole in the roof, claimed to be a chimney for the smoke from sacrificial burnt offerings.

► Stavrós   179B2
The main town in the north of the island has a small but excellent **Archaeological Museum►►** (*Open* Tue–Sun 9–3. *Admission free*) showing objects from excavations at nearby Polí Bay and Pelikáta, another possible site for Odysseus's palace, which fits Homer's description 'between three mountains and overlooking three seas.' On display is a terracotta mask engraved 'Dedicated to Odysseus' – one of the few pieces of archaeological evidence for a connection between Odysseus and Itháki, his reputed home.

Beaches
The sandy and pebble beach at Filiátro is accessible by boat from Itháki. The cove below the Arethoúsa Fountain (see Walk opposite) is idyllic. In the north, Polí Bay has rocky swimming, but access is easier (and there are more facilities) at Fríkes and Kióni, both attractively situated little ports with a few low-key tourist developments.

Walk

Walk across the south of Itháki to the **Arethoúsa Fountain▶▶**, where Odysseus met his swineherd Eumaus. The English poet Lord Byron thought that this walk alone was worth the journey to Itháki. There are no facilities *en route*, so take food, water and suitable clothing (approximately 6km; allow two hours).

The road to the Arethoúsa Fountain is signposted on the waterfront in Itháki Town, near the Yacht Club. The town is soon left behind as the dirt road leads into a valley of olive groves. After 15 minutes or so the road splits, but the Arethoúsa path is still signposted. It is easy to imagine

The Arethoúsa Fountain

Odysseus or Telemachus hurrying into town along a path like this, between vines, olive and fig trees. Another 40 minutes of gentle climbing gives wonderful views back to Itháki's bay. Then a signposted track leads down the hill to the sea. The Arethoúsa Fountain, as Homer describes it, beneath the rock of Korax (the Raven), gives some shade and, usually, clean water. Continue down the path to the lovely cove below for a welcome swim.

181

Walk

Sites associated with Odysseus are the theme of this walk in northern Itháki, crossing the island from east to west (5–6km; allow two hours).

Leaving Fríkes waterfront at the northern end, a road leads up the fertile valley to Láchos. At the next village, Platrithias, a right turn after the playground leads to the (unmarked) archaeological site known locally as 'Homer's School' (although there is no evidence that Homer visited Itháki). The most easily identified ruins belong to the Byzantine church of St Athanasius.

Continuing along the main road towards Stavrós, another right turn leads 2km up to Exogí, a remote village with excellent views from its belltower. Five minutes further on the main road, a left turn on Odós Aredátis leads to Stavrós **Archaeological Museum▶▶**, while the next left turn leads to the ongoing excavations at Pelikáta (see under Stavrós, opposite). A few minutes further brings you to **Stavrós▶** (shops and cafés) and another road back downhill to Fríkes.

Fríkes to Stavrós

Top right: Follow the Odysseus trail!
Above: The small port of Fríkes on the northeastern coast

Of all the great stories that have survived from antiquity, Homer's Odyssey *is among the most popular. While the* Iliad *tells us much about Greek warfare, the* Odyssey *provides an insight into Greek society. And as if that were not enough, it is also a great story.*

ODYSSEUS ON ITHAKI

'My home is Ithaca, that bright conspicuous isle, with Mount Neriton rising clear out of the quivering forests. Round it lie many islands clustering close, Dulichion and Samê and woody Zacynthos. My island lies low, last of all in the sea to westwards, the others away towards the dawn and the rising sun. It is rough, but a nurse of good lads; I tell you there is no sweeter sight any man can see than his own country.' Homer, *Odyssey* Book IX

182

Homer, whose epics continue to confuse scholars: are they fact or fiction?

Odysseus In the *Iliad* (see pages 240–1), Homer describes the events of the Trojan War, in which an alliance of Greeks, among them Odysseus, the king of Itháki, set out to avenge the kidnapping of Helen by the Trojan prince Paris. Odysseus, Homer tells us, is 'never at a loss' and it is he who devises the wooden horse which ultimately leads to the downfall of Troy. After Troy is sacked, the army disperses. But Odysseus's trials are not over yet, for he blinds a Cyclops, the son of the seagod Poseidon and the god is determined to punish him.

Travels and homecoming Poseidon is determined that Odysseus shall not reach his home. After wandering for many years throughout the Mediterranean (some say he even crossed the Atlantic), Odysseus is trapped on an island (perhaps Corfu) by the nymph Calypso until his ally, the goddess Athena, forces the great god Zeus to intervene and Odysseus is released. But Poseidon has not finished with him. Next there is shipwreck and seduction, while at Odysseus's palace on Itháki his faithful wife Penelope is being courted by 108 eligible men from the islands: while she stalls, they slowly eat away at Odysseus's wealth. But with Athena's help Odysseus does return home, bringing with him enough treasure to restore the family's fortunes. Arriving in his house in disguise, Odysseus and his son Telemachus take their revenge on Penelope's suitors, killing every one of them.

Homer Little is known about the poet called Homer, but this has not deterred speculation ever since the 2nd-century Greek historian Herodotus wrote Homer's biography. Homer is believed to have lived around 800 BC, 400 years after Odysseus. Where he came from is not known, though several islands – including Itháki and Chíos – now claim him. His name is said to mean 'cannot see', from which comes the tradition that he was a blind poet. Not that his eyes would have helped him in telling the story, for in Homer's time epics like this were consigned to memory. It would not have been written down until several centuries after his death, perhaps in Alexandria or another centre of learning.

But is it true? Unlike the story of the *Iliad*, which is supported to some extent by excavations at Troy, the story of Odysseus's 20-year journey home is not borne out by archaeology. He is believed to have reached Itháki in 1174 BC, but so far, although artifacts bearing the name of Odysseus have been found – suggesting that he was worshipped on Itháki long after his death – no physical evidence has yet been uncovered to prove the events that Homer describes. Professor Sarantis Symeonoglou of Washington University, St Louis, Missouri, who has been digging on Itháki since 1984, explains it like this: 'There are those who believe Homer – and believe that this [Itháki] is the island he was talking about – and there are those who think it's all a myth. I believe in it. Of course I do...'

In the absence of proof...

Until more tangible evidence for Odysseus's story comes to light, we only have Homer's text, as it has come down to us, to go by. Although there are inconsistencies and inaccuracies in describing the island – for instance, he calls Itháki the most exposed of its group of islands, whereas it is sheltered behind Kefalloniá – some experts point out that Homer was a storyteller, not a conscientious historian. Still, his description of the location of Odysseus's palace is exact enough – beneath three peaks and within sight of three seas – and both Alalkómenes near Váthi and Pelikáta near Stavrós fit that description.

CAVE OF NYMPHS

'[Here] is a beautiful dusky cave, sacred to the nymphs who are called Naiads. In the cave are great bowls and two-handled jars of stone and in these the bees hive their honey. There are also tall poles of stone like the beams of a loom, where the nymphs weave webs of sea-purple wonderful to behold...'

Homer, *Odyssey*
Book VIII

Left: A precious early edition of Homer's masterpiece, the Odyssey

Below: Odysseus forced out the eye of Polyphemus, the most famous of Cyclops, after making him drunk with wine

The west coast of Kefalloniá

USEFUL NUMBERS (ARGOSTOLI)
Port Authority
tel: 0671 22224
Hertz Rent-a-Car
tel: 0671 25114 or 25116
Airport tel: 0671 41510
Tourist information
tel: 0671 22248

KEFALLONIAN WINES
Notable among Keffalloniá's often excellent wines are those made by Nicholas Cosmetatos, whose family have been on the island for many centuries. His best-known wines are Gentilini and Gentilini Fumé.

THE RICHES OF NATURE
As well as thyme-scented honey, quince jelly and rabbit stew, Kefalloniá is famous for its ewe's milk feta cheese, which is put to good use in the local speciality *riganata*, where it is mixed with bread, oil and oregano.

KEFALLONIÁ

The 1953 earthquake hit Kefalloniá, the largest of the Ionian Islands, particularly badly, devastating most of the towns and villages and reducing to rubble many beautiful Venetian buildings. Their modern replacements may sometimes lack character, but it could partly be this – and partly the infrequency of international flights – that has saved the island from mass tourism. As a result, it has preserved much of its beauty and its people (despite their reputation for being insular) can be more welcoming than those of the more frequently visited islands. Kefalloniá is a great place for walking: many Greeks come here in spring and autumn to do just that. A free leaflet, *Trails of Kefalloniá*, is widely available from the island's hotels and tourist agencies.

▶ Argostóli   179B2

Kefalloniá's main town was almost completely destroyed by the 1953 earthquake, but was rebuilt more or less according to the same plan. The stone bridge running across Argostóli's bay and the commemorative obelisk in the middle, are rare reminders that Britain controlled these islands in the 19th century. For more insight into 19th-century life on the island visit the **Historical and Cultural Museum▶▶▶** (*Open* Mon–Sat 9–2. *Admission charge*) at the Corgialénios Library (corner of Rokkoy Vérgoti and Ilia Zérvou). As well as costumes and antiques, there are excellent photographs of Kefalloniá before and immediately after the earthquake. For a look at modern life take an excursion to Argostóli's beach resort, Lássi, which has a good but crowded beach: unless you are staying there, a glimpse may be enough.

▶▶▶ Ásos   179B2

The ancient Greeks built a stronghold on this rocky promontory, joined to the island by a small causeway and successive conquerors have added to it. The present castle, so spectacular when seen from the approach road, is Venetian, built in the 16th century, its ruined interior converted into a park. The drive to Ásos, particularly the section from Angónas onwards, is among the most beautiful on the islands.

▶▶▶ Fiskárdo   179B2

A lovely fishing town which escaped relatively undamaged from the 1953 earthquake, Fiskárdo is one of Kefalloniá's main tourist attractions, so hotels and restaurants are more expensive. Still, it is worth making the trip north to see the 18th-century houses and to imagine how the rest of the island must have looked before the disaster.

▶▶ Kástro (Ágios Geórgios)   179B2

The Venetian capital of Kefalloniá, with its looming castle of Ágios Geórgios, was a sizable town until it was wrecked by a 17th-century earthquake. Its ruins still look good and the English poet Lord Byron is said to have waxed lyrical about the views from the castle (*Open* Jun–Oct Tue–Sat 8.30–7, Sun 8.30–3. *Admission charge*), which was built over an earlier Byzantine fort. Under British rule, the terrible dungeons beneath the inner fort were used as a prison for Kefallonians of liberal persuasion.

To the southeast of Kástro, Lourdas offers an excellent sandy beach backed by lovely walking country. Archipelagos, an environmental protection organisation supported by the World Wide Fund for Nature, has laid out a beautiful and environmentally friendly trail along the coast here, involving about two hours of easy walking.

▶▶ Sámi   179B2

The east-coast port of Sámi is a forlorn-looking place. In 1571, a fleet assembled here which defeated the Turks at Lepanto and changed the course of history. It is still a useful transit point for ferries and as a centre for visiting the nearby Drogaráti and Melissáni caves. In the hills immediately above the modern port lie the ruins of ancient Sámi, the capital in Homer's time, destroyed by the Romans after a long siege. From Karavomílos beach, 2km north of Sámi, boats leave for the **Spiliá Melissáni (Melissáni cave)▶▶** (*Open* daily summer only 9–8. *Admission charge*). Here an underground saltwater lake is fed by water from the other side of the island near Argostóli. A hole in the cave roof lets in sunlight which brings out beautiful shades of blue and violet from the water. A short ride from Sámi is the equally extraordinary **Drogaráti cave▶▶** (opening times as for Melissáni), with yellow and orange stalactites. One of its chambers has excellent acoustics and was used for concerts, most famously one given by the *diva* Maria Callas.

Beaches

Kefalloniá has many wonderful beaches. Best of all is the dramatic, white-stone Mírtos, although occasionally tar and pieces of rubbish are blown onto it. Further north, Ásos is picturesque. Andisámos is quiet; the more developed Plátis Giálos, Póros and Skála in the south are still enjoyable, while sandy Potomákia beach, near Skála, is a breeding ground for loggerhead turtles, so access is forbidden at night.

In Markópoulo, locals claim that on 15 August, the Assumption of the Virgin, small, non-poisonous snakes with crosses on their heads slither towards the church

CONNECTIONS
Ferries run all year round from Argostóli and Póros to Kyllíni (Peloponnese), from Sámi to Itháki and Pátra and from Fiskárdo to Itháki and Lefkáda. There are additional summer sailings from Sámi to Paxoí, Igoumenítsa (Epirus) and Ancona (Italy) and from Pessáda and Argostóli to Zákynthos. Hydrofoils link Póros with Itháki, Zákynthos and Pátra and there are summer services to Corfu, Paxoí and Lefkáda.

USEFUL NUMBERS
Port Authority
tel: 0661 32655
Airport
tel: 0661 30180/37398
Hertz Rent-a-Car
tel: 0661 38388 or
20557
Tourist information (Odós
Voulefton. *Open*
Mon–Fri 8–2)
tel: 0661 37520/37638

KÉRKYRA (CORFU)

According to mythology, the seagod Poseidon fell in love with Corcyra, a daughter of the river-god Asopos and brought her to this island, which then took her name. Homer credited the islanders with being among the most civilised in the world – a view based on the story that, 3,000 years ago, when his hero Odysseus was washed up on the island, he received wonderful hospitality. Earlier this century the writers Lawrence and Gerald Durrell recorded a similar warmth among the islanders. Blessed with fertile land, an idyllic coastline and some fascinating architecture, Corfu is still a beautiful island, but rapid development means you must now choose your spot carefully.

The two forts of Corfu Town

PUBLISHED INFORMATION
Look for *The Corfiot* and the *Ionian Times*, both English-language monthly papers.

ÁGIOS SPIRIDON CELEBRATIONS
There are large celebrations at the church four times a year when the saint's relics are taken in procession around the city: on Orthodox Holy Saturday (to commemorate his help in averting a famine), on Palm Sunday and the first Sunday in November (to commemorate an end to plagues in 1629 and 1673) and on 11 August (to celebrate the defeat of a Turkish attack in 1716).

▶▶▶ **Kérkyra (Corfu Town)**   *187C4*

To understand Corfu history, step away from the arcades of Odós E Voulgaréos or Odós N Theotóki and head for the wonderfully atmospheric **Old Town**▶▶▶. You would be forgiven for thinking yourself in Italy. The houses, now with peeling plaster, date from the Venetian period. The **church of Ágios Spirídon**▶▶, Corfu's patron saint, is cool and dark, full of shadows and incense. The remains of the saint, a 4th-century Bishop of Cyprus, were smuggled to Corfu from Istanbul. The elaborate 17th-century **town hall**▶▶ (not open) enhances the sloping main square of the old town – where some of Corfu's most elegant restaurants are to be found. When the Venetians designed the town and its fortifications, they left a large open area for defensive purposes, the **Spianada**▶▶▶ (Esplanade), which covered one third of the town's area. The arcaded building known as the Liston was designed by a Frenchman, De Lesseps, father of the engineer of the Suez Canal, who graced Paris's rue de Rivoli with a similar construction. There is undeniably a Parisian air to the line of cafés, the stone terrace, the tables under the trees; and it is a mark of Corfu's cosmopolitan character that cricket is still played on the grass beside it. The British developed this area during their occupation and the **Maitland Rotunda**, a bandstand with Ionic columns built in 1816, commemorates the first British High Commissioner.
Continued on page 189.

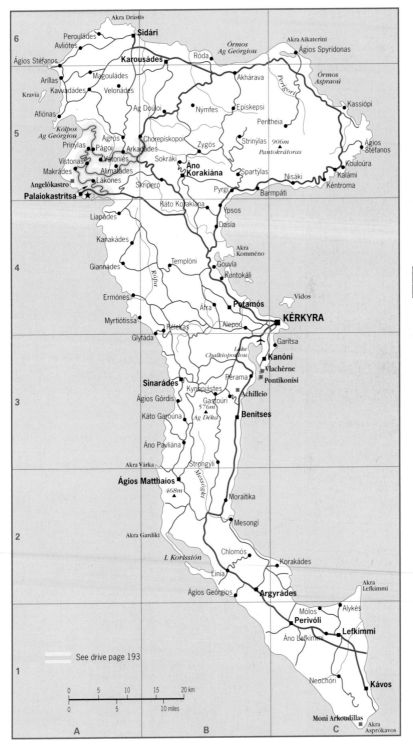

See drive page 193

0 5 10 15 20 km
0 5 10 miles

From culture to cooking, many aspects of life in the Ionian Islands have been influenced by the country that faces the islands across the Adriatic. Not surprisingly, four centuries of Venetian rule have also left their mark on these islands and on their people.

THE NOBLE GRAPE

The Comoútos family were given the title of count by the Venetians, perhaps in appreciation of their wine. Their Zákynthos winery, founded in 1638 and still family-run, is now the oldest in production in Greece. While many Ionian wineries have closed in recent years, the Comoútos have improved the range and the style of their products.

IONIAN MURDERERS

'In habit they imitate the Italians, but transcend them in their revenges and infinitely lesse civill. They will threaten to kill a Merchant that will not buy their Commodities and make more conscience to breake a Fast, than to commit a Murther...He is weary of his life that hath a difference with any of them and will walke abroad after day-light.'
George Sandys, an English traveller on Zákynthos (1610)

Venetian rule When Constantinople fell to the Crusaders in 1204, the Ionian Islands were given to various noble Venetian families to control. Corfu, however, was ruled by the Greek despots of Epirus. After the Venetians moved on Corfu, in 1386, they ruled all the Ionian Islands directly until the arrival of Napoleon Bonaparte in 1797.

The look Many Venetian buildings survive, but there were many more before 1953, when the islands were hit by disastrous earthquakes. Zákynthos Town was, until then, regarded as even more exceptional than Corfu Town. Still, churches, *kastri* and town houses survive throughout the Ionian Islands with an occasional coat of arms or Catholic motif as a reminder of the builder.

The sound Not having been colonised by the Turks, the Ionian islanders have an Italian-influenced musical tradition unique in Greece. *Kantádes* and the particular form known on Zákynthos as *arékias*, are ballads played on guitar and mandolin, with lyrics of a political, topical, or extremely personal (and sometimes sexual) nature being improvised.

The taste of Italy Traditional Ionian cooking shows Italian influence and is all the better for it, as in the Corfiot dish *pastitsatha*, which combines veal and pasta, or *mandolato*, a nougat from Zákynthos. The islanders also owe the quality of their wines, some of which are highly regarded, to the influence of the Italians.

The most atmospheric part of Corfu Town is Campiello, with its tiny alleyways and Venetian houses

Continued from page 186.

Beyond the bandstand is a statue of **Ioánnis Kapodístrias**, first president of modern Greece. At the top of the Spianada is the finest building of the British period, the neoclassical **palace of St Michael and St George**▶▶ (not open), former residence of the High Commissioner and seat of the Ionian Senate. It is partly occupied by a museum of Far Eastern art (*Open* Tue–Sat 8.30–3, Sun 9.30–2.30. *Admission charge*).

There was a fortified settlement on Cape Sidaro in ancient times but it was the Venetians who built the impressive **Old Fortress**▶▶▶ (*Open* daily 9–9. *Admission charge; free* Sun), which has wonderful views from its highest point. The fort's British-built Church of St George is now used as an exhibition centre and a nearby café serves refreshments.

Following the road past the British palace, Odós Arseníou rounds the headland towards the new port. Steps off it lead to the **Antivouniotissa Byzantine Museum**▶▶▶ (*Open* Tue–Sun 9–3. *Admission charge*), a collection of rare icons housed in a late 15th-century church with an extraordinary carved-wood ceiling.

The modern port is dominated by the impressive **New Fortress**▶▶ (*Open* daily 9–9. *Admission charge*), also built by the Venetians and nowadays used as a base by the Greek navy.

The newly extended **Archaeological Museum**▶▶, to the south of the Spianada (5 Odós Vraila. *Open* Tue–Sun 9–3. *Admission charge; free* Sun), has some spectacular antiquities including the famous Gorgon Pediment, found near Kanóni, a 7th-century BC stone lion, a clay head of Artemis (6th–5th century BC) and a 1st-century BC marble head of the poet Meander.

▶ Achilleío (Achilleion Palace)   187B3

A must if you love kitsch, the palace was built in 1890 for the Empress Elizabeth of Austria, popularly known as 'Sisi'. Her enthusiasm for Homer led her to fill the place with second-rate neoclassical sculpture. The gardens, however, are beautiful. The palace is open as a museum by day (*Open* daily 9–3. *Admission charge*) and becomes a casino at night.

The Austrian Empress 'Sisi' named the Achilleío (above) after her hero Achilles, whom she identified with her son Rudolph

ON YOUR BIKE
An alternative to hiring a car or motorcycle is to cycle on Corfu. Several companies rent cycles to help escape the crowds and explore the island.

COLONIAL TASTE
The ghosts of Corfu's colonial past seem to congregate around the Spianada, especially when cricket is being played. To enjoy the experience to the full, sit at one of the tables under the mature trees and order a *tzntzi* (ginger beer), a tasty relic of the days of British occupation.

UNDERWATER
Scuba diving is forbidden in most Greek waters, often due to the possibility of divers finding (and keeping!) antiquities on the seabed, but there are opportunities on Corfu. Dive Med, operating out of Gouvía Marina, offers trial days and excursions. Various recognised courses are available.

DURRELL'S KALAMI HOUSE

'A white house set like a dice on a rock already venerable with the scars of wind and water. The hill runs clear up into the sky behind it, so that the cypresses and olives overhang this room in which I sit and write. We are upon a bare promontory with its beautiful clean surface of metamorphic stone covered in olive and ilex: in the shape of a *mons pubis*. This is become our unregretted home. A world. Corcyra.'
Lawrence Durrell, *Prospero's Cell* (London, 1945/1962)

As you often see in Greece, the summit of Mount Pantokrátoras is graced with a lovely church

CORFU CLICHÉ

One of the most familiar images of Corfu is of the two islets off the south of Kanóni, on one of which stands the Vlachérne Convent, linked to the mainland by a causeway, while on the other the 12th-century church of the Pantokrator is surrounded by greenery (and, in season, by visitors).

OLIVES

There are 3–4 million olive trees on Corfu, covering 30 per cent of the island. Corfiots have cultivated the olive for 5,000 years, but do so by letting the olives fall to the ground naturally. They also do not prune their trees. The result is that they have some of the largest trees in Greece.

►►► Ermónes, Myrtiótissa, and Glyfáda *187A4/B4*

A rival to Palaiokastrítsa as a possible site for King Alcinoös's palace (see panel opposite), cliffside Ermónes has a pebble beach and notoriously cold water due to nearby streams. Myrtiótissa beach, accessible only on foot, is one of the island's most beautiful and secluded. Glyfáda is something less of a secret. Its wonderful beach caused a rush of construction, making it one of the island's larger resorts.

►►► Kalámi and Kouloúra *187C5*

Kalámi is a must for Lawrence Durrell fans, for this is where he lived, as described in his book *Prospero's Cell* (see panel). Durrell's 'white house' is now rented out to visitors and has a taverna downstairs. The neighbouring cove of Kouloúra, thick with cypress and palm trees, has a pebble beach and great views of Albania. Most of this stretch of coast is beautiful but less developed than elsewhere and has clear water.

►► Kanóni *187B3*

The ancient settlement was based on the peninsula south of Corfu Town, but little remains. Some 3km from the town, **Mon Repos Palace►►** was built by British High Commissioner Sir Frederick Adam in 1831 and was at one time used as a retreat by the Greek royal family (*Open daily 8–3. Admission free*). Opposite the palace gate is the site of the ancient *agora*. Nearby is one of Corfu's more interesting Byzantine churches, the 11th-century **Ágios Iassonos and Sosipáter►►**.

▶ Kassiópi   187C5

The pretty harbour at Kassiópi is used to invasion. Julius
Caesar landed here in 31 BC, Venetians later destroyed the
fort and then the Turks came and massacred the population in 1537. Now the fishing community has been
transformed into a resort town, though it has kept some of
its village atmosphere. Remains of the Byzantine fortress
stand on the hill behind the resort. There is swimming in
the town, but the pebble beaches are a walk away.

▶ Kávos   187C1

No place to get away from it all, Kávos has become one of
Greece's rave centres, suiting those who want to dance all
night and sleep on the beach all day, without seeing Greece.
  Close by, near Ákra (Cape) Asprókavos, the southern-
most point of the island, lies the fortified **monastery of
Arkoudíllas▶**, surrounded by beautiful landscape.

▶▶ Mount Pantokrátoras   187C5

Various rough tracks approach Corfu's highest mountain
(906m): from the north, a road leads to Perítheia, a remote,
partly deserted village, lovely in spring when blossom
covers the trees. From the east coast, tracks leave from
Kouloúra and Nisáki. The easiest way up is the track from
the windswept inland village of Strinýlas. The view from
the top (on a clear day) is stunning evidence of why Corfu
is called the emerald island.

▶▶▶ Palaiokastrítsa   187A5

Tradition sets the ancient palace of King Alcinoös here,
though no remains have been found. One of the most
beautiful bays on Corfu (discovered by visitors long ago),
Palaiokastrítsa has developed into a major resort. Off season, however, it makes a good base, offering excellent
watersports facilities, including a rare chance to scuba-
dive. **Theotókos monastery▶▶** (*Open* daily 7–1 and 3–8.
Admission free), out on the edge of the bay, deserves a visit.

*Palaiokastrítsa has been
identified with Homer's
Scheria, where Nausica
took Odysseus to the
palace of her father*

**KING ALCINOÖS'S
PALACE**
'Round the courtyard,
walls of bronze ran this
way and that way... and
upon them was a coping
of blue enamel; golden
doors and silver
doorposts stood on a
threshold of bronze, with
silver lintel and golden
crowlatch. Golden and silver dogs were on either
side, which Hephaistos
had made by his clever
brain to guard the
mansion of proud
Alcinoös...Within the hall
were seats fixed along the
wall on both sides, from
the threshold right to the
inner-end; and spread
over these were soft cov-
erings of fine-spun stuff
which the women had
made. There the leaders
of the Phaiacians used to
sit, eating and drinking,
for they had plenty which
never failed.'
Homer, *Odyssey* Book VII

Founded around 1225 and reconstructed in the 18th century, it has a good display of rare icons.

To the north, **Angelókastro**▶▶ is a 13th-century castle built by the Byzantine despot Michael Angelos II. The fort looks formidable up on its rock – a half-hour walk from the nearest road – and proved so on many occasions, being the home of the Venetian governor of Corfu and a place of refuge for thousands of villagers.

▶ **Sidári**   *187A6*

A lively town with shallow water and soft sand, Sidári is understandably popular as a family resort, but beautiful it is not. Hotels, shops and house rentals abound, but the main natural attraction is the sea-eroded rock formation, famous for its **Canal d'Amour**, a passage through which it is possible to swim and about which there are several traditions ensuring eternal love.

Beaches

Looking for an idyllic, empty stretch of sand on Corfu during the summer is a hopeless task, but the island does have some wonderful beaches. The northern half of the island is more developed: north from Corfu Town, developments are shoulder to shoulder for some distance. The north coast, from Kassiópi to the other side of Sidári, has a string of family-orientated resorts with sandy beaches and good bathing, but the land is largely featureless. Ágios Geórgios, in the northwest, is a large and lovely sandy bay, around which package tourism is creating a village.

CONNECTIONS
Corfu Town has ferry links with Igoumenítsa, Pátra, Kefalloniá, Paxoí and Syvota; also with Italy (various parts).
There are summer hydrofoil services to Paxoí, Lefkáda, Itháki and Kefalloniá. Excursion boats also run, in season, to the offshore islets of Ereíkoussa, Othoní and Mathráki.
Buses run to Athens (under 12 hours) from the terminal on Odós Solomoú in Corfu Town.

192

Tourism has taken over the stunning bay of Palaiokastrítsa in a big way

Palaiokastrítsa is the next in a string of excellent sandy beaches, including Glyfáda and Ágios Górdis, but they can be windy. Palaiokastrítsa has good watersports facilities. Ágios Geórgios, further south (increasingly referred to as St George South to distinguish it from the northern bay of the same name), has a fine beach backed by a vast array of package hotels. The east coast, which is more sheltered, has a medley of villages, resorts and mostly mediocre beaches which have been hideously developed, even to the end of the airport runway.

Drive

Palaiokastrítsa and Ágios Geórgios

A drive through the hills and cultivated valleys of northwestern Corfu, passing traditional villages and offering wonderful coastal and rural views. (About 40km; allow two to three hours. See the map on page 187. The rough track between Prinýlas and Vístonas is not suitable for mopeds and bicycles.)

The road to Lákones climbs steeply out of **Palaiokastrítsa▶▶▶**, a beautiful bay with a number of hotels and restaurants. The hillside is covered with olive trees to Lákones. Beyond it is the Bella Vista, a café-restaurant (closes at sunset) announcing 'Where the kings of Greece have eaten, as well as Kaiser, Tito and Nasser'. A less contentious claim is that this is the best **view of Palaiokastrítsa▶▶▶**. Some 2km further, in Makrádes, a right turn leads inland. Above the village is a fertile plain with vines and roadside shrines; 5km

A view of the Byzantine fortress of Angelókastro, near Palaiokastrítsa. A path leads up to it from Krini

from Makrádes, ignore the left turn to Alimatádes and continue for 3km to the junction at Troumbetás. Ignoring the road to Corfu Town, turn left towards Sidári and after 1km, follow signs right for a 2km detour to **Chorepískopoi▶▶**, as traditional as any village on Corfu can be. Back on the main road, follow signs to Págoi, along a **country road▶▶▶** through the villages of Arkadádes and Vatoníes. In **Págoi▶▶**, where you may see women wearing traditional costume and, in summer, herbs in their hair, veer right at the church. Immediately, there are signs down to the large, sandy bay of **Ágios Geórgios▶▶**. Returning to the road out of Págoi, continue to Prinýlas (1.5km) from where Palaiokastrítsa is signposted. The road beyond Prinýlas is unsurfaced but has **wonderful views▶▶▶** of Ágios Geórgios and Graviá island, said to be the ship that took Odysseus to Itháki, turned to stone by Poseidon. Turn right after 3.5km in Vístonas and return through Makrádes and Lákones to Palaiokastrítsa. (Alternatively take the left turn, east of Lákones, onto the main road for Corfu Town.)

Walk down the steep slopes of many an island village and you could well hear the tapping of typewriter keys as another foreign writer sets out to emulate Lawrence Durrell and Henry Miller. Whether it is because of their fecundity, their rich vein of history, or their easy living, the Ionian Islands have seen their fair share of foreign writers and none more so than Corfu.

Above: the writer, Samuel Clemens (Mark Twain)

BYRON'S ISLANDS

'The isles of Greece, the isles of Greece!
Where burning Sappho loved and sung.
Where grew the arts of war and peace
Where Delos rose and Phoebus sprung!
Eternal summer gilds them yet,
But all, except their sun, is set.'
Lord Byron, from *Don Juan* (written 1811)

194

FURTHER READING

Gerald Durrell, *My Family and Other Animals* (London, 1956)
Lawrence Durrell, *Prospero's Cell* (London, 1945)
Gustave Flaubert, *Letters, 1830–57* (London, 1954)
Edward Lear, *Selected Letters* (London, 1988)
Henry Miller, *The Colossus of Maroussi* (London, 1942)

Lawrence Durrell (below) lived in The White House, Kalámi (above right) – less isolated now than when he described it in Prospero's Cell

Earlier travellers The most famous of all foreign writers to visit Greece must surely be the British poet, Lord Byron, not because he wrote most beautifully about it – most of his writings in Greece were notes and letters – but because he came to help the Greeks fight for their independence in the 1820s and died of fever (and the local doctors' attempts to cure it) in 1824 at Missolonghi in western Greece. After Greek independence, as a result of the rest of the Mediterranean being pacified after the Napoleonic campaigns, there was a flow of inquisitive writers visiting the Greek Islands as part of a grander tour: Herman Melville, Mark Twain, Edward Lear and William Thackeray were among them.

The 20th century During this century, the names of three foreign writers in particular have been linked with Corfu. Gerald Durrell described his childhood on the island in *My Family and Other Animals*, giving a unique and often comical insight into Corfu wildlife and creating some entertaining pen-portraits of local people he knew. His elder brother Lawrence wrote *Prospero's Cell*, a beautiful evocation of northern Corfu, after he had been evacuated before the Nazi invasion in World War II. The American novelist Henry Miller recorded his visit to Lawrence Durrell before the war in *The Colossus of Maroussi*. But not everyone was passionate about Corfu: Evelyn Waugh, passing through in 1927, found it 'a very clean and rather attractive town' which reminded him of Brighton.

Sailing is the ideal way to discover and enjoy Kýthira's splendid and isolated beaches

USEFUL NUMBERS
Port Authority
tel: 0735 33280
Airport tel: 0735 33297

CONNECTIONS
Ferry services run (weather permitting) from Agía Pelagía to Piréas and Neápoli (southern Peloponnese). Hydrofoils operate to Piréas in summer.

195

KÝTHIRA

Out on its own off the southern coast of the Peloponnese, nearer to Crete than to the other Ionian Islands, Kýthira nevertheless shared Venetian and subsequently British occupation with the Ionians. In antiquity, the Phoenicians and Minoans had bases here. After massive emigration in the 1950s (many islanders now live in Australia), Kýthira is quiet and in some places even abandoned, attracting Athenians and foreigners to its fine beaches.

▶▶ Kýthira Town (Chóra)   *179A1*

The island capital is a quiet place with wonderful views over its port, Kapsáli and the islet of Avgó, reputed birthplace of Aphrodite. The nearby fort, **Kástro tis Chóra▶**, was built by Venetians in the 13th century and restored later – hence the inscription of 1503. The small museum (*Open Tue–Fri 8.45–3, Sun 9.30–2.30. Admission charge*) has evidence of the island's various occupiers. Below the *kástro*, **Kapsáli** – popular with yachts rounding the Peloponnese – is Kýthira's most visitor-oriented village.

▶▶ Potamós   *179A1*

The largest settlement on the island is quiet and has some accommodations to rent. To the east lies **Palaiochóra▶▶** or Ágios Dimítrios, the medieval town. Built on a strong site, invisible from the sea, it was a flourishing fortress-town in 1500, with 72 churches and a population swelled from the fall of Mýstra, a Byzantine city in the Peloponnese. In 1537 the Turkish admiral Barbarossa destroyed the fort, killing thousands and capturing 7,000 islanders.

▶▶ Mylopótamos   *179A1*

This beautiful village near the west coast is set in a lush valley near a ruined **Venetian fortress▶**. A half-hour walk leads to the cave of Agía Sophía (*Open summer only, Tue–Thu, Sat–Sun 11–3, Wed and Fri 4–8 pm. Admission charge*). Formerly used as a church, it has stalactites and stalagmites and a chamber where, locals say, Aphrodite slept.

Beaches

Kýthira has a number of sandy beaches, good if it is not too windy. Kapsáli has pebbles and sand and is busy in summer. Diakófti is a beautiful strip of sand, Platiá Ammos in the north is served by a summer taverna, while sandy Limiónas on the west coast is quiet but hard to reach.

Detail, the Venetian kástro

DROIT DE SEIGNEUR
In the 13th and 14th centuries there was a custom at Palaiochóra that new brides must first sleep with the local ruler. When a young man of noble Venetian descent objected, the ruler agreed to waive his rights if the young man would throw himself off a nearby cliff. The young man accepted, but when he jumped he took the ruler with him. Both men died and the custom was dropped.

LEFKÁDA

Lefkáda, connected to the mainland by a causeway, hardly feels like an island. Its towns, which have been badly damaged by earthquakes, are unspectacular but there are excellent beaches and, particularly in the south, dramatically beautiful scenery.

A series of fortresses is proof that Lefkáda was long an important strategic base

USEFUL NUMBERS
Port Authority (Lefkáda)
tel: 0645 22322
Olympic Airways (Lefkáda)
tel: 0645 22881
Tourist information,
contact regular police
(Lefkáda) tel: 0645 22346
Hertz Rent-a-Car (Nydrí)
tel: 0645 92289

▶▶ Lefkáda Town   179B3

Along the causeway is the impressive **Fortress of Santa Maura▶▶▶**, built by Giovanni Orsini in the 13th century and, because of its strategic position, repeatedly enlarged. However, the castle was of no use against the biggest threat to the island in this century: earthquakes. The upper storeys of many buildings are now constructed from wood or corrugated iron to minimise damage if they fall.

▶ Nydrí   179C3

German archaeologist Wilhelm Dörpfeld claimed, earlier this century, that Nydrí, not Itháki, was the site of Odysseus's palace – his evidence being some Bronze Age tombs he had found nearby. His theory was never accepted, but his statue still stands on the quay at Nydrí. From this growing resort, there is a wonderful view of several green, offshore islets including Skórpios, famous as the playground of Jackie Kennedy and Aristotle Onassis (landing is forbidden) and Meganísi, a short ferry ride away but retaining a surprising atmosphere of the real, agricultural Greece.

▶▶ Ákra Doukáto (Cape Lefkádas)   179B2

Lefkáda's southernmost point is a thin and dramatic ribbon of rock high above the sea, where, according to tradition, unrequited love could be cured by throwing yourself off the 72m-high cliff. The most famous casualty was the great poet Sappho, rejected by the boatman Phaon. She is said to have died by jumping (the place is known as Sappho's Leap), although it is likely that she died a more natural death in Sicily. A lonely and spectacular spot. Bring poetry.

Beaches

Windsurfers enjoy the high rollers at Vasilikí, while sand-and-pebble Póros beach is beautiful and quiet. A dirt road leads to Pórto Katsíki, one of Greece's most spectacular beaches, the white stones giving the water an extraordinary brilliance, but there are currents and high waves. Further north, Ágios Nikítas has access to an expanse of pebble and sand at Mílos beach.

CONNECTIONS
Ferry services operate
from Nydrí to Kefalloniá
and Itháki and also to
Meganísi and other islets.

PAXOÍ

Lacking an airport and with a shortage of water, tiny Paxoí has kept mass tourism at bay. With an excellent hotel, a range of rental properties, a good anchorage and a gently rolling interior dominated by olive trees, it is one of the most relaxed and charming Ionian islands.

▶▶ Gáïos (Paxoí Town)   *179B3*

The main pleasure in this mostly car-free town is strolling around or visiting the islet of **Ágios Nikólaos**▶▶, with its windmill and a ruined 15th-century Venetian fort. Behind it lies another islet, **Panagía**▶, whose monastery is a popular place of pilgrimage for the 15 August celebrations.

▶▶ Lákka   *179B4*

The island's main road runs to Lákka. The pretty, enclosed harbour has been taken over by apartment- and villa-rental companies, but it is a quiet and pleasant place.

▶▶ Longós (Loggós)

Paxoí's third small town clusters round a tiny harbour, where there are several excellent restaurants.

▶▶ West-coast caves   *179B3*

Famous even in antiquity – Homer mentions one, Ipparándi, as being covered in gold – Paxoí's caves make a good excursion by boat from Gáïos or Lákka. Kastanída and Ortholíthos are the most extraordinary.

▶▶ Antipaxoí   *179B3*

A short boat ride from Gáïos, Antipaxoí has few hotels but is a welcome day trip from Paxoí. While Paxoí is famous for its olives, Antipaxoí produces powerful wine. Agrapídia, the main settlement, is the anchorage. The island has fine, sandy beaches.

Beaches

Paxoí's beaches are mostly pebble or rock. The Paxos Beach Hotel has the best swimming cove in Gáïos, while Kaki Lagada, north of the town, has good bathing. Orkós, off the Lákka–Longós road, is worth the excursion.

The cliffs of Erimítis on Paxoí's northern shore

USEFUL NUMBERS
Port Authority (Gáïos)
tel: 0662 31259
Information and accommo-
dation: Paxos Sun
Holidays, tel: 0662
31201 and Paxos
Holidays Agency,
tel: 0662 31381

Life on Paxoí revolves around its olive groves

CONNECTIONS
Paxoí has ferry links with Corfu, Párga, Igoumenítsa and Antipaxoí. A summer hydrofoil service operates to Corfu.

USEFUL NUMBERS
Port Authority
tel: 0695 42417
Tourist information
Tzoulati 1
tel: 0695 27307
Airport
tel: 0695 28688/28322
Hertz Rent-a-Car
tel: 0695 45706

DIONYSIOS SOLOMOS
Born into a Hellenised
Venetian family and edu-
cated in Italy, Solomós
began writing verse in
Italian but then became
the first poet to use the
demotic Greek language
and Greek legends – and
this at a time when
Greece was fighting for its
independence. He dedi-
cated poems to the
independence fighters and
to the British Lord Byron,
who died while helping
them and his *Ode to
Liberty* was used as the
Greek national anthem.

CONNECTIONS
Zákynthos has ferry links
with Kyllíni (Peloponnese)
and Kefalloniá. There is
also a summer hydrofoil
service to Kefalloniá.

ZÁKYNTHOS (ZÁNTE)

If you are looking for streets lined with disco-bars and
beaches thick with comatose bodies sleeping off hang-
overs, then Zákynthos in high season (especially the south
of the island) is for you. Otherwise, come in spring or
autumn to enjoy the island's other considerable attractions, which include spectacular landscapes, several
unspoiled villages, beautiful sandy beaches and, especially in spring, the blossoms that earned it the label 'the
flower of the East'. Whatever your reasons for coming,
make time to appreciate the plight of the island's special
wildlife, particularly the threatened loggerhead turtle (see
panel opposite) and the rare Mediterranean monk seal,
which return to the island to breed.

▶▶ Zákynthos Town   *179B1*

The Venetians prided themselves on Zákynthos Town, but
the 1953 earthquake brought it all crashing down. Many
houses were rebuilt in an Italianate style, most successfully
around **Plateía Solómou▶▶**, a grand open space fronting
the water, surrounded by the 16th-century church of Ágios
Nikólaos Molou and the **Byzantine Museum▶▶** (*Open
Tue–Sun 8.30–3. Admission charge; free Sun*). Among orna-
ments salvaged from ruined churches are the 1681
iconostasis of the Church of the Pantokrátor and the walls
of the 17th-century church of Ágios Andréas with their
frescos of Judgement, Heaven and Hell. There is also a collection of icons and a model of the town before 1953.

In the neighbouring square, the **Solomós Museum▶▶**
(Plateía Ágios Márkou. *Open Mon–Sat 9–12. Admission free*)
is dedicated to local poet Dionysios Solomós (1798–1857)
and his brother. On display are memorabilia of their lives
and times, the most bizarre being part of the tree under
which Solomós composed his great works of May 1823.
The beautiful Byzantine church of Kyrias ton Angelou
(Odós Archiepiskópou Kokkiní), reconstructed after the
earthquake, is closed, but the waterfront **cathedral of Ágios
Dionysios▶** (*Open daily 7–noon and 4.30–9*) survived the
earthquake and has a profusion of frescos and a silver reli-
quary for the saint's bones.

A steep climb above the town, the walls of the **Venetian
kástro▶▶** (*Open daily 8–4. Admission charge; free Sun*) survived the 1953 earthquake, unlike the buildings inside,
now replaced with a park com-
manding excellent views
over the beautiful bay.

*The loggerhead turtles'
only hope for survival is
probably to be considered
a tourist attraction in
their own right*

▶▶ Ákra Skinári (Cape Skinári)   *179C1*

Between the northern cape of Zákynthos and the port of Ágios Nikólaos, the **Blue Caves**▶▶ make a popular excursion. The combination of diffused light, rock and water makes the sea in the caves appear a brilliant blue.

▶ Laganás   *179C1*

If Zákynthos Town goes quiet at night it is because the noisy ones have come to this exploding and brash resort for dancing, drinking and sex. Even if the barman has just poured a bottle of vodka down your throat (they do), remember that the beach belongs to the loggerhead turtles at night; it is forbidden to go on it after dark (see panel).

▶▶ Machairádo   *179B1*

A place of pilgrimage, Machairádo is one of the most interesting inland villages for its **church of Agía Maura**, a survivor of the 1953 earthquake. Ornately decorated, its wall and ceiling painted with biblical themes, it is accompanied by its separate belltower, another happy survivor.

▶▶ Volimés   *179B1*

This rather sprawling village in the northwest of the island is known for its handicrafts and local produce, often enthusiastically marketed to visitors. Several kilometres to the south is the monastery of **Anafonítria**, an earthquake survivor which has retained some of its frescos. A well-advertised tourist attraction nearby is the **wreck of a ship**, smashed off the inhospitable west coast and now mostly buried in sand. It can be seen from the cliffs above and is often combined, on boat excursions from Ágios Nikólaos and elsewhere, with a visit to the Blue Caves (see Ákra Skinári, above). In summer, with your own transport (mopeds are not suitable), drive to Pórto Vrómi, on a bay near the wreck and take a boat from there, making time to eat at Uncle Yanni's Cantina on your return.

Beaches

Zákynthos's beaches can be overrun in the summer. Pórto Róma, south of Zákynthos Town, has good gentle bathing and a good taverna. Gerákas can be quieter but is also a nesting ground for loggerhead turtles, as are the next two beaches, smaller pebble-and-sand Kalamáki and the many kilometres hemmed in by hotels at Laganás. Órmos Álikon (Álikon Bay) in the northeast has a long sandy beach on which are the unexciting resorts of Alikanás and Alikés.

SAVE THE LOGGERHEAD TURTLES

Tourism has been a disaster for the loggerhead turtle – a species that is very sensitive to disturbance. Threatened in the water by speedboats and fishermen, the turtle, *Caretta caretta*, now finds its breeding grounds on the beaches invaded by sun-worshippers. Conservation groups have begun to make some headway: night flights into Zákynthos are being curtailed, since that is when the turtles come up onto the shore to lay their eggs and some beaches have been put off limits. The Greek Animal Welfare Fund reported that visitors are responding to their appeals, but some local landowners and businessmen are not. Buildings, walls and beach kiosks at Laganás were constructed without permission, while noise and lights from nearby bars confuse and, indirectly, cause the deaths of the newly hatched turtles, which need to reach the sea quickly. Numbers of the turtles have fallen dramatically and, unless immediate action is taken, the loggerhead turtle will soon be a fond memory in this part of the world.

What you can do:
● Observe notices to keep off the beach at night and encourage others to do so. Do not pollute beaches or disturb the sand in any way.
● Contact the campaign co-ordinators for more information: MEDASSET (the Mediterranean Association to Save the Sea Turtles) Odós Licavitou 1c, 10672 Athens; tel: 01 364 0389; fax: 01 724 3007 email: MEDASSET@hol.gr website: http://www.hol.gr/greece/medasset

Thásos is popular with northern Greeks for its excellent sandy beaches

NORTHERN AND EASTERN AEGEAN Unlike the Cyclades or the Ionian Islands, the islands in this group have no common identity. Sometimes separated into the Northern Aegean (Límnos, Samothráki, and Thásos) and the Eastern Sporades (Chíos, Ikaría, Lésvos, and Sámos), they cling like barnacles to the Turkish coast. Sometimes hard to reach and spartan in accommodations, they offer visitors who make the effort a wonderful range of possibilities, from antiquities on Samothráki to a genteel resort atmosphere on Thásos, from the volcanic drama of Chíos to the lush countryside and unspoiled villages of Lésvos.

EARLY HISTORY In antiquity, visitors came to Thásos and Límnos for gold, stone, and wine, and for theatre, while everyone from emperors to pious citizens visited Samothráki to take part in the sacred mysteries connected with its Great Gods. But of these islands, Sámos and Lésvos were most renowned in the ancient world. When the Greek historian Herodotus visited Sámos he thought

that the defences of the city of King Polycrates (6th century BC), the water tunnel that fed them and the nearby temple to Hera (the Heraion) were among the greatest architectural achievements of the Greeks. Lésvos's claim to fame was more literary and cultural. The third largest Greek island, with a wealth assured by its fertility, it was the homeland of Terpander (the father of Greek music) and of the lyrical poets Arion, Alcaeus, and of course the famous Sappho, while in its schools the great Aristotle and Epicurus came to teach. There is still a hint of this cultural achievement about the island, a touch of pride in the islanders' character, especially in the main town of Mytilíni, home to several modern painters and writers.

ITALIAN AND TURK Like so many other islands, those of the Northern and Eastern Aegean came under Venetian or Genoese influence in the 13th century after the fall of Byzantium, but, being so close to the Turkish mainland, many were quickly retaken by the Turks. The Genoese Gattilusi family held Thásos and Samothráki throughout

The Northern and Eastern Aegean Islands
Chíos (ΧΙΟΣ)
Ikaría (ΙΚΑΡΙΑ)
Lésvos (ΛΕΣΒΟΣ)
Límnos (ΛΗΜΝΟΣ)
Sámos (ΣΑΜΟΣ)
Samothráki (ΣΑΜΟΘΡΑΚΙ)
Thásos (ΘΑΣΟΣ)

the 14th and 15th centuries, but Límnos, at the mouth of the Dardanelles and the shipping lane to Constantinople (Istanbul) and Asia, was not so secure. The fate of Límnos became a gauge of Turkish power and it was only in 1912, after the Balkan War, that the Greeks finally won it back, along with Lésvos, Sámos, and Chíos, held by the Turks since the 15th and 16th centuries.

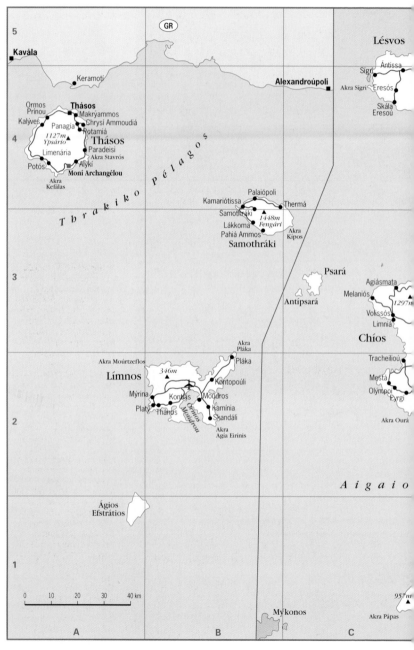

GREEK WARINESS The islands are too close to Turkey not to be an issue – Sámos, for instance, is only 3km from the Turkish mainland. There were still sizeable Turkish communities on these islands until the exchange of citizens in 1924. The Greeks remain wary of Turkish intentions and Límnos continues to be a place of contention, with the Turks calling for the large Greek garrison to be removed.

▶▶▶ REGION HIGHLIGHTS

Agiássos
see pages 208–9
Mastic villages
see pages 204–5
Mólivos see page 212
Néa Moní see page 205
Palaiópoli see page 216

BEST BEACHES
- Empóreio (Chíos)
- Aktí Mýrina (Límnos)
- Alykí and Paradise (Thásos)
- Tzamadoú (Sámos)

203

INTER-ISLAND TRAVEL
Recent improvements in sea communications mean that it is at last feasible to hop through these islands in a single trip without taking months over it, as Ptolemy or Anthony and Cleopatra would have done.
However, although in summer frequent boats and hydrofoils connect the islands, the distances between them make it necessary to think carefully about your itinerary. If travelling from the mainland, note that the port of Keramóti is closer than Kavála to 'Megas Alexandros' (Alexander the Great) Airport and to Thásos island. An unreliable hydrofoil service connects Samothráki to Límnos in the summer, otherwise it is a long boat ride from Kavála or a hydrofoil from Alexandroúpol. Connections, however, made from Límnos down through the other islands are both more frequent and more reliable.

The sticky sweet smell of mastic resin still pervades the air in villages where mastic is cultivated

CHÍOS

The economy of Chíos depends much more on its shipowners, on mastic production and on citrus groves than on tourism. Although there are a few tour groups, the island has most to offer the more adventurous traveller.

▶▶ Chíos Town

203D3

Chíos, the capital and port, is a lively commercial centre that has not compromised itself for tourism. Beyond the ferry landing is a busy bazaar, very Asian in atmosphere, where everything from mastic and metal cheese-cupboards to live animals is on sale. The **Philip Argenti Museum**▶▶ (2 Odós Kórai. *Open* Mon–Sat 8–2. *Admission charge*) houses an amazing collection of local folkloric costumes, maps and family paintings. The **Byzantine Museum**▶ in the old Mecidiye Mosque (Plateía Plastíra. *Open* Tue–Sun 10–1. *Admission charge; free* Sun) has heaps of marble fragments from buildings and tombs. Just outside the town is the **Kámpos**, settled in the 14th century by the Genoese aristocracy who built magnificent villas in the middle of olive and citrus groves. Many made way for the airport or fell into ruin, but a few have been beautifully restored, the most famous being the Villa Argenti which offers the most exclusive (and expensive) hotels on these islands. Just outside the suburb of Vrontádos, in an olive grove, is the 'Stone of Homer' where the great poet supposedly composed his famous epics. Of the many contenders for the birthplace of Homer, Chíos makes the most credible claim – though none of the evidence is conclusive.

▶ Kardámyla

203D3

Káto Kardámyla, the island's second town, set in a fertile plain, is a welcome sight after 'Homer's Crags', the rugged mountains of the north. There is little to interest visitors beyond some excellent beaches.

▶▶▶ Mastikochoriá (mastic villages)

202C2

Traditionally used in many products from varnish to chewing gum, the resin of the mastic tree (a relative of the pistachio) was the basis of much of Chios's early prosperity. The mastic business in this part of the island was profitable until the discovery of petroleum-based products and now most of the mastic trees have made way for olives and apricots. The medieval villages, however, preserve their unique character. **Pyrgí**▶▶ is famous for its houses elaborately decorated with *sgraffito*, geometric patterns in white and grey paint. The cathedral is of little interest, but the 12th-century church of Ágioi Apóstoloi (*Open* Tue–Thu and Sat 10–1), in the corner of the square, is a gem. **Olýmpoi**▶▶, the least pretty of the villages, is still worth a visit for its old town. **Mestá**▶▶▶, the finest, is a walled-in village with dark streets which often feel like underground tunnels built by ants. The main square has some excellent tavernas serving local specialities.

▶▶▶ Néa Moní   *203D3*

Néa Moní (*Open* daily 8–1 and 4–8), one of the most famous Greek Orthodox buildings in all Greece, was founded in 1042 by the Emperor Constantine Monomachos after three hermits discovered a miraculous icon of the Virgin. The setting is superb, but reminders of a troubled past are close at hand: beyond the main gate, an

ossuary contains the bones of the victims of a savage Turkish attack in 1822. The church suffered from Turkish ransacking and a later earthquake, but happily some magnificent mosaics have survived. Before 1822 the monastery supported over 600 monks, but only a handful of nuns are in residence today.

▶▶ Volissós   *202C3*

Most of Volissós's older inhabitants live in new houses around the main square, but their old stone houses, dramatically set beneath the crumbling Byzantine castle, are slowly being restored. Traditions have been well preserved in Volissós; the local baker, who can never make enough bread, still bakes on olive wood. The nearby port of Limniá has a few good fish tavernas.

Beaches

Near Chíos Town are the sandy beach at the resort of Karfás and two lovely pebble beaches at Vrontádos. Emporeió's black-stone beach, on the south coast, has good snorkelling. The best beach in the north is Nagós – not the crowded main black-sand beach but the small beaches beyond it. There are good white-pebble coves near Tracheilioú and below Volissós.

WOMEN'S AGRICULTURAL-TOURIST COOPERATIVE
This women's cooperative offers visitors the opportunity to stay with local families, in very simple houses in the mastic villages and share their lives and work. The bathless rooms are quite cheap, especially for a double, and it is a unique experience. For reservations write to the cooperative: Pyrgí 82102, Chíos.

Ax-clefts in children's skulls are a painful reminder of the brutality of 1822

205

LIVE THE VILLAGE LIFE
Old stone houses are being restored on Chíos, particularly in the lovely mastic village of Mestá and in Volissós. Some of these are being done by and for local people, but others are available for rent and make wonderful places to stay if you want to get a feel for village life. Many are decorated with traditional old furniture, to give them an authentic look. In Mestá you can make reservation through Dimitris Pipidis (tel: 0271 76319), or in Volissós with Argyris Angelou (tel: 0274 21421). For other villages, contact the Women's Agrotourist Cooperative (tel: 0271 72496).

CONNECTIONS
Chíos has ferry links with Piréas, Lésvos, Sámos, Léros, Thessaloníki, Kavála, Límnos, Oinoússes and Cesme (Turkey). Hydrofoil services operate to Sámos, Ikaría, Pátmos, Foúrnoi and Lésvos.

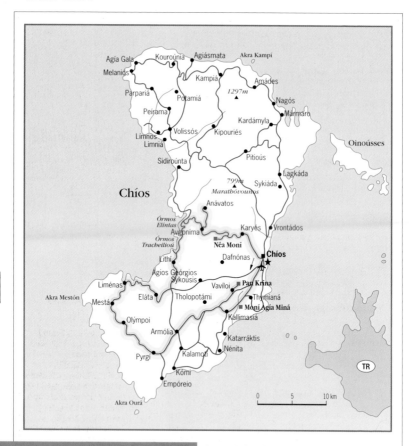

Drive

To the mastic villages

Cross the island to explore the mastic-growing country of the southwest, with its well-preserved villages. (Approximately 55km to Mestá; allow all day, with a good lunch stop.)

Leave Chíos Town on the road for the airport, following signs for Nénita and Kallimasiá and passing through the Kámpos (see page 204). Follow the sign for Kalamotí, heading uphill. About 3km further on, pass windmills and the monastery of Ágía Miná. Continue through Kallimasiá, following a sign (right) by the church to Tholopotámi

and after 3km drive between the windmills to the right, back towards Chíos. Go through Vavíloi and, after 2km, a small yellow sign in Greek leads to a dirt track on the right which leads through an olive grove to the amazing 13th-century **church of Panagía Krína▶ ▶** with splendid wall paintings. Return to the main road at Vavíloi and follow signs for Pyrgí. The road winds through olive and mastic groves, past the first mastic village of **Armólia**, famous for its pottery. After about 16km, reach **Pyrgí▶ ▶** (see page 205). The main road leads on to the other mastic villages of Olýmpoi▶ ▶ and **Mestá▶ ▶ ▶**, a good lunch stop. Either return the same way or continue along the scenic west coast to Elínta, where the road cuts inland to Chíos Town, passing the lovely villages of **Anávatos▶** and **Avgónima▶** and the monastery of **Néa Moní▶ ▶ ▶** (see page 205).

IKARÍA

The prosaic explanation of Ikaría's name is that it comes from the Phoenician word for fish. Locals prefer to link it with the famous legend of Icarus, whose home-made waxen wings melted when he flew too near the sun. The island (which some claim to be wing-shaped) is not exceptionally beautiful and has no important sights, but it does offer an increasingly rare commodity: peace and quiet. With few visitors to serve, facilities are minimal outside the main towns. Roads are rough and public transport practically nonexistent, apart from the daily school bus between Armenistís and Ágios Kírykos.

► Ágios Kírykos   203D1

The waterfront, with its tree-shaded cafés, provides the greatest excitement in Ágios Kírykos, but even in summer it remains a sleepy fishing town. Most visitors stay here for the nearby spas. The baths in Thérma are a strange sight: while invalids bathe in the thermal springs, their partners sip coffee by the side. The hot springs at nearby Thérma Lefkádas, boiling up in a seawater pool formed by volcanic rocks, are more attractive.

► Évdilos   203D1

The bus ride over the long ridge to Évdilos is truly spectacular. After the empty, rugged landscape, Évdilos can appear to be a lively place, but it is a very relaxed resort. In nearby Kámpos is the site of ancient Oinon (*Open* daily. *Admission free*), once Ikaría's main town and the charming 11th-century church of Agía Iríni.

► Armenistís   203D1

The island's two best sandy beaches, Livádi and Messakhtí, are within walking distance of this fishing village. In Nás, 4km further, are the ruins of the temple of Artemis Tavropoleio, overlooked by a small hippie community. The older residents in the nearby village of Christós still speak an ancient Homeric dialect.

► Foúrnoi   203D1

The island of Foúrnoi, a popular Sunday lunch excursion from Ágios Kírykos, offers the opportunity for a walk or an afternoon swim. Most people stay in the port or walk to the small village of Kámbi, 15 minutes away.

One of the more secluded coves on the splendid Livádi beach

USEFUL NUMBERS
Port Authority tel: (Ágios Kryikos) 0275 22207; (Évdilos) 0275 31007
Airport tel: 0275 23888
Tourist Police
tel: 0275 22207
Ikariada Travel (waterfront in Ágios Kyrikos) tel: 0275 23322 (for general information, reserving ferry tickets and hotels). In Évdilos try Blue Nice tel: 0275 31990

CONNECTIONS
Ikaría has ferry links with Piréas, Sámos (Vathí or Pythagóreio), Páros, Pátmos, Náxos, Foúrnoi, Mýkonos and Sýros. Hydrofoil services operate in summer to Pátmos, Lésvos, Sámos, Chíos, Foúrnoi, Leípsoi, Léros, Kálymnos and Kós and summer boat services also run to Foúrnoi.

USEFUL NUMBERS
Port Authority
tel: 0251 24115
Aeolic Cruises (tickets to
Turkey) tel: 0251 23960
Hertz Rent-a-Car tel:
0251 42576
Airport
tel: 0251 61234/61212
Tourist information
(Mólivos) tel: 0253 71347;
(Eressós) tel: 0253 53214;
(Plomári) tel: 0252 32535
Tourist Police and
information (Mytilíni:
Plateía Teloniou, near the
ferry boat landing.
Open daily 8.30am–8pm)
tel: 0251 22776

POETRY AND MUSIC
Lésvos, always a prosperous island, has since antiquity been a haven for artists and poets. In the 7th century BC Terpander, the father of Greek music, lived in Ántissa and the poet Arion, from Mólivos, wrote for the first time personal poetry instead of long epics. Both of them inspired the two great poets of the next century, Sappho from Eresós and Alcaeus from Mytilíni. In the 4th century BC the famous School of Philosophy was founded where Aristotle and Epicurus often lectured. Poetry is still alive at the *Vallia* in Agiássos where, every year on the Monday before Shrove Tuesday, villagers try to outdo each other in exchanging satirical verse.

LÉSVOS

Lésvos is the third largest Greek island after Crete and Évvoia. Although it is rapidly replacing its traditional industries – olives, *oúzo*, fishing and shipbuilding – by mass tourism, it still has its Greek character, unspoiled villages, good beaches and lovely countryside.

▶▶ Mytilíni   203D4

Mytilíni, the capital and main harbour, has a bustling waterfront with plenty of sophisticated cafés and *ouzerí*. The modern city is built on the ruins of ancient Mytilíni, of which only the large Hellenistic theatre has survived. A huge 6th-century *kástro*, repaired by the Genoese in 1373, divides the two harbours. Despite the modern character of the town, its busy Old Market still has the feel of a bazaar. The **Archaeological Museum▶▶▶** (Odós Arg. Eftalídi. *Open* Tue–Sun 8.30–3. *Admission charge; free* Sun) has fine Roman sculpture, mosaics with scenes from the comedies of Menander, pottery and well-arranged jewellery. The **Museum of Theophilos▶▶▶** (*Open* Tue–Sun 9–1 and 4.30–8. *Admission charge*), recently moved to the Pinakothíki, corner of Odós Mikras Asias and Odós Andramitíou, has over 80 primitive paintings by the native Theophilos depicting old traditions or historical events. Just to the south of the town, past many of its grand old mansions, is the **Thériade Museum▶▶▶** (Odós Alice Thériade, Variá. *Open* Tue–Sun 9–2 and 5–8. *Admission charge; free* Sun). This collection of book illustrations by Picasso, Chagall, Matisse and others, published by the Lésvos-born art critic Elefteriades (better known under his French name Thériade), is delightful and unexpected.

▶▶▶ Agiássos   203D4

This charming village in the foothills of Mount Ólympos makes an enjoyable day excursion. The stalls in the bazaar filled with religious and kitsch souvenirs are aimed at the many Greek tourists. The village has maintained its

The north coast of Lésvos has some pretty bays and harbours, including Skála Sikaminéas

Walk

Mytilíni's busy waterfront is devoted to business by day, but turns into a pleasant and breezy place to walk in the evenings

At the foot of Mount Lepétimnos

A long but easy walk through some inviting villages overlooked by Mount Lepétimnos, with good views over the surrounding countryside. The route follows one of several signposted trails laid out by the Mytilíni tourist office (21km; allow most of a day. Buses leave Mytilíni every morning around 8 or 9 for Kallóni and Mólivos. A bus returns from Mantamádos at 4.30).

Start at the spring on the road from Kallóni to Mólivos, just before the junction to Stypsí. Follow the signpost to Stypsí, taking the paved road into the heart of the village. There are a few tavernas on the way and good views over the sea. Walk through Stypsí's main street, with its lively kafeneía and tiny old shops. Follow the sign in the centre for Mantamádos, along a dirt track past a little church. From the road there are fine views over the abundant valley of Kallóni, with its orchards. A drinking fountain, after half an hour, announces the peaceful village of Ipsilométoro, with its kafeneía in the shade of the trees and a minaret but no mosque. The road leads on to the scenic village of Pelópi which is built around a ravine and is very lush. Its mosque has now been turned into a warehouse. The road continues to Kápi, a small village with cobbled streets, from where you continue to nearby Mantamádos. This lovely village is famous for its pottery and its huge monastery of the Archangel Michael (*Open* daily until 10 pm in summer, 7 pm in winter). Believers offer tin slippers full of money to the eerie 'black icon' of the archangel, because they believe that he often wears out his shoes while fulfiling all the wishes of his devotees.

special atmosphere along with its grey stone houses with Ottoman balconies, its noisy *kafeneía* and its quaint butchers' shops which sell, among other things, a local cheese in goatskin. The church of the Panagía Vrefokratoússa provides plenty of interest before a good lunch in one of the tavernas.

▶ Eresós   202C4

Famous as the birthplace of Sappho, Eresós and its nearby beach resort Skála Eresoú have become fully developed because of the wonderful beach. Between here and Sígri, little remains of the Petrified Forest, but the Turkish castle at Sígri, near the island's most westerly point, is still standing and open to visitors.

CONNECTIONS
Lésvos has ferry links with Piréas, Chíos, Límnos, Kavála, Thessaloníki, Sámos, Pátmos and Ayvalik (Turkey). Summer hydrofoil services run to Sámos, Chíos and Pátmos and less frequently to Kavála and Límnos.

The Greeks invented poetry and their political security created an environment in which a poetic tradition flourished. Literature students around the world study the early Greeks today, but some modern Greek poets find this legacy more of a hindrance than a help.

Memorial stone to British poet Rupert Brooke on Skíros

**SOME MODERN
GREEK POETS**
Constantine Cavafis
Odysseus Elytis (Nobel prizewinner)
Níkos Kazantzákis (Nobel nomination)
Takis Papatsonis
Yannis Ritsos (Nobel nomination)
Angelos Sikelianos (Nobel nomination)
George Seferis (Nobel prizewinner)

SAPPHIC LOVE
' – so sobbing, many times, she left me
and she said this [to me]
'My god! what awful things are happening to us:
Sappho, I swear I am leaving you against my will.'
And I replied to her in these words:
'Go with a light heart and with memories
of me, for you know how we cherished you'.
Sappho, from Fragment No 94

Origins of poetry There is little evidence today of Greece's once-thriving oral tradition, but storytellers everywhere know that it is easier to remember lines that are sprung with a rhythm. Perhaps it was from the simple need for an aid to memory that poetry developed. The origins of written poetry are lost, although Homer is usually placed at the beginning, with his *Iliad* and *Odyssey*. Even if he did compose those epic poems – and their authorship is in doubt – their content was the product of a long-established oral tradition.

Establishing the tradition The earliest surviving poems took as their subject the behaviour and attitudes of men faced with the often incomprehensible activities of the gods. Hesiod (c8th century BC) continued this didactic tradition in his *Theogony*, which explained the creation of the world and recounted the history of the gods. His *Works and Days*, however, praised honest labour, attacked corrupt judges and gave a vivid picture of village life. Of the early poets, Sappho (c7th century BC) stands out, although she is almost as well known now for her lifestyle and sexual preferences as for her poetry. As a lyrical poet she is believed to have led a female literary circle in her native

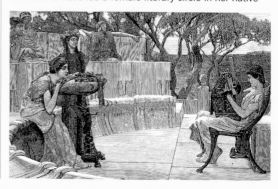

The poetess Sappho had a school of poetry on Lésvos

Mytilíni (Lésvos). Not everyone admired her poetry, some of which was said to be very erotic and addressed to women; her work was burned and, of the original nine volumes, only fragments survive.

Change of content As Greek society evolved, so poets focused increasingly on the activities of their contemporaries. Their popularity hardly suffered: Pindar (*c*520–*c*440 BC), probably the finest of ancient Greece's lyric poets, was composing celebratory odes from an early age for victorious athletes at the Olympic Games – poems which the 17th-century British poet Dryden was quite happy to imitate more than 2,000 years later.

In the 5th and 4th centuries BC, the public imagination was caught by dramatists like Aeschylus, Sophocles and Euripides (see pages 218–19) and by the great historian Herodotus, who created the first prose masterpiece in Greek. By the time cultural preeminence passed to Alexandria in Egypt, poets were looking back fondly to the glory days of Greek poetry.

A language problem With the rise of Greek nationalism in the late 18th century, poets were faced with the problem of having to choose between Greek as spoken by farmers and islanders (demotic) and the official and literary language known as *katharévousa*, a simplified version of classical Greek. Controversy raged throughout the 19th century and the Greek government fell in 1901 after the New Testament was translated into demotic. The move away from the élitism of *katharévousa* was inevitable – the Alexandrian-Greek Constantine Cavafis was writing his great works in demotic early in the 20th century – but the controversy rumbled on: in 1963 the Nobel laureate George Seferis called *katharévousa* 'some kind of Esperanto masquerading as [Greek].'

A perennial subject Some of Cavafis's poems take their subjects from ancient Greek history and myth. This shows up one of the ironies of Greek poetry: myths and symbols of ancient Greece – the subject matter of the first poets – still form part of the raw material of poetry today. Two recent Nobel prizewinning poets have been Greek: Odysseus Elytis, who wrote primarily about the natural world and George Seferis, who revisited ancient myths.

A famous episode in Homer's Iliad: *Hector saved from Achilles by the god Apollo*

THE WEIGHT OF TRADITION
'In a land which has produced so many masterpieces in architecture, sculpture and literature, the Greek creative temperament has constantly to struggle against the crushing precedents set by its ancestors. For some, the Parthenon is not so much a symbol of the glorious past as an overbearing weight that suffocates inspiration and stunts expression.'
Kimon Friar, *Modern Greek Poetry* (Athens, 1993)

THE *EROTOKRÍTOS*
The masterpiece of Greek literature during the Turkish occupation was an epic poem called the *Erotokrítos*. Written on Crete around 1646 by Vincenzo Kornaros, it tells of the love between a princess and a commoner. Written in the Cretan vernacular rather than the more literary *katharévousa*, the *Erotokrítos* became as important Greek heritage as the Parthenón.

THEOPHILOS'S BREAD
This is a story told by the poet Seferis about the Lésvos-born artist Theophilos and his painting of a baker: 'When he came to putting in the baker's rake, instead of following the laws of perspective and making it horizontal, he drew it perpendicular, showing the whole breadth of its surface; then, in the same way, he drew a loaf of bread on the rake. A clever man came past and said to the painter, "That loaf of bread is going to fall down, the way you've painted it". Without bothering to turn his head around, the painter replied, "Don't worry. Only real loaves fall down; the painted ones stay put and in a picture one ought to show everything".'

The pretty town of Mólivos has been declared a protected monument, but lost part of its character during recent restorations

▶▶▶ Míthymna (Mólivos) 203D5

It is easy to see why many visitors to Lésvos choose to stay in this lovely old town on the north coast of the island. The dramatically situated medieval chora, with its Macedonian-style houses and delightful streets, was declared a protected monument, so has been spared new development. Above the chora towers an impressive Genoese *kástro*▶ (*Open* Tue–Sun 8.30–3. *Admission charge*), where the island's most prestigious cultural events take place. The views are especially stunning towards sunset, sometimes extending as far as Mount Áthnos, rising from the sea in the far distance, with the Turkish coast much closer at hand. From the top of the town it is a pleasant walk, through cobbled, vine-covered streets, down to the fishing harbour and its choice of tavernas.

To the east of Mólivos, beyond the developing resort of Eftaloú, are the pretty village of Sykamineá and the island's most attractive fishing harbour, Skála Sykamineás, with some excellent restaurants.

▶ Plomári 203D4

Known to produce the best *oúzo* on Lésvos, this relaxed resort with its scenic fishing harbour is especially popular with Scandinavian visitors.

Beaches
Peaceful, unspoiled beaches can still be found on Lésvos. Pétra has a good sandy beach, but it is noisy and crowded in season. The beaches are quieter further west; Ambélia has a long bay with a sandy beach. Between Míthymna (Mólivos) and Skála Sykamineás there are many little pebble-stone bays, one of the nicest being at Eftalóu. Ágios Isídoros is the best beach in the south, with pebbles and good bathing. The long sandy beach of Vatera is also very good, but in places really crowded. Skála Eresoú beach has good dark sand and is also very popular.

LÍMNOS

Its position near the entrance to the Dardanelles has long guaranteed Límnos great strategic value; it was from here that the World War I Gallipoli campaign was launched. Greek troops are still among the island's most frequent visitors and archaeologists also come here to explore the ancient sites. For the rest, Límnos has some good beaches, a wonderful resort hotel and one of the Aegean's most atmospheric ports.

USEFUL NUMBERS
Port Authority
tel: 0254 22823
Pravlis Tourist Travel
Agency (tickets and information) tel: 0254 22471
Airport tel: 0254 31204

Mýrina may be provincial (Greeks call it boring), but it's a pleasant place to spend an afternoon

213

▶▶ Mýrina   *202B2*

The main town on Límnos is literally divided in two by a ruined *kástro*. Built by 14th-century Venetians over the temple of Artemis and rebuilt under Turkish occupation, the *kástro* offers excellent views over the sea and island. Running around the *kástro*, from the port to the beach, is a lively shopping street with a distinctly eastern feel to it. This is where Limniotes stroll in the evening.

On this street, opposite the beach, finds from the island's three ancient sites are housed in a Turkish mansion, the **Límnos Archaeological Museum**▶ (*Open* Tue–Sun 8.30–3. *Admission charge; free* Sun). Among the well-presented chronological displays, the 6th- to 8th-century BC vases from Kabeirion and grave goods from Hephaistia are outstanding.

▶ Moúdros   *202B2*

Central Límnos arches around the bay of Moúdros (Órmos Moúdrou), one of the finest natural harbours in the Aegean. This was the starting point for the 1915 Anglo–French attack on Gallipoli, intended to force Turkey out of World War I, which left about 36,000 Commonwealth soldiers dead: the **Commonwealth War Cemetery**, just outside unexciting Moúdros Town, contains the graves of 887 of them, most of whom died in the base hospitals around the bay. Sikh and Muslim casualties are buried at the side of the cemetery.

Beaches

Límnos has some good sandy beaches. Mýrina has an excellent large public beach to the north of the kástro; beyond it is the private beach of the wonderful Ákti Mýrina Hotel. Out of town, the villages of Platý and Thános overlook fine sandy beaches, which are usually less crowded than Mýrina.

A LÍMNIOT HEROINE
In 1475, after the fall of Byzantium, the victorious Turkish general landed on Límnos with an army carried in 300 ships. The Venetian garrison fought bravely but were outnumbered and talking of surrender when a Límniot girl called Maroula picked up the sword and shield of her dying father and rushed at the Turkish forces. The invaders fled, the fortress was saved (for a while) and Maroula was rewarded by a dowry and her choice of Venice's young aristocrats.

CONNECTIONS
Límnos has ferry links with Kavála, Piréas, Lésvos, Thessaloníki, Chíos and Ágios Efstrátios; in summer with Sámos, Samothráki, Pátmos and the Sporades.

> TO THE IMMORTAL MEMORY
> OF THOSE WHO DIED
> FOR THE EMPIRE
> DARDANELLES CAMPAIGN
> 1915 – 1916.

The Allied military cemetery in Moúdros commemorates the 36,000 Allied soldiers who died here in 1915

Vourliótes, in the hills near Kokkári

USEFUL NUMBERS
Port Authority (Sámos Town) tel: 0273 27318
Port Authority (Pythagóreio) tel: 0273 61225
Hertz Rent-a-Car tel: 0273 24771 (Vathi) or 61550 (Pythagóreio)
Airport tel: 0273 61222
Tourist information Sámos Town: off the waterfront on Odós I Martíou, *Open* Mon–Fri 11.30–2, longer in season, tel: 0273 28530.) Tourist information Pythagóreio: booth on main street (tel: 0273 61389).

PYTHAGORAS
The great philosopher and mathematician Pythagoras came from Sámos. At the age of 18 he was a champion wrestler at the Olympic Games, but he is better known for being the first to claim that the sun was the centre of the universe and for founding the basis of the system of logarithms. Pythagóreio (formerly Tigáni, or 'frying pan') was named after him only in 1955.

SÁMOS

Lush and green Sámos was once the wealthiest island in the Aegean, where the arts and sciences flourished. Its coastal resorts become more popular every summer, but the interior remains comparatively untrodden.

▶ Sámos Town (Vathí)   *203E1*

With its perfect horseshoe-shaped harbour, this is the main port and provincial capital. It has a busy pedestrianised bazaar area and some good neoclassical mansions. The excellent **Archaeological Museum**▶▶▶ (Plateía Ágios Spyridónos, behind the little park. *Open* Tue–Sun 8.30–3. *Admission charge; free* Sun) is the town's main attraction. The old wing has griffin-heads, for which 7th-century BC Sámos was famous; other exhibits show foreign influences on local artwork. The new wing was specially constructed to house a magnificent 5m-high *kouros*, the largest free-standing statue known from ancient Greece. Picturesque old Vathí, on the slopes behind the modern town, is worth a visit.

▶ Karlovási   *203E1*

Karlovási, the island's second town and port, is little more than a cluster of four small villages. Limáni, the port itself, has hotels and a waterfront lined with terraces and tavernas. Meséo and Paleó are residential areas with a few friendly *ouzerí*, while Néo is only a wasteland.

▶▶ Kokkári   *203E1*

Once a quaint fishing village, Kokkári has good beaches which attract the crowds. For some island atmosphere, head for the nearby hills where good walking trails link villages in a countryside of cypresses, orchards and pine forests. The most atmospheric villages are Vourliótes – a maze of narrow streets with a pretty central square – and Manolátes with its flowering gardens.

▶ Mytilinioí   *203E1*

Mytilinioí has a pleasant main square with some old kafeneía and a disorganised **Palaeontological Museum**▶ (*Open* Mon–Fri 9–12, 5–8. *Admission charge*).

▶▶ Pythagóreio 203E1

Sámos's ancient capital, Pythagóreio, was built by the 6th-century BC autocrat Polycrates; and his two great engineering projects, which astonished the ancient world, are still more or less visible: the ancient port, exactly where the harbour and jetty are today and the amazing **Efpalinion Tunnel▶▶** (*Open* Tue–Sun 8.45–2.30. *Admission charge; free* Sun). This 1km-long aqueduct was cut through the mountain to bring water to ancient Sámos.

The **Roman baths▶** (*Open* Tue–Sun 8.30–3. *Admission free*) are less impressive and the **Archaeological Collection▶** (*Open* Tue–Sun 8.30–3. *Admission free*) is small. Far more interesting is the **Temple of Hera▶▶▶** (*Open* Tue–Sun 8.30–3. *Admission charge; free* Sun) at nearby Iréon, a huge shrine dedicated to the Mother Goddess. Although only foundations and a reerected column have survived, they do give an impression of how important this temple once must have been.

▶ Votsalákia 203D1

Votsalákia has a long beach backed by a sprawling resort. If the beach gets too crowded, or for a change of scene, try climbing Kerketéfs (Mount Kérkis) for some fabulous views. Neighbouring Marathókampos, dramatically built on a hillside, overlooks its port, Órmos Marathókampou. Tavernas in villages like Vourliótes often serve local specialities which are worth trying out: *tirópita*, cheese pastries made with fresh goat's milk; *revithokefthédes*, fried chick-pea balls; and syrupy *moskháto*, a white dessert wine.

Beaches

Good beaches can be found almost all around the coast, but you will need to choose carefully to avoid the crowds, especially in high season. The best beach near Sámos Town is at Kalámi. The good sandy beaches past Logothetis castle are used by several big hotel complexes. Near Kokkári, Tzamadoú beach has good bathing, with nude sunbathing at the west end. There are excellent beaches on the unspoiled coast past Karlovási. Potámi is lovely, with sand and pebbles – a pleasant walk away from Karlovási. A further one-hour walk leads to Megálo Seïtáni, a wildly beautiful beach. Votsalákia is a rapidly growing resort with a good but crowded beach; Psilí Ammos, 3km away and one of two beaches on the island to share this name, is quieter.

CONNECTIONS

Sámos has ferry links with Piréas, Ikaría, Foúrnoi, Chíos, Kálymnos, Pátmos, Páros, Náxos, Leipsoí, Sýros, Agathónisi, Léros, Lésvos, Mýkonos and Límnos. Hydrofoils run in summer to Pátmos, Kós, Léros, Kálymnos, Ikaría, Chíos, Leipsoí and Lésvos. Excursion boats go to Kusadasi (Turkey) in the summer.

215

The crescent-shaped Tzamadoú beach features on almost every poster of Sámos

HERODOTUS ON SAMOS

'I have written somewhat at length concerning the Samians, because they have the three greatest constructions of all the Greeks: first a channel with two mouths dug beneath a mountain a hundred and fifty fathoms high...The architect of this channel was Megarian, Eupalinos son of Naustrophos. This is one of the three and the second is a breakwater in the sea around the harbour, twenty fathoms in depth. Their third construction is the greatest of all known temples, of which the first master-builder was Rhoikos son of Phileus, a Samian.'
Herodotus, *The Histories* (London, 1972)

USEFUL NUMBERS
Port Authority
(Samothráki)
tel: 0551 41305
Tourist Police
tel: 0551 41218 41790

The Hieron, in the sanctuary of the Great Gods, is all that is left of a large Doric temple from the 4th century BC

SAMOTHRÁKI

Samothráki is dominated by mountains and lashed for much of the year by fierce winds and high seas. It was the site of one of the ancient world's most enduring rituals, the 'mysteries' at the Sanctuary of the Great Gods. The sanctuary's ruins are among the most impressive to be found in the Greek islands.

SOLVING THE MYSTERIES
No writer in antiquity dared record exactly what went on at the sanctuary, but the Samothráki mysteries were based on the worship of the Great Gods – the Great Mother, a lesser male figure called Kadmilos and the Kabeiroi. The first stage of initiation involved a ritual based on the cycle of life and rebirth, while higher initiation required purification and then a baptism with animal's blood. Samothráki's Great Gods were later assimilated with gods in the Greek pantheon, so the Great Mother became Demeter, Kadmilos became Hermes and the Kabeiroi became the Dioscuri – the twins Castor and Pollux (Gemini in the constellation).

▶▶ Samothráki Town (Chóra)   202B3
There is nothing in particular to see in the island capital, but its quiet alleys, clinging attractively to their hillside, are the best place to stroll or have lunch if the weather forces you off the coast.

▶▶ Thermá (Loutrá)   202B4
The road along Samothráki's rough and rugged north coast towards Thermá gives no hint of what is to come: the little spa is a place of soft beauty. The air is inspiring, sunlight filters through aged trees and sulphur-rich springs fill the therapeutic baths (*Open* May–Oct daily 8–1 and 5–7. *Admission charge*).

▶▶▶ Palaiópoli   202B4
Philip of Macedonia and the Roman emperor Hadrian went straight to the sanctuary, but lesser mortals should start at the **museum**▶▶ (*Open* Tue–Sun 8.30–3. *Admission charge*. Here, objects like the 3rd-century terracotta Eros, a dancing-girl frieze and a cast of the famous Winged Nike (Victory), the original of which is in the Louvre in Paris (see panel opposite), help to give the place a human proportion. A path leads to the clearly marked **Sanctuary of the Great Gods**▶▶▶ (*Open* Tue–Sun 8.30–3. *Admission* same ticket as museum), where the Arsinoeion, named after the wife of Ptolemy of Egypt, is Greece's largest ancient rotunda. Most impressive are the reerected columns and architrave of the Hieron. Above here stood the fountain and statue of Nike; below is the wild sea and all around there is an extraordinary atmosphere of power and desolation.

Beaches
Kamariótissa's stone beach, in the northwest, is very exposed. Much better is Thermá (Loutrá) with sand and stone. In the south, the large sandy beaches at Pachiá Ámmos and Kípos require private transport.

CONNECTIONS
Samothráki has ferry links with Kavála, Alexandroúpoli and Límnos, which can also be reached by hydrofoil in summer.

THÁSOS

A short hop from the mainland, Thásos is a popular resort island with Greek and foreign holiday-makers. Small and hilly, with good beaches and important antiquities, its character has been transformed by tourism.

▶▶ Thásos Town (Liménas) 202A4

The beauty of the capital is assured by the surrounding pine-covered hills, by its pretty port and by its antiquities. The **Agora▶▶**, fenced off but often open, covered with mostly Roman ruins and shaded by trees, makes a wonderful, peaceful retreat from the tourist shops. Nearby is an excellent Archaeological Museum (*Open* Tue–Fri 8–7, Sat–Sun 8.30–3. *Admission charge*) and a Greek Theatre which has fabulous views. The acropolis is topped by a **fort▶▶**, originally built in the 5th century BC and enlarged over the centuries. The **ancient walls▶▶** repay closer inspection.

▶ Moní Archangélou 202A4

The original 12th-century church here was built by an ascetic who had a vision of St Michael; the icon of St Michael and the natural spring were credited with healing powers. The spring has dried up, but the church is still a popular sight. The convent was established in 1974.

Beaches

Thásos has excellent sandy beaches with good bathing, especially on the east and south coasts. Chrysí Ammoudiá is convenient from Thásos Town, but Paradise Beach, further south, is worth the extra effort. Alykí is in a beautiful cove but is impossibly crowded in high season. Potós is the best beach near Limenária.

217

The acropolis of ancient Thásos was converted into a medieval fortress, first by the Venetians in 1204 and a hundred years later by the Genoese

Before the Ancient Greeks there was no theatre; some would claim that there has been little theatrical innovation since then. Exploding out of the extraordinary celebrations for Dionysos at the time of Athens's greatest power, wealth and prestige, theatre quickly developed into the exchange between actors and audience that we continue to enjoy today.

The mask of a tragic actor from Piréas, 4th century BC

218

AESCHYLUS'S EGG
Tradition has it that the great poet Aeschylus, who was bald in his old age, was killed at the age of 69 when an eagle mistook his head for a rock and dropped a tortoise on it from some height.

ANCIENT THEATRES TODAY
Only the foundations of Athens's Theatre of Dionysos are now visible, but elsewhere in the country fine examples of early Greek auditoriums have survived. One of the most spectacular theatres built in Ancient Greece was at Epídavros. It is still known for its extraordinary acoustics. The popularity of the works of Sophocles, Euripides and their rivals is clear from the fact that this theatre could seat up to 13,000 spectators. Set in thick pine woods, it was hidden for many centuries, but since 1955 Epídavros has been the venue for a summer theatre festival. There are similar theatre festivals at several other places, including Thásos.

The birth of Tragedy Tragedy, strangely enough, has its origins in the most carefree of all Greek festivals, the Dionysia – a time of orgiastic celebration. It was at the Dionysia in Athens in 536 BC that Thespis first put in front of the festival audience an actor and a chorus. The success of his venture can be gauged by the popularity of tragedies at subsequent festivals.

Aeschylus's revolution Aeschylus (525–456 BC), the first great tragic poet, went against tradition by putting several actors on stage at the same time, creating drama between them and by giving the chorus more of a background role. He is believed to have composed more than 80 plays, although only seven survive, the most famous being *The Persians*, about the the Greek victory at Salamis and the *Oresteia*, a trilogy of plays about Orestes, who avenged the murder of his father Agamemnon.

Human failings At the festival of 468 BC, Aeschylus found himself competing with a younger poet by the name of Sophocles, who won the laurels that year and became the Athenians' favourite. Sophocles (496–406 BC) stands out as the master of Greek tragedy. Where the characters of Aeschylus are doomed from their opening lines, Sophocles's characters are plausible human beings who bring tragedy on themselves. They are brilliantly drawn, with all their human desires and failings. As a dramatist, Sophocles also understood that he could move his audience with pathos, as is obvious in his masterpieces, *Antigone*, still popular today and *Oedipus Rex*, on which Aristotle based his poetic theory and from which Freud named the Oedipus complex.

The development of the theatre In the 6th century BC, when Thespis was putting on his tragedies, 'theatres' were little more than open spaces in front of the tent in which actors and chorus prepared themselves for the performance. By the 5th century BC, a more permanent theatre was evolving in Athens to meet the demands of this changing art form; a stone auditorium on the side of the Acropolis, near the temple of Dionysos, was finally completed around 330 BC. It could seat more than 20,000 people. (All that can be seen today are its foundations.) As dramas became more complicated and as audiences became larger, so the design of theatres needed to be changed, until the stage was raised, the orchestra sunk and the place began to look like something that we would recognise as a theatre.

Having a laugh One of the reasons for the growing popularity of theatre was the advent of a poet called Aristophanes (c448–c380 BC), who abandoned the familiar legends about heroes and gods and instead staged satires about contemporary issues and characters. In one of them, *The Frogs*, he has Euripides (see panel) and Aeschylus competing against each other for the tragic prize in the afterworld – and so comedy was born out of tragedy.

The legacy When the Romans conquered Greece they maintained the theatres and Roman poets and playwrights continued Greek traditions. Virgil's *Aeneid* traces the founding of Rome back to a character Homer mentions at the sack of Troy. However, the fall of the Roman Empire brought an end to classical theatre. Plays were not performed again in Europe until the 15th century, initially accompanying religious festivals, as in early Greece. The texts of some early Greek plays survive and are now performed at theatres throughout the world.

The renowned Hellenistic theatre of ancient Thásos

THE THIRD GREAT TRAGEDIAN

The third of the great Attic tragic poets, Euripides (c480–406 BC), brought to tragedy his gift for plot development. Although not as popular in his lifetime as his contemporary Sophocles – it is significant that he died outside his native land, in Macedonia – his work increased in popularity after his death. Of the 90 or so dramas that he wrote, 18 have survived, more than the surviving works of both Aeschylus and Sophocles together.

ARISTOPHANES'S HUMOUR

In his comedy *Wasps*, Aristophanes showed that no subject was taboo in his theatre. A character called Xanthias has the following lines:
'Like that prostitute I visited yesterday at midday, When I told her to get on top, she got mad at me And asked if I wanted to set up a tyranny like Hippias'.

Classical artists often represented theatre scenes on ceramics

The Saronic Islands

The Saronic Islands
Aígina (ΑΙΓΙΝΑ)
Póros (ΠΟΡΟΣ)
Salamína
 (ΣΑΛΑΜΙΝΑ)
Spétses (ΣΠΕΤΣΕΣ)
Ýdra (ΨΔΡΑ)

Saronic Islands

Pages 220–1: the Póros Strait, so lyrically described in Henry Miller's The Colossus of Maroussi

Temple of Aphaia
see *page 224*

Ýdra Town
see *page 231*

THE SARONIC ISLANDS Sitting just south of Athens and its busy port, Piréas, the islands in the Saronic Gulf were among the first to be visited by pleasure-seekers. But although some of them have become almost a commuter belt for Athenians, the five main islands in this group have maintained some of their character and offer plenty of opportunities within reach of the capital.

WAR AND PEACE Although the islands are so close to the mainland, their history has been dominated by the sea. Ýdra was uninhabited in antiquity, but Salamína, Aígina and Póros (known as the island of Poseidon) were home to important seafaring communities. Salamína is famous for the sea battle that took place in 480 BC off the narrow strait between it and the mainland, when the much smaller Greek navy outmanouvered the ships of the Persian King Xerxes. Neighbouring Aígina sent 30 ships to join the Greek fleet, an indication of its strength. The islanders were renowned for their skill at sea – ships from Aígina traded throughout the Mediterranean and the island was

Tiers of white-walled, red-tiled mansions around the idyllic horse-shoe harbour of Ýdra

BEST BEACHES
The Saronic Islands are not the best place to go for that idyllic seaside vacation since their beaches tend to be crowded with both Athenians and foreign visitors. However, the best of the lot is at Ágioi Anárgyroi on Spétses.

wealthy and powerful. But 50 years after the Persian defeat, the people of Aígina made the mistake of siding with the Spartans against Athens; after the Spartan defeat, Aígina was destroyed. The rest is history: Athens had all the glory, the Saronic Islands lived in her shadow, but Aígina's Temple of Aphaia serves as a reminder of just how grand the island was in the 5th century BC.

MODERN HISTORY During the War of Independence against the Turks, the Spétsian heroine Laskarína Bouboulína saved her native island in dramatic fashion (see panel on page 229). Aígina's past glory was recalled a few years later when Ioánnis Kapodístrias was sworn in as first governor of the free Greek state in Aígina's cathedral. The island's main town acted briefly as the first state capital and the first modern drachma was minted there.

LANDSCAPES AND FARMING The islands in the Saronic Gulf might be rocky, with poor volcanic soil, but they do support agriculture and, in some places, an abundance of wildlife. Aígina is the most fertile and its pistachio crop is so renowned that it has given the nut its Greek name, *aígi-nas*. Ýdra's fine houses are known for their gardens, while Spétses is famous for its woods of Aleppo pine.

CHOOSING YOUR SEASON Because of the number of Athenians who stay there and the even greater number of day-trippers, some Saronic Island ports have a cosmopolitan air, with the sort of cafés, restaurants and expensive boutiques that you would expect to see in Mýkonos. In summer, as elsewhere, beaches are crowded and discos noisy. So if island life and archaeology are what you are looking for then consider visiting off season. The sea may be too cold or rough for bathing, but the views will be unobstructed and you might have the privilege of hearing the islanders speaking their native language – a mix of old Albanian and Greek – instead of *kafeneía* English.

MYTHOLOGICAL ISLANDS
According to mythology the first king of Aígina was Aeacus, offspring of the liaison between Zeus and Aígina. Aeacus had three sons, Peleus, Telemon and his favourite, Phocos. When Phocos was killed by his jealous brothers, the latter were exiled, Peleus to Thessaly and Telemon to Salamina, where they proceeded to establish their dynasties. Peleus's son Achilles and Telemon's son Ajax were among the greatest warriors of the Trojan war.

223

THE ISLANDS IN A DAY
The Saronic Islands are known as the 'offshore islands' because of their proximity to Athens. They are close enough for it to be possible to visit an island for the day and be back in the city by nightfall. Athenian travel agents also offer a one-day cruise, usually to three of the islands; Aígina, Ýdra and Póros.

HENRY MILLER ON ÝDRA
'Hydra is a rock which rises out of the sea like a huge loaf of petrified bread. It is the bread turned to stone which the artist receives as reward for his labours when he first catches sight of the promised land.'
Henry Miller, *The Colossus of Maroussi* (London, 1942)

USEFUL NUMBERS
Port Authority (Piréas)
tel: 01 451 1311
Port Authority (Aígina)
tel: 0297 22328

A GOOD ESCAPE
The small island of Agkístri, only a short boat ride away from Aígina and the latest to be included in travel brochures, still offers some authentic island life, especially off season. The main town Skála is already seriously overbuilt, but Mílos still has an attractive village centre with a good beach close by.

224

CONNECTIONS
Aígina has ferry links with Piréas, Méthana, Póros, Ýdra, Spétses, Agkístri, Ermióni and Portochéli. Hydrofoil services operate to most of these places and one-day cruises to Póros, Ýdra and Spétses are also offered by local travel agents.

The Temple of Aphaia is one of the best preserved in Greece

AÍGINA

Athenians often regard Aígina as their nearest clean beach. Many visitors come only to visit the Temple of Aphaia.

►► Aígina Town 223B3

Aígina harbour is always busy with hydrofoils, fishermen and the boats bringing fresh produce from the mainland. North of the port stands the *Kolóna*, a lone column from the ruined **Temple of Apollo►** (*Open* Tue–Sun 8.30–3. *Admission charge*). The town has some grand houses from the brief period, in the 19th century, when it was the first capital of Greece.

An Archaeological Museum (*Open* Tue–Sun 8.30–3. *Admission charge*) exhibits the island finds that have not been removed to Athens. It was built on the site of what was the very first Archaeological Museum in Greece.

►►► Naós Afaía (Temple of Aphaia) 223B3

Open: Mon–Fri 8.30–7 (5 pm closing in winter), Sat, Sun and public holidays 8.30–3. Admission charge
Regular buses from Aígina Town and Agía Marína
This Doric temple, the best-preserved classical temple in the Greek Islands, was built around 490 BC, on the site of a more ancient cult place. It was dedicated to the Cretan nymph Aphaia, who was connected with Artemis and was worshipped as the protector of women. The temple's pediments, depicting the battles of Troy, were found intact but were removed to Munich.

► Pérdika 223B3

This quiet fishing village, overlooking the island of Moní, is renowned for its waterfront fish tavernas. Daily boats leave here for Moní, mainly a nature reserve but with some bays for bathing.

Beaches
The best places to swim include the small beach near the Kolóna (near Aígina Town), in west-coast Marathóna, or on Moní islet.

Cycle ride

To the Temple of Aphaia (Naós Afaía)

A steep ride, either by motorcycle or by bicycle for the more energetic, takes you from the present capital Aígina to the old capital Palaiochóri and from the modern monastery of Ágios Nektários to the ancient site of worship, Naós Afaía (Temple of Aphaia) (12km each way; allow half a day. Bicycle and motorcycle hire agencies line the waterfront, but shop around since prices can vary).

Leave the waterfront in Aígina Town, going away from the ferry landing, passing the Hotel Brown and then taking the second street to the left, at the Hotel Miranda. Follow signposts for Agía Marína and, uphill, take the second street on the right. The road winds through pistachio orchards, past pretty villas and small villages. Turn right at the end of the road. About 5km from Aígina, on the left, you will see the monastery of Ágios Nektários. The enormous church, dominating the landscape, houses the tomb of a bishop from Aígina who died in 1920 and was canonised in 1967. Pass the signpost for Ágios Nektários and continue for 500m to the deserted old island capital of Palaiochóri, an extraordinary place where only 20 of the supposed original 365 churches and monasteries remain. A few are open in the morning. Returning to the main road, turn left towards the pretty village of Mesagrós in the middle of vineyards and pine woods, whose products are combined to make excellent local retsina. Go past the churchyard taking the straight (slightly towards the left) road for Agía Marína and soon the Temple of Aphaia (see page 224) will come into sight, towering over the landscape and offering an interesting stop with magnificent views over the island. Make the return to Aígina Town by the same route.

The modern church of Ágios Nektários is dedicated to a rather controversial saint, only recently canonised

Many visitors to the Greek Islands expect to encounter mosquitoes or butterflies and to find some fish or squid on their plates, but few take time to find out about the islands' rich and varied wildlife. Sadly the visitors themselves are unwittingly one of the biggest threats to a fragile wildlife environment which is home to a number of endangered species.

A southern festoon, one of the most striking butterflies to be seen in the islands

WILDLIFE REHABILITATION

226

Aígina has one of the most successful animal rehabilitation centres in Greece. The Hellenic Wildlife Hospital, beside the Hotel Danae in Aígina Town, takes care of numerous birds and wild animals, as well as stray cats and dogs, often from Athens. Once animals have recovered, they are released if at all possible. (To arrange a visit or give a donation, tel: 0297 22882.)

FOREST FIRES

Every summer many acres of Greek forests are destroyed by fires, sometimes started accidentally but too often lit on purpose by shepherds wanting more grazing, or by developers with their eye on another stretch of land. Repeated fires result in a barren, desert-like scrubland which, without ground cover, is very vulnerable to erosion. Wildlife also suffers in fires, as amphibians and reptiles rarely move fast enough to escape the flames and birds are asphyxiated by the smoke.

Marine life Mainland Greece has its fair share of nature reserves and wildlife sanctuaries, but it is the marine life around the islands which is most under threat. The Northern Sporades have been chosen for the first (and long overdue) National Marine Park, where several endangered creatures including the Mediterranean monk seal will find protection. Of special interest are the loggerhead turtles, still quite numerous but seriously threatened by tourism. Playful dolphins often follow yachts and ferries, but sharks are seldom spotted near the islands' coasts. The Greek seas, like other parts of the Mediterranean, are heavily overfished and their fish stocks are decreasing.

Birdwatching in the islands The Greek Islands and Crete in particular, are fascinating for birdwatchers, who can see both resident Mediterranean species and, primarily from mid-March to mid-May, migratory birds on their way from East Africa and the Nile to Northern Europe, from where they return south in the autumn. In the mountains it is common to find rock nuthatches, buzzards, smaller eagles, alpine choughs and Griffon vultures. With some luck it is possible to spot a rare vulture found mainly on the plateaus of Crete, the Lammergeier. Near the coast are found several species of egret and heron, black-winged stilts and marsh harriers. Outside villages and in the hills, swallows, nightingales, crows, crag martins, kestrels, tiny Scops owls, golden orioles and lovely black and white hoopoes can also be seen.

The hoopoe

Insects Most people would probably rather not encounter insects on their holiday, but they can be beautiful and fascinating to watch. Even if you do not see them, the noisy presence of grasshoppers and cicadas will not go unnoticed. A great variety of beetles, flies, mosquitoes and wasps all make their home here, but probably the most beautiful of Greece's insects are the butterflies, especially visible in spring and summer. Crete, again, has some very colourful species such as the southern festoon with red, yellow and black zigzags; big bright yellow Cleopatras; and tiny green hairstreaks.

Reptiles Lizards of various species are found everywhere but they can be shy, darting away as you approach. However, look for them basking among the stones of ancient sites in the midday sun. The almost fluorescent Balkan green lizard, which can grow up to 50cm long, is quite common and unmistakable. In the Dodecanese and northern Cyclades it is possible to find the brown-greyish, iguana-like agama or Rhodes dragon and Crete is one of the few places in Europe where chameleons can be spotted. At night, geckoes come out to devour mosquitoes. Of several species of snake, only the cat snake is poisonous.

Mammals Comparatively few mammals are found in the islands but there are some endemic species especially in Crete, such as the Cretan spiny mouse and the island's mascot, the rare kri-kri or wild goat, now surviving mainly in nature reserves on deserted islets. Skýros has a rare variety of small wild horse and monk seals can sometimes be spotted around Alónnisos (see page 236). Most islands are home to smaller mammals, such as hares, badgers, weasels, mice, rats and bats.

Threats Fish stocks are limited in the seas around the islands and until recently fishermen often killed the monk seals, which sometimes damaged their nets while looking for food. Pollution from fast-growing industries and forest fires is another danger as well as the undoubted threat from the large number of visitors, causing pollution and habitat loss as coast and countryside are lost to development. The most well-publicised example is the plight of the loggerhead turtles on Zákynthos (see panel on page 199). The tourist industry has grown very quickly and protecting the environment from its more undesirable consequences has often been ignored until it was too late to prevent damage.

A bee-eater

ARCHIPELAGOS
Archipelagos, a private conservation group based in Argostóli on Kefalloniá, aims at the preservation of the marine and coastal environment in the Ionian Islands and throughout Greece. It is particularly concerned about the endangered Mediterranean monk seal and with marine pollution. Together with local people it has produced brochures with walking trails on the Ionian Islands as part of a plan to help build a complementary relationship between the natural world, non-intrusive tourism, local culture and the economy. (For more information contact Gerasimos and Susanne Dimitratos, tel: 0671 24565.)

The Balkan green lizard

THE STRAIT OF PÓROS
'If there is one dream
which I like above all others it is that of sailing on
land. Coming into Póros
gives the illusion of the
deep dream. Suddenly the
land converges on all
sides and the boat is
squeezed into a narrow
strait from which there
seems to be no
egress...To sail slowly
through the streets of
Póros is to recapture the
joy of passing through the
neck of the womb. It is a
joy too deep to be remem-
bered.'
Henry Miller, *The
Colossus of Maroussi*
(London, 1942)

THE BATTLE OF SALAMIS
On the stretch of water
between the mainland and
the bleak town of
Paloúkia, a battle took
place which changed the
course of European his-
tory. In 480 BC the Persian
fleet under King Xerxes,
who was already occupy-
ing Attica, was all set for
victory over the Athenians
and Peloponnesians who
had retreated to the
waters near Salamína.
The Greek fleet was out-
numbered by about two to
one, but thanks to the
Athenian strategist
Themistocles, the Persian
fleet was outmanoeuvered
and forced to retreat.

PÓROS

Póros, separated from the mainland only by a 350m-wide
strait, is in fact two islands: Sferiá, a small, crowded island
occupied almost entirely by the bustle of Póros Town and
the larger and until recently much wilder Kalávria. Both
Póros and the nearby mainland town of Galatás have
opened their doors to package tourism. Most of the hotels
are on Kalávria, but Póros Town has plenty of more basic
accommodation and a wide choice of places to eat, both on
the busy quayside and up in the town.

▶▶ Póros Town   223B2

Looking across to the mainland, Póros Town has a lively
and atmospheric waterfront – a good place to linger over a
meal or a drink, or simply watch the world go by. There is
a small **Archaeological Museum▶** (*Open* Mon–Sat 9–3.
Admission free) and a blue-domed clocktower from where
there are fine views over the mountains and sea. The
Greek Navy has a training college on the north side of the
town – evidence of the island's long and continuing maritime tradition.

▶▶ Galatás   223B2

Galatás is a fast-developing mainland resort across the
strait from Póros, with two good beaches, Pláka and Alíki.
The **Limonódassos**, just beyond Alíki, is a vast lemon
grove with more than 30,000 trees and a taverna serving
fresh lemonade. From Galatás it is possible to travel by bus
to the renowned ancient theatre at Epidavros and other
mainland sites.

▶▶ Kalávria   223B2

On a longer visit to Póros, it is worth crossing the bridge to
Kalávria – though not, perhaps, for its beaches. Up in the
hills, well away from the ranks of seaside hotels, there are
some fine views over the sea and the Peloponnese. Places
to visit include a ruined 6th-century BC **Temple of
Poseidon** and the abandoned 18th-century monastery of
Zoodóchos Pigí▶.

Beaches

Kanáli has the best beach, but an admission fee is charged
to all who wish to use it. Further down Askéli Bay there is
good bathing, but even more hotels are currently under
construction here.

SALAMÍNA

Salamína sees few tourists, as its beaches are too close to
the pollution of Athens and Piréas to be recommended.
The island is remembered historically for the Battle of
Salamis, a momentous victory by Athens over the Persians
in 480 BC (see panel).

▶ Salamína Town (Kouloúri)   223B4

Most people live here in the island's capital, a sprawl of
concrete buildings. There are no facilities for visitors and
nowhere to stay, but there is a good bus system to the villages. Bus No 8 passes near the **monastery of Panágia
Faneroméni▶**, whose two churches have good 18th- and
19th-century wall paintings.

▶ Aiánteio 223B4

This cosy village has a small pebble beach. The charming Hotel Gabriel is owned by Mr Tzimas, an enthusiastic poet and journalist, who will recite from his work when the mood takes him.

▶ Paloúkia 223B4

Paloúkia is the port of arrival and an important military base, but there is nothing worth staying for.

▶▶ Selínia 223B4

Selínia is a summer resort popular with Greeks. There are several daily ferry connections to Piréas. The waterfront is quite pleasing and has a few tavernas.

SPÉTSES

Group tourism has reached Spétses, the farthest from Athens of the Saronic Islands, but away from the main town and the noise of the mopeds, there are still cool pine forests and some fine beaches waiting to be explored. There is talk of lifting the ban on private cars, which will inevitably transform the island's character. At present, apart from a few taxis, transport is by hired bicycle or moped, by boat, or (in Spétses Town) by horse-drawn carriage. An erratic bus service operates and the island is small enough for walking to be practicable (and pleasant).

▶▶ Spétses Town 223A1

On summer days the port (Dápia – a name often used to refer to the town itself) is mobbed by hordes of day trippers, so locals and resident visitors tend to emerge only in the early evening, after they have gone. The **Spétses Museum▶** (*Open* Tue–Sun 8–2. *Admission charge*), in the beautiful Hadziyánnis Mexís mansion (follow signposts from the waterfront), has a small collection of local costumes, memorabilia from the War of Independence and the bones of the local heroine Laskarína Bouboulína. Her statue, dressed in baggy pirate trousers, stands to the west

A few boatyards on Spétses still build sturdy kaíki, a familiar sight in the islands' harbours

CONNECTIONS
The easiest way to reach Salamína is by ferry from Pérama (near Piréas) to Paloúkia. Póros and Spétses have ferry links with each other and with Piréas, Aígina, Ýdra, Ermióni, Portochéli and Méthana. Hydrofoils operate to Piréas and the other Saronic Islands (except Salamína).

LA BOUBOULINA
In 1821, Laskarína Bouboulína led the uprising of Spétses against the Turks with her own fleet and army. Considered the local Jeanne d'Arc, she is remembered for her courage, having lost two husbands in pirate raids and subsequently losing two sons during the War of Independence. Accounts of her bravery include the story of her placing hats on bushes along the shore, to make the Turks think that soldiers were hiding there.

Laskarína Bouboulína overlooking the comings and goings of ferries in Spétses' harbour

of the new harbour. The **Laskarína Bouboulína House▶ ▶** is now a private museum (guided tours only; for times see the boards at the harbour. *Admission charge*).

On the same square is the grand, slightly crumbling villa of the island's benefactor, Sotírios Anárgiros (see panel on page 231). Nearby on the waterfront is the impressive Possidonion Hotel. A 20-minute walk towards the east past some fine villas leads to the old harbour, Palaió Limáni, still with a boatyard and some good fish tavernas. Watching over all the activity is the old cathedral of Ágios Nikólaos, from whose clocktower the Greek flag was raised in April 1821, heralding Spétses' entrance into the War of Independence.

Beaches

Boat trips run to the bigger beaches in summer, so do not expect to have a beach all to yourself. West of Spétses Town are some hidden coves and pleasant beaches with tavernas, particularly Vrelloú and Zogeriá. Agía Paraskeví is a pretty beach with a little church, but Ágioi Anárgyroi is definitely the finest of all, a long bay with fine sand which fills up quickly in summer. Heading east, Agía Marína has good bathing and a taverna.

Walk

Spétses' pine forests

A walk along part of the road that rings Spétses island, built by the millionaire Sotírios Anárgiros to reveal its beauty, tranquillity and wonderful beaches. Instead of completing the circle on the road, return by climbing through the pine forests at the centre of the island (approximately 6km; allow a whole day, including stops for bathing).

Start from Spétses Town, head west past the Possidonion and Spétses Hotels. The imposing Anárgiros College soon appears on the left. The road winds on through pine trees, with views below of wonderfully clear coves and rocky sunbathing spots, to reach Vrelloú. The beach here (though sometimes litter-strewn) is pleasant and there are some good coves suitable for bathing.

Return to the road and walk on to Zogeriá, which has lovely coves, trees for shade and a few small tavernas. Off the road as it continues towards Agía Paraskeví there are larger coves for bathing, worth the long walk down small paths. Agía Paraskeví has a small, easily accessible beach with a white chapel. On the hill above is the Villa Yasemia, which appears in John Fowles's *The Magus* (see panel on page 231).

Further on, the road suddenly reaches a residential area and the fine sandy beach of Ágioi Anárgyroi. Tasos's taverna here is a popular lunch spot and the beach is a good place to rest before heading inland. Walk to the main road and turn left. After about 200m, past the villas on the right, look for a small path heading uphill. Beyond here directions are difficult to give, but at the top of the hill keep to the path that veers to the right. The pine forests are slowly recovering from the fires which destroyed them in 1990, so the vistas are not always clear, but if you get lost you can always orient yourself by following the direction of the boats heading for the new harbour. Depending on the path you have taken, you will arrive back in town either at the Spétses Hotel or further on at the Lazaros Taverna.

ÝDRA

Wild rocky shores and one of the most beautiful and sophisticated harbours in the Aegean, mean that Ýdra Town is completely overrun in summer. But as there is no transport apart from donkeys and boats, few visitors venture beyond the edge of the town.

▶▶▶ Ýdra Town   223B1

Arriving in Ýdra is truly magnificent; savour the view of the town descending dramatically into the perfect crescent-shaped harbour. The waterfront has many fine mansions, the homes of the 19th-century shipbuilders and sea captains who made the island famous. (A town map, available from local bookshops, indicates the most important ones.) West of the waterfront, in a peaceful courtyard, the **monastery of the Panagía Mitropóleos**▶▶ has a remarkable clock tower.

▶▶ Monasteries   223B1

Paths lead from the town to isolated monasteries inland. About an hour uphill are the **convent of Agía Evpraxía**▶ and the **monastery of Profítis Ilías**▶ and, further away, the **monastery of Agía Triáda**▶, where women are not admitted. The views alone justify the climb.

Beaches

Mandráki is the island's only sandy beach, but it belongs to the Miramáre Hotel. A path west of the harbour leads to a small, popular, pebbly beach just before Kamíni and, further on, to Kastéllo, another pebbly beach. The south coast has beautiful coves for bathing, such as Bísti and Ágios Nikólaos, most easily reached by boat from Ýdra Town.

THE GOOD MILLIONAIRE
Sotírios Anárgiros, a 19th-century native adventurer who made his fortune in America, came back to Spétses not only with plans for developing the island as his playground but also with enough money to realise them. He built a circular road around the island to make it more accessible, dug wells and planted the pine forests which enhance Spétses today. He founded the Anárgiros College, inspired by English private schools, which attracted children of rich families from all over Greece (and the novelist John Fowles, who taught here, see below). He also built the Possidonion Hotel, hoping to attract wealthy tourists to stay on the island.

231

Once the daytrippers leave, Ýdra town regains its delightful mixture of peace and joie-de-vivre

CONNECTIONS
Both ferries and hydrofoils link Ýdra with Piréas and the other Saronic Islands.

THE MAGUS
The English writer John Fowles lived for a while on Spétses, while teaching English at the Anárgiros College. His famous novel *The Magus* was set on the island and both the Possidonion Hotel and the college are mentioned. On top of the hill near Agía Paraskeví is the Villa Yasemia, where the late Alkis Botassis resided. He prided himself on having inspired Fowles to write *The Magus*.

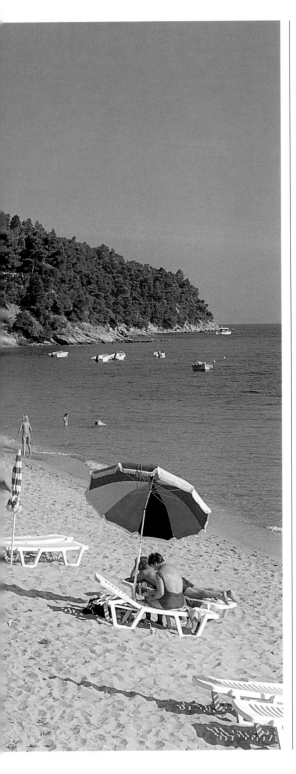

The Sporades and Évvoia

The Sporades and Évvoia

THE SPORADES AND ÉVVOIA The Sporades are aptly named. The 'scattered ones' lie off the eastern coast of Thessaly and, perhaps because of their location, were overlooked by foreign fun-seekers. The Greeks have long preferred them for their great beaches, clean water and wooded hills. Now, direct charter flights have transformed Skíathos and Skópelos and are changing the face of Alónnisos and Skýros. Even so, there is still plenty of scope to get away from it all and if the Sporades seem too busy, nearby Évvoia beckons.

SPORADIC MYTHS The Minoans from Crete colonised the Sporades around the 16th century BC and brought with them the olive and the vine, which the islanders soon learned to cultivate with skill: wine from ancient Alónnisos was traded throughout the region. The islands were later settled by the Dolopians, seafaring Mycenaeans. Among them was Peleus, whose son, the great Achilles, led the Dolopian warriors in the Trojan

Pages 232–3: Vromólimnos, one of Skíathos's more popular beaches

Below: the landscape of southern Évvoia

234

War. Skýros, especially, is rich in mythology from this period, for this was where Achilles's mother hid him to stop him going to Troy, where it had been prophesied that he would die. As another prophecy had announced that the Achaeans would not win at Troy without Achilles, he went to fight. During his stay on Skýros, he fathered a son, Neoptolemus, out of a liaison with King Lycomedes's daughter. After Achilles's glorious death, another prophecy announced that the Greeks would not win at Troy until Neoptolemus was fighting with them: Troy fell after his arrival on the scene.

BEST BEACHES
● Koukounariés and Banana beaches (Skíathos)
● Lalaria beach (Skíathos)
● Magaziá and Mólos (Skýros)
● Kokkinókastro (Alónnisos)

THESEUS'S REVENGE When Theseus, the king of Athens who had killed the minotaur in Knosós (see panel on page 85), arrived on Skýros, King Lycomedes, fearing for his throne, killed the hero. The incident was without consequence for several centuries, until 476 BC, when the oracle at Delphi insisted that Theseus's bones must be returned to Athens. An army was then sent, the islanders were made slaves and the other islands in the group, including Évvoia, were colonised. The hero's bones were then reinterred in his city. From Athens to Rome, Byzantium and Venice, the Sporades knew many masters, but, thanks finally to Turkish indolence, after the pirate Barbarossa had sacked the islands, they managed to retain their individual identity.

THE FIRST GREEKS
It was from Évvoia that the Greeks got their name, for one of the tribes from the island was known as the Graeci. Under the Roman occupation, all people of the area began to be referred to as the Graeci, or Greeks.

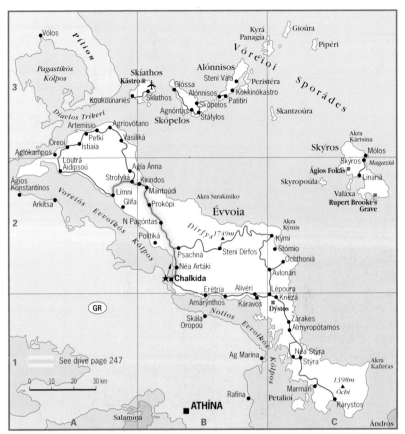

ISLAND LANDSCAPES There is great variety in the look of the islands. Alónnisos is the most remote, untamed and the least developed, an earthquake in 1965 having scared off prospective developers. Its mountainous interior provides excellent if demanding walking, while the coast offers wonderful snorkelling. On Skíathos, other visitors are never far away, even in the hills, but the island has some of Greece's finest beaches. There are beautiful walks through hilly farmland on Skópelos, which still earns more from olives than from visitors. This island is also noted for its plums, pears and almonds, but at sea level it is getting harder to avoid the developments. Skýros has a greater variety, with barren mountains in the south and gentle walking through pine-clad hills and fertile valleys in the north.

THE FERTILE ISLAND Évvoia is the second largest Greek island, separated from the mainland by a narrow channel and near enough to the capital for Athenians to come just to eat, but its fields, hills and villages are a world away from the city's noise and pollution. Although the main town, Chalkída, is industrial, the rugged northeast, the mountainous centre, the open farmlands and the hidden coves make Évvoia one of the most fascinating islands to explore. This one, perhaps more than any, needs time.

Cats are a familiar sight on Alónnisos

THE MONK SEAL
The Mediterranean monk
seal is near extinction.
There are only about 800
left, of which 30 live
around Alónnisos. Until
recently (and still
occasionally) the seals
were being killed by fishermen because they can
damage their nets. The
sea to the north of
Alónnisos has been
declared a marine wildlife
park and the Hellenic
Society for the Protection
of the Monk Seal in Stení
Vála on Alónnisos has
won strong local support.
Little by little, seal pups
from a seal crèche in
Holland are being
released into the park.
But in spite of growing
numbers, there is still little chance of seeing the
seals, as they often hide
in sea caves. If you do
spot them, try not to get
any closer as they are
easily scared away from
their habitat.

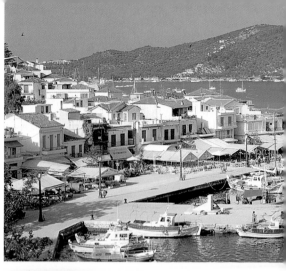

ALÓNNISOS

This mountainous island, the quietest and most remote of
the Sporades, is a paradise for walkers. Although the
island suffered badly in the 1965 earthquake, there is
plenty to discover if you have time and energy to spare:
large areas are accessible only on foot, as roads on
Alónnisos are few.

▶ Patitíri   235B3

Most islanders live in Patitíri, an unattractive concrete
development with a few waterfront bars and tavernas. As
most visitors also stay here or in adjacent Vótsi it is usually
packed in summer. A bus (or a 30-minute walk) goes up to
the picturesque **Palaiá Alónnisos▶▶**. Abandoned in the
1960s, following earthquake damage, the old village with
its narrow, cobbled streets is coming to life again as its
houses are being restored for the summer by Athenians,
British and Germans.

▶▶ Stení Vála   235B3

This is a small, tranquil village with nearby pebbly
beaches. There are some rooms for rent, a campsite and a
few restaurants.

▶▶ Nearby islets   235B3/C3

In summer there are daily excursions to neighbouring
islets. Peristéra has fine sandy beaches which are often
empty. Kyrá Panagía, home to a few wild goats, has good
sandy beaches and two empty monasteries. Gioúra, a
reserve for wild goats, claims to have the cave where the
Cyclops imprisoned Odysseus. Pipéri is a reserve for
monk seals (see panel).

Beaches
The best beaches, most of which are on the more sheltered
east coast, are reached by boat. Chrysí Miliá, crowded in
summer, has pine trees and a taverna. Kokkinókastro has
a lovely pebbly beach, remains of ancient Ikos and a taverna. Stení Vála has good pebbly beaches and Ágios
Dímitrios, further up the coast, is often empty. In the south
of the island is Vithísma, a good sand and pebble beach, as
well as Vrisítsa, on the west coast.

The best view of lively Skíathos Town is from a distance. Close-up, the centre of town looks very tourist-orientated and soulless

SKÍATHOS (Skiáthos)

With the best beaches in the Sporades, if not in all Greece, Skíathos gets very crowded in summer. Although this is no longer the place to find the 'real Greece', a walk inland soon reveals the island's striking nature.

▶▶ Skíathos Town   235B3

What was left of Skíathos Town after World War II has been taken over by the tourist trade. More bars and tavernas open every year and even the Boúrtzi fortress now has a bar. The **Papadiamántis House▶** (off Odós Papadiamántis, near the harbour. *Open* Tue–Sun 9.30–1 and 5–8. *Admission free*), now a museum, is filled with memorabilia of the native author who wrote about customs and traditions on the islands.

▶▶▶ Kástro   235B3

The sight of this 16th-century village is a great reward after the two-hour walk from the harbour. Abandoned in 1830 when the inhabitants moved to the main town after Greek independence, most houses fell into the sea and only three churches have survived, some with original frescos. It remains a charming site.

▶▶ Monasteries   235B3

A paved road off the road to the airport leads to the lovely **Evangelístria monastery▶▶** (*Open* daily 8–12 and 4–8. *Admission free*). A small track leads further to the uninhabited but beautifully situated **monastery of Ágios Charálampos▶**, from where it is possible to reach Kástro. Before Evangelístria, a signpost points the way to the 15th-century **Panagía tis Kehrias**, believed to be the oldest monastery on the island.

Beaches

Some say Koukounariés is the best beach in Greece – it's certainly one of the most crowded. The nearby nudist Banana Beach is the island's trendiest. Vromólimnos is a lovely big sandy bay. Paths lead to Mandráki and Elia, less packed – even in summer. Lalaria beach, accessible only by boat, is dramatically surrounded by steep cliffs.To avoid the crowds you could head for the islet of Tsougriá.

237

USEFUL NUMBERS
Port Authority
tel: 0427 22017
Airport
tel: 0427 22945/22376
Tourist Police
tel: 0427 23172

WONDROUS CAVES
Some of the many spectacular caves in Skíathos's rugged rocky coastline can be visited by boat from the town. The most beautiful and most accessible are Spíliá Káminari and the caves near Lalária beach: Skotiní, Glázia and Hálkini.

CONNECTIONS
Alónnisos and Skíathos are connected by ferry to each other and to Skópelos, Vólos and Ágios Konstantínos. Alónnisos also has ferry links with Kými (Évvoia), while from Skíathos ferries run to Oreoí (Évvoia), Tínos, Mýkonos, Páros, Thíra, Crete and Skýros. Both islands have hydrofoil links with Ágios Konstantínos, Vólos, Skópelos, Oreoí, Skýros and Thessaloníki and with each other. From Alónnisos, hydrofoils also run to Kými and from Skíathos to Chalkída and Aidipsoú (Évvoia).

The monasteries offer a welcome, shady escape from sun and sea

238

OLIVE TREES
Olives, not tourism, are
the main source of
income on Skópelos. In
November most of the
islanders get ready for the
picking season. Many stay
in the *kahlevi*, shelters
originally built for the olive
season, now often
restored as rural homes.
During the harvest,
tourists are forgotten and
the talk in town is all
about how big and how
plentiful the olives will be
and how much oil they will
yield. Once harvested, the
olives are taken to the
refinery, just off the waterfront, where olive oil is
produced for local use.

CONNECTIONS
Skópelos has ferry links
with Skíathos, Vólos,
Ágios Konstantínos,
Alónnisos, Oreoí or Kými
(Évvoia) and Thessaloníki.
Hydrofoil services operate
to Alónnisos, Ágios
Konstantínos, Skíathos,
Vólos, Thessaloníki,
Skýros and Chalkída or
Oreoí (Évvoia).

SKÓPELOS

Skópelos's coastline is rugged, with steep cliffs and rocky
bays, while its interior is lush, with olive groves and fruit
orchards. The resorts are growing steadily, but Skópelos
still has a traditional feel and offers a welcome escape
from its crowded neighbour Skíathos.

►►► Skópelos   235B3

The waterfront in Skópelos Town, lined with tavernas,
bars and souvenir shops, is where most visitors congregate. A walk through the streets behind, winding up to the
ruined Venetian *kástro*, will reveal the true character of the
town. Many of the pretty whitewashed houses have
wooden balconies. There are supposedly 123 churches in
the town and three monasteries stand just outside it (see
Walk opposite).

►►► Glóssa   235B3

Skopelos's second town, Glóssa has a more traditional
feel. Perched high above the fishing harbour of Loutráki, it
is a charming Greek town with a few guest houses, some
kafeneía and fantastic sea views. A pleasant walk east leads
to the rather ugly **monastery of Ágios Ioánnis**, set on a rock
above a small cove with good bathing.

Beaches

The beach in Skópelos is sandy but far from clean.
Stáfylos, a 40-minute walk away, is quite rocky and very
popular. Pánormos is a crowded resort, but the pebbly
beach between there and Miliá, facing the islet of Dasía, is
one of the best, with pines coming down to the beach.
Sáres, reached by boat from Skópelos, is pleasant and not
too crowded.

Walk

From Skópelos Town

A quiet walk through olive groves to two monasteries perched on the hills overlooking the town (approximately 5km; allow two hours for the monastery of Evangelístria, or a good half-day for both monasteries). Take enough water and food for a picnic if you are planning the half-day trip. In summer start early to avoid motorcycles and midday heat.

Walk along the harbour front and the bay, past the row of hotels towards the hills opposite the town. At the end of the bay follow the paved road uphill through the olive groves.

At the Taverna Dilina the road forks and there are signs, left to the monastery of Evangelístria and right to Metamórfosis and Pródromos monasteries. Turn left and follow the dirt road, passing a fountain under two enormous sycamore trees, from which the local people get their drinking water.

Walk up 11 steep bends, or cut through on the even steeper goat paths, to the monastery of **Evangelístria**▶▶ (*Open* daily 10–1 and 4–7), which has stunning views over Skópelos Town. The monastery, rebuilt in 1712, has a gold-plated altar screen and a lovely 15th-century icon. The nuns make craft items which they sell to visitors. From here, either walk back down to town, or go as far as the Taverna Dilina and then walk uphill towards Metamórfosis.

The more adventurous can follow the goat tracks from Evangelístria (ask the nuns for directions). The 16th-century monastery of **Metamórfosis**▶ is closed up for most of the year, but some monks from Mount Áthos stay there each August to celebrate the big annual *panagía*.

From Metamórfosis, either walk back down the road, or continue up the hill from the monastery and at the next bend take the small track along the rocks, which offers some magnificent views on the way back into Skópelos Town.

Bronze of Homer

The *Iliad*, *the oldest surviving work of Greek literature, tells of the war between the Greeks and the Trojans. While many of the events described in its 15,693 lines remain a matter of legend without historical evidence, Homer's evocation of the mighty warriors brings alive one of the ages of ancient civilisation. Alexander the Great took the book with him when he set out to conquer the known world.*

PARIS

Also known as Alexandros, Paris is blamed by Homer for providing the cause for the Trojan War – the abduction of Helen – and thereby bringing about the downfall of his people and their city. Before this, he was famous for having been obliged to judge the beauty of Aphrodite, Hera and Athena; he chose Aphrodite, who promised him the most beautiful woman in the world: Helen. After the death of Hector, it was Paris who killed Achilles with an arrow in his heel.

ACHILLES

When Achilles's mother Thetis heard that her son was fated to die at Troy, she disguised him as a girl and hid him in the *kástro* of Skýros Town, the probable site of King Lycomedes's palace. When Odysseus came looking for Achilles, he brought gifts of jewellery, dresses and a sword. On leaving, Odysseus raised the alarm and while the ladies grabbed the jewellery and ran, Achilles instinctively seized the sword. Achilles became the most brilliant and feared of the Greek warriors, but for all his divine protection, he still died young.

The Trojan War Excavations at Truva in Turkey, close to Límnos, have uncovered what might be the fabled city of Troy, which once controlled the waterway between the Black Sea (and Asia) and the Mediterranean. Beyond that, there is very little evidence to authenticate the events of the Trojan War, believed to have taken place in the 12th century BC.

Homer's Trojan War Homer probably lived in the 8th century BC, over 300 years after the Trojan War. As most of his information about the war came from earlier tales and legends, historical accuracy was neither possible nor of interest, although the world he described would have been very real to him and his audience. The war, as he tells it, started when Paris, Prince of Troy, abducted Helen, wife of Menelaus of Sparta. Menelaus's brother, Agamemnon, the most powerful Greek ruler, collected an army of heroes and warriors – Achilles and Odysseus among them

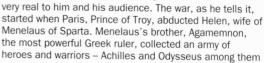

– and laid siege to Troy. The siege lasted ten years and even then Troy's defenses were only breached by Greek trickery: warriors hid in a massive wooden horse, presented to the Trojans as a gift, from which derives the saying, 'Beware of Greeks bearing gifts'.

The story of the *Iliad* Homer's companion work, the *Odyssey*, for all its suffering, is a comedy with a happy ending. The *Iliad* is a tragedy, ending in death and heartbreak beneath the negligent gaze of the gods, busy enjoying themselves up on Mount Olympus. And yet in telling the story, Homer makes us laugh, complain and feel elation before the tears roll. His interest is not in relating the events of the Trojan War: his story begins and ends during the tenth year of the siege and concerns a quarrel between Agamemnon and Achilles over a girl. As a result of Agamemnon taking the girl, Achilles withdraws his warriors from the Greek ranks. The Trojans take advantage of this rift and almost drive the Greeks into the sea. In response, Achilles allows his men to fight under the command of his friend Patroclus. The counter-attack is successful, but Patroclus is killed by Hector, King Priam's son and bravest of the Trojans. Seeking revenge, Achilles rejoins the war and kills Hector, dragging his corpse around the walls of Troy tied to his chariot. The Trojans pay a ransom to recover Hector's body, King Priam gives him a solemn burial and the *Iliad* ends with the line: 'Such were the funeral rites for Hector, tamer of horses'.

The islands and the *Iliad* The Greek Islands play an important part in the *Iliad* and their heroes are often mentioned. The most famous and the main character in the *Odyssey*, is Odysseus, prince of Ithảki (see pages 182–3). Others are the Abantes from Évvoia, with their long hair and ash spears, the proud-hearted men of Rhodes who filled nine ships, warriors from Aígina, from 'Crete of the Hundred Towns' as Homer calls it, from Kós, Kárpathos and a number of other islands.

241

Achilles dragging the corpse of brave Hector round the walls of Troy

HECTOR
Hector is one of Homer's most moving characters. The eldest son of King Priam and Queen Hecuba, brother of Paris, whose abducting of Helen was the primary cause of the war, Hector is described as the ideal of the hero – brave as a warrior, tender as a husband and father, attentive as a son. In earlier stories about the Trojan War, Paris was presented as the Trojan general, but Homer appears to have promoted Hector, finding in him the qualities that made him the equal of the leader of the Greeks, Achilles.

Heinrich Schliemann started uncovering the site of Troy using Homer as his guide

Sporades

Isolated and far from Athens, Skýros has retained its traditions

USEFUL NUMBERS
Port Authority (Skýros)
tel: 0222 96474
Olympic Airways (in Skýros Travel, also good for hotels and information about Skýros) tel: 0222 91600/91123
Ferry information (Skýros)
tel: 0222 91790 or 91789
Port Authority (Evvoia)
tel: 0221 22236

242

DANCING WITH THE GOATS
Skýros is renowned for its traditional festivals, the most intriguing being the Carnival, held seven weeks before Easter, at which a 'goat dance' is performed. Géros, the main character, wears a goatskin mask and dances with strings of sheep's bells attached to his costume. The second figure is a transvestite, while the third – the Frangi – is a figure dressed up as a foreigner.

TRIS BOUKÉS
The English poet Rupert Brooke, who died near Skýros in 1915 from blood poisoning on a ship bound for Gallipoli, knew the island only vaguely. Even so, he became something of a local hero and was buried in Tris Boukés, one of Skýros's most atmospheric spots. Only a year before he died, he wrote, somewhat prophetically, the famous lines:
'If I should die, think only this of me
That there's some corner of a foreign field
That is forever England...'
Tris Boukés can be reached on foot, or by boat from Linariá or Kalamítsa, or by taxi.

SKÝROS

Skýros is one of the most interesting islands to visit if traditional island life appeals to you. There is a theory that it was once two islands; the enormous difference between the green and hilly north and the barren mountainous south gives it credibility.

▶▶ Skýros Town   235C2

The island's capital is built like an amphitheatre at the foot of the **kástro**▶ (*Admission free*), a mostly Byzantine fortress covering the site of the ancient acropolis. There is a good walk up to the *kástro*, past traditional whitewashed cubist houses; there is little to see once you reach the top, but the great views over the town compensate for this. At the northern end of the town is a bronze **statue of 'Immortal Poetry'**▶, a memorial to the young English poet Rupert Brooke who is buried under an olive tree in Tris Boukés, at the southern end of the island (see panel). The **Archaeological Museum**▶ (*Open* Tue–Sun 8.30–3. *Admission charge*), below Brooke's memorial, has a small collection of objects from local excavations. More interesting is the nearby **Faltaitz Museum**▶▶▶ (*Open daily 10–1 and 5.30–8. Admission free*), founded by the charming sociologist, artist and poet Manos Faltaitz in his family home to display his collection of local embroideries, pottery, carved woodwork, costumes and fine old photographs. One display is devoted to the island's famous spring Carnival and its extraordinary 'goat dance' (see panel).

▶ Linariá   235C2

Linariá, little more than the harbour across the island from Skýros Town, is where ferries dock. In the summer, boats visit the caves of Gerania and Pentekáli as well as the islet of Skyropoúla, where wild ponies roam.

Beaches

Called 'paradise' by the locals, the pebble beach at Ágios Fokás north of Linariá does come pretty near to deserving the name and it is probably almost as difficult to reach as its heavenly namesake – access is only by boat or a tricky hike. The sandy beach between Magaziá and Mólos, north

CONNECTIONS
Skýros has ferry links with Kými (Évvoia), Mýkonos, Páros, Thíra, Crete and Tínos. Hydrofoil services operate to Alónnisos, Skíathos, Skópelos and Vólos. (Regular buses link Kými with Athens.)

of Skýros Town, is being developed, but is still good. Ahíli, south of the town, was an excellent beach until the new marina was built there. Atsítsa, across the island from Skýros Town, is a lovely bay with rocks and pine trees – though beaches on the west coast tend not to be very clean.

243

WILD HORSES OF SKÝROS
Skýros has a unique breed of very small horse, believed by some to be related to the Shetland pony and much like the horses depicted on the Parthenón frieze. On 15 August there is a children's race, near Magaziá, when competitors ride tame horses.

ÉVVOIA

The second largest Greek island, after Crete, Évvoia remains one of Greece's great unknowns. Although it sometimes seems like an extension of the mainland to which it is connected by bridge, Évvoia is an island with a rich, independent history. It is very fertile and the relatively prosperous islanders have so far done little to encourage tourism.

▶ Chalkída (Chalkís) 235B2

The heavily industrialised capital of Évvoia is also its biggest town, with more than 50,000 inhabitants. It has little going for it at first sight, but it is the scene of one of the liveliest evening promenades in the islands and it has excellent fish restaurants on the waterfront, to which Athenians will drive for the evening.

It is said that Aristotle threw himself in the water here in frustration at his inability to explain the flow of currents in the narrow **Évripos Channel**, which separates Évvoia from the mainland. Even today people stare in amazement at the current: some days it fails to change direction at all, while on others it changes up to 14 times. Not surprisingly, the Évripos (whose name means 'swift current') has always been a notoriously difficult passage for boats. the present **Évripos Bridge**, dating from 1962, replaced a Venetian structure called Negroponte (black bridge), which had a fort halfway across (see panel). Previous bridges were built by the Boeotians (*c*410 BC) and the Emperor Justinian (6th century AD).

Near the bridge, in the old Ottoman quarter, is a fine 15th-century mosque, the church of Agía Paraskeví and the scattered remains of the *kástro*. This neighbourhood is still inhabited by some Turks, a few gypsies and a small Jewish community.

The **Archaeological Museum▶** (Odós Venizélou 13. *Open* Tue–Sun 8.30–3. *Admission charge*) houses a small collection of artifacts, most of them from ancient Erétria.

A TRAVELLER'S VIEW
'Khalkis was the showpiece of the Venetian Aegean and in old prints it is drawn bristling with towers and turrets, surrounded entirely by moat and sea-wall and tight-stacked upon the water's edge. Its site remains extraordinary. The Euripos is one of the world's enigmas...The Venetians built actually on top of the channel, in the middle of a double drawbridge, a fortified tower that marked their imperial frontier. It was a romantic, Rhenish-looking construction, if we are to believe the old pictures and so remarkable was the place, so suggestive the movements of waters beneath it, that local rumour held it to be an enchanted castle, guarded by fairies or demons'.
Jan Morris, *The Venetian Empire: A Sea Voyage* (London, 1980)

THE NOEL-BAKER ESTATE

On the outskirts of Prokópi is an estate owned by the Noel family, who are descendants of the English poet Lord Byron. The house, in its lovely surroundings, is used as a centre for all kinds of residential holiday courses, from pottery to creative writing. (For information, contact Elysian Holidays tel: 01797 225482, in the UK.)

MOUNT DÍRFYS

If the busy town ambiance or the summer heat gets too much, head west from Kými or east from Chalkída for Évvoia's highest mountain, Mount Dírfys (1,743m). Buses from Chalkída go as far as the pretty village of Stení Dírfos, from where a trail leads up the mountain. Telephone the Hellenic Alpine Club (tel: 01 364 5904) for more information and to make arrangements to stay overnight in their refuge.

MOUNTAIN HONEY

Prokópi is famous for its honey, which is widely sold in the village. In George Vassos's shop on the corner of the church square, it is possible to taste it before buying. Mr Vassos speaks some English and will happily explain about the different local varieties such as thyme (the most expensive), orange-flower and pine tree.

▶▶ Erétria   235B1

A rival city to Chalkída in ancient times, Erétria is now a sprawling resort. As the modern town was built over the ruins of the ancient one, little has survived of Évvoia's most important classical site – though the ruins of a Doric temple of Apollo and part of the agora are easy enough to spot in the town centre. Of more interest in the northeastern corner of the town, behind the museum (not often open), is a Hellenistic theatre, with an underground passage from where a *deus ex machina* could suddenly appear on stage. Also on the site is a 4th-century BC palace with a clay bath tub and a gymnasium. The site is open to the public, but feels very neglected.

▶ Kárystos   235C1

Kárystos is an unexceptional 19th-century town built over an earlier site. All that remains of the earlier fortifications is a 14th-century Venetian tower. On the hill above the town is the **Castello Rosso**▶▶, a huge medieval castle on the site of an ancient acropolis. The castle is ruined inside, apart from an Orthodox chapel, but commands magnificent views over the town and sea. Kárystos waterfront, lined with bars and pleasant tavernas, livens up after dark when the entire population comes down for the *vólta* or promenade. There are lovely beaches nearby and good hiking to the hill villages around Óros Óchi (Mount Óchi; 1,398m), of which Míli and Grábia are the best. Marmári, the nearest town to Kárystos, is a scenic fishing harbour where many Athenians have built summer houses.

▶▶ Kými   235C2

Perched high on a rock, Kými is a pleasant, undistinguished town surrounded by vineyards, orchards and forest. The pretty **church of Panagía Koímisis**▶, whose blue domes rise out of a garden, has an important 7th-century icon of the Virgin with Child. At the bottom of the town, the **Folklore Museum**▶ (*Open* Tue–Sun 9–1. *Admission charge*) has a vast collection of local costumes and old photographs of Kymians both in Kými and in the USA, where they have formed a large community. The town overlooks Paralía Kýmis, from where ferries and

Friendly nuns at the Moní Nikoláou Galatáki are proud of their spectacularly set convent

Legend has it that dragons moved these enormous blocks of masonry

WINE AND PINE
The retsina from fertile Évvoia is highly regarded everywhere in Greece. Retsina is a protected Greek speciality and no other country is allowed to make it commercially. It is not known if the ancients drank it for pleasure, but they certainly knew of the antiseptic properties of resin and used it as a disinfectant seal. It is possible that the origins of retsina can be traced to the need to preserve wine during transport. There is a popular belief that retsina gets its taste from pinewood barrels in which it is stored. In fact its unique flavour comes from the addition of a few pieces of Aleppo-pine resin during fermentation. Perhaps surprisingly, the largest consumers of retsina are visitors, not Greeks.

hydrofoils leave for the Sporades, especially Skýros. Nearby is **Moní tou Sotírou**▶, a 17th-century convent set in a lush garden (men not admitted).

▶▶ Límni 235A2

Límni, a small harbour where, legend claims, Zeus and Hera married, is a pleasing town with neoclassical houses and good beaches nearby. A little way south of the town, the 16th-century convent of **Moní Nikoláou Galatáki**▶▶ is spectacularly set above the rocky shore, on the site of a classical temple of Poseidon. The convent was damaged by the Turks, but fine frescos have survived in the chapel.

▶▶ Loutrá Aidipsoú 235A2

The spa of Loutrá Aidipsoú has been known since antiquity for its therapeutic qualities. Fashionable and somewhat exclusive in the 19th century, it is now a boom town with over 100 hotels attracting crowds of mostly older Greeks. Loutrá is a long drive away from the capital, but can be reached by ferry from the mainland.

▶▶ Prokópi 235B2

At the foot of Mount Pixaria, in the middle of pine forests, lies the tranquil village of Prokópi, famous for its mountain honey and the huge **church of Ágios Ioánnis Róssos** which dominates the main square. Greek refugees from Turkey, who settled in Prokópi in 1923, brought with them the relics of their patron saint, St John the Russian, a Russian soldier enslaved in Turkey and built this rather unattractive church for him.

▶▶ Stýra 235C1

Néa (New) Stýra is a package resort, with a ferry connection to Rafína. Old Stýra, inland up the hill, is famous for its Drakóspita ('dragon houses') – strange towers built with enormous blocks which, according to legend, were carried here by dragons (if not by slaves).

It is the resin tapped from pine trees that adds the distinctive flavour to retsina wine

Sporades and Évvoia

The tower of the 14th-century Bourtzí is the only reminder of the once vast fortifications around Kárystos

CONNECTIONS
Trains run regularly from Stathmós Laríssis in Athens to the mainland side of the channel at Chalkída. Buses run regularly from Liossíon 260 terminal to Chalkída and Kými. Ferries link Kými with Skýros, Alónnisos and Ágios Ioánnis; Kárystos with Rafína; Erétria with Skále Oropoú; Loutrá Aidipsoú with Arkítsa; and Oreoí with Skíathos. Hydrofoil services operate between Chalkída and Loutrá Aidipsoú, Oreoí, Límni and (summer only) Skíathos and Skópelos; between Kárystos and Rafína, Mýkonos and Tínos; between Loutrá Aidipsoú and Skíathos; and in summer between Oreoí and Vólos, Skíathos, Skópelos and Alónnisos.

Psilí Ámmos beach, near Kárystos

Beaches
Évvoia is within easy reach of Athens and, although still not visited by many foreigners, it has become very popular with Athenians. Many of them have built summer villas along the coast, so on a summer weekend the best beaches can be crowded. Emptier beaches are here to be found, but are often accessible only on foot or after a long, slow drive. The nearest beach to Chalkída, Astéria, has a taverna and boats run from Astéria to the tiny islet of Tonnoíron which has a good beach, usually less crowded. Just below Moní Galatáki, outside Límni, is Glífa, one of the best beaches on this side of the island, with several long, clean bays of pebble and sand which can only be reached by footpaths. Angáli beach near Agía Ánna in the north is lovely but sometimes dirty, while the much smaller Elliniká is cleaner and prettier. The beaches in the north, such as Pefkí and Oreoí, are nothing special. Stómio, near Kými, is a fine sandy beach near a river with good bathing, while the magnificent beach of Psilí Ámmos is sufficient reason to stay in Kárystos.

Drive

Northern Évvoia

Évvoia has lived off its agriculture for centuries; the north of the island is especially fertile. This drive from Chalkída to Límni goes through some magnificent scenery with impressive mountains, narrow ravines and pretty villages. (About 72km one way; allow four hours. See the map on page 235. Most signposts on Évvoia are in Greek, so brush up on your Greek alphabet before setting off.)

Leave **Chalkída**▶ by the main road that leads north out of the town past the central market, following signposts for Mantoúdi. The road first crosses saltmarshes and farmland and then, after about 5km, passes the dull development of Néa Artáki. After 12km, the road forks: take the right turn, towards **Psachná**, a pretty little market town with the Technical High School towering above it. From here follow signs for Prokópi. The road winds up through olive groves and pine forests, eventually giving

splendid views over the island and the mainland. By the village of Néo Pagóntas (37km) the scenery is positively alpine, but roadside shrines serve as reminders that this is not Austria. The landscape becomes even more dramatic, the road following a small river around steep rocks in a narrow ravine. Then the river broadens and there is flat farmland again. At **Prokópi**▶▶ (see page 245) keep right, following signposts to Límni. There are several good picnic spots between here and the lively town of **Mantoúdi**. Drive through Mantoúdi, with its whitewashed houses and flower-filled gardens and follow signs for Strofyliá.

Kírindos▶, 4km further on, has lovely summer villas in the middle of vines and cornfields, while nearby Paralía Kírindos has a few remains of 6th-century BC Kírindos, as well as a small beach.

Back on the main road, continue to **Strofyliá** whose houses have pretty gardens. Where the road forks, bear left through some quiet villages before returning to the main road, which suddenly descends towards **Límni**▶▶ (see page 245).

Life still runs at a slow pace in the more remote parts of Évvoia

Ever since Zorba the Greek, it has been tempting to think that all there is to Greek music is the sound of the bouzouki. But Greek music has a long and varied tradition and is an intriguing mix of east and west.

ZORBA'S DANCE
'He threw himself into the dance, clapping his hands, leaping and pirouetting into the air, falling onto his knees, leaping again with his legs tucked up – it was as if he were made of rubber. He suddenly made tremendous bounds into the air, as if he wished to conquer the laws of nature and fly away. One felt that in this old body of his there was a soul struggling to carry away this flesh and cast itself like a meteor into the darkness'.
Níkos Kazantzákis,
Zorba the Greek
(London, 1959)

THE RISING EAST
'The modern Greek...when he begins to sing...breaks the crust of Greek logic; all at once the East, all darkness and mystery, rises up from deep within him'.
Níkos Kazantzákis

THE POWER OF SONG
Nicholas Gage, in *Hellas*, his excellent portrait of modern Greece, quotes the composer Manos Hadjidákis describing the feeling he had on first hearing *rembétika*: 'Dazed by the grandeur and depth of the melodic phrases, a stranger to them, young and without strength, I believed suddenly that the song I was listening to was my own, utterly my own story'.

Many Greeks, like Zorba, love spending the evening eating, drinking, singing and making music

The sound of the city First: the bouzouki. A bouzouki is a stringed instrument, like a lute, and is common throughout the region. The tradition seems to have come from Asia Minor, particularly Smyrna, earlier this century. When the Greeks of that area were expelled in 1923, they brought bouzouki music with them, as well as the more troubled sounds of *rembétika*. While bouzouki music has a certain insistent joy about it, *rembétika* is full of despair, its lyrics concentrating on broken love and brutal death. It is the music of urban repression and, since its birth in the tavernas and music cafés of the region's cities, it has developed into one of the most widespread and compelling of Greece's many musical styles.

Country music In contrast to the traditions of the city, country music is localised. On Crete, country music is played on a three-stringed fiddle with accompaniment from a lute-player. On Kárpathos, the bagpipes are still played. Zákynthos Town is proud of its Venetian-inspired *arekias*, whose lively and much repeated melodies are used as a background for improvised lyrics. Kazantzákis's Zorba played the *sandoúri*, a dulcimer, when he needed to express himself in music.

Music places Many Greek restaurateurs seem to believe that foreigners want only to hear the music of Míkis Theodorákis, link arms and throw plates. But Greece's musical tradition is both popular and varied: if you ask, you will often find more satisfying music to listen to. However, you will need to be in the right place at the right season, for Greek musicians tend to install themselves in Athens and Piréas in winter and then move with their audience to the islands for the summer.

Arriving and departing

By air

There are daily scheduled flights to Athens from most European capitals as well as a daily direct flight to Thessaloníki from London Heathrow. The Greek national carrier Olympic Airways offers the widest choice of scheduled flights, as well as connections from Athens to many islands. Domestic flights should be booked in advance, as they are in much demand, especially over weekends and around public holidays, when half of Athens moves to the islands. From May to October the cheaper option is to take a charter flight either to Athens or direct to one of the major islands such as Mýkonos, Thíra, Rhodes, Crete, Corfu or Skíathos. If you plan to stay on one island, check out flight-and-hotel package offers from tour operators, which can be real bargains, especially out of season (see page 262). All Olympic Airways flights – both international and domestic – operate from the western terminal of Athens airport, Ellinikón. All other flights depart from the eastern terminal. The terminals are linked by a shuttle bus or taxis.

By sea

Regular car and passenger ferries operate between Ancona, Venice, Bari and Brindisi in Italy, and Igoumenítsa, Corfu and Pátra, some also calling at other Ionian islands. Less frequent ferries connect Trieste and Otranto to Igoumenítsa, Corfu and Pátra. The problems with road access to Greece through the former Yugoslavia have led more travellers to use these ferry routes, and it is necessary in summer to book ferry tickets in advance. Tickets are considerably cheaper out of season. In summer there is also a four-hour hydrofoil service between Brindisi and Corfu. A ferry also sails from Venice to Bari, Piréas, Irákleio (Crete) and Alexandria (Egypt) weekly for most of the year. In summer, ferries and hydrofoils run from the Dodecanese and the north-eastern Aegean islands to coastal towns in Turkey. From Rhodes and Crete there are also connections to Israel and Cyprus in summer.

By train

Many young travellers arrive in Greece by train, using an InterRail or Eurail pass. The traditional route through the former Yugoslavia is hardly in use since the problems in that area over the last few years, so most people go through Italy and take a ferry from Bari or Brindisi to Pátra (see **By sea**, above). The alternative is to take a train from Budapest via Sofia to Thessaloníki.

By bus

For those who believe that travel should still include suffering it is possible, in the good old 'hippie tradition', to take a bus from several European capitals to Athens, also via Italy. It is a long journey and, although considerably cheaper than the train, it is not the most reliable or comfortable way to travel.

By car
It is possible to drive to Greece and take car ferries to the islands, but if you intend to go island-hopping it is probably easier and cheaper to rent a car locally. If you are set on taking your own car contact the Automobile Association (AA) in the UK (tel: 01256 20123) for information. You need an EU driving licence, vehicle registration documents and insurance. A green card is recommended.

Customs regulations
Since July 1999 people travelling within the European Union are no longer entitled to import duty-free goods. It is also forbidden to bring in plants with soil, bulbs, flowers or fruit and pets must have a valid health and rabies inoculation certificate, issued between 6 days and 12 months (six months for cats) before arrival.

Exporting antiquities without a permit is a serious offence, as is drug-smuggling.

Passports and visas
EU nationals need a valid passport to enter Greece. Most non-EU Europeans and Australian, US, New Zealand and Canadian citizens will be issued on arrival with an entry visa permitting a stay of up to 90 days. There is no time limit for EU nationals, but they report to the authorities every 6 or 12 months. A resident permit for 6 months can be obtained from the Aliens Bureau in Athens (tel: 01-646 8103 or check with your embassy). If you overstay your time, a hefty fine will be charged upon departure.

Hydrofoils are fast and reliable but lack romance

251

Essential facts

Climate and when to go

Greece has a generally mild Mediterranean climate. Most islands are far more pleasant out of season than during the busy weeks from late June to the end of August when the heat is intense and the crowds often unbearable. The islands are at their best at the beginning of June and in September, when the temperature is pleasant and most facilities are available. May and October are good too, but you may find establishments closed and ferry connections less frequent. Many island hotels and restaurants are closed from late October till Easter, especially in the more northerly islands. Out of season the evenings can still be cold, and few hotels have heating. The spring warms up slowly and even in May the sea can be cold. The traditional holiday month of August is best avoided if possible, as space is short in hotel rooms and on beaches.

What to take

In summer, take light cotton clothing and swim-wear, as one is never far from a beach. A good protective sun-cream, a hat and comfortable sandals are essential. A pair of walking shoes never goes amiss. Always bring a sweater or a light jacket for those evenings when the *meltemi* blows, or for late-night ferries. Out of season bring warmer clothes as the nights can be damp and cold. Be modestly dressed (no shorts or vests) when visiting monasteries and chapels.

Smaller hotels lack soap and towels, and even bigger hotels often omit the shampoo. Colour-print film is widely available but is generally more expensive than in other countries. Slide film can be more difficult to find. A small flash-light can be useful for exploring archaeological sites and caves, and for a stroll on a moonless night.

National holidays

Although government offices and businesses close on national holidays, some shops and tourist sites remain open. There are also many local festivals, when some shops and businesses close.

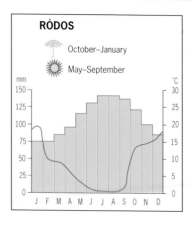

RÓDOS

October–January

May–September

1 January: New Year's Day
6 January: Epiphany
Lent Monday (precedes Shrove Tuesday)
25 March: Greek Independence Day
Good Friday, Easter Day and Easter Monday
1 May: May Day
15 August: Assumption of the Virgin
28 October: *Ochi* Day (celebrating Metaxas saying 'no' to Mussolini)
25 December: Christmas
26 December: Gathering of the Virgin (Sinaksis Theotokou)
(for religious festivals, see pages 20–1)

Time differences

Greek time is usually two hours ahead of GMT. Clocks in Greece go forwards one hour at 4 am on the last Sunday in March, and back one hour at 4 am on the last Sunday in September.

Money matters

The monetary unit, the Greek drachma, is circulated in coins of 100, 50, 20 and 10 drachmas and in notes of 100, 200, 500, 1,000, 5,000 and 10,000 drachmas. Most banks exchange foreign currency, as do most medium-priced and expensive hotels.

It is possible to exchange money in some post offices, which is handy on smaller islands which have no bank. On many islands there are also exchange offices which are open longer and often offer better rates (but do check commission charges).

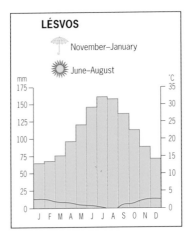

LÉSVOS

☂ November–January

☀ June–August

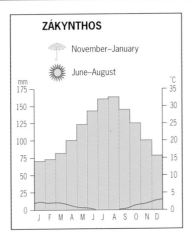

ZÁKYNTHOS

☂ November–January

☀ June–August

Many exchange places now accept credit cards, and most cash dispensers will accept Visa and American Express cards for obtaining local currency; fewer take other cards. Travellers' cheques and Eurocheques can be cashed at hotels and banks. Exchange rates are published in daily newspapers. Some banks will still demand to see your passport before changing money.

Travel insurance

In theory, all EU citizens can receive free medical treatment in Greece upon presenting an E111 form (available from most post offices in your home country). Unfortunately hospital staff will often make you pay,

leaving you to reclaim the money after your holiday. Travel insurance is often a more reliable option and is certainly indispensable for non-EU nationals. There are comprehensive travel policies which cover accidents, illness, delays, cancellation etc. In the case of medical care, keep all receipts and ask for a full medical report. In the event of loss or theft, you will need a police report giving details of the loss and stating how it happened. The police will issue a case number, which will allow the insurance company to follow up the case.

Exchange offices often offer better rates for foreign currency than banks, but charges may be high

253

Getting around

Domestic flights Olympic Airways
and Olympic Aviation connect
Athens with many islands and also
operate some inter-island flights,
although for island-hopping the
hydrofoil services are usually the
fastest way to travel. During the summer season or around public holidays
book seats as far ahead as possible –
generally at least a week – as flights
fill up quickly. In peak season delays
are common, luggage often gets sent
elsewhere and flights can be cancelled
due to bad weather. Domestic air tickets are non-refundable, but you can
change your flight details. All internal
flights are non-smoking.

Ferries and hydrofoils Hydrofoils,
which generally cost twice as much as
ferries, are becoming more frequent
in the summer and offer a fast and
convenient service, but rough seas
and high costs make it impossible for
them to operate out of season. Ferries
operate all year round to all inhabited
Greek islands, although some smaller
islands might only be served once a
week. Timetables are published, but
are not widely available, and tend to
be unreliable anyway. There are several classes, the cheapest being Deck
and the most expensive a private

*On smaller islands the only bus, out of
season, is often the schoolbus, one in the
morning and one late in the afternoon*

cabin. Food and drinks on ferries are
often highly priced. Ferry and hydrofoil tickets can be bought in advance.

Buses Buses, operated by the
privately owned KTEL company, are
popular and cheap. Regular services
link Athens to the main ports and
even to Corfu. Long-distance tickets
can usually be bought in advance;
otherwise tickets are paid for on the
bus. Even on the smallest islands a
service will be provided, often by the
school bus making a tour of the island
and linking port and main town. If it
is the school bus, be prepared to start
early and to come back when classes
are over. On larger islands, buses will
also run from the main town in time
to catch ferries.

Taxis Greek taxis are generally good
value when they use the meter (obli-
gatory only in towns), but tariffs
double between midnight and 5am
and out of town. Surcharges apply for
large bags and for entering harbours
or airports. Greek taxi drivers have a
bad reputation: be sure that the correct rate is being applied and if you

are riding without the meter, agree the fare per car before setting off. If you are dissatisfied, insist on your right to consult the Tourist Police.

Trains There are no trains on the islands but useful trains from Athens include services to Évvoia (almost hourly), Pátra (though the Athens bus service is more useful) and Kavála, for connections to the north-eastern Aegean and Dodecanese islands.

Driving
Car hire Driving on the islands can be a great pleasure and hiring a car will certainly open up the larger islands like Rhodes, Crete and Corfu. However, it can be an expensive and, if you break down, an infuriating

Rural scenery away from the coast rarely disappoints

experience. Before you start, a few things should be carefully considered.

There are two ways of going about car hire – through an international or a local agency. Of the international agencies (Avis, Holiday Autos etc.) Hertz have the largest network. Telephone several companies to compare rates, as a price war is being waged at the moment. Although prices are often higher than for renting from local firms, large agencies can at least offer peace of mind. They also usually have agents at international airports, so if you book ahead you can pick up your car on arrival. Local agencies are usually cheaper and you will often be served by the person who owns the cars. Out of season, it should be possible to talk down the rates of local agencies, something that can seldom be done with the international groups.

255

❏ Island driving can be different from driving elsewhere in Greece, especially in more remote places. In tourist centres the main problem might be traffic congestion and a shortage of parking places, obliging you to park in the sun while you are on the beach, for example. While island main roads are usually in good condition, remoter ones can be rutted, rarely have cat's eyes and are more often used by goats, men on donkeys and agricultural vehicles than by cars. It is wise to be off twisting mountain roads by nightfall. ❏

However, local-agency cars are often kept longer and some are not as well maintained, which can lead to problems: be sure you test the car before handing over money. The range of cars available for hire has been extended and on larger islands you will be offered everything from basic Fiat Panda to air-conditioned, new-model, top-of-the-range Mercedes. An international driving licence is not required for EU licence holders, but it can be useful if you get into difficulties. Most agencies will accept valid American, Australian and Canadian licences. Drivers must be at least 21 years of age (25 for some vehicles).

Breakdowns Whoever you hire from, be sure you know what to do if you break down or are involved in an accident (Greece has one of the highest accident rates in Europe). Proof of membership of the AA or RAC entitles you to free roadside assistance from ELPA, the Greek national breakdown service, which has centres on Crete and Corfu (dial 104 for service). Many agencies have agreements with ELPA's rivals, Hellas Service or Express Service, but it is essential that you have the agency's membership details when you telephone for the service, as their call-out charges for non-members are astronomical.

Freedom of the Greek roads The Greeks have embarked on a major road-improvement programme since

Renting a car or scooter is recommended as public transport is limited on most islands

joining the European Community, and while this makes it easier to get around on the islands, it also makes it easier for people to drive faster. Wherever you are, be sure to keep an eye on your petrol tank, especially if you are running on lead-free fuel as not all petrol stations will stock it.

Although some of the international petrol companies accept credit cards, many of the island petrol stations are still run by local companies which

will insist on payment in cash, so make sure you are carrying notes.

Motorcycle, moped and bicycle hire
Mopeds and motorcycles are usually readily available in tourist centres and can be an excellent and economical way of getting around. A wider range of motorcycles is available in more developed tourist centres and, with luck, you might even find a Harley-Davidson. Whatever you rent, be sure to check the machine before you hire for signs of previous damage and for faulty brakes. Although feeling the breeze in your hair may seem to go with the 'easy rider' image, helmets are recommended, even on mopeds, as last year's tourist casualties will tell you. Rates for hire can usually be talked down out of season.

Hitch-hiking
Public transport can be very erratic on some islands and hitching a short lift with a local is usually no problem as people are used to it, although taxi drivers might complain. Hitching can be a good way to meet some local people and try out a mouthful of Greek. Longer rides might be less easy but should not be a problem.

The media

International newspapers are widely available in Athens and at major resorts. The *Athens News* is a local English paper with good listings, and both Corfu and Rhodes produce an English paper for the expatriate community. The *Athenian* is an English-language monthly with excellent features on the islands and Greek culture, and listings of events.

There is a wide variety of regional radio stations in almost every town in Greece, and the BBC World Service can be picked up on short-wave frequencies. The government-controlled TV station ET1 has news summaries in English (check papers for timing), and foreign soaps and films are broadcast in the original language with subtitles.

Post offices

Most post offices are open Monday–Friday 7.30–2, in larger cities often until 8 pm and in the capital also during summer weekends, usually 9–2. Post offices will usually exchange money and travellers' cheques.

Air mail letters take over a week from the islands to Europe, and two weeks to North America; postcards are slower. The express service cuts the time by a few days. Poste restante should be addressed to the main post office of any larger town, with your name underlined. It is usually held for a month, and a passport is needed upon collection. In Athens, Pátra, Irákleio, Corfu, Mýkonos, Rhodes, Thíra and Skíathos, American Express cheque- or card-holders can use the mail service in the Amex offices.

Telephone and fax

Although it is possible to telephone from any moderate or more expensive hotel, it is much cheaper to use a phone card in a telephone booth. Phone cards are available from OTE offices, newsagents and street kiosks, with 100, 500 or 1,000 units. Local calls are cheap but long-distance calls are quite expensive. For calls within Greece, cheap-rate times are 3–5pm, 9pm–8am and all weekend. Long-distance calls can also be made at OTE offices, as well as reverse-charge calls.

Faxes can be sent from larger OTE offices and from some travel agents or hotels. To call abroad from Greece, dial 00 + country code (Australia 61, Canada and USA 1, Ireland 353, New Zealand 64, UK 44) + area code (minus initial 0) + number.

Language

The Greek alphabet

Alpha	A, α	a, as in rather
Beta	B, β	v, as in very
Gamma	Γ, γ	y, as in yes, before i or e; g, as in get, before o, a, ou
Delta	Δ, δ	th, as in that
Epsilon	E, ε	e, as in yes
Zita	Z, ζ	z
Eta	H, η	ee, as in meet
Theta	Θ, θ	th, as in thing
Iota	I, ι	i, as in lid
Kappa	K, κ	k
Lambda	Λ, λ	l
Mu	M, μ	m
Nu	N, ν	n
Xi	Ξ, ξ	ks
Omicron	O, o	o, as in pot
Pi	Π, π	p
Rho	P, ρ	rolling r
Sigma	Σ, σ (mid-word) ς (end of word)	s
Tau	T, τ	t
Upsilon	Y, υ	e, very similar to eta
Phi	Φ, φ	f
Chi	X, χ	h, as in loch
Psi	Ψ, ψ	ps, as in corpse
Omega	Ω, ω	o, as in bone

Pronunciation

αι	e, as in met
αυ	av/af
ει	ee, as in reed
ευ	ev/ef
ου	ou, as in tour
γγ	ng, as in angel
γκ	g, as in goat, at beginning of word; ng in the middle
μπ	b at beginning of word; mb in the middle
ντ	d at beginning of word; nd in the middle
σι	sh, as in shelter
τζ	j, as in Johnny

Numbers

1 énos, éna, mía	14 dekatésseres
2 dío	20 íkosi
3 trís, tría	30 triánda
4 tésseres, téssera	40 saránda
5 pénde	50 penínda
6 éksi	60 eksínda
7 eftá	70 evdomínda
8 októ	80 oghónda
9 enyá	90 enenínda
10 déka	100 ekáto
11 éndeka	200 diakóssies
12 dódeka	1,000 hílies
13 dekatrís	2,000 dío hiliádes

Greetings

hello (informal)	hérete (yásu)
good morning	kaliméra
good evening	kalispéra
good night	kaliníkhta
goodbye	adío
please/you're welcome	parakaló
thank you (very much)	efharistó (párapolí)
okay, all right	endáksi
how are you?	ti kánis (ti káneteh)?
I'm fine	kalá ímeh

Essentials

yes (formal yes)	né (málista)
no	óchi

I don't understand	then katalavéno
how many?	póssi, pósses?
how much?	póso?
sorry	signómi
what can I do for you?	oríste?
be careful	ópa
take your time	sigá sigá
open	aniktó
closed	klistó
left	aristerá
right	deksiá
far	makriá

Time

what time is it?	ti óra íne?
today	símera
yesterday	kthés
tomorrow	ávrio
now	tóra
later	argótera

Travel

airport	arothrómio
harbour	limáni
bus station	praktorío leoforíon
how far is it?	póso makriá íne?
where is...?	pou íne...?

Nudism is strictly forbidden on most islands, but some local authorities are tending to ignore it on more isolated beaches

Crime and the police

Greece is one of Europe's safest countries, with a relatively low crime rate. As you will notice, Greeks themselves often leave cars or houses unlocked or their bags unattended, but it is advisable to be reasonably careful.

Pickpocketing is increasingly common in crowded tourist areas in cities or resorts. Violent crime or rape is less common, but women travelling on their own can expect some minor harassment from the almost professional machos who operate in tourist resorts.

If you are involved in an incident, contact the Tourist Police immediately: there is an office on every island and in every major town.

Embassies and consulates

Australia Odós D Soutsoú 37, Athens (tel: 01 644 7303)
Canada Odós I Gennadióu 4, Athens (tel: 01 725 4011)
Ireland Leóforos Vas. Konstantínou 7, Athens (tel: 01 723 2771)
New Zealand Xenia 24, Athens (tel: 01 771 0112)

United Kingdom Athens: Odós Ploutárchou 1 (tel: 01 723 6211); Irákleio: Odós Papalandroú 16 (tel: 081 224012); Kavála: Odós Thessaloníkis 45 (tel: 051 223704); Corfu: Odós Menekrátous 1 (tel: 0661 30055); Rhodes: Odós Amerikis III (tel: 0241 27306/27247); Sámos: Odós Themistoklí 15, Vathí (tel: 0273 27314).
United States of America Odós Vasilissís Sofías 91, Athens (tel: 01 721 2951)

Emergency telephone numbers

Ambulance–medical help	166
Police–emergencies	100
Fire	199
Road assistance	104
Tourist Police	171

Lost property

Report losses to your hotel and to the local police station. Most larger bus and train stations have a lost property office. If you lose your papers or

The traditional taverna is a family-run affair, with mother or father behind the stove

passport contact the police and your nearest embassy or consulate as soon as possible. If you lose travellers' cheques or credit cards, report the loss to the police and the issuing company immediately.

Health
There are no mandatory vaccination requirements but it is wise to be up to date with tetanus and polio immunisations. A typhoid-cholera booster is recommended. Tap water is safe in most places, but can be in short supply on drier, further-flung islands. Bottles of mineral water are widely available.

For medical help in an emergency, telephone 166. If you are on an island with some tourist facilities, it is worth asking whether your hotel could contact an English-speaking doctor. The Tourist Police can also help with providing this information, as can your nearest consulate. Emergency treatment in state hospitals is free, but facilities can be pretty basic. Outpatient clinics (*iatreía*), which usually operate in the morning, are slightly better. If you have travel insurance including medical cover, you may be able to use one of the more comfortable private hospitals. Keep the receipts of all bills and receipts for drugs. (See also page 253.)

Chemists
Chemists can usually help with minor ailments and it should be quite easy in the major resorts to find one who speaks English. A Greek chemist (*farmakeío*) can supply a wide range of drugs without a prescription. Chemists are usually closed in the evenings and on Saturday morning, but a notice should always be displayed outside showing the nearest one open.

Holiday hazards
More and more people visit the Greek Islands for sun and sex, both of which can be dangerous unless proper precautions are taken. One of the most common health problems suffered by visitors is sunstroke or over-exposure to the sun. Use a strong protective suncream, wear a hat, drink plenty of fluids and try to acclimatise gradually to the sun. Sex plays a major part in the holiday scene at some resorts, and here as well it is advisable to be prepared. Condoms are cheap and available everywhere at chemists, kiosks and supermarkets.

The sea can hide some dangers as well, such as sea urchins (on rocky shores) or jellyfish. Chemists sell remedies for stings. The spines of the urchins should be removed, with care, immediately.

Mosquitoes in Greece are nothing to worry about, but they can be irritating in the evenings. Repellents and electric devices are widely available. When sleeping or lying on the beach you may encounter sandflies, and when walking or climbing watch out for the odd snake or scorpion.

Hayfever sufferers should take precautions during the April to June pollen season.

Eating meals al fresco is one of the great joys of summer on the Greek Islands

261

Camping

The Greek Camping Association publishes a yearly guide to all the official camp sites in Greece, available from GCA, 102 Odós Solonós, GR-10680 Athens (tel: 01 362 1560; fax: 01 346 5262) or from tourist offices. The EOT runs some of the best organised sites. Most places offer hot showers, electricity, a restaurant and cooking facilities, and some also have a swimming pool. Greek camp sites accept people without tents, but you will need a sleeping bag – even summer nights can be chilly.

Some sites will add a government tax to the bill (often not mentioned on arrival), so be sure to check what is included in the price. Camp sites often insist on keeping passports. Free camping outside designated areas is strictly forbidden by a law which the police enforce more diligently every year.

Camping outside authorised campsites is illegal

Self-catering holidays

Houses, flats and self-contained studios are usually rented by the week or month. It can be a more pleasant and sometimes cheaper option than a hotel if there are several of you to share. Out of season it should be possible to find a house or flat on arrival on the island, at the ferry pier or in the nearby *kafeneía*, but in the summer season it makes sense to book ahead through a tour operator; many packages are available. Self-catering is becoming more and more common on the islands as it appeals to families.

Some specialist tour operators in the UK are:
Elysian Holidays, 14 Tower Street, Rye, East Sussex, TN31 7AT (tel: 01797 225482, fax: 01797 225483). Hand-picked high-quality houses and villas on Chíos, Évvoia, Skýros and Spétses; various creative courses on Évvoia.
The Best of Greece, 23–4 Margaret Street, London W1N 8LB (tel: 0171-255 2320). Rather exclusive hotel and villa arrangements.
Laskarina Holidays, St Mary's Gate, Wirksworth, Derbyshire DE4 4DQ (tel: 01629 822203). Specialists in several of the more remote and unspoilt Greek islands.
Simply Crete and Simply Ionian, Chiswick Gate, 598–608 Chiswick High Road, London W4 5RT (tel: 0181-994 4462). Specialists in hotels, houses and flats on Crete and the Ionian Islands.

Children

Greeks love children, so the islands are a good place for travelling with a family. You can take children everywhere, as the Greeks do, and expect hotels, restaurants and shops to be very welcoming. Children love the island life: beaches, ferries, sailing boats, the pedestrian streets of the old towns or *chóra*. Pushchairs can prove difficult to use in the steep, cobbled streets of these old towns, or on rough paths in the countryside, where a good backpack-seat is a better option. Except on the more remote islands, most necessities for babies and children are available from supermarkets or pharmacies, but do bring a total sunblock cream

for children as this can be hard to find. A sun hat is also essential. When choosing a destination look out for shallow, sandy beaches, as pebble or rocky beaches are uncomfortable for the very young. Take warm clothes for the evening as it can be chilly even in summer.

Visitors with disabilities
Changing boats, visiting old towns or *chóras*, and walking around archaeological sites can be daunting for travellers with disabilities. Several package-tour operators, including Thomson and Horizon, will advise on suitable trips. For independent travellers, the following organisations offer advice and help: **National Tourist Organisation of Greece** (see page 268); **Association Hermes** (Odós Patriarchoú 13, Grigourioú E, 16542 Argyroúpolis; tel: 01 996 1887, is good for advice; **Evyenia Stavropoulou, Lavinia Tours** (Odós Egnatía 101, 54110 Thessaloníki; tel: 031 240 041) tried out many of the islands in her wheelchair and is very helpful; **RADAR** (12 City Forum, 250 City Road, London EC1V 8AF; tel: 020-7250 3222) publishes fact sheets and an annual guide to international travel for people with all kinds of disabilities; **Twin Peaks Press** (Box 129, Vancouver, WA 98666; tel:

Children are guaranteed a warm welcome on their Greek holiday

206-694 2462) publishes a worldwide *Directory of Travel Agencies for the Disabled* and other useful books for people with disabilities.

Electricity
Current is 220 volts AC throughout the country and the islands, with two-pin continental plugs.

Etiquette and local customs
Greeks, in a very Asian way, take their time with greetings and will often ask about the health of the entire extended family. It is considered rude to ask something without at least saying hello. Mastering the basic social graces, such as 'please' and 'thank you', in Greek, will always be appreciated (see page 259). When visiting a monastery or sacred chapel always dress modestly, which means covering up legs and arms. Apart from on the few official nudist beaches, nude bathing is illegal and some police are quite strict about it, especially on public beaches or near monasteries. Topless bathing has become acceptable on most of the islands, but use your discretion on beaches where the more traditional Greek families congregate.

CONVERSION CHARTS

FROM	TO	MULTIPLY BY
Inches	Centimetres	2.54
Centimetres	Inches	0.3937
Feet	Metres	0.3048
Metres	Feet	3.2810
Yards	Metres	0.9144
Metres	Yards	1.0940
Miles	Kilometres	1.6090
Kilometres	Miles	0.6214
Acres	Hectares	0.4047
Hectares	Acres	2.4710
Gallons	Litres	4.5460
Litres	Gallons	0.2200
Ounces	Grams	28.35
Grams	Ounces	0.0353
Pounds	Grams	453.6
Grams	Pounds	0.0022
Pounds	Kilograms	0.4536
Kilograms	Pounds	2.205
Tons	Tonnes	1.0160
Tonnes	Tons	0.9842

MEN'S SUITS

UK	36	38	40	42	44	46	48
Rest of Europe	46	48	50	52	54	56	58
US	36	38	40	42	44	46	48

DRESS SIZES

UK	8	10	12	14	16	18
France	36	38	40	42	44	46
Italy	38	40	42	44	46	48
Rest of Europe	34	36	38	40	42	44
US	6	8	10	12	14	16

MEN'S SHIRTS

UK	14	14.5	15	15.5	16	16.5 17
Rest of Europe	36	37	38	39/40	41	42 43
US	14	14.5	15	15.5	16	16.5 17

MEN'S SHOES

UK	7	7.5	8.5	9.5	10.5	11
Rest of Europe	41	42	43	44	45	46
US	8	8.5	9.5	10.5	11.5	12

WOMEN'S SHOES

UK	4.5	5	5.5	6	6.5	7
Rest of Europe	38	38	39	39	40	41
US	6	6.5	7	7.5	8	8.5

Maps

Locally available maps are sometimes seriously inaccurate and hard to use. Free maps are usually available from tourist offices or local travel agencies. The two most reliable road maps are the German-published Geo Center maps of Greece and the Islands, and Greek Islands & Aegean Sea, available in the UK and the USA but hard to find in Greece.

Opening times

It is hard to be precise about open - ing hours, especially for sites or museums, as the hours change from winter to summer, from early sum-mer to peak season and, at some sites, according to the mood of the keeper. Opening times for individual sites are usually given in the A-Z section of this book, but changes occur frequently. Some sites and museums on the islands are closed all winter.

Government offices usually open from 8 until 2, although the rule is not to expect to get anything done after 1. In general, shops in the summer are open Monday to Saturday from 9 to 2.30 and on Tuesday, Thursday and Friday they reopen from 6 to 9 in the evening. In the winter businesses start later and close earlier. In major tourist resorts shops stay open all day and until late at night. Most shops are closed on the many national holidays (see page 252).

All state-run archaeological sites and museums are free on Sundays and public holidays to all European Union nationals, which can mean a good saving. Student-card holders get a reduction of 50 per cent, and EU student-card holders may be admitted free.

Photography

There is usually no charge for taking photographs in museums, but an extra charge is levied for the use of tripods or video-cameras. Most brands of film are widely available, but slide films are expensive and hard to find.

Places of worship

There are Greek Orthodox churches and chapels on almost every street corner. The Muslim communities are

A simple Greek meal: choriátiki *or Greek salad and bread*

very small now, but a few mosques in Rhodes Town and on Kós are still open for prayer. The Jewish community in the islands is almost non-existent, although there is still a synagogue in Rhodes. There are some Catholic churches on Náxos, Tínos and Syros, remnants of the Venetian or Genoese occupation.

Student and youth travel
Students are well catered for on the islands, with budget food and accommodation, although prices are rising. Inter-Rail is a cheap way of getting to Greece, and camping and youth hostels offer cheap accommodation.

Tipping
A service charge is almost always included in restaurant bills but it is common to leave a small tip for the waiter who brings the bread and clears the table.

Toilets
The first thing you will notice in many Greek toilets is that paper should be dropped only in the appointed waste bin. Plumbing is seldom a strong point, and toilets easily get blocked. As public toilets tend to be fairly dirty, it is often better to use a toilet in a hotel or restaurant.

Watersports
Watersports are increasingly popular and most major resorts offer windsurfing, water-skiing, pedaloes, jet-ski and paragliding. Prices to hire equipment are lower than in most other Mediterranean resorts. The islands are a wonderful place for sailing. It is possible to

JET SKI PARAGLIDING RINGO'S CRAZY BANANA

book tailor-made cruises or to charter boats on arrival. The Hellenic Yachting Federation, Odós Aktí N Koundouríti 7, 18534 Piréas (tel: 01 413 7351) issues a brochure Sailing the Greek Sea, also available from tourist offices.

Scuba-diving is allowed only on Mykonos, in certain parts of Crete, on Kálymnos and in the Ionian Islands; this is to prevent visitors from finding and unlawfully keeping submerged archaeological treasures. For more information, contact the Union of Greek Diving Centres in Athens (tel: 01 922 9532).

Women travellers

Greece has low rates of street crime, but it is a patriarchal society, which means that Greek women are usually less liberated than females elsewhere in Europe. Encouraged by past success, Greek men will often pursue foreign women in the hope of a liberating experience of their own, but a polite, firm refusal will usually deter them. If you do have difficulties with harassment, report them at once to the Tourist Police.

Women travelling on their own have become a common sight on the islands

Greece in books

Archaeology and art
John Boardman, *Greek Art* (London, 1989). A classic on the subject.
Reynold Higgins, *Minoan and Mycenaean Art* (London, 1981). Well-illustrated exposé.
Colin Renfrew, *The Cycladic Spirit* (London, 1991). Useful explanations of the meaning and purpose of the mysterious Cycladic objects.
David Talbot Rice, *Art of the Byzantine Era* (London, 1963). Exhaustive and comprehensible study.
Suzanne Slesin, *Greek Style* (London, 1993). Elegant and beautiful interiors from the mainland as well as from Corfu, Rhodes and other islands.

Biography
Nicholas Gage, *Eleni* (London, 1983). Moving story of a Greek-born American journalist who returns to his native Epirus and is condemned to death in 1948.
George Psychoundákis, *The Cretan Runner* (London, 1955). The story of the World War II invasion of Crete and the resistance, told by a message-runner for the British (translated by Patrick Leigh Fermor).

Foreign fiction about Greece
John Fowles, *The Magus* (London, 1966). Acclaimed novel, inspired by Spétses in the 1950s.
Louis de Bernières, *Captain Corelli's Mandolin* (London, 1994). Set during the Italian occupation of Kefalloniá.

Modern Greek fiction and poetry
C P Cavafy, *Collected Poems* (London, 1968). A translation of all the work of the celebrated poet who spent most of his life in Alexandria, Egypt.
Eugenia Fakinou, *Astradeni* (Athens, 1991). Tale of a teenage girl moves with her family to Athens hoping for a better life, but then remembers the good life and old traditions on her native Symi.
Nikos Kazantzákis, *Zorba the Greek* (London, 1961), *Report to Greco* (London, 1965), *Freedom and Death* (London, 1956) and *Christ Recrucified* (London, 1954). Just a few of the novels of the famous Cretan writer.
Kimon Friar (ed.), *Modern Greek Poetry* (Athens, 1993). A good anthology.
George Seferis, *Collected Poems, 1924–1955* (London,1967). Excellent works from the Nobel Prize-winning islander.
Didi Sotiriou, *Farewell Anatolia* (Athens, 1991). The tragic story of the fall of Hellenism in Asia Minor. A bestseller in Greece.
(It is worth noting that Kedros Publishers in Athens have an interesting list of contemporary Greek writers in translation, widely available on larger islands.)

Specialised guides
Marc Dubin, *Trekking in Greece* (London, 1993). A good hiker's guide to both the mainland and the islands.
Frewin Poffley, *The Thomas Cook Guide to Greek Island Hopping* (Peterborough, annually). Excellent guide to ferry schedules and connections (although the ferries often break the rules).
(Lycabettus Press Guides in Athens produce a series of excellent local guidebooks to the more visited islands. Páros and Pátmos are especially good.)

Travellers' tales
Gerald Durrell, *My Family and Other Animals* (London, 1956). Durrell recounts his childhood on Corfu and his adventures with the local fauna.
Lawrence Durrell, *Prospero's Cell* (London, 1945). Lovely account of the life the young writer led with his wife Nancy on Corfu, before World War II. *Reflections on a Marine Venus* (London, 1952). Durrell's experiences during the war on Rhodes and the other Dodecanese. *The Greek Islands* (London, 1978). A romantic vision of the islands as they are no more.
Henry Miller, *The Colossus of Maroussi* (London, 1942). Miller at his happiest on Corfu and other islands.
Patricia Storace, *Dinner with Persephone* (London, 1997). Well-received account of a woman traveller in Greece.
Sara Wheeler, *An Island Apart* (London, 1992). A traveller's account of one of the least known islands, Évvoia.

Tourist Offices

Abroad

The National Tourist Organisation of Greece (NTOG, known in Greece as EOT) has offices in Austria, Belgium, Denmark, Finland, France, Germany, Italy, Japan, the Netherlands, Norway, Spain, Sweden, Switzerland, the UK and the USA.

Australia 51 Pitt Street, Sydney NSW 2000 (tel: 029241 1663; fax: 029235 2174)

Canada 1300 Bay Street, Toronto, Ontario M5R 3K8 (tel: 416-968 2220; fax: 968 6533)

1233 rue de la Montagne/ Suite 101, Montréal, Québec H3G 1Z2 (tel: 514-871 1535; fax: 514-871 1498)

United Kingdom 4 Conduit Street, London W1R 0DJ (tel: 020-7734 5997; fax: 020-7287 1369)

USA Olympic Tower, 645 Fifth Avenue, New York, NY 10022 (tel: 212-421 5777; fax: 212-826 6940)

168, North Michigan Avenue, Suite 600, Chicago, IL 60601 (tel: 312-782 1084; fax: 312-782 1091)

611 West Sixth Street, Suite 2198, Los Angeles, CA 92668 (tel: 213-626 6696; fax: 213-489 9744)

In Greece

The head office of the EOT is in Athens. There are EOT offices on several major islands (officially open 10.00–1.30), as well as local munici-pality information booths. Where there is no official tourist information,

a local travel agency dealing with ferry tickets, excursions and accom-modation often assumes the role. Sources of tourist information are listed in the A-Z sections of this book. Main EOT offices are as follows:

Athína (Athens) Odós Amerikís 2 (tel: 01 322 3111); east terminal, Athens airport (tel: 01 969 4500)

Kefalloniá Customs Pier, Argostóli (tel: 0671 22248)

Kérkyra (Corfu) Odós Voulefton, Corfu Town (tel: 0661 37520/37638)

Kríti (Crete) Odós Xanthídou 1, Irákleio (tel: 081 228225); Megáron Panthéon, Odós Kriári 40, Chaniá (tel: 0821 92943); Odós S Venizélou, Réthymno (tel: 0831 29148)

Kavála Odós Filéllinon 5 (tel: 051 228762; information line tel: 051 222425)

Kós Akti Miaoulia, Kós Town (tel: 0242 29200)

Lésvos Odós 8 Novemvríou 57, Mytilíni (tel: 0251 42511)

Piréas Zea Marina (tel: 01 413 5730/413 5716)

Ródos (Rhodes) Odós Archiepiskópou and Odós Papagoú, Rhodes Town (tel: 0241 23655)

Sámos Odós 25 Martíou, Vathí (tel: 0273 28582)

Syros Dodecanissiou 10, Ermoúpoli (tel: 0281 86725)

Some words of Greek will come in handy, and are sure to be appreciated by local people

Hotels and Restaurants

HOTELS

A disturbing number of hotels has been constructed on the islands over the past few years. Most are aimed at package tourists and are booked in advance through travel agents; few of these have been included in this listing. Most of the hotels listed below were chosen for their good value, atmosphere and standards of cleanliness, and/or for their views. Relatively few cheaper hotels are included, because at the lower end of the market it is often better (and in Greece far more usual) to rent a room in a private house. We have not included specific room-rentals, as these change by the season. The best way to find a room is to ask the owners, many of whom usually meet incoming ferries in search of custom; failing that, tourist offices will usually be able to provide a list of available rooms.

Most Greek hotels fall into one of five categories – de luxe, A, B, C and D – but the ratings mean very little. Prices seldom include breakfast: few Greeks take a proper breakfast, so it is often the least interesting meal, even in more expensive hotels. If a room in the cheap or medium categories seems expensive, try bargaining, especially if the hotel is not full. Prices are very much lower out of season, but remember that, as there are few visitors on the islands in winter, many hotels close from October or November until Easter or even May. There are no fixed dates for opening: that depends on the weather and on the mood of the owners. On the other hand, during Easter and the peak months of July and, especially, August, it can be very difficult to find a room at all without booking in advance.

The *Greek Travel Pages* is Greece's monthly travel guide. It includes most hotels, with phone and fax numbers, as well as flight and ferry schedules. It is available from International Publications in Athens (tel: 01 324 7511; fax: 01 323 3384).

The hotels recommended below have been divided into three price categories:

(£) = budget
(££) =moderate
(£££) = expensive

ATHÍNA (ATHENS)
(telephone area code 01)

Acropolis House (££)
Odós Kodroú 6–8, Pláka tel: 322 2344
This is a friendly family-run hotel in a restored 19th-century villa. It is very conveniently located, in a pedestrianized street on the edge of the Pláka district. Spotless rooms with more character than most, some with good views.
Athenian Inn (£££)
Odós Cháritos 22, Kolonáki tel: 723 8097
In a lovely residential area very near the city centre, this is a favourite with regular visitors to the capital. Small and cosy, with friendly service.

Grande Bretagne (£££)
Plateía Syntágmatos (Syntagma Square)
tel: 323 0251; fax: 322 8034
The city's oldest and most elegant hotel. Since the mid-19th century, royals and celebrities have occupied its suites, some of which have magnificent views of the Acropolis. Fun for a drink if nothing else, or a meal at the excellent GB Corner.
Student and Travellers Inn (£)
Odós Kydathinaíon 18, Pláka tel: 324 4808
Simple, clean rooms and friendly service in a very central location. Front rooms are noisy.

KRÍTI (CRETE)

Irákleio
(telephone area code 081)

Dedalos (££)
Odós Daidaloú 15 tel: 244812
Newly refurbished central hotel on a quiet street. Higher rooms have attractive views.
Galaxy (£££)
Odós Dimokratías 67
tel: 238812; fax: 211211
The city's best, a few minutes' walk from the Archaeological Museum, with all facilities including sauna, a good pool, and a popular summer café (see Restaurants).
Marin (£)
Bofort 12 tel: 224736
In one of the quieter streets in this noisy town, the Marin is close to the Archeological Museum and the harbour. It has 48 simple but pleasant rooms, and very helpful staff.

Ágios Nikólaos
(telephone area code 0841)

Green House (£)
Odós Modátsos 15 tel: 22025
Six quiet, clean rooms around a flowering courtyard near the resort's main square.
Panorama Hotel (££)
Odós Ioúsif Koundouroú tel: 28890
Pleasant rooms with excellent views over Mirabello bay and the port, and therefore a little noisy.
St Nicolas Bay Hotel (£££)
tel: 25041; fax: 24556
Luxurious, well-equipped resort hotel with impressive service, 2 km north of Ágios Nikólaos port, overlooking the town and islands in the bay. Three restaurants, several pools and a small private beach.

Chaniá
(telephone area code 0821)

Casa Delfino (£££)
Odós Theofánous 8 tel: 93098; fax: 96500
Beautiful 17th-century Venetian mansion in the Old Town converted into apartment suites, some overlooking the old harbour. Many of the rooms are split-level, with the bed on the upper level, and all are tastefully decorated. Close to the harbour but in a quiet, elegant area.

Monastiri (£)
Odós Ágios Márkos 18 tel: 54776
Simple guest house surprisingly located among the amazing ruins of a Venetian monastery in the Kastélli, overlooking the harbour and town.
Theresa (££)
Odós Angeloú 8 tel: 40118
In an old house, rooms decorated with local crafts and antiques. Nos 1 and 4 have good sea views, No 3 for its style. Kitchen facilities and a roof terrace are a bonus.

Réthymno
(telephone area code 0831)

Byzantine (££)
Odós Vospórou 26 tel: 55609
Attractive rooms in a renovated palace close to the minaret.
Zanya (£–££)
Odós Vlatoú 3 tel: 28169
Wonderful hotel in an old Turkish house with spacious rooms, friendly atmosphere, and a communal bathroom.

Siteía
(telephone area code 0843)

Arhontiko (£)
Odós Kondilákis 16 tel: 28172
Spacious, friendly, wooden guest house with orange and lemon trees in the courtyard.
El Greco (££)
Odós Arkadioú 13 tel: 23133
Well-run family hotel with 19 impeccable rooms and superb views over the harbour.

THE CYCLADES
Amorgós
(telephone area code 0285)

Aegiális (£££)
Órmos Aigiális tel: 73393; fax: 73395
A modern hotel with all facilities, a wonderful pool and good views over the bay.
Minoa (££)
on the harbour square, Katápola tel: 71480
Pleasant rooms in traditional-style hotel, but can be noisy.
Grypso's Hotel (£)
Aegiali tel: 73502
Villa-style hotel whose architecture is in the typical blue and white Cycladic style.

Anáfi

There are only a few rooms for rent, so take any offers made upon arriving, especially in the busy summer season.

Ándros
(telephone area code 0282)

Avra (£)
Batsí tel: 41216
One of the cheaper guest houses in the town, with well-kept rooms.

Chryssí Aktí (££)
Batsí tel: 41236
The most popular hotel for its location, in the city centre and across from the beach. Advance reservation is recommended in summer.
Paradise (£££)
Ándros Town tel: 22187; fax: 22340
Elegant, well-run neoclassical hotel near the town centre, with airy rooms and superb views.

Folégandros
(telephone area code 0286)

Anemomylos (£££)
on the edge of Folégandros Town tel; 41309; fax: 41407
Fully equipped apartments built in traditional style on the cliff's edge, with stunning views. One is equipped for visitors with disabilities.
Fani-Venis (££)
Folégandros Town tel: 41237
Comfortable hotel in a neoclassical mansion, with rooms overlooking the sea (summer only).
Odysseus (££)
Folégandros Town tel: 41276
Pleasant, friendly hotel, a long-time favourite with visitors to Folégandros.

Íos
(telephone area code 0286)

Homer's Inn (££)
Mylopótamos tel: 91365
Breakfast room actually overlooking the port; others look out on the countryside. Swimming pool and bar, but open summer only.
Íos Palace (£££)
Mylopótamos tel: 91269
Modern, traditional-style hotel near the beach with comfortable rooms overlooking the sea.
Philippou (££)
Plateía Filippoú, Íos Town tel: 91290
Small hotel in the centre of the nightlife. Bring ear plugs if you want to sleep early.

Kéa
(telephone area code 0288)

Ioulis (££)
Kéa Town Ioulída tel: 22177
Wonderful quiet spot in the *kástro* with gorgeous views from the terrace.
Iy Tzia Mas (£££)
Korissía tel: 21305
The island's only motel, near the beach, fills up quickly in summer, so reserve in advance.

Kímolos
Not many stay on Kímolos, but there are a few rooms for rent in Psáthi and Kímolos Town.

Kýthnos
(telephone area code 0281)

Anagenissis Xenia (£–££)
Loutrá tel: 31217
Clean rooms overlooking the beach in this once-fashionable spa.

271

Hotels and Restaurants

Possidonion (££)
Mérichas tel: 32100
One of the few hotels. Unatmospheric, modern, and expensive for what it offers.

Mílos
(telephone area code 0287)

Corali (££)
Adámas tel: 22204
Excellent rooms a little walk uphill from the ferry landing. Someone will pick you up from the ferry if you call in advance. Open all year.

Kapetan Tassos (£££)
Apollónia tel: 41287
Modern apartments in traditional blue and white island architecture, with good sea views.

Panorama (£–££)
Klíma tel: 21623
Small sea-front hotel with friendly service. The boss sometimes takes clients fishing.

Mýkonos
(telephone area code 0289)

For rooms in Mýkonos in the summer, reserve well in advance, as room prices can treble. Mýkonos Accommodation Centre (MAC – tel: 23160; fax: 24137) helps with accommodation, for every budget, but charges 10 per cent of the room price or a minimum fee.

Apollo (££)
Paralía, Mýkonos Town tel: 22223
Small but long-established, in the heart of the fun. Ten spotless, good-value rooms with bath.

Cavo Tagoo (£££)
*past the new harbour, Mýkonos Town
tel: 23692; fax: 24923*
Prize-winning Cycladic architecture, a uniquely friendly atmosphere, sharp service, and wonderful views over Mýkonos Town and the Aegean make the Cavo Tagoo, in its hillside setting, one of Greece's most special hotels. Swimming pool. Highly recommended.

Philippi (££)
*Odós N Kalogerá 32, Mýkonos Town
tel: 22294*
A converted traditional house, central but quiet, with a charming garden, friendly service and spotless rooms.

Zorzis (££)
*Odós N Kalogerá, Mýkonos Town tel: 22167;
fax: 24169*
Jonathan Varnalis has taken over his father's small hotel, one of the island's oldest, in a quiet street in the heart of the old town, and has turned it into a characterful and pleasant place to stay.

Náxos
(telephone area code 0285)

Anixis (£)
Kástro, Náxos Town tel: 22932; fax: 22112
There are 16 rooms, mostly ensuite, in this simple but spotlessly clean little hotel, which is centrally located near the Venetian tower.

Chateau Zevgoli (£££)
*Boúrgo Kástro, Náxos Town
tel: 22993; fax: 24525*
The island's most interesting hotel: ten rooms, tastefully decorated, high up in the old town. Good views and great atmosphere.

Grotta (££)
Grotta, Náxos Town tel: 22201; fax: 22000
Modern, Cycladic-style hotel, with sparkling clean rooms and great views over the sea and the *kástro*. The best mid-range hotel in town, within easy walking distance of the port.

Páros and Antíparos
(telephone area code 0284)

Páros is absolutely packed during the summer months and it can be hard to find any accommodation at all. Make reservations in advance or take up an offer of a room at the ferry arrival. Remember that rooms north of Páros Town are often a long walk from the centre.

Anargyros (£)
Kastro, Antíparos tel: 61204
Basic but well-kept rooms.

Astir of Paros (£££)
*on the beach, Náousa, Páros tel: 51797;
fax: 51985*
One of the best deluxe hotels in Greece, with a large pool and a three-hole par 3 golf course. Spacious rooms with all facilities.

Chrysí Aktí (££)
*east coast of Antíparos, near Kástro
tel: 61220*
An elegant beach hotel with good rooms.

Dina (£)
Agorá, Old Town, Páros tel: 21325
Eight very clean rooms in the heart of the Old Town, set around a lovely flowered courtyard. Recommended, but reserve in advance!

Golden Beach (££)
Chrysí Aktí (Golden Beach), on the east coast of Páros tel: 41366; fax: 41195
Modern low-rise hotel with excellent service and good, balconied rooms overlooking the beach. Very popular with windsurfers.

Kontes (££)
*Plateía Mavrogénous, Páros Town, Páros
tel: 21246*
Slightly older but well-kept hotel with upstairs rooms opening on to a sun deck. Great views over the windmill and the sea.

Mandalena (£)
Kástro, Antíparos tel: 61206
Clean but simple rooms, with harbour views.

Náousa (££)
by the sea on the southern approach to Náousa, Páros tel: 51207
Faded hotel with rusty balconies but well-maintained rooms and very friendly service.

Yria (£££)
*near the beach of Parásporos,
3km south of Páros Town
tel: 24154; fax: 21167*
Pretty, traditional-style village with characterfully furnished bungalows. Quiet terrace and large swimming pool.

Sérifos
(telephone area code 0281)

Areti (££)
Livádi tel: 51479; fax: 51547
A very enjoyable hotel, near the ferry landing,
built on a hill and with superb views.
Pansion Chrysti (££)
Livádi tel: 51775
Pleasant and quiet rooms with lovely views over
the bay.

Sífnos
(telephone area code 0284)

Sífnos is very popular with young Athenians on
weekends, so book ahead.

Apollonía (£)
Apollonía tel: 31490
Small hotel with pleasant, clean rooms.
Artemon (££)
near the main square in Artemón tel: 31303;
fax: 32385
Lovely family hotel with rooms that overlook
fields rolling towards the sea. Recommended.
Moní Chrysopigí (£)
near the beach of Apokoftó tel: 31255
This 17th-century monastery rents out simple
cells in summer. Reserve well in advance.
Platýs Yialos (£££)
Platýs Gialós tel: 71324; fax: 71325
Excellent and very popular hotel with wood-
carvings and wall-paintings. Good views.
Sifnos (££)
off the main square in Apollonía tel: 31624
Charming, quiet little hotel with nine rooms with
bathrooms, in traditional island architecture.

Síkinos
(telephone area code 0286)

Flora (£)
Aloprónoia tel: 51214
Simple, pleasant rooms, some with bathrooms.
Kamares (££)
Aloprónoia tel: 51234
Traditional-style, affordable hotel with comfort-
able but average rooms.
Porto Sikinos (£££)
on the beach in Aloprónoia (tel/fax: 51220
The best accommodation available, a new,
small resort hotel with traditional-style rooms.

Sýros
(telephone area code 0281)

Dolphin Bay Hotel (£££)
*on the beach at Galissás tel: 42924;
fax: 42843*
The largest and most modern hotel on the
island, with all facilities, a large swimming pool
and lovely views. Family-orientated.
Europe Hotel (££)
*Odós Proíou 24, Ermoúpoli tel: 28771;
fax: 23508*
Pleasant hotel with a Rhodian-style pebbled
courtyard and spacious rooms. Open all year.

Ksenon Ipatias (££)
Odós Babagiótou 3, Ermoúpoli tel: 83575
Delectable little hotel in a restored 19th-century
mansion. High-ceilinged rooms with stone
floors, wall-paintings, and brass beds.
Omiros (£££)
*Odós Omiroú 43, Ermoúpoli tel: 84910;
fax: 86266*
Newly restored neoclassical mansion, with
good views over the lively harbour.

Thíra
(telephone area code 0286)

Hotels with a view over the caldera are expensive. Many of the cheaper rooms are in
modern, characterless house extensions, often
a long walk from town. Prices more than double
in summer and reservations are essential.

Atlantis (£££)
Thíra Town tel: 22232; fax: 22 821
Luxurious hotel, built in the 1950s but recently
renovated. Spacious rooms, most with bal-
conies overlooking the town and the volcano.
Kamari Beach (££–£££)
*is right on the black sands of Kamari Beach
tel: 31243*
Large airy rooms and large pool.
Lauda (££)
Oía tel: 71204
Pleasant Cycladic-style rooms with superb
views over the caldera.
Loucas (££)
Thíra Town tel: 22480
Long-established hotel perched on the cliffs. All
rooms have bathroom and simple furnishings.
Excellent terrace overlooking the caldera.
Perivolas Traditional Homes (£££)
Oía tel: 71308
Former cliff-face dwellings turned into simple
but tasteful suites with cooking facilities.
Stunning views, a cliff-top pool, a well-run café,
excellent buffet breakfast and a relaxed atmo-
sphere. Highly recommended.
Tataki (£–££)
Old Town, Thíra tel: 22389
One of the cheaper hotels in the centre, with
simple rooms around a courtyard. Central heat-
ing and private showers. Open all year.

Tínos
(telephone area code 0283)

Eleana (£)
Plateía Ierarchón, Tínos Town tel: 22561
Spacious, bright rooms with balconies
overlooking the lovely square.
Porto Tango (£££)
Pórto Ágios Ioánnis tel: 24411; fax: 24416
New, Cycladic-style hotel. Swimming pool
overlooking the sea and surrounding country-
side. A little too expensive in the high season.
Tinion (££)
*Odós Konstantínou Alavanoú 1, Tínos Town
tel: 22261; fax: 24754*
Charming old-world hotel with tiled floors, lace
curtains, and a large balcony.

273

Hotels and Restaurants

THE DODECANESE

Astypálaia
(telephone area code 0243)

Astynea (£)
on the harbour tel: 61040
A modest little hotel, recently renovated.
Paradissos (£)
on the harbour, Gialós tel: 61224
Clean, comfortable rooms, but does not live up
to its name.

Chálki
There are no hotels in Chálki, only rooms or
apartments for rent. Reserve in advance.

Captain's House (£)
Chálki Town tel: 0241 45201
A lovely restored mansion with a few rooms for
rent. The management may be able to help you
to find a room elsewhere if the house is full.

Kálymnos
(telephone area code 0243)

Atlantis (£)
Myrtiés tel: 47497
Friendly, cosy hotel with large sea-view rooms.
Manolis (£)
Vathýs tel: 31300
Lovely, well-equipped rooms in a blue and white
house with a flowery garden.
Olympic (££)
Póthia tel: 28801; fax: 29314
Modern hotel with spacious rooms and
balconies over the (often noisy) harbour.
Panorama (£)
Amoudára, Póthia tel: 23138
Worth its name, as this hotel was built on the
high centre of the town, overlooking the har-
bour. If you reserve in advance, someone will
come and pick you up.

Kárpathos
(telephone area code 0245)

Avra (£)
Odós Ektovrioú 28, Kárpathos Town
tel: 22388
Friendly family hotel. Clean rooms have
bathrooms and balconies.
Dolphin Hotel-Apartments (££)
opposite the ferry landing, Kárpathos Town
tel: 22665
Charming modern hotel with airy, very clean
rooms and studio apartments overlooking
the port and the town. Advance reservations
are necessary.
Karpathos (£–££)
Odós Dimokratías 25, Kárpathos Town
tel: 22347
Pleasant rooms, some with bathrooms.
Krinos (££)
Léfkos tel: 71410
Pleasant new hotel facing the sea and set in a
pleasant garden. Offers good value; necessary
to reserve in advance.

Possirama Bay (££–£££)
Vróntis beach tel: 22511, fax: 22929
A five-minute walk from Kárpathos Town. Quiet,
spotless, spacious apartments have balconies
overlooking the beach and the port.

Kásos
(telephone area code 0245)

Anagennisis (££)
on the waterfront in Frý tel: 41495; fax: 41036
Probably the best place to stay on Kásos. Run
by a Greek-American. Comfortable rooms, the
most expensive with harbour views.
Anessis (£££)
Frý tel: 41201
Slightly cheaper and smaller hotel, good rooms.

Kastellórizo (Megísti)
(telephone area code 0241)

Mavrothalassitis (£)
Kastellórizo Town tel: 49202
Simple rooms in a restored mansion, run by the
family of the same name.
Megístis (££)
harbour of Kastellórizo Town tel:49272
Has pleasant, cosy rooms overlooking the port.

Kós
(telephone area code 0242)

Most hotels on Kós are used by package
companies and are often noisy.

Afendoulis (££)
Odós Evripiloú 1, Kós Town tel: 25321
Small, modern hotel with balconied rooms. One
of the few hotels which has not given in to
package tourism. Reserve in advance.
Panorema (££)
at Kéfalos tel: 71524)
Lovely gardens and wonderful views out to the
Kástri islet.
Pension Alexis (£)
Odós Irodotoú and Omiroú 9, Kós Town
tel: 28798
Friendly central guest house. Good value.

Leipsoí
(telephone area code 0247)

Kalypso (££)
Leipsoí tel/fax: 41242
This is the only hotel on the island (but there
are quite a few cheaper rooms for rent). All
rooms have bathrooms.

Léros
(telephone area code 0247)

Chryssoula (££)
Alínda tel: 22451
Comfortable rooms with great views.
Elefteria (£)
Plátanos tel: 23550
Pleasant and quiet hotel with acceptable rooms
and good views.

Malias Beach (££)
Alínda tel: 22834
Spacious and sunny, overlooking the bay and
pebble beach.

Nísyros
(telephone area code 0242)

Nisyros (£)
near the monastery in Mandráki tel: 31052
New, well-equipped rooms.
Romantzo (£)
by the ferry landing at Mandráki tel: 31340
Clean rooms with good harbour views and a big
shady terrace.
Porfiris (££)
Mandráki tel: 31376
Comfortable modern hotel with well-maintained
rooms, gardens, and a swimming pool.

Pátmos
(telephone area code 0247)

There are no hotels or rooms in lovely Pátmos
Town, but private houses can be rented for
longer periods through travel agents in the port
or through Emanouel Fallieras (tel: 31398).

Artemis (££)
Grígos tel: 31555
Traditional-style hotel with a pleasant garden
and simply furnished rooms with sea views.
Captain's House (££)
Skála tel: 31793; fax: 32277
New but lovely hotel overlooking the sea, with
sparkling and bright rooms.
Knossos (£)
Skála tel: 32189
Good-value hotel with ten rooms in a villa over-
grown with bougainvillaea. Just off the port.
Patmion (£–££)
Skála tel: 31313
Well-established old-style hotel with good-value
rooms in a charming villa.
Skala (££–£££)
Skála tel: 31343; fax: 31747
This quiet and welcoming hotel, drowning in
bougainvillaea, is on Skála's increasingly busy
waterfront. Excellent breakfast terrace and
pool. Recommended, but reserve in advance.

Ródos (Rhodes)
(telephone area code 0241)

For individual travellers the most atmospheric
option is to stay in the Old Town. It is possible
to rent rooms there through the tourist
information office (tel: 0244 31900).

Casa de la Sera (££)
Odós Thiséos 38, Rhodes Old Town tel: 75154
Peaceful hotel in an old restored villa in a more
residential area of the Old Town. Very clean
rooms.
Cavo d'Oro (££)
Kisthiríou 15, Rhodes Town tel: 36980
Handy for ferries, this 13th-century house has
recently been sympathetically restored.

Kastro (£)
*Plateía Ariónos 14, Rhodes Old Town
tel: 20446*
Friendly hotel in the Old Town. Clean rooms,
and various decorations by the owner.
Minos (£)
Odós Omiroú 5, Rhodes Old Town tel: 30815
Simple guest house with friendly atmosphere;
lovely views from the roof terrace.
San Nikolis (££–£££)
*Odós Ippodámou 61, Rhodes Old Town tel:
34561; fax: 32034*
Delightful hotel, in the most attractive area of
the Old Town, with comfortable rooms, friendly
service and great breakfasts.

Sými
(telephone area code 0241)

Aliki (££)
Yialós, Sými Town tel: 71665; fax: 71655
The island's best, with elegant and comfortable
rooms, some with excellent sea views. Advance
reservations necessary.
Hotel Fiona (££)
Chorió, Sými Town tel: 72088
Bright rooms with good views in the Old Town.

Tílos
(telephone area code 0241)

Irini (££)
Livádia tel: 44293
Charming small hotel with beautiful gardens
and helpful owners. Reserve in advance.

THE IONIAN ISLANDS
Itháki
(telephone area code 0674)

Mentor (££)
Itháki Town tel: 32433
Most people's choice; spacious rooms over-
looking the beautiful harbour. Open all year.
Nostos (££)
Fríkes tel: 31100
A small, family-run hotel in a quiet valley behind
the port of Fríkes, with atmosphere and wonder-
ful cooking. Guests tend to return year after
year. Recommended.

Kefaloniá

Fiskardona (££)
Fiskárdo tel: 0674 41436
A 19th-century villa near the port in Fiskárdo,
with character and cooking facilities.
Melissani (£–££)
*a couple of minutes south of Sámi
tel: 0674 22064*
Backed by the hills, facing the sea, a calm
hotel with large balconies.
Olga (££)
Paralía Metaxá 82, Argostóli tel: 0671 24981
A year-round modern hotel run by a local. Good
value and friendly service.

Hotels and Restaurants

White Rocks (£££)
Platí Gialós tel: 0671 23167 or 28332
Kefallonians speak with pride of this expensive resort hotel. Surrounded by pines, with access to excellent beaches.

Kérkyra (Corfu)
Bella Venezia (££)
N Zampelí 4, Corfu Town tel: 0661 46500
A restored mansion in a quiet street, with a lot of atmosphere and a friendly staff.
Corfu Palace (£££)
*Leofóros Demokratías 2, Corfu Town
tel: 0661 39485*
Luxury on the sea a few minutes' walk from the Old Town. Prices are high, so the Palace attracts an older clientele.
Cyprus (£–££)
*Agíon Patéron 13, Corfu Town
tel: 0661 40675*
The best of the town's budget hotels (if you can get in). Popular with Americans.
Green House (£–££)
Palaiokastrítsa tel: 0663 41311
A small and basic guest house in this popular resort. Reserve well in advance.

Lefkáda
(telephone area code 0645)

Byzantio (£)
Dörpfeld 40, Lefkáda Town tel: 22629
The budget choice: clean communal facilities, high-ceilinged rooms and a terrace over the harbour. Only 15 rooms, so book ahead.
Lefkatas (££–£££)
Vasilikí tel: 31801
Modern comfort and helpful staff, together with taverna and *kafeneío*.
Odyssey (£££)
Ágios Nikítas tel: 97351
A 37-room hotel with sea views, near excellent beaches in this new resort.
Pension Ostria (£££)
in Ágios Nikítas tel: 97483
This is a lovely blue and white hotel away from the village centre.
Santa Maura (££)
Dörpfeld, Lefkáda Town tel: 21308
In the centre of town, can be noisy. Spacious rooms, some with private bathroom.

Paxoí
(telephone area code 0662)

Paxos Beach (£££)
Paxoí Town tel: 32211
The island's first and best, with simple rooms and good beach, water sports, and tennis. Pretty restaurant serves unexceptional food.

Zákynthos
(telephone area code 0695)

Crystal Beach (£££)
Kalamáki tel: 42788
The only building on Kalamáki beach, very calm and quiet for a Zákynthos beach hotel.

Montreal (££)
Alíkes tel: 83241
A 31-room hotel right next to the beach in a quiet resort.
Palatino (££–£££)
*Kolokotróni 10 and Kólyva, Zákynthos Town
tel: 45400*
A block back from the sea, this modern, elegant city hotel has sea views and a good bar. One of the quietest hotels in town.
Zenith (£)
Odós Tertséti 48 tel: 22134
Ten basic rooms above a supermarket.

NORTHERN AND EASTERN AEGEAN ISLANDS

Chíos

Kardamyla (£££)
Kardámyla tel: 0272 23353; fax: 23354
A quiet beach resort with good rooms overlooking the Marmara bay. A range of water sports are available.
Kyma (££)
*Odós Evgenías Chandrís 1, Chíos Town
tel: 0271 44500*
Characterful hotel in a 1917 shipowner's villa with rooms, completely modernized a while ago and now distinctly old-fashioned. Very helpful manager. Excellent breakfasts.
Perleas Mansion (£££)
Kámpos tel: 0271 32217
Next to one of Greece's most expensive hotels, surrounded by orange groves, this lovingly restored mansion offers quiet, comfortable rooms with antique furnishings.
Phaedra (£)
*Odós Livanós 13, Chíos Town
tel: 0271 41130*
Small hotel with clean rooms in an old mansion run by young people.
Zorba apartments (££)
Volissós tel: 0271 21436; fax: 21720
Sparkling clean rooms and self-contained apartments overlooking Limniá harbour. Simply furnished. Quiet choice.

Ikaría
(telephone area code 0275)

Akti (£)
on the waterfront in Ágios Kírykos tel: 22694
Simple but well-maintained rooms with views over the bay from the garden.
Cavos Bay (££–£££)
Armenistís tel: 71381
Luxurious, quiet hotel set on a hillside.
Daidalos (££)
Armenistís tel: 71390
Traditional-style, very airy hotel, in blue and white, overlooking the bay. Good views, relaxed atmosphere. This hotel tends to be popular with Athenians.
Evdoxia (££)
Évdilos tel: 31502
Modern hotel with balconied rooms overlooking the harbour and the bay.

Lésvos
(telephone area code 0251)

Blue Sea (££)
Odós Kountourióto 91, Mytilíni tel: 23995; fax: 29656
Comfortable rooms, many with balconies overlooking the harbour.
Delfinia (£££)
Mólivos tel: 71315; fax: 71524
Pleasant resort hotel overlooking the town and harbour with simple rooms, swimming pool and sports facilities. Open all year.
Sea Horse (££)
near the beach at Mólivos tel: 71320
Modern hotel below the old town with unfussy, clean rooms and friendly service.
Villa 1900 (££)
Odós Vóstani 24, Mytilíni tel: 23448
Small hotel in a restored *belle-époque* villa.

Límnos
(telephone area code 0254)

Aktaion (£)
Odós Arvanitáki 2, Mýrina tel: 22258
A two-storey hotel on the port, somewhat noisy and run down, but open all year.
Aktí Mýrina (£££)
Mýrina tel: 22681
One of the finest and most expensive hotels on the Greek Islands. Simple but spacious accommodation in bungalows, each with its own small private garden. Marvellous beach, several excellent restaurants, and all water sports.

Sámos
(telephone area code 0273)

Avli (£)
Odós Aréos and Kaloméri, Sámos Town tel: 22939
Wonderful hotel in an old monastery in the quiet back streets near the harbour. Recommended.
Doryssa Bay (£££)
Pythagóreio tel: 61360; fax: 61463
Large and modern, just outside town. The resort cleverly replicates a Greek village, complete with taverna and *kafeneío*.
Labito (££)
Pythagóreio tel: 61085; fax: 61086
New hotel near the harbour, built in neoclassical style with quiet, spacious rooms in pastel colours.
Paradise (££)
Odós Kanarí 21, Sámos Town tel: 23911
New, elegant hotel set in a lush garden with a swimming pool, away from the tourist hubbub, but still central. Recommended.

Samothráki
(telephone area code 0551)

Aeolos (££)
Kamariótissa tel: 41595
A new hotel, a short walk up from the port and waterfront restaurants. Quiet.

Kaviros (£££)
Thermá tel: 98277
Surrounded by lush greenery, only a short walk from cafés and restaurants and within easy reach of an attractive pebble beach.

Thásos
(telephone area code 0593)

Prinos (££)
Skála Prínos tel: 71374
A clean, friendly, small hotel on Prínos beach. Reserve ahead for rooms with sea views.
Villa Chrysalis (££)
on Golden Beach tel: 61979
The best of available accommodation on the better side of the sandy bay.

THE SARONIC ISLANDS

Aígina
(telephone area code 0297)

Eginitiko Arhintiko (££)
Odós Nikólaou and Thomáidou 1, Aígina Town tel: 24968
This is a charming traditional guest house in a neoclassical house with tastefully decorated rooms around two flower-filled courtyards.
Ippokampos (£)
Pérdika tel: 61363
Friendly hotel overlooking the small fishing town and a courtyard with bougainvillaea.
Moondy Bay (£££)
5km south of Aígina Town tel: 61622; fax: 61147
Friendly resort hotel with frequent bus services into Aígina Town and Pérdika. Lovely gardens, with a good private beach and swimming pool.

Póros
(telephone area code 0298)

Latsi (£–££)
Odós Papadopoúlo 74, Póros Town tel: 22392
Simple, slightly worn but clean rooms; balcony overlooking the Peloponnese. Good deal.
Pavlou (££)
Neório bay tel: 22734
Pleasant and quiet hotel on Kalávria.
Sirene (££–£££)
Askéli tel: 22741; fax: 22744
Very popular with tour groups but nevertheless an excellent hotel with swimming pool and private beach. Spacious rooms with magnificent views.

Salamína
(telephone area code 01)

Gabriel (£–££)
Aiánteio tel: 466 2223; fax: 466 2275
Definitely the best guest house on the island, with simple rooms.
Votsalakia (£)
Odós Themistokléous 64, Selinia tel: 467 1334
Pleasant, simple hotel with swimming pool.

Hotels and Restaurants

Spétses
(telephone area code 0298)

Possidonion Hotel (££–£££)
Spétses Town tel: 72006
Slowly fading but still grand, an Edwardian hotel overlooking the waterfront. Once legendary for its wealthy and famous clientele.
Spetses Hotel (££)
1km west of the harbour in Spétses Town tel: 72602
Very quiet but large hotel away from the crowds, with comfortable rooms overlooking the town and the sea. The hotel has its own jetty.
Villa Christina (££)
54m uphill from the ferry landing in Spétses Town tel: 72218
Secluded hotel with comfortable and clean rooms around a courtyard.

Ýdra
(telephone area code 0298)

Miranda (£££)
Mandráki tel: 52230
First-class hotel in a beautifully renovated 19th-century mansion. Some rooms have old hand-painted ceilings and balconies with exceptional views over the town.
Orloff (££)
Odós Rafália 9 tel: 52564
Another tasteful renovation of a typical Hydriot mansion, with ten differently designed rooms.
Sofia (£)
on the waterfront, on the corner of Odós Miaoúlis tel: 52313
Quite noisy but charming hotel, right in the heart of the place.

THE SPORADES AND ÉVVOIA

Alónnisos
(telephone area code 0424)

Alkyon (£–££)
Alónnisos Town tel: 65450
Pleasant guest house with sparkling rooms. Good value, but reserve in advance.
Liadromia (££)
Patitíri tel: 65521; fax: 65096
A modern hotel overlooking the harbour, a few minutes' walk from tavernas and shops.
Paradise (££)
Magnísias, adjacent to Patitíri tel: 65213; fax: 65161
Lovely, family-run hotel built on the rocks, above the harbour and with sea views from many rooms. Great terrace.

Skíathos
(telephone area code 0427)

Karafelas (£)
Odós Papadiamánti 59, Skíathos Town tel: 21235
Pleasant little hotel with quiet rooms and garden and very friendly owners. Reserve in advance!

Meltemi (££)
Skiáthos Town tel: 22493
Comfortable modern hotel, overlooking the yacht harbour. Reserve well in advance: this is a popular place even in spring and autumn.
Skiáthos Princess (£££)
Agía Paraskeví tel: 49226; fax: 49666
Luxurious resort hotel with large rooms overlooking the lovely beach, swimming pool, and tavernas.

Skópelos
(telephone area code 0424)

Archontiko (££)
Xánthou 1, Skópelos Town tel: 22765
Well-situated guest house in a stylish mansion with comfortable rooms.
Drossia (£–££)
Skópelos Town tel: 22490
Built on top of the hill overlooking the town. The tidy rooms have excellent views.
Prince Stafylos (£££)
Livádi tel: 22775; fax: 22825
Lovely hotel, built like a country house within walking distance of the town. Swimming pool and perfumed garden. Advance reservations necessary. Recommended, despite being expensive.

Skýros
(telephone area code 0222)

Angela (££)
Mólos tel: 91764
Spotless rooms, all with balconies.
Nefeli (££)
Skýros Town tel: 91964
Best choice in the town, modern but with Skyrian-style architecture and tastefully decorated bedrooms, most with lovely views. Recommended, but reserve beforehand.
Skyros Palace (£££)
Acheroúnes tel: 91994
Big resort built in traditional style with a good swimming pool.

Évvoia
Als (££)
Kotsika 96, Kárystos tel: 0224 22202
Very well situated on the waterfront.
Kentrikon (£)
Odós A Gotsioú, Chalkída tel: 0221 22375
Old-fashioned hotel near the Évripos bridge with clean but simple rooms.
Krineion (£)
Plateía Papanikoláou, Kými tel: 0222 22287
Charming hotel with large-rooms. The equally large balconies overlook the village square.
Limni (£)
Límni tel: 0227 31316
Offering good value, this hotel has spotless rooms overlooking the quiet bay.
Lucy (££–£££)
Odós Voudóuri 10, Chalkída tel: 0221 23831
Lovely 1950s-style hotel with comfortable rooms and splendid views over the Évripos strait and the evening *volta*.

RESTAURANTS

On many islands, particularly the smaller ones, the choice of restaurants is limited to the two or three on the waterfront. As space here is limited, we have only mentioned tavernas and restaurants that we think stand out, or ones which are more difficult to find. Telephone numbers are given only for establishments where advance reservations might be appropriate.

Greeks almost never look at the menu, preferring to ask the waiter what's cooking, because often the specialities or more interesting items are not written down. If you do not know the names of Greek dishes, and if you would like to see the prices, it may be sensible to look at the menu. If not, ask to have a look in the kitchen, and also take note of what your Greek neighbors are eating. Part of the pleasure of eating out in the islands is wandering around to find the place right for your mood. Remember that many restaurants are closed out of season, from October to March or April. The restaurants recommended below have been divided into three price categories:

(£) = budget
(££) = moderate
(£££) = expensive

ATHÍNA (ATHENS)
(telephone area code 01)

Brazilian (£)
one block behind the Grande Bretagne hotel on Plateía Syntágmatos (Syntagma Square) tel: 323 5463
Elegant 1930s stand-up coffee bar with excellent cappuccino, good croissants, and pastries. Try the terrace in the alley for an open-air lunch.
Eden (££)
Odós Lysioú 12, Pláka tel: 324 8858
First vegetarian restaurant in Athens. Greek with tasty Middle Eastern influences.
Gerofinikas (£££)
Odós Pindaroú 10, Kolonáki tel: 362 2719
Very elegant restaurant, with excellent Greek and international specialities.
Sigálas (£)
Plateía Monastiráki tel: 321 3036
Ancient taverna with boisterous atmosphere. Simple, cheap, good.
Socrates' Prison (££)
Odós Mitséon 20, Koukáki tel: 922 3434
Atmospheric restaurant with good fresh Greek and more continental dishes.

KRÍTI (CRETE)

Irákleio
(telephone area code 081)

Ionia (££)
Odós Evans 3 tel: 283213
Popular restaurant near the market, with a wide selection of fresh dishes. Snails and artichokes are a particular speciality.

Kyriakos (££)
45 Odós Dimokratías tel: 224649
Rated as Irákleio's best by residents, with a wide variety of Greek specialities. Reservations necessary. Closed Wed.

Ágios Nikólaos
(telephone area code 0841)

Cretan Restaurant (££–£££)
Odós Koundouroú tel: 28773
Standard Greek food and fisherman's décor, but a great place to sit and watch the port.
Pelagos (££)
corner of Odós Koraká and Katecháki 10 tel: 25737
Atmospheric taverna in an old villa, with fish specialities and an interesting menu. Dining also on the terrace.

Chaniá

Bon Appétit (£)
inside the Central Market
A no-nonsense restaurant with a range of fresh dishes on display. Excellent vegetables, grilled octopus. Closed Sun.
Falasin Ageri (££–£££)
Odós Chaléppa Viviláki 35 tel: 0821 56672
Excellent seafood and fish restaurant. Only open in the evenings.
Tamam (££)
Odós Zambelioú 49
Very popular and good-value restaurant in part of an old hammam. Among the most imaginative food in town. Closed Sun.

Réthymno

Apostolis (£–££)
Odós Kallirons Sigánou 10 tel: 0831 24401
Long-established, family-run taverna with modest Cretan specialities, away from the tourists.

Siteía

Kali Kardia (£–££)
Odós Foundalídou 20 tel: 0843 22249
Excellent Greek food with all the standards on the menu. Try the *mezédes* with ouzo or one of the daily specials. The decoration is wild.

THE CYCLADES

Amorgós

Akrogiali (£–££)
Katápola
The most atmospheric of the tavernas, with good fresh Greek specialities.
Toh Limani (Katerina's) (£–££)
Aigiális
Popular taverna with good food, wine from the barrel and excellent music.
Vitzentos (££)
seafront, Xylokeratídi, Katápola tel: 71518
Very popular seafood restaurant with a more inventive menu than most.

279

Hotels and Restaurants

Andrós

Oasis (££)
Batsí (a 10-minute walk from the beach
Pleasant taverna specialising in chicken and
grilled meat. Dine under shady vines.
Ti Kalo (££)
Batsí
Small restaurant with excellent fish and
seafood, especially lobster.

Folégandros

ly Melissa (£)
Plateía Kondaríni, Folégandros Town
Go for breakfast: fresh juices, omelettes, and
delicious yoghurt with honey or fruit.
Niko's Ouzeri (£–££)
near the bus stop in Folégandros Town
Cosy place run by an Italian. Good food.

Íos

Dolidoros (££)
Koumpára beach
Popular restaurant with well-prepared
traditional dishes. Evenings only.
Pithari (£–££)
*Plateía Filíppou
Íos Town*
Elegant restaurant with some unusual dishes.
Windmill (££–£££)
top of Íos Town tel: 0286 91284
Wonderful Greek food. Try the excellent stuffed
aubergine or the tender goat's meat.

Kýthnos

Toh Kandouni (££)
end of the beach in Mérichas
Excellent food served beside the water, with
cool island wine and local dishes.

Mílos

Trapatselis (££)
on the Apollónia road in Adámas
Large variety of well-prepared dishes.
Renowned locally for fresh fish.
Zygos (££)
*Adámas (a five-minute walk east along the
seafront, then follow sign for restaurant grill*
Lovely view over town, good Greek fare and
better value than in the port.

Mýkonos
(telephone area code 0289)

Niko's Taverna (££)
*near Paraportiani church in Mýkonos Town
tel: 24320*
One of the better tavernas, popular with locals
and visitors. Large, good-value menu.
Philippi (£££)
Odós Mitropóleos, Mýkonos Town tel: 22295
Romantic and elegant setting, with tables
under the olive trees and excellent continental
dishes. Reservations recommended.

The Sesame Kitchen (££)
*next door to the Marine Museum on Odós
Matogiánni tel: 24710*
Cosy atmosphere and imaginative dishes with
Greek and Middle Eastern inspiration.

Náxos
(telephone area code 0285)

Good Heart (£–££)
Paralía, Náxos Town
Fresh grilled fish, octopus, and standard Greek
food. Unfussy waterfront restaurant.
Kastro (££)
by the castle walls in Náxos Town tel: 22005
One of the best in town: excellent *stifado*.
O Lefteris (££)
main street, Apeírados tel: 61333
Delicious, simple home cooking, with excep-
tional local cheeses and pastries.
O Nikos (££–£££)
*above the Commercial Bank, Paralía, Náxos
Town tel: 23153*
The most popular restaurant overlooking the
harbour, with fish, lamb, and other dishes.

Páros
(telephone area code 0284)

Levantis (££–£££)
Odós Ágora, Páros Town tel: 23613
Really good food inspired by Turkish and Middle
Eastern cuisine. Recommended.
To Tamarisko (££–£££)
Odós Ágora, Páros Town tel: 22170
Fresh Greek food and grills in a whitewashed
house with a garden.
Tsitsanas (£–££)
*between the villages of Pródromos and
Mármara*
Though this restaurant is hard to find (ask for
directions), the food is well worth the search.

Sérifos
(telephone area code 0281)

Ouzerie Meltemi (££)
by the yacht harbour
A wide range of unusual and filling *mezédes*.

Sífnos
(telephone area code 0284)

Apostolis (££)
Apollonía
The best of the tavernas. Also a great find for
those seeking vegetarian dishes.
Captain Andreas (£–££)
Kamáres tel: 32356
Excellent fish and seafood taverna directly on
the beach.
Liotrivi (££)
Artemón tel: 32051
A favourite with Sifniots. Local specialities
served here include caper salad and chickpea
beignets. Only open in summer, but its sister
restaurant, **Manganas** (££), on the central
square in Artemón, is open all year round.

Sýros

Boubas (£)
left of the ferry landing, Ermoúpoli
Pleasant *ouzéri*.

Cavo D'Oro (££)
Paralía, Ermoúpoli tel: 0281 81440
The best and most popular fish and seafood taverna on the waterfront.

Il Giardino (££)
near Apollon theater, Ermoúpoli
Delightful restaurant in a restored villa. Pasta and Italian specialities. Recommended.

Thíra
(telephone area code 0286)

Helidoni (££)
in an alley off the main square in Thíra Town tel: 22859
Fresh grilled fish and octopus served in a courtyard – notably simple for Thíra.

Kukumavolos (£££)
Oía tel: 71413
One of the island's best. Elegant dining on a beautiful terrace overlooking the sea. Imaginative food.

Kyma (£–££)
Ammoúdi waterfront, Oía
The latest fish taverna on the waterfront below Oía, with the freshest of fish.

Tínos
(telephone area code 0283)

Pantelis (££)
Odós Drossoú 13, Tínos Town
Popular Greek cuisine, well prepared and with plenty of variety. Busy at weekends.

Pelekani (£)
first street on the right as you go inland from the taxi stand in Tínos Town tel: 23375
Cosy, old-style *ouzéri*: octopus is on the menu.

Peristeronias (££)
behind the Lido Hotel, Tínos Town tel: 23425
Tasty dishes served in an interior decorated like a Venetian dovecote. Only open in summer.

THE DODECANESE

Kálymnos

Ouzeri Meris (£)
Paralía, Chrístos
The signpost is hard to find, but look for the octopus drying outside. Good octopus dishes.

Yacht Club (£–££)
Póthia tel: 0243 29239
Delightful fisherman's-style restaurant with good food and harbour views.

Kárpathos

Iy Kali Kardhia (££)
on the waterfront, a short walk from town towards Vróntis bay tel: 0245 22256
Pleasant outdoor taverna by the sea, known for its fresh fish and seafood.

Kafeníon Halkia (£–££)
Odós Apod. Karpathíon, Kárpathos Town
The menu features traditional food like stifado with green beans, or fried fresh sardines. These are served with lots of retsina in the only old house left in town. A lively atmosphere and sometimes has live *rembetika* music.

Kafeníon Posidon (£)
by the windmills, Ólympos
Lovely *kafeneío* with perfect views and traditionally prepared cheese and spinach pastries as well as delicious *loukoumádes* in local honey.

Kós
(telephone area code 0242)

Arap (Platanio) (£–££)
Platáni tel: 28442
One of the few Turkish restaurants on the island: excellent Turkish and Greek specialities.

Mavromatis (££–£££)
on the coastal road east of Kós Town, before Psalídi beach tel: 22433
A favourite on Kós, with a terrace on the beach. Specialises in lobster and deliciously prepared fish, as well as other Greek classics.

Petrino (££)
Plateía Theológou 1, Kós Town tel: 27251
Lovely Greek specialities served on a quiet terrace next to the Western Excavations.

Pátmos
(telephone area code 0247)

Pantelis (£–££)
one street back from the harbour in Skála tel: 31230
Long-established traditional restaurant, a favourite with locals and foreign residents. Friendly service. Open all the year round.

The Patmian House (££–£££)
Pátmos Town tel: 31180
New York-trained chef Viktor Gouras, his wife Irene and their sons have made this restaurant something really special. The Greek specialities are simply divine. Reserve.

Ródos (Rhodes)
(telephone area code 0241)

Despina's (£)
Odós Agíou Fanourioú 30, Rhodes Old Town tel: 74540
Small, family-run taverna, good for cheap beer and the daily specials.

Dodekanisos (££)
Plateía Martyrón Evraïón 45, Rhodes Old Town tel: 28412
Excellent fish restaurant popular with locals for its fresh seafood and local specialities.

Efterpi (£–££)
Charáki waterfront
Simple taverna with a Turkish flavour.

Palia Istoria (£££)
Odós Mitropóleos 108, corner Dendrínou, Rhodes New Town tel: 32421
The best restaurant on Rhodes, with Greek cuisine served on a stylish patio. Reserve.

Hotels and Restaurants

Sými

Neraida (£–££)
main square in Gialós, Sými Town
Atmospheric taverna with tasty grilled fish and an array of mouthwatering *mezedes*.

THE IONIAN ISLANDS

Itháki
(telephone area code 0674)

Fatouros (also known as **Kasiani**) (£–££)
main square in Stavrós tel: 31385
Open all year for grilled meat and fish.
Gregory's (££)
Paliocaravo, Itháki Town tel: 32573
A little out of town, on Vathí bay. Taverna food.
Symposium (£)
Fríkes
On the waterfront, this offers some imaginative dishes, with many vegetarian options.

Kefalloniá

Patsouras (££)
Odós Israel (off Odós Vassiléos Georgíou), Argostóli tel: 0671 22779
Escape from the *plateía* to this garden restaurant. Good home-from-home cooking.

Kérkyra (Corfu)

Aristos (also known as Yioryias) (£–££)
Odós Guildford 16, Corfu Town
tel: 0661 37147
Good fresh food at this neighbourhood taverna.
Bella Vista (££)
on the road from Palaiokastrítsa to Lákones
'Where the kings of Greece have eaten', says the sign. Go for the sea views. Lunch only.
Chambor (££–£££)
Odós Guildford 71, Corfu Town
tel: 0661 39031
Fancy Greek and international cooking.

Lefkáda
(telephone area code 0645)

Regentos (£–££)
Dimárchou Veríoti 17, Lefkáda Town
tel: 22855
Fresh food simply prepared in a long-established family taverna. Excellent value.
No Problem (££)
on Sývota waterfront tel: 31182
The best of the waterfront tavernas.

Paxoí
(telephone area code 0662)

Rex's Taverna (££)
Paxoí Town tel: 31268
Fixed-price meals and fresh fish.
Vassilis (££)
Longós tel: 31587
Waterfront taverna serving exceptionally good food. Long wine list too.

Zákynthos
(telephone area code 0695)

Arekia (££)
Odós Kryeneniou (off Plateía Solómou)
Zákynthos Town tel: 26346/23471
Greek food at low prices. Come early for a quiet dinner, or later to see the local musicians.
Mantalena (££)
Alikanás tel: 83487
Some of the best food on the island.
Uncle Yanni's (£–££)
Pórto Vrómi beach
Mobile kitchen in a secluded cove: fresh fish, lobster and *mezedes*.

NORTHERN AND EASTERN AEGEAN ISLANDS

Chíos

Dimitrakopoulos (£)
Odós Sgritá (near KTEL bus stop) Chíos Town
Tiny restaurant with freshly cooked dishes.
Iannis (££)
about 6km out of Chíos Town, in the Kambos, on the road to Kallimasiá
Marvellous outdoor taverna: good-value dishes.
Mesaronas I and II (£–££)
main square in Mestá
Excellent food. Open all year round.

Lésvos

Dagellis (££)
on the approach to Agiássos tel: 0251 22241
Simple taverna. Wonderful cheese fritters.
I Skamnia (I Moyria) (££)
Skála Sykaminéas tel: 0253 55319
Delicious food and quiet setting.
Seal Nautikos (£)
far end of the harbour, Mytilíni
Cheap beer and oúzo, served with *mezedes*.

Límnos
(telephone area code 0254)

Hotel Akti Mýrina (£££)
Mýrina tel: 22681
Excellent Greek and international cuisine.
Glaros (££)
Mýrina harbour tel: 22220
Typical harbour fish taverna. View of the *kástro*.

Sámos
(telephone area code 0273)

Avgo Tou Kokora (££)
Kokkári tel: 92113
Range of *mezédes* and fish and meat dishes.
Café Museum (£)
next to the Archaeological Museum in Vathí
tel: 23053
Pleasant and elegant terrace in the shade of palm trees, with good Greek music.
I Varka (£–££)
by the ferry landing in Pythagóreio
A kitchen built into a small fishing boat.

Samothráki

Chora Taverna (££)
Samothráki Town
High above the port, perfect for lunch when you have had enough of the beach and ruins.
To Kyma (£)
Kamariótissa waterfront tel: 0551 41263
A simple waterside taverna serving fish and grills. Rooms to rent.

Thásos

Beautiful Elena (££)
Alykí beach
Out of the water and straight to the table for customers and fish alike.
Delfini (£–££)
Skála Prínos tel: 0593 71341
Well-prepared fresh fish dishes.

THE SARONIC ISLANDS

Aígina

Ouzeri Ta Vrahamena (£)
Odós Leonárdou Ladá (inland from the ferry landing), Aígina Town
Small *ouzeri* with tables in an alley, popular with local fishermen. Good flow of wine and oúzo, grilled octopus.
Vatsouliali's (££)
Ágioi Assomati, on the road to Agía Marína tel: 0297 22711
Very popular and good-value taverna with succulent Greek food including rabbit. Open only evenings on Wed, Sat and Sun.

Póros

Lucas (££)
Paralía, Póros Town tel: 0298 221945
Good value fresh seafood and friendly service.

Spétses

(telephone area code 0298)

Exedra (££)
Palaío Limáni, Spétses Town tel: 73497
Excellent fish and seafood taverna overlooking the Old Harbour.
Lazaros (££)
on the Dápia in Spétses Town
Genuine taverna food, specialities of goat in lemon sauce and chicken in tomato sauce, and good barreled retsina.
Tasos (££)
near the beach at Agía Anargýri
Very popular and friendly taverna with good typically Greek fare.

Ýdra

Kondilenias (££–£££)
Vlýchos
Popular fish and seafood taverna serving fresh grilled fish and squid as well as excellent risotto with shrimp. Strongly recommended.

To Steki (££)
Odós Miaoúlis, Ýdra Town tel: 0298 53517
Friendly traditional taverna.

THE SPORADES AND ÉVVOIA

Alónnisos

Kamaki (££)
Patitíri tel: 0424 65245
The best food in town, away from the more touristy establishments. Speciality: grills.

Skíathos

Ilias (££–£££)
Skíathos Town (from Odós Papadiamánti, turn right into Odós Evangelístrias and follow the arrows to Ilias) tel: 0427 22664
Traditional taverna dishes, excellent roast beef with prunes and lamb with vegetables in filo.
Mesogia (££)
Odós Grizóriou, Skíathos Town tel: 0427 21440
One of the few tavernas with a Greek feel.
The Windmill (££)
Skíathos Town tel: 0427 21105
Superior cooking in a fabulous setting.

Skópelos

Anatoli Ouzeri (£)
in the ruins of the Venetian kástro at the top of Skópelos Old Town
Perfect *ouzéri*. Inexpensive *mezédes*.
Dilina (££)
1km out of Skópelos Town on the road to the monasteries
Standard taverna but with superb views.
Ta Kymata (££)
on the waterfront by the ferry landing in Skópelos Town tel: 0424 22381
The best of the waterfront tavernas.

Skýros

Kabanero (£)
Skýros Town
Popular place for traditional fare well prepared.
Kristina's (££)
Skýros Town tel: 0222 91778
Great garden restaurant with both Greek and continental delights. Evenings only. Reserve.

Évvoia

Avra (££)
waterfront at Límni
The best of Límni's fish tavernas, but grilled meats are also on the menu.
O Gouveris (££–£££)
No 22 on the waterfront at Chalkída
Excellent seafood and grilled fish. Specialities are crayfish, lobster, and other shellfish.
Stavedo (£££)
Odós Karaóli and Dimitríou 1, Chalkída tel: 0221 77977
Pleasant restaurant with Greek specialities.

Index

285

Index

Index/Acknowledgements

288

Picture credits

The Automobile Association would like to thank the following photographers, libraries and associations for their assistance in the preparation of this book: **ASSOCIATED PRESS** 138a; **THE BRIDGEMAN ART LIBRARY** 28b Sculpture of Aphrodite (Hermitage, St Petersburg); **THE BRITISH MUSEUM, LONDON** 26b, 37, 108b, 126a, 126b, 219b, 240a; **BYZANTINE MUSEUM, ATHENS** 38a; **MARY EVANS PICTURE LIBRARY** 36a, 36b, 40b, 44a, 84/5, 86a, 210b, 211, 240b, 241; **R GAULDIE** 102, 103; **C GORDON** 49b; **RONALD GRANT ARCHIVES** 135a, 135b; **TERRY HARRIS** 9a, 22b, 152/3, 184, 185, 197a, 209, 232/3, 236/7, 238/9; **HISTORIC MUSEUM, CRETE** 42a, 70c; **THE HULTON GETTY PICTURE COLLECTION LTD** 44b, 44c, 46b, 47a, 47b, 49a, 194c; **THE MANSELL COLLECTION LTD** 34a, 41, 42b, 48a, 86b, 86/7, 87, 116b, 155b, 182a, 182b, 183b, 194a, 210/1, 240/1; **MUSEUM OF IRÁKLEIO, CRETE** 31b; **NATIONAL ARCHAEOLOGICAL MUSEUM, ATHENS** 34b, 58, 59a, 218a; **NATURE PHOTOGRAPHERS LTD** 79a (R Burbidge), 198 (J Sutherland), 226b (P R Sterry), 226c (R Tidman), 227a (P R Sterry); **PICTURES COLOUR LIBRARY LTD** 111, 117, 118, 120; **SPECTRUM COLOUR LIBRARY** 101, 192.

All other pictures are held in the Association's own library (**AA PHOTO LIBRARY**) with contributions from the following photographers: **S L DAY** 2b, 6, 8, 9b, 11, 12a, 13a, 14a, 16b, 17a, 19a, 20b, 21b, 25a, 25b, 40a, 43, 48b, 140a, 142/3, 144, 145, 147, 148b, 149, 150, 151, 153, 154, 155a, 156, 157, 158, 159a, 159b, 160/1, 161, 164, 167, 168a, 168b, 168c, 169, 170, 171, 173, 174/5, 226a, 248b, 249a, 250/1, 255, 256/7, 259, 269a; **P ENTICKNAP** 13b, 28a, 30a, 32a, 39a, 46a, 63, 68, 72/3, 72, 78a, 78b, 84b, 88, 91a, 92, 108a; **T HARRIS** 2a, 3, 4a, 10a, 14b, 20a, 21a, 22a, 26a, 27b, 29a, 35b, 98/9, 104, 105a, 105b, 105c, 106/7, 107, 113, 114, 115a, 115b, 119, 121, 123, 124/5, 125, 128, 129, 130, 131, 133, 136, 137a, 138b, 139a, 139b, 140/1, 141, 253, 254, 261, 266, 268; **T LARSEN-COLLINGE** 38b, 91b, 166, 172, 262, 265a; **R MOORE** 10b, 19b, 183a, 234, 235, 242, 243, 244, 245a, 245b, 246a, 246b, 247; **K PATERSON** 5, 12b, 15a, 15b, 17b, 18a, 18b, 23b, 24a, 27a, 33b, 35a, 62/3, 62, 64, 66, 69, 70a, 70b, 71a, 71b, 74, 75, 76/7, 77, 79b, 80, 81, 82, 89a, 89b, 90, 91c, 93, 94, 95, 96/7, 97, 140b, 188a, 197b; **A SATTIN** 126c, 181a, 181b, 196, 199, 200/1, 204a, 204b, 205, 207, 208, 212, 213a, 213b, 214, 215, 216, 217, 219a, 249b, 265b; **R SURMAN** 29b, 39b, 50/1, 54, 60a, 127, 132a; **J A TIMS** 6/7, 16a, 45, 148a, 176/7, 176, 178, 186, 188b, 189, 190, 191, 193, 194b, 195a, 195b, 200/1, 224, 225, 229, 230a, 231, 263; **M TRELAWNY** 260, 269b; **P WILSON** 23a, 24b, 24c, 31a, 51, 53, 56, 57, 59b, 61a, 61b, 109, 132b, 222, 248a.

Acknowledgements

The authors would like to thank the following individuals and organisations for their help during the research of this book: Olympic Airways, Autohellas Hertz, National Tourist Office of Greece, Maxine Harrison of Elysian Holidays, the management and staff of the Cavo Tagoo, St Nicholas Bay, Grotta, Nostos and Mentor hotels.

Contributors

Revision Editor: Grapevine Publishing Services   Verifier: Mike Gerrard